Christianity, Social Justice, and the
Japanese American Incarceration
during World War II

# Christianity, Social Justice, and the Japanese American Incarceration during World War II

. . . . . . . . . . . . . . . . . . . . . . . . . . . . . . . . . . . . . . . . . . . . . . . .

ANNE M. BLANKENSHIP

The University of North Carolina Press   Chapel Hill

This book was published with the assistance of the Anniversary Fund of the University of North Carolina Press.

The University of North Carolina Press has been a member of the Green Press Initiative since 2003.
Library of Congress Cataloging-in-Publication Data

Names: Blankenship, Anne M., author.
Title: Christianity, social justice, and the Japanese American incarceration during World War II / Anne M. Blankenship.
Description: Chapel Hill : University of North Carolina Press, [2016] | Includes bibliographical references and index.
Identifiers: LCCN 2015046029| ISBN 9781469629193 (cloth : alk. paper) | ISBN 9781469629209 (pbk : alk. paper) | ISBN 9781469629216 (ebook)
Subjects: LCSH: Japanese Americans—Evacuation and relocation, 1942–1945. | World War, 1939–1945—Japanese Americans. | Christianity and justice—United States—History—20th century. | Human rights—Religious aspects—Christianity. | Japanese Americans—Religion. | Concentration camps—West (U.S.)—History—20th century. | Japanese Americans—United States—Social conditions—20th century.
Classification: LCC D769.8.A6 B58 2016 | DDC 940.53/1773—dc23
LC record available at http://lccn.loc.gov/2015046029

Cover illustration: Entrance to Catholic chapel (V), Manzanar Relocation Center, California (photo by Ansel Adams; courtesy of the Library of Congress).

*To my parents*

# Contents

# Figures

# Acknowledgments

My gratitude first goes to Cheryl and Lee Blankenship, my parents, to whom this book is dedicated. Without their unwavering support, pride, and confidence, this project would not have been completed. The high value placed on education in our family oriented me toward a profession in teaching and research, and they encouraged me to continue even when my interests veered in unexpected directions. They also allowed me to write for months at their home on Puget Sound while filling me with fresh salmon, Dungeness, halibut, clams, oysters, shrimp, and garden produce. My mother accompanied me to the sites of incarceration camps around the country and read numerous manuscript drafts. Mitch, Tara, and Zoe Gray, my brother, sister-in-law, and niece, put me up while I dug through the University of Washington archives. Their company at the end of each day made the work even more enjoyable. My grandparents, Delbert and Delsie Clampitt, also deserve credit for this project, as they helped inspire its conception. They farmed in southern Idaho from 1943 to 1977 and likely interacted with Nikkei from the nearby Minidoka incarceration camp, which features prominently in this book. I would also like to thank my friends who have listened to me talk about this project for years: Aaron Klink, Dusty Hoesly, Katie DeVore, Christina Mortillaro, Scott Libson, and my graduate school cohort—Kathy Foody, Vince Gonzalez, Megan Goodwin, and Matt Grey. You all made this a fun and endurable process.

Numerous colleagues helped me realize the broad potential of this project. Laurie Maffly-Kipp, Grant Wacker, David Morgan, Eric Muller, Yaakov Ariel, and Barbara Ambros all provided feedback on full drafts of this project at different stages of its evolution. Commentary from the anonymous readers of my manuscript helped fine-tune the argument. My colleagues at the John C. Danforth Center on Religion and Politics at Washington University in St. Louis asked prodding questions to help me see this topic in new ways and allowed me to absorb some of the center's condensed wisdom. Marie Griffith, Leigh Schmidt, Darren Dochuk, Mark Jordan, Laurie Maffly-Kipp (again!), Hannah Hofheinz, Rachel Lindsey, Lerone Martin, Emily Johnson, Rachel Gross, Karen Smyth, and others all read chapters during my two years at the center. I shall not list them all for fear of overlooking half a dozen, but I would also like to thank the many guest speakers and scholars who engaged me and other members of the center in thought-provoking conversation during that time. Beth Hessel, with her knowledge of the primary source material, proved an excellent conversation partner as well.

In addition to the brilliance of my colleagues, a two-year postdoctoral fellowship at the Danforth Center on Religion and Politics amplified my work by supporting research in Seattle, New York, Washington, D.C., and Philadelphia and conferences in Oxford, Chicago, Baltimore, Washington, D.C., and Banff, Canada. Grants from the University of North Carolina and its Center for the Study of the American South allowed me to plunder archival sources in California, Idaho, and Arkansas. North Dakota State University, my current institution, contributed generous funds to finalize the creation of this book.

This project would not have been possible without the assistance of archivists and my editor. It benefited from resources at special collection libraries and archives at the University of Washington; the Graduate Theological Union; the University of California, Los Angeles; the University of California, Berkeley; the Presbyterian Historical Society; the Maryknoll Mission; the American Friends Service Committee; the National Archives; Haverford College; Quincy College; the University of the Pacific; the College of Southern Idaho; the University of Arkansas; and the Japanese American National Museum. Densho, a digital archive and resource center, is doing a magnificent job preserving experiences and artifacts of the incarceration; its collections made my project markedly richer and more manageable. My editor at UNC Press, Elaine Maisner, helped pull all this together. Thank you.

Finally, I wish to acknowledge the Nikkei and white activists who fill these pages; I am privileged to share your stories with the world.

Christianity, Social Justice, and the
Japanese American Incarceration
during World War II

# Introduction

· · · · · · · · · · · · · · · · · · · · · · · · · · · · · · · · · · · · · · · · · · · · ·

The forced mass evacuation . . . creates a special responsibility for us
to help preserve the ideal of brotherhood and of political and religious
freedom in our country.

—"A Message to the Society of Friends and Our Fellow Christians"

While purportedly fighting a war against ideas of racial supremacy propagated by fascist regimes, the U.S. government incarcerated nearly
120,000 legal residents and American citizens of Japanese descent on the
sole basis of their ancestry.[1] When President Franklin Delano Roosevelt's
Executive Order 9066 allowed the military to remove people of Japanese
descent from the West Coast, American citizens, residents, and orphaned
children alike packed their bags, sold their belongings, and attempted to
build functional lives in the desert camps or swampy deltas where they
were sent.

Seizo and Ben Itoi had managed the Carrollton Hotel near Seattle's
waterfront for twelve years when the government cast them out of the
city. Mr. Itoi had laid railroad ties, harvested potatoes, cooked on Alaskan
fishing vessels, and operated a dry cleaning shop for fourteen years
before saving enough money to buy the hotel in *Nihonmachi* (Japan Town).
Their four children attended public schools, and the family worshiped
together at the Seattle Japanese Methodist Church. The Itois visited
family in Japan once, but the children failed to make friends or acclimate
to the different customs. Their youngest son, Kenji, died there. The Japanese attack on Pearl Harbor stole the family's sense of security and comfort. In the spring of 1942, the U.S. government imprisoned the Itois in an
incarceration center, and the family settled into a single room furnished
only with army cots. The barracks, flimsy wooden structures covered in
tar paper, baked inhabitants in the heat of summer and allowed cold
winds to enter throughout the winter.[2]

*Nikkei* (people of Japanese descent) could leave the camps for jobs or
school east of the western exclusion zone but remained banished from
the coast until January 1945. Ben and Seizo Itoi's remaining son, Henry,

married in camp and left for St. Louis with his new wife after being rejected from the army for health reasons. Monica, their eldest daughter, left camp in the summer of 1943 to work in Chicago and enter college. Their youngest daughter, Sumiko, entered the Cadet Nurse Corps on Long Island. With their children scattered across the nation, Mr. and Mrs. Itoi remained behind barbed wire until government officials permitted them to return home to Seattle. They were lucky; trustworthy friends managed the Carrollton in their absence, so unlike most Nikkei, the Itois had jobs and a place to live upon their return. Having scraped together a life as young immigrants, many *Issei* (first-generation immigrants) lacked the ability to begin again as old men and women. Variations of the Itois' story transpired throughout the American West as the U.S. government withdrew basic civil rights from nearly an entire ethnic population. A government commission later concluded that "race prejudice, war hysteria, and a failure of political leadership," not legitimate security concerns, fueled this action.[3] Not a single spy or saboteur of Japanese descent was ever discovered.

Nikkei Christians like the Itois turned to their faith to reconcile their loss of civil rights, and many white Christians felt a "special responsibility" to amend the injustice out of compassion, patriotism, and Christian brother- and sisterhood. When the government incarcerated Japanese Americans in direct defiance of opposition and recommendations from Federal Bureau of Investigation (FBI) director J. Edgar Hoover, Attorney General Francis Biddle, and other government officials, Nikkei and white Christians faced a serious conundrum: confront the government during a time of national crisis or stand aside as the injustice unfolded. Many progressive Protestants and Catholics discerned the true roots of the incarceration and the dire precedent set by the race-based policy. The incarceration played into the hands of Japanese propaganda that heralded the intractable racism of America and Europe. It also shared frightening similarities with Hitler's anti-Semitic policies. Christians feared that the incarceration would irreparably damage foreign missions and America's chance to establish global peace by destabilizing domestic race relations and damaging diplomatic ties with Asian nations.

Decades before civil rights struggles peaked in the American South, Christian leaders began determining the ethics and pragmatism of fighting against or acquiescing to an unjust social system. Negotiating conflicting images of a united church, nation, and future world became a high-risk game when leaders disagreed with government officials and most of their congregants. This book explores how Christian leaders faced this dilemma and how Christians of Japanese descent responded to their incarceration. The experience inspired new approaches for liberal American Christians confronting inequality within the nation and their own ranks. The injustice challenged white Christian leaders and Japanese Christians as Americans and as people of faith.

The Japanese American incarceration tested the willingness of Christians to challenge government policies on race and ultimately convinced many individuals to join secular and religious social justice and civil rights movements after the war. Up until this point, one of the few objective goals of Christian race relations was to end lynching, pleading for people to respect established judicial systems and follow the law. The severity and suddenness of the incarceration provoked Christians to respond immediately. Unlike the status quo of segregation, the incarceration represented an egregious deterioration of race relations.

Examining Christian responses to the Japanese American incarceration stretches and diversifies perceptions of the civil rights movement and American churches' role within it. Until recent years, scholarship on civil rights activism had focused on relationships between white and black Americans.[4] This obscures the complexity of race relations work prior to and during World War II, when churches faced the overwhelming task of tempering negative public perceptions of Japanese and Japanese Americans. Invoking Jacquelyn Hall's concept of the long civil rights movement, this book stretches narratives to acknowledge activism prior to the 1950s and diversifies narratives that limit the movement to a struggle for African American rights.[5] Although the role of religion in the African American civil rights struggle of the 1960s is well documented, the role of churches in this expanded understanding of the civil rights movement remains unclear. Mainline Protestants, Quakers, and Roman Catholics devoted significant resources to addressing the harms caused by the unconstitutional incarceration of American citizens of Japanese descent.

*Christianity, Social Justice, and the Japanese American Incarceration during World War II* intertwines a cultural history of Nikkei Christians from 1941 to 1946 with institutional histories of the organizations working with Japanese Americans. Parallel narratives of mainline Protestant, Quaker, and Roman Catholic experiences delineate national liberal responses to a crisis of domestic racial persecution. Surveying the diversity of Christian responses highlights commonalities and conflicts over race, church–state relations, and the global role of American religionists in the mid-twentieth century. Quakers' resistance to the incarceration reveals an alternative to mainline Protestants' strategy of closer cooperation with government agencies. Roman Catholic experiences expose their resolute independence and the extent to which government programs inadvertently favored Protestantism. Leaders of the three groups sought to aid all Nikkei, not just Christian adherents, but their white congregants disagreed with their sympathetic approach. Lacking connections with white Americans, incarcerated Buddhists faced even greater trials. However, their experiences crossed or closely paralleled those of Christians at times.[6]

The previously unexplored intersection of religion and the incarceration exposes shifting understandings of race and diversity within mid-twentieth-century liberal Christianity.[7] This research expands existing conversations about the racial integration of churches, which focus almost exclusively on white and African American dichotomies.[8] It also complements recent scholarship on mainline Protestantism, such as David Hollinger's *After Cloven Tongues of Fire*, Matthew Hedstrom's *The Rise of Liberal Religion*, and Elesha Coffman's *The Christian Century and the Rise of the Protestant Mainline*, by further exploring liberal Protestants' struggles with racial boundaries.[9] The 1940s were transitional years for U.S. race relations and the participation of American churches in social justice campaigns, but inadequate scholarship bridges the two issues. This work will further sharpen the history of American Christianity and begin transforming the nation's and churches' narratives to include the stories of Asian Americans, decisions made on their behalf, and the outcomes of related conflicts.

The incarceration challenged religious and racial boundaries within American churches. Attempting to unify American Christians, Protestant leaders instructed Nikkei to abandon denominational loyalties in the camps and join established, predominantly white churches as they reentered society. The incarceration strained intrachurch relationships as leaders pressured Japanese American and white Christians to embrace unity while limiting the autonomy of ethnic minorities. Attempts to heal racial divisions by eliminating ethnic churches and ethnic intradenominational organizations failed spectacularly, challenging Protestant denominations and ethnic groups to redefine justice within their own institutions. It also helped certain groups recognize the breadth of racial discrimination in the United States. In response to these demands,

Japanese Americans began to negotiate their place within the church more actively.

This book clarifies the roots of Asian American liberation theology. The experience of confinement and its unusual worship structures encouraged lay Christians to develop new lived theologies and influenced the formative professional years of young Nikkei ministers. These pastors shaped novel approaches to ministry during and after the war. Subsequent reflections on those experiences accelerated the evolution of new church structures and theologies, building a foundation for Asian American liberation theologies articulated in the 1960s and 1970s.

Most books about the incarceration mention the three authorized religions in the camps—Buddhism, Protestantism, and Catholicism—but no one has looked inside the church doors to see what was happening, why it looked the way it did, or what happened afterward.[10] The wealth of historical, sociological, legal, and visual studies of the Japanese American incarceration fails to adequately address religion.[11] This book adopts an approach to the incarceration delineated by Lon Kurashige that attempts to do more than unearth the tragedy.[12] Like the complicated work of the War Relocation Authority, which functioned as incarcerees' jailer and protector, religious groups cannot be judged simply as doing right or wrong. While Christians certainly could have done more to confront this unconstitutional act, this book will show that their more questionable actions were intended, if misguidedly, to shape a more just and peaceful world.

This study's discussions of activism, race, and ecumenism, alongside examinations of memorial services in the camps and Japanese Americans' arguments for pacifism, will contribute more generally to scholarship on the role of religion during World War II.[13] The government worked to preserve religious liberty during the war as one of Roosevelt's Four Freedoms, obliquely defining and categorizing religion through these efforts.[14] With the aid of religious and governmental propaganda, government officials instituted ethnic and religious pluralism often credited to the Cold War and Dwight D. Eisenhower's presidency.

· · · · ·

The incarceration was a harsh blow to Japanese immigrants who had built thriving communities, businesses, and farms despite anti-alien land laws and other discrimination. In every major West Coast city, Nikkei opened their own barber shops, newspapers, movie theaters, banks, and depart-ment stores and operated hundreds of hotels and restaurants.[15] Japanese midwives, dentists, and physicians cared for the community's medical needs. Ethnic Christian churches and Buddhist temples organized com-munity life by sponsoring Japanese language schools, Boy Scout troops, athletic teams, and social clubs. Outside of the cities, the yield of Japanese farms dominated the West Coast production of numerous crops.[16] Their success drew envy and resentment from white farmers who had not accomplished so much in so little time, though the population of Nikkei in the United States never exceeded 140,000 prior to World War II.[17] Nearly 7,000 Nikkei lived in Seattle by 1940, half of Washington's total Nikkei population, a special focus of this book.[18] As part of the Gentle-men's Agreement, Japan curtailed the emigration of Japanese laborers in 1908 but allowed women to join their husbands in America. Family members and matchmakers exchanged photographs and held weddings in Japan—minus the groom—before the bride departed to join her new husband in the United States. The immigration of thousands of picture brides led to a boom in the second generation; 25,170 *Nisei* (second-generation Japanese Americans) were born between 1910 and 1920.[19] They became U.S. citizens by birth as mandated by the Constitution, but the Naturalization Law of 1790 barred their parents from citizenship.

Nisei grew up listening to swing bands and playing baseball with friends of various ethnicities. Issei saw opportunities for their children that were unreachable within their own lives and encouraged them to perfect their English, attend university, and join American society. Most Nisei attended public schools, but 9 percent obtained schooling in Japan, and some parents sent their children to one of several Catholic schools in coastal Japanese communities.[20] Largely segregated, the Catholic schools' required Japanese language curriculum appealed to many families, only 10 percent of whom were Catholic.[21] A greater percentage of Nisei at-tended college than the general U.S. population, but racism prevented most graduates from obtaining professional, white-collar work. A dejected college graduate wrote, "I would much rather be a doctor or lawyer . . . but my aspirations were frustrated long ago. I am only what I am, a pro-fessional carrot washer."[22] Only a quarter of Nisei worked in the profes-sional field for which they had trained; many returned discouraged to family farms or businesses.

A small number of Japanese were already Christian when they arrived in the United States, but most immigrants encountered the religion through the work of Christian aid societies and home mission programs on the Pacific Coast. Christian missions provided families with child care, employment services, financial aid, and English lessons, not unlike Protestant organizations operating among Catholic and Jewish immigrants in eastern cities. They functioned as support systems for Japanese immigrants, particularly women, who had lost the tight-knit social groups of their hometowns and extended families.[23] As states increasingly restricted the rights of immigrants, Christian and Buddhist organizations also provided opportunities for leadership. Nikkei staffed nearly all Japanese churches in the United States by 1940, and Japanese pastors led many, perhaps the majority.[24] Churches founded by Japanese missionaries retained even greater autonomy and sustained ties with congregations in Japan.[25] Depending on the region, 20–25 percent of the nation's Nikkei identified as Christian by the beginning of World War II, and nearly all of those adherents attended ethnic denominational churches formed by home mission societies.[26] Most ethnic churches belonged to mainline Protestant denominations, but Japanese Holiness, Salvation Army, and Roman Catholic churches also prospered.[27] At least a quarter of Seattle's Nikkei population identified as Christian and attended one of seven ethnic churches: the Japanese Baptist Church (founded in 1899), the Japanese Methodist Church (1904), St. Peter's Episcopal Church (1906), Japanese Presbyterian (1907), Japanese Congregational (1907), the Catholic Maryknoll Mission—Our Lady Queen of Martyrs (1925), and a Japanese Holiness church (1935). A similar number of Buddhists were affiliated with the city's Nichiren or Shinshu Buddhist temples.[28]

Japanese parents frequently sent their children to Sunday school and encouraged them to join Christian churches while they themselves retained Buddhist customs. They often made this decision out of convenience, since church groups provided safe recreational opportunities to occupy children's attention or out of a desire to provide moral instruction, assuming "any church is good for [them]."[29] An Issei parent explained another commonly held understanding: "I'm Japanese. Buddhism is a Japanese religion. But my children are American. Christianity is an American religion. My children should be Christian."[30] Some immigrants identified Christianity with American society and thought conversion would help their children succeed in that world.

Foreign and domestic missionaries contended that discriminatory immigration barriers and prejudice in America were the greatest hindrances to foreign and domestic missions. They wrote editorials to educate the public and petitioned the president to oppose immigration quotas for the benefit of peaceful international relations and "Christian" race relations at home.[31] While proselytization and hopes for spreading Christianity across the globe influenced missionaries' work, these Christians were among the few people who knew immigrants intimately, believed in their potential, and sympathized with their plight. Missionaries became one of the primary champions of immigrant welfare. The prolific Congregational missionary Sidney Gulick led the campaign against anti-Japanese legislation, fighting scientific racism with evolutionary science.[32] Catholic missionaries united theology with American democracy to bolster the rights of immigrants, describing the denial of naturalization as a violation of natural law, and worked with Japanese consulates to block anti-alien land laws.[33] The Federal Council of Churches (FCC), the Catholic Maryknoll Missionary Society, and the Quaker American Friends Service Committee (AFSC) denounced the Immigration Act of 1924 on grounds of racial justice, human dignity, and Americanism.[34]

The public, including many Christian pastors, regularly dismissed missionaries' ideas, rationalizing that time abroad negatively altered a person's perception of the world and America's priorities. Nativist groups like the Know Nothing Party, the Asiatic (later Japanese) Exclusion League, and the Native Sons and Daughters of the Golden West accused Gulick and other Christian activists of promoting "the mixing of all Asiatics with our race in our country by means of citizenship, intermarriage, and social assimilation." Arguing that the aims of liberal Protestant leaders were "wholly political and entirely without relation to the spiritual mission of the Churches of Christ," white supremacists like Montaville Flowers warned church members to question the peaceful rhetoric heard from the pulpit.[35]

Liberal Christians did not deny their political goals, and a central component of interwar Christian campaigns for global peace focused on U.S.–Japan relations and the difficulties facing Japanese Americans. America's Catholic and mainline Protestant churches' calls for the "banishment of war" promoted international law, disarmament, and a "new international morality" that would "subordinate narrow self-interest to the interests of all." The FCC's Joint Committee on Right Relations between America and Japan advocated specific policy reforms for disarmament, trade, and immigration and the cultivation of a "more wholesome public opinion on American Japanese relations." Christian peace activists argued that discrimination against Japanese Americans exacerbated international tensions by bolstering Japan's claim that the United States would never treat Asian and African nations and people fairly. Renamed the National Committee on American Japanese Relations, the FCC committee explained Japan's growing aggression as "the inevitable and necessary response to Western militarism." While condemning militarism on both sides, they believed better "insight and sympathy" for Japan's problems would strengthen the power of Japan's liberal politicians. Progressive Christians blamed anti-Japanese domestic policies on "unscrupulous politicians and ill-informed promoters of race prejudice," the future perpetrators of the incarceration.[36]

Mainline Protestant peace efforts culminated in the work of future secretary of state John Foster Dulles, illustrating the intertwining agendas of Protestant ecumenism and U.S. foreign policy during the mid-twentieth century. As the founding chair of the FCC's Commission to Study the Bases of a Just and Durable Peace, Dulles developed the "Six Pillars of Peace," a less institutional revision of Woodrow Wilson's League of Nations. The treatise outlined "the ethical principles upon which world order must be based" to establish a "just and durable peace." They included moral, political, and economic reform. Politicians, church leaders, and media outlets in the United States and abroad admired the "Six Pillars" and remarked on the plan's practicality in the face of growing global strife. Associated programs mobilized laity within mainline denominations around the world to foster support for the FCC's peace campaigns.[37]

Christians felt the need to build a new national faith based on moral law. In 1938, the Japanese American pastor Bill Hata wrote that Americans could "do much toward the establishment of peace among the nations of the world," but this would require "a resurrection of Christian ideas and principles." His thoughts reflected Dulles's belief that Christians bore a "supreme responsibility" to lead the country—and the world—as exemplary ethical models. While Dulles insisted that the moral law forming the foundation of his new world order could be accepted by Christians and non-Christians, Catholics argued that the world must embrace a Christian worldview with Christian foundations for democracy to establish lasting peace. In comparison, President Roosevelt lauded freedom of religion as the foundation for democracy.[38]

The calls for peace and moral order from foreign missionaries and peace workers consistently connected triumph abroad with domestic harmony among races. FCC president Robert Speer sought a "Christian . . . solution" to racial discord and forecasted the "undreamed of access of power to the Church on the foreign field" were they to be successful.[39] Many Christians believed reconciliation could be achieved only through the church, but mainline Protestant race work did not progress beyond white and African American Christian relations until World War II. When the FCC founded its Commission on the Church and Race Relations in 1921 to join the "Christian men and women of the two races," negative attitudes toward Asians largely remained the concern of missionaries and global peace commissions.[40] Headlines about African Americans dominated the mainline "Interracial News Service" and the Quaker "Interracial News Letter" through the 1930s, though Quakers integrated several ethnic groups within their race awareness programs.[41]

Campaigns to spread an ideology that bound global peace and harmonious race relations succeeded in many cases. Arguing for the Grange membership of a Japanese American in 1944, a Methodist farmer in Vermont declared that such prejudice was "an attack upon the four freedoms that we are supposedly fighting for, and . . . blasphemy against our Lord."[42] Conflating the values and aims of the nation with those of Christianity, some Americans saw racial divisions as a threat to both institutions. Protestants and Catholics addressed racial tensions that threatened to undo iconic American and, as they saw them, Christian values of equality, tolerance, and even pluralism. Such sentiments heightened the urgency to build a unified national faith based on moral law.[43]

But the Reverend Hata and John Foster Dulles feared Americans were not up to the task of leading a peaceful world. Leopold Tibesar, a Catholic missionary working with Japanese, agreed as he wrote, "I pity our poor country, forced by the very nature of things to take a leading role in world affairs when its citizens are totally unprepared in their most ordinary thought processes to assume and help in such a role."[44] Despite efforts to involve laity, progressive Christian leaders' advocacy for Nikkei resembled their leadership on other social issues of the twentieth century—they led "where few of [their] flock would follow."[45] The unconstitutional, race-based incarceration of Nikkei confirmed that America was ill equipped to be the world's model nation.

Many American Christians disapproved of churches' efforts to end the incarceration and aid its victims. Popular evangelist Aimee Semple McPherson made virulent anti-Japanese remarks before and during the incarceration, warning politicians and the public that Issei might poison their crops and commit sabotage.[46] Progressive Christians sought to overcome such voices through personal interactions between Nikkei and white Americans and education utilizing American and Christian tropes of tolerance and democracy, but numerous Christian pastors supported the incarceration and opposed Nikkei's return to the coast in 1945.

Christian commissions for foreign missions, global peace, and race relations drove responses to the Japanese American incarceration philosophically and administratively. Quaker aid to Japanese Americans initially came from the American Friends Service Committee's Inter-Racial Relations Committee and the Friends Mission Board. Both continued to contribute to the effort, but the AFSC soon founded a dedicated program for Nikkei aid. At the request of the government, AFSC workers organized and operated the National Student Relocation Council and helped resettle Nikkei as they left the camps.[47] Other Christian pacifist groups like the Fellowship of Reconciliation and Church of the Brethren also assisted Nikkei.

Mainline Protestant aid came from a jumble of national and regional ecumenical and denominational aid committees, councils, and programs. The FCC and the Home Missions Council of North America chartered the Protestant Church Commission for Japanese Service to oversee worship in the camps and the Committee on Resettlement of Japanese Americans to help Nikkei leave the camps. Mark Dawber, executive secretary of the Home Missions Council, organized the Committee on Administration of Japanese Work to oversee everything. Several denominations also organized their own committees to aid Nikkei. The list of denominations constituting mainline Protestantism, an anachronistic term for this era, varies with regularity, but the mainline denominations most committed to alleviating the harms of the incarceration included United Methodists, American Baptists, Episcopalians, Presbyterians (U.S.A.), Congregationalists, and, to a lesser extent, Disciples of Christ.

While the National Catholic Welfare Council contributed a limited amount of funds, the Catholic Foreign Mission Society of America, more commonly known as Maryknoll missionaries, organized Catholic aid to Nikkei. Subject to local dioceses, Maryknoll's priests, brothers, and sisters ran most of the prewar Catholic missions and schools for Nikkei living on the West Coast. Like the white pastors of Japanese Protestant churches, several Maryknoll priests and brothers entered the camps to provide ministry and material support for their parishioners and other incarcerees. The hierarchy of Maryknoll and the Catholic Church determined Catholic engagement, while individual Protestant workers were not monitored as closely.

Regional ecumenical councils, congregations, denominations, youth groups, and numerous individuals acting independently complemented the work of these national organizations, as did the YMCA, YWCA, the American Bible Society, and other interdenominational groups. Christians coordinated their efforts at times, but overlapping responsibilities frequently put them at odds with one another.

Few Mormons, African Americans, or Jews appear in this book for the simple fact that none organized support for Nikkei. Despite a history of missions in Japan, Mormons provided no organized aid to Nikkei beyond individual wards welcoming resettlers to the neighborhood. Utah's senator Elbert E. Thomas, having spent his mission in Japan, spoke in favor of Nikkei rights but did so on political, not religious, grounds. Similarly, controversial Japanese American Citizens League leader Mike Masaoka never suggested that his Mormon faith directly influenced his actions, despite the title of his autobiography, *They Call Me Moses Masaoka*. He later criticized the Mormon Church for failing to protect the rights of Nikkei.[48] Cheryl Greenberg's study of African American and Jewish responses, or rather the lack thereof, concluded that most did not see the incarceration as an issue of racial discrimination and prioritized their own concerns.[49]

In addition to analyzing national organizations, the book's narrative follows the white and Nikkei clergy, congregants, and Christian organizations of Seattle, Washington, from the months prior to the attack on Pearl Harbor, on 7 December 1941, to 1946, the year following the war. The study moves in and out of the camps, as did many of its subjects, both white and Nikkei. Focusing on Seattle's Christian community reveals the effects of national policy decisions on West Coast communities, Japanese Americans, and white pastors. Similar negotiations occurred throughout the country, but Seattleites left unparalleled textual records, oral histories, photographs, and material artifacts that detail the tensions among white and Nikkei Catholics, Quakers, mainline Protestants, regional ecumenical councils, and government officials. This focus also helps fill a gap within incarceration studies, which frequently overlook the experiences of Nikkei in the Pacific Northwest. Following the Seattle community to Minidoka, an incarceration center in southern Idaho, allows me to follow the lives of several individuals continuously to show how the war and church policies changed their secular and spiritual lives. Unique factors affected every community, but the book's general conclusions and the experiences of the Seattle community resonate with the national story. Notable deviations and unique experiences in other camps are duly noted.

Religious experiences within the Department of Justice detention centers are beyond the range of this study because these Nikkei were legally interned, and the regulation of religious practices differed from that in the civilian incarceration camps.[50] The draft, Nikkei chaplains, and other elements of the war are discussed in chapter 4, but the religious experiences within the segregated Japanese American army units are beyond the scope of this book. The white chaplains who served these units had no previous connection to the communities and could comment only on their experiences in Europe and the South Pacific.[51]

Chapter 1 sets the scene for the rest of the book by mapping the initial reactions of Japanese and white Christians to the bombing of Pearl Harbor and incarceration of coastal Nikkei. Progressive Christians leapt to the defense of Nikkei, but the East Coast leaders of mainline Protestant and Catholic organizations instructed their constituents to cease protests when the military announced its decision to incarcerate all West Coast Nikkei. Many leaders on the West Coast agreed that dissent might limit their ability to provide aid, or they deemed protest during a time of national crisis inappropriate. While diversity existed within each religious group, this chapter compares the bold, decisive actions of individual Quakers and the American Friends Service Committee, the cooperative inclinations of well-intentioned but cautious Protestant leaders, the independent solutions of Catholics, and the determined perseverance of Japanese Christians. Identifying the initial perspectives of Christians helps make sense of their later choices.

Chapter 2 surveys the actions of concerned Christians outside of the camps. Once Nikkei were confined, a proliferation of Christian organizations formed to aid incarcerees. Their greatest efforts went toward supporting worship in the camps and resettling Nikkei outside of the camps during the war. The latter required the transformation of public opinion in addition to finding employment and housing for former incarcerees. Publications and speakers encouraged Americans to welcome Nikkei as they left the camps. Seeking to decrease racism nationally, activists faced resistance from fearful and racist congregants and pastors. The FCC, the Home Mission Council, the AFSC, regional church groups, Christian missionaries, and churches around the country contributed organizational support, pastoral guidance, and material aid.

Chapter 3 returns to Seattle's Nikkei and white pastors who worked at Minidoka incarceration center. They fashioned sacred space in bare, overcrowded barracks, helped Nikkei resettle outside of the camp, and tried to raise the camp's morale in addition to their usual pastoral duties. Catholic priests protested the limits of religious liberty in the camps, while Protestants attempted to form ecumenical churches. Some men and women in the camps reveled in what they believed was a spiritually superior united church, while others refused to redefine denominational boundaries as dictated by white authorities. Generational barriers, a constantly shifting population, and material limitations challenged pastors to develop innovative strategies.

Nikkei Christians frequently thanked God for giving them the strength to endure the incarceration and developed a variety of faith communities to provide additional support. The focus of chapter 4 turns away from church leaders to examine how lay (non-ordained) Christians experienced camp life. Buddhists joined Protestants and Catholics to organize interfaith memorial services for Nikkei soldiers killed in action, while pacifists and others resisted the military draft. This chapter expands the book's focus to highlight Christian youth culture at a camp in Arizona and the hardships at Tule Lake, where incarcerees attacked Japanese Christians for cooperating with camp officials. The roots of Asian American theologies began growing in the camps in response to this rejection and suffering.

As Nikkei Christians left the camps, white church leaders instructed them to join established churches and prevented them from re-forming their prewar ethnic congregations. Chapter 5 analyzes attempts to mend the nation's racial divisions by ending the segregation of white and Japanese Protestant worship. Efforts to drastically restructure the racial divisions within American Protestantism incited extensive debate about the role of racial minorities within the church. As with the decision to form ecumenical churches, leaders thought the long-term benefits of fewer divisions in the church outweighed the temporary challenges to the subjects of their experiment. Most Japanese Americans formed ethnic fellowship groups or left the church rather than join predominantly white churches. The results of this experiment revealed the limited extent to which American Christians were interested in, capable of, and willing to reform definitions of race in order to unite the Christian church.

The epilogue reflects on the long-term effects of Christian activism during the Japanese American incarceration and considers the subsequent rise of Asian American theologies. The status of Nikkei in American churches shifted as the minority demanded autonomy.

# 1 The Attack on Pearl Harbor and Executive Order 9066

On a peaceful Sunday morning, December 7, 1941, Henry, Sumi and I were at choir rehearsal singing ourselves hoarse in preparation for the annual Christmas recital of Handel's "Messiah." Suddenly Chuck Mizuno . . . burst into the chapel, gasping as if he had sprinted all the way up the stairs.

"Listen, everybody!" he shouted. "Japan just bombed Pearl Harbor . . . ! It's war!"

The terrible words hit like a blockbuster, paralyzing us. Then we smiled feebly at each other, hoping this was one of Chuck's practical jokes. Miss Hara, our music director, rapped her baton impatiently on the music stand and chided him, "Now Chuck, fun's fun, but we have work to do."

But Chuck strode vehemently back to the door, "I mean it, folks, honest! I just heard the news over my car radio. Reporters are talking a blue streak. Come on down and hear it for yourselves."

With that, Chuck swept out of the room, a swirl of young men following in his wake. . . . The rest of us stayed, rooted to our places like a row of marionettes. I felt as if a fist had smashed my pleasant little existence, breaking it into jigsaw puzzle pieces. . . . I knew instinctively that the fact that I was an American by birthright was not going to help me escape the consequences of this unhappy war.

—Monica (née Itoi) Sone, *Nisei Daughter*

Once news of the attack on Pearl Harbor sunk in, Monica Itoi and her siblings careened home from the Seattle Japanese Methodist Church to be with their parents. They found their mother "sitting limp in the huge armchair as if she had collapsed there, listening dazedly to the turbulent radio, . . . her face . . . frozen still." Their father deemed the story false propaganda until he heard the news on both American and Japanese radio broadcasts. Knowing that other Americans would associate Japanese immigrants with their homeland, Nikkei rushed to burn, bury, or otherwise destroy items from Japan: Buddhist shrines, texts, and statues, language textbooks, Japanese flags, kimonos, photographs, and anything else with Japanese writing or obvious ties to Japan. Some Japanese Christians congregated at home like the Itois, while others gathered in their churches, waiting to learn their fate within the global calamity.[1]

The news shocked the white men and women who worked with Seattle's Nikkei community as well. Several miles north of Nihonmachi, Floyd Schmoe, a botany professor at the University of Washington, hurried home from his Quaker meeting house to find five Nisei women "huddled in the basement listening to the radio; they were frightened beyond tears." His family regularly hosted university students, and their current boarders feared leaving the protection of the Schmoe house. Soon after the Reverend Emery Andrews's Sunday morning benediction at the Seattle Japanese Baptist Church, members of his congregation returned to the church with news of the attack. Father Leopold Tibesar, the priest of the city's Japanese Catholic community, heard the news over the radio as he waited for breakfast after the morning's Missa Cantata in honor of the Immaculate Conception.[2]

Andrews, Tibesar, and Everett Thompson, the Itois' Methodist pastor, quickly set to work calling and visiting their parishioners. White missionaries all along the coast translated instructions and interrogations as the police and FBI agents raided Japanese homes that evening. Seizo Itoi packed a bag in anticipation, but he was not arrested. By 9 December, 116 of Seattle's Japanese citizens, including Buddhists priests, Japanese language school teachers, and other community leaders, sat behind bars. Tibesar met with officers of the Japanese American Citizens League, led by James Sakamoto, a Nisei under instruction for baptism. The priest helped them arrange meetings with the FBI and organize an Emergency Defense Council.[3]

Nikkei faced increasing, unpredictable government restrictions. Closure of Japanese banks and the frozen accounts of all Issei caused chaos in Nihonmachi as businesses could not function without funds or access to their accounts. On 29 December, federal agents and local law enforcement confiscated "contraband" material, including shortwave radios, hunting rifles, cameras, ceremonial swords, binoculars, and dynamite used for clearing land.[4] A curfew for Issei instituted on 4 February 1942 expanded to include Nisei on 27 March. It forbade Nikkei from traveling more than five miles beyond their homes or staying out past eight P.M.[5] Nikkei truck farmers ignored the law or employed non-Nikkei to bring their produce to market. Doctors and midwives received special passes from city officials, and many others risked arrest to visit patients or parishioners. The University Friends Meeting moved gatherings to the house of their one Japanese member because the curfew made it impossible for him to attend otherwise.[6] With the belief that Christians would face less discrimination, an unknown number of Nikkei began attending Catholic and Protestant services.[7] Protestant pastors reported that most of these visitors soon returned to their Buddhist temples.[8]

Anti-Japanese voices grew in January, pressuring the government to expel people of Japanese descent from the West Coast, if not the entire country. The majority of newspaper editorials calling for eviction came from politicians, many seeking reelection, but labor unions and nativist groups like the Native Sons and Daughters of the Golden West also made their voices heard.[9] Many white farmers hoped to physically excise their greatest competition from the marketplace. The Salinas Grower-Shipper Vegetable Association bluntly stated, "We're charged with wanting to get rid of the Japs for selfish reasons. We might as well be honest. We do. It's a question of whether the white man lives on the Pacific Coast or the brown man. . . . We don't want them back when the war ends, either."[10] Aggressors based their claims on nearly a century of anti-Asian sentiments. William Randolph Hearst's yellow journalism fanned the flames of prejudice, inventing stories of sabotage, fabricating interviews, and distorting the reality of wartime America. Even the typically progressive children's author Theodor Geisel, better known as Dr. Seuss, drew cartoons criticizing the government's naive lack of action that allowed fifth column Japanese plots to grow.[11]

On 19 February 1942, President Roosevelt signed Executive Order 9066, which permitted military officials to exclude whomever they deemed a threat from sensitive security zones. Lieutenant General John DeWitt made immediate plans to evict men, women, and children—anyone with one-sixteenth or greater Japanese ancestry—from the West Coast and Alaska.[12] The War Relocation Authority (WRA), the civilian agency established to manage the incarceration, obtained land and hastily built two incarceration centers in California (Tule Lake and Manzanar), Arizona (Poston and Gila River), and Arkansas (Jerome and Rohwer) and one each in Idaho, Wyoming, Utah, and Colorado (Minidoka, Heart Mountain,

Topaz, and Granada, respectively). From March to June 1942, Nikkei families packed their bags—only what they could carry—and sold or rented their houses, businesses, farms, and belongings at immense financial and personal loss. Nearly 115,000 people moved to fairgrounds or race tracks converted into temporary "assembly centers" or directly to one of ten large "relocation centers" in the western deserts or Arkansas's poverty-ridden deltas. Another 6,000 Japanese Americans were born in the camps.[13] Despite their proximity to Pearl Harbor, the government did not incarcerate Nikkei living in Hawaii. In Seattle, Nikkei moved into the ironically named Camp Harmony at the Puyallup fairgrounds, forty minutes southeast of the city.

Having attempted to alleviate the tensions between Japan and America for decades, progressive Christian leaders leapt to the defense of Japanese Americans, but mainline Protestant and Catholic leaders hesitated to challenge the authority of the president or military at a time of war.

### Quaker Responses

Quaker leaders publically recognized the pending threat to Nikkei well before the United States entered the war. Seven months before the bombing of Pearl Harbor, the West Coast section of the American Friends Service Committee circulated a letter warning of the domestic emergency that would follow the United States' entry into a Pacific war. At this early date, Quakers predicted that all Japanese Americans will become " 'Japs' and . . . find it impossible to avoid the caustic backwash of war hysteria."[14] Under the auspices of the Fellowship of Reconciliation (FOR), an interfaith pacifist group committed to social justice, Floyd Schmoe organized conferences in Seattle, Los Angeles, San Francisco, and Honolulu to bring attention to the challenges facing Nikkei in the spring of 1941.[15]

Quakers' definitive condemnation of the incarceration, frequent admissions of responsibility, commitment to action, and requests for forgiveness set them apart from other Christian denominations. Quaker leaders never accepted the excuses of military necessity or the need to protect Nikkei from angry mobs, swearing, "We cannot concede the right of a government for such arbitrary mass action against a group as a whole."[16] The AFSC warned of the incarceration's ramifications for American democracy and the future world.

Despite having fought discriminatory legislation, Quaker publications never suggested they bore less guilt than other Americans: "The fault rests squarely upon us as a people who have permitted prejudice, fear, and hatred to flower into intolerance and violence." The AFSC's May 1941 letter listed the things "we" have denied them, such as "full freedom in a free land," equal social and economic opportunities, legal rights to naturalize and own property, and "chiefly . . . our friendship and willingness to understand." Acknowledging a tendency to believe they innocently assumed the guilt of other, notices cautioned Friends to examine their own prejudices. As the war stretched into years, internal correspondence reminded AFSC workers, "Let us never forget that we threw these people behind barbed wire. We wiped out their savings, and their means of livelihood. We destroyed their financial security. . . . For the sake of our own integrity, we still have a debt to pay." Another proclaimed, "We have failed as a society because we have failed as individuals. As individuals we must begin to make amends." Taking full responsibility, Quakers exhorted readers that aid was an obligation, not simply charity.[17]

Pledges to remedy the situation always accompanied Quaker confessions: "The forced mass evacuation . . . creates a special responsibility for us to help preserve the ideal of brotherhood and of political and religious freedom in our country." AFSC workers promised to "share in the sufferings and sacrifices of the evacuees." These vows professed the inadequacy of "simply making life as comfortable as possible . . . in the detention camps," perhaps an allusion to mainline Protestant aid. They promised to restore Nikkei's full rights and status in all American communities. Consistent with their historical approach, Quakers sought to remedy the source of the problem rather than just alleviate its symptoms.[18]

The AFSC addressed letters to Nikkei communities conveying their regret and disagreement with the government. One such letter confessed, "Had there been real understanding [the incarceration] would not have come about and it is to our shame and regret that we failed to build that understanding in time to avert this tragedy." They "acknowledge[d] this mistake and [took their] share of the blame" for the incarceration. The AFSC sent these apologies to community leaders and printed them in publications read by the Nikkei community to "humbly ask forgiveness."[19]

Quakers began working to sustain Nikkei's civil rights immediately after the Pearl Harbor attack. AFSC executive secretary Clarence Pickett declared their commitment to "breaking the force of this calamity which has come upon the Japanese population." Within two weeks of the attack, the AFSC had commissioned a new branch office in Seattle, Washington and hired Floyd Schmoe to lead it.[20]

Individuals working for mainline Protestant and Catholic aid organizations had established careers within the church, but Quaker aid workers came from diverse occupations. The University of Washington granted leaves of absence to several Quaker faculty members who decided to spend the war helping Japanese American students and other Nikkei. Schmoe's work exemplified that of many Friends who coordinated their efforts through the AFSC. Raised in a Quaker family on the Kansas prairie, Schmoe's love of natural beauty led him to the Pacific Northwest. He and his family lived in Mount Rainier National Park for years after he became the park's first naturalist and spent summers on a sailboat in the San Juan Islands, where he studied underwater ecology. His work at the University of Washington ended when Japan bombed Pearl Harbor. Foreseeing the magnitude of challenges Nikkei would face, Schmoe took a temporary leave of absence without delay. Schmoe's detailed survey of the Pacific Northwest's Japanese population in 1941 gave him valuable contacts within the imperiled communities. These connections led dozens of Nikkei to seek his advice as many knew no other sympathetic white people. Members of the Seattle Friends Center mentioned this experience in their request to hire Schmoe. AFSC headquarters in Philadelphia consented and augmented their offer to include Thomas Bodine, a young worker on the East Coast. The Social Industrial Section of the AFSC funded offices to work with Nikkei in Southern and Northern California and Hawaii that December as well. Esther Rhoads, a Quaker missionary in Japan, arrived in California on 11 February 1942 to lead the AFSC's efforts in that region. Beginning that month, bulletins updated American Quakers on current developments and recommended specific actions that individuals could take to help Nikkei.[21]

In the early weeks of the war, Schmoe worried about the amorphous nature of the AFSC's support because it had no precise agenda beyond managing the rising crisis. Schmoe prioritized efforts to calm public fears and squelch rumors before they did serious damage. He described this as "paddling a canoe against Niagara" as the roar of incriminations against Japanese Americans rose. When Canada began removing Nikkei from British Columbia in January 1942, Schmoe wondered whether Seattle's AFSC workers should remove themselves to this greater emergency to arrange housing and be with the persecuted Canadians. But the financial quandaries of Issei in America soon filled Schmoe's schedule. AFSC workers organized food deliveries, arranged legal assistance, and met with state attorneys general to reactivate bank accounts. AFSC leaders on the

Pacific Coast met in January to compare experiences, explore approaches to the increasing problems, and pool resources for public relations and fund-raising. Throughout the war, the AFSC petitioned Quakers and other civic-minded people for financial support.[22]

As rumors of Executive Order 9066 spread, the Seattle AFSC office protested the policy in telegrams to the secretary of war, the attorney general, Eleanor Roosevelt, and three congressmen. Preparing for the worst, they requested money from AFSC headquarters to expand their office staff and install additional telephone lines. They also made plans to visit the communities where Nikkei would be sent to reduce anti-Japanese activism and welcome the new arrivals. Two weeks after FDR signed Executive Order 9066, the AFSC sent delegates to Washington, D.C. as "a last-minute effort to revoke the evacuation scheme." When that plea failed, AFSC workers turned to resettlement plans: designing cooperative farms and housing projects just outside the military zone. Throughout March and April, Friends arranged housing and employment for Nikkei east of the exclusion zone.[23]

Americans living along the Pacific Coast had an opportunity to express their views on the incarceration in February and March of 1942. Under the auspices of the House Select Committee Investigating National Defense Migration, Representative John Tolan of California held hearings to gauge tensions and attitudes related to Japanese Americans. Anyone from the community could present their view of the situation at the Tolan Committee hearings. Fifty-five people came forward in Seattle, twelve of whom opposed a total incarceration. Friends, classmates, and university professors joined the eight supporters from Christian organizations. Religious leaders avoided the use of religious arguments, instead focusing on empirical data and American values. By framing their arguments around practical concerns, religious leaders attempted to prevent accusations that they based their support for Nikkei on idealistic, naive notions of Christian love.

The Tolan Committee testimony of Floyd Schmoe and AFSC board member Bernard Waring turned into a circus as Congressman George Bender, a Republican from Ohio, interrogated them about America's integrity, their personal religious beliefs, and even Herbert Hoover's standing within the Quaker church. Schmoe regularly interjected, defending Nikkei liberty on the basis of the American way of life and human dignity. Because government officials had asked the Tolan Committee to ascertain means of support for a mass incarceration, Representative Carl

FIGURE 1 Gordon Hirabayashi, University of Washington undergraduate. Source: University of Washington, Special Collections, UW36485.

Curtis of Nebraska asked whether the AFSC would provide financial support and service to Nikkei harmed by the eviction. Waring verified that the AFSC would support Nikkei wherever the military sent them before an irate Bender interrupted to continue his tirade against pacifism. Bender's belligerence and suspicion about pacifism and the loyalty of people unwilling to fight for their nation undermined what might have been a strong testimony against incarceration.[24]

By late April, Schmoe knew the incarceration could not be stopped but encouraged further resistance. He and other workers on the West Coast pleaded for the AFSC headquarters to do more. He preferred to fail rather than do too little. E. Stanley Jones, a Methodist missionary who worked closely with the AFSC during this time, agreed that efforts to "bring about real peace" should continue "even though it may mean failure."[25] Both Japanese and white Quakers sought legal solutions to the diminishing rights of Nikkei.

The Quaker and Japanese Christian beliefs of Gordon Hirabayashi (Figure 1), a University of Washington undergraduate, led him to challenge the injustice directly. Hirabayashi grew up at White River Garden, a Mukyōkai farming commune in Thomas, Washington, hearing his parents' emphasis on Jesus's message to "turn the other cheek" and observing their choice to lead by example. Though the majority of Japanese Christians converted through the guidance of Western missionaries in Japan or the United States, others belonged to independent Japanese Christian sects formed by Japanese in Japan. Uchimura Kanzō's Mukyōkai movement, founded in 1901, was the most prominent form of Japanese Christianity in the early twentieth century. In Uchimura's words, the promotion of Mukyōkai, literally an "absence of church," "does not set up institutions or attempt to control other people but rather practices mutual love, encouragement and assistance among its members." He rejected the denominational politics he witnessed in the United States, seeing no reason for Japanese Christians to inherit the historical divisions and quarrels within Western Christianity. Instead, Uchimura turned to the Japanese value of *giri*, a sense of moral obligation to the group or others. His rendition of this obligation included a commitment to pacifism, which he considered to be the "touchstone" of true Christian faith. The centrality of giri defined the community where the Hirabayashi family lived.[26]

When the United States began a peacetime conscription in 1940, Gordon Hirabayashi realized that his upbringing had given him a strong "pacifistic orientation." After two years in the Reserve Officers' Training Corps, Hirabayashi registered as a conscientious objector because he could not reconcile a "military solution" with a "peaceful way of life." He joined FOR and became an active member of the university YMCA. After over a year of visiting different pacifist churches, Hirabayashi joined a Quaker meeting house. It most closely resembled his parents' tradition, as he explained to them: "You never heard of Quakers 'til I became one, but your beliefs and your way overlap so strongly to the Quaker way that I found it very easy to adapt." The church's lack of hierarchy, commitment to pacifism, frequent interactions with other Christian groups, and emphasis on each believer's responsibility to find his or her own way paralleled Uchimura's teachings.[27]

Curfew restrictions provided an opportunity for Hirabayashi to act on his religious beliefs. After weeks of dutifully following regulations, the unfairness of the situation dawned on Hirabayashi, and he began intentionally violating the eight P.M. curfew. He described such racial discrimination as "unchristian, undemocratic [and] un-American."[28] As the date to register for eviction approached, Hirabayashi turned himself in to the

FBI. Despite their willingness to overlook the offenses, he persisted and refused to register for eviction or go to Camp Harmony, the assembly center where Nikkei Seattleites were initially confined. As one of only a few Nikkei to refuse to comply with laws associated with the incarceration nationally, Hirabayashi wrote a statement explaining his actions to the public: "Over and above any man-made creed or law is the natural law of life—the right of human individuals to live and to creatively express themselves. . . . If I were to register and cooperate under those circumstances, I would be giving helpless consent to the denial of practically all of the things which give me incentive to live. I must maintain my Christian principles. I consider it my duty to maintain the democratic standards for which this nation lives. Therefore, I must refuse this order for evacuation."[29] Years earlier, the Hirabayashi family and others at White River Gardens had litigated against alien land laws on similar grounds, feeling the obligation to support democracy and Mukyōkai principles.[30] Fellow Friends and other acquaintances admired Hirabayashi's stand and deep religious belief, drawing parallels between his prison experience and those of early Quakers. M. D. Woodbury, executive secretary of the University of Washington's YMCA, wrote, "I am not exaggerating when I say that Gordon in my opinion has more depth and sincerity in his religious life than any student that I have had the privilege of working with during the past twenty years."[31]

Hirabayashi initially approached the American Civil Liberties Union (ACLU), assuming it would take his case, but the ACLU's national board declined when it became apparent that the lawyers' approach would question the president's decision.[32] The AFSC, FOR, and state senator Mary Farquharson founded the Gordon Hirabayashi Defense Committee to organize and finance his defense. Their fund-raising and a grant of $1,000 obtained by the AFSC through the Robert Marshall Civil Liberties Trust paid for the first two trials, after which the AFSC's fund-raising efforts spread throughout the nation.[33] Clarence Pickett saw Hirabayashi's case as a way to show that Friends' "interest in the Japanese problem goes beyond simply assisting in relocation."[34] Floyd Schmoe vigorously supported Hirabayashi's case, writing a stirring article, "I Know Gordon Hirabayashi."[35] It reminded readers that racist stereotypes do not fit individuals; when you know a person, you realize that he or she rarely resembles racial or ethnic stereotypes.

After a short jury trial in Seattle declared Hirabayashi guilty, the circuit court of appeals offered no ruling and sent the case to the U.S. Supreme Court. Opting to rule only on the curfew violation, the Supreme Court sidestepped the question of mass removal. Pressure from President Roosevelt and Chief Justice Harlan Fiske Stone resulted in a unanimous decision to uphold the law on 21 June 1943.[36] Hirabayashi spent six months in the King County jail before being released to work with the AFSC. He then hitchhiked to an Arizona prison camp to serve the rest of his sentence.[37]

In addition to supporting legal challenges to the incarceration, one of the AFSC's most significant contributions to relief efforts for Nikkei was the relocation of university students to schools east of the restricted region. In the hope that some students could transfer schools before entering the camps, AFSC activists began this work as soon as the government announced the incarceration. With University of Washington sociologist Robert O'Brien and home economist Margaret Terrell, Schmoe facilitated the transfer of university students to schools in the country's interior.[38] During the months following the bombing of Pearl Harbor, Schmoe visited nearly one hundred schools to find placements for Nikkei students. Only three schools turned him down, including Princeton University and a Bible college in Caldwell, Idaho. Princeton's president claimed they could not protect Nikkei students, while representatives of the Christian school replied blatantly, "We don't want any Japs here."[39] Schmoe's job also entailed sneaking students to the train station after curfew. Describing this process, he later wrote, "We hid our 'criminal' students under a blanket in the back seat of the car. . . . Their only crime was that they had not been born white."[40] He continued these efforts throughout the war, visiting incarceration camps to encourage college-age students to take advantage of student relocation.

AFSC leaders walked a fine line between standing with victims of persecution and cooperating with the perpetrators in order to help Nikkei. Having first navigated this boundary while helping World War I European refugees, Quaker representatives carefully negotiated the distance they kept between themselves and the government. The AFSC issued orders to "be careful not to actually assist in the evacuation and . . . do nothing that might destroy the Japanese confidence" in Quaker volunteers.[41] The organization retained this cautious attitude throughout the war and continually questioned the legitimacy of collaborative ventures with the U.S. government. Friends organized and managed some programs at the government's request, but only projects that helped Nikkei leave the camps.

Individual Friends stood at the extremes of this stance. Some Quakers reconciled working for the WRA, knowing they could provide sympathetic aid from within that agency's ranks, while others refused to aid Nikkei in any manner on the grounds that this encouraged the government to do an inadequate job. The Quaker Robert O'Brien, for example, could only obtain military leave from the University of Washington, so he took an unpaid position from the WRA in order to support the AFSC's work. He laughed that it "may have looked ridiculous to my Quaker Meeting but it made it possible for me to do the things that I wanted to do." When approached by the WRA, Quaker George Townsend, Minidoka's future assistant project director of community activities, immediately rejected the offer of employment. The request surprised him, he later wrote: "I could save their time and mine since I could not in good conscience be a part of a program which I thought might be unconstitutional." The government recruiters had done their homework, however, and reminded him of his duty to find "sacrifices . . . consistent with his conscience." They convinced him of the need to retain compassionate, unprejudiced people like himself.[42]

Similarly, many Quakers answered the WRA's plea for teachers in the camps, but others declared, "That's helping the government, and you ought to resist!"[43] These arguments resembled critiques that the Quakers should not operate work camps for conscientious objectors, a responsibility of the government. Critics thought they should direct their energy elsewhere to avoid complicity with the military draft. Gordon Hirabayashi later cautioned that such work under the auspices of Quaker organizations led Quaker youth to accept these options without critiquing the larger mechanism involved.[44] These discussions reflected the open debate and individual discernment encouraged by Quakers. Friends rejected the incarceration unanimously but disagreed how to support Nikkei.

Prepared for the vilification of Japanese Americans, Quakers in the United States took decisive actions to defend Nikkei's civil rights and minimize the damage caused by the incarceration. In public and internal statements, the AFSC apologized for the injustice and pledged solidarity and material support. The group quickly mobilized to transfer university students out of the exclusion zone before they could be sent to camps. Quakers like Floyd Schmoe quit their jobs to volunteer independently or work through the AFSC, while the Quaker and Japanese Christian principles of Gordon Hirabayashi led him to oppose the discriminatory laws and bring his case to the Supreme Court. Other Quakers thought any aid or cooperation with the government was ill advised. Seeking to aid Nikkei without supporting unjust government actions, the AFSC and individual Quakers disagreed what constituted "collaboration" with government agencies.

## Mainline Protestant Responses

Redolent of the canyon splitting the prewar assumptions of Quakers and other Protestants, a statement from the Seattle Council of Churches prior to December 1941 expressed radically different suppositions than those found in the prewar AFSC notice. According to its website, the council formed in 1919 as "the worldwide ecumenical movement began to flourish." Like other ecumenical groups of the early twentieth century, the council presented itself as an activist organization committed to peace, economic justice, and religious and racial tolerance. Toward that end, it released a "Message to the Japanese in the Pacific Northwest" in November 1941 to commend the ethnic community for its good citizenship. The incarceration soon contradicted the council's assurance that Nikkei had "nothing to fear from the American government or the American people." Observing the growth of local and international tensions, Protestant leaders hoped to inform Nikkei Washingtonians of the "sympathy and co-operation of the Churches." They "urged" the minority group to "confer with any Christian Church pastor" if "any problem . . . [arose]." This greatly exaggerated the support Nikkei could find among Christian ministers; many pastors were as racist as anyone else. The council's message hoped to calm and offer support to Nikkei—not alert the public or white congregants to a pending crisis. Members of the Federal Council of Churches's Inter-Council Committee on Japanese Christian Work in the United States felt more pessimistic about the future of Nikkei and urged the FCC to release a statement in support of Japanese Americans in April 1941. The FCC declined because several minority groups faced "condemnation," and it did not want to single out Nikkei.[45]

Mainline Protestants immediately defended Nikkei after the attack on Pearl Harbor. Worried for their physical safety, Protestant groups invoked Christian and patriotic responsibilities in an attempt to dampen flames of racist hysteria. The FCC, the Home Missions Council of North America, and the Foreign Missions Conference of North America released a joint statement on 9 December. It "call[ed] upon the church people of this country to maintain a Christian composure and charity in their dealings with the Japanese among us." Similarly lucid and placid, the Seattle Council of Churches published this statement the day following the attack: "We urge our people to remain calm and not be carried away in a wave of hysteria. Sane thinking and a sober, prayerful attitude now will save us. . . . It would be most unfortunate if our Christian people would . . . add to the difficulties and trials of the Japanese-Americans who now become victims of unfortunate circumstances because of the present situation. . . . We urge that as long as the Japanese people within our borders remain loyal to our country, we shall not be guilty of discriminating against them in our community life, and particularly in holding of jobs, and in enjoying the privileges of this country. . . . This is no hour to forget the traditions and principles of our great nation." This statement addressed Christians specifically but invoked patriotic ideals to counter violent and discriminatory actions of those who might—and did—attack Japanese Americans. It attended to immediate economic concerns that white employers would fire Nikkei workers. The council did not use forceful language to halt potential discrimination but encouraged calm rational actions. This statement contrasted with the FCC's piece by invoking civic duty, not moral obligations. Both secular and religious media used concepts of American and Christian morality and ideals interchangeably, affirming and equating the righteousness of the church with that of the nation.[46]

Consistent with prior declarations, the Seattle Council of Churches's statement to the Tolan Committee in March 1942 used mild language and did not criticize the government. The council first dismissed the idea of incarcerating Nisei by saying that it saw "no reason why American citizens of enemy alien lineage should be involved in the discussion of evacuation" and expressed its faith that the government would not base its decision on ethnic heritage. In his concluding remarks, the council's representative, Harold Jensen, clarified that council members "feel very definitely opposed to mass evacuation" but qualified, "unless it is a military necessity." The Seattle Council hurriedly interviewed 327 Japanese Christian families in Seattle to ascertain their thoughts on the potential incarceration and shared the results with the committee. Most families, not surprisingly, wished to remain in Seattle. As with the interview with AFSC members, Representative Curtis stressed the "golden opportunity" for American churches to "render a great deal of service" to the soon-to-be-evicted Nikkei. Military officials had made plans for the total eviction of Nikkei before these proceedings concluded, so committee members tried to steer conversation toward productive discussion about the incarceration.[47]

Using more deliberate language, the Reverend Everett Thompson of Seattle's Japanese Methodist Church and the Reverend U. G. Murphy, a Methodist from the Northwest Oriental Evangelization Society, submitted letters to the Tolan Committee on behalf of Nikkei. Thompson stated bluntly, "In mass evacuation we should be repeating the deed that Hitler perpetrated against the Jews. . . . Thus we should be conquered by Hitler's spirit and methods even though not by his military machine. . . . The basic injustices would be the same." Comparisons to Hitler's actions appear in several mainline sources as numerous people saw the incarceration as a direct threat to American values of equality and justice. Murphy recommended a parole system whereby Nikkei could remain on the coast while monitored by local (white) citizens. Thompson and Murphy drew authority from their years of close relations with Nikkei and limited their arguments to democracy and fair play, not mentioning Christianity. This line of argument placed many white supporters under FBI investigation.[48]

Religious leaders along the West Coast gave a similar range of testimonies. The YWCA recommended eviction on an individual basis since "the worth and rights of the individual" were the "very thing [sic] our country is fighting for." Speaking for the Los Angeles Committee for Church and Community Cooperation, George Gleason questioned the necessity of evicting all enemy aliens and their descendants but pledged full confidence in the army and other government agencies and cited the serious security threats posed by enemy nationals living on the coast. The Portland Council of Churches's brief statement to the Tolan Committee asked the federal government to respect family units, cover the financial costs of the move, and provide schools and health care but offered no judgment of the eviction. In San Francisco, a panel composed of white Protestant leaders working with Nikkei argued against wholesale incarceration and submitted a loyalty pledge signed by 1,400 Japanese Christians. While representing Christian institutions, pastors refrained from calling the injustice "unchristian" or citing religious justifications for their argument. Since the 1800s, labor organizers and politicians had attacked liberal Protestants on the West Coast for their soft, naive perspectives on race and immigration. Avoiding religious language, invoking patriotism, and providing factual evidence helped avoid such accusations.[49]

Few Nikkei shared their views at the Tolan hearings. Though not addressing the question of incarceration specifically, the national Japanese

Church Federation attested to their loyalty and acknowledged their obligation to "bear the cross of Christ; to give [their] lives for those great principles for which Christ gave His life."[50] The use of biblical imagery suggested submission to the government's decision but pointedly reminded people of their Christian, and by association American, identity. Moreover, the metaphor placed the government in the role of Herod persecuting the innocent.

Many mainline Protestant churches skirted condemnation of the incarceration during its first months. A group of ministers in Southern California publicly expressed their regret in April 1942 but "did not criticize the policy, . . . contented . . . with deploring its apparent necessity and wishing well . . . its victims." Congregational churches judged the act to be "favoritism among God's children" but conceded that national security "justified" the eviction of Japanese nationals. The FCC sent a letter to President Roosevelt to express its "grave concern" about this situation that "jeopardizes . . . democracy" but did not directly condemn the incarceration or acknowledge its unconstitutional nature. Instead, the FCC wrote that the incarceration "savor[ed]" of discrimination and warned that Nikkei "conclude that we are practicing race discrimination." Although the letter noted its dissatisfaction, the FCC did not send the letter until late April 1942, when the military had already evicted thousands of Japanese Americans. Some mainline Christian leaders feared that open criticism would harm their cause and relationship with the federal government and urged pastors to temper their words. Others may have felt that the issue was hopeless or believed vociferous opposition would limit their ability to help in other ways.[51]

Conversely, a group of ministers in Santa Maria, California, argued that the "highest patriotism" requires Christian citizens to reject the incarceration for its "totalitarian methods." Most likely through the leadership of Clarence Gillett, the group's statement cited both practical and ethical reasons why an incarceration should not occur. Significantly, the Santa Maria group released this statement in February 1942, showing that at least one mainline organization, though small, tried to prevent the incarceration from occurring. The Northern Baptist Convention registered its "deep concerns" for a democracy that "placed racial discrimination . . . above the law," denying "full citizenship rights," ignoring the Fifth and Fourteenth Amendments of the Constitution, and violating "Christian principles." Three months later, the Northwest Oriental Evangelization

Society "deplore[d]" the removal of citizens to "concentration camps" and urged the government to allow Japanese Americans "who wish to" do so to return home, particularly women married to non-Nikkei men. This brief resolution did not explain why Nikkei should be released, but the message was clear: release citizens now. Fremont Baptist Church in Seattle also offered decisive views on the incarceration. The church expressed "deep concern" for the un-Christian and unconstitutional precedent set by this case, where "democratic rights have been infringed upon and racial discrimination placed above law."[52]

Behind closed doors, Seattle Church Council members acknowledged the injustice of the government's actions and tabulated the true motives. They correctly determined that the pending incarceration was "an afterthought and undoubtedly . . . a result of pressure from various patriotic groups" and their "economic jealousy." Members concluded that government officials and their own congressional representatives "have washed their hands of the question of civil liberty." Despite these clear critiques, the council's efforts and plans emphasized alleviating the stress of incarceration, not preventing or ending its reality. The public could not access the minutes from this meeting, and the council never shared these convictions publicly. In lieu of direct condemnation, the Seattle Council and most other religious groups criticized how the government organized the eviction.[53]

The articles and editorials within *Christian Century*, a magazine posited as the voice of mainline American Christianity, reveal the approaches of progressive Protestants toward Japanese Americans and the incarceration. The magazine educated East Coast and Midwest readers exposed to pugnacious media representations of Nikkei. Most articles came from Californian authors, but letters to the editor provided a broader view of national opinions of the Japanese incarceration. The *Century* exhibited more compassion than could be found in most secular sources. West Coast subscribers shared stories about honest, loyal Nikkei to reduce blanket prejudices against the minority and personalize the growing injustices. A Japanese American recommended an issue of *Century* to a Nisei friend, citing his "relief" after reading so many negative attitudes in other sources. But like the mainline churches it represented, *Century* did not condemn the government's decision or fight to end the incarceration in the late spring of 1942. Like the FCC and the Seattle Council of Churches, its editors avoided direct confrontation with the injustices perpetrated by the federal government. Historian Elesha Coffman's work has shown that *Century* helped define the mainline and its beliefs more than convince readers of certain views.[54]

Full of pertinent questions about pacifism and the church's role in a future, postwar world order, the *Christian Century* gave minimal attention to the situation of Japanese Americans until Nikkei began filling the assembly centers. From December 1941 to February 1942, *Century* editors printed a few cautionary tales of discrimination, but most reports suggested that the situation was under control. By late March, the magazine revealed tragic stories of violent harassment and suicide. The 11 March issue cautioned against conniving politicians, racist labor unions, unfounded rumors, and misplaced anger, but President Roosevelt had signed Executive Order 9066 weeks earlier. *Century*'s call for the federal government to control local political forces with "axes to grind" was too late. A week later, *Century* articles warned that the United States might be "convert[ing] a difficult minority problem into an incurable cancer" by aggravating loyal Japanese American citizens and inflicting the "kind of wound which goes deep and festers long." Articles and editorials voiced criticism and warnings like "Hitlerism Threatens the California Japanese," but editors softened their tone once U.S. officials announced the decision to incarcerate West Coast Nikkei. They avoided direct condemnation of the government and the incarceration but praised proactive Christian individuals.[55]

Congregationalist Galen Fisher, cofounder of the Northern California Committee for Fair Play for Citizens and Aliens of Japanese Ancestry, wrote *Century*'s longest and most articulate articles about the incarceration. He presented facts about the situation and allowed readers to draw their own conclusions. This tactic avoided criticizing the government and may have fostered the sympathy and understanding of readers more effectively. Prior to the war, Fisher had worked for the YMCA in Japan.

Fisher's article "Our Japanese Refugees" considered why more people did not speak out against the government action. In a rhetorical attempt to gain supporters, Fisher provided the "mass of intelligent people in the churches" an excuse for allowing the injustice to occur: Americans "could hardly conceive that the authorities would adopt" such a program when the attorney general and head of the FBI denied its necessity. They did not oppose incarceration because they believed it could never happen. Fisher's hypothesis likely explained the inaction of some people but contrasts with Quaker statements that accepted full blame for the injustice. By providing a generous explanation why Americans allowed the incarceration to happen, Fisher structured his prose in a way that expressed an assumption that readers would be more vigilant now that they knew all the facts. With ignorance no longer an excuse, active support was the only ethical response. He recommended they "follow every stage . . . with a cooperative but a critical eye" in case an opportunity to aid Nikkei arose. Again, his conclusion is lighter and vaguer than Quaker publications that demanded specific actions from readers. The Seattle Council of Churches similarly worried about people's complacency and hoped that the Christian citizenry would "express itself quickly before it becomes a custom to accept whatever the government does as being the correct way."[56]

While messages like Fisher's helped balance the inflammatory nature of other news sources, such voices remained singular and isolated. Few mainline Christian organizations approached Fisher's criticism, but their leaders recommended his articles to congregations, journalists, and social organizations seeking information on the incarceration.[57] Galen's Committee on American Principles and Fair Play reprinted the *Christian Century* articles in a 1943 pamphlet, "A Balance Sheet on Japanese Evacuation."

The editors of *Christianity and Crisis*, a publication founded by Reinhold Niebuhr to counter the more pacifist *Christian Century*, expressed decisive criticism of the incarceration. While Niebuhr accepted aggressive military actions like the firebombing of Dresden and the use of nuclear weapons, he did not see the incarceration as an "unfortunate necessity." The *Christianity and Crisis* article "A Blot on Our Record" states that the government had no legitimate excuse for its action. Editors did not publish this article until late April 1942, when the course of events could not be changed, but critical attention to the issue became a regular topic in *Christianity and Crisis* until the end of the war. Niebuhr wrote the most substantial critique in May 1942. John Bennett, an editor for *Christianity and Crisis*, and other mainline Protestants working with Nikkei disapproved of the magazine's approach, arguing that opposing the government was "not good policy." In late April 1942, Bennett wrote that it would be wiser to "assume evacuation" rather than try to prevent it.[58]

On behalf of multiple interdenominational Protestant organizations, Frank Herron Smith, superintendent of the Japanese Methodist churches in California, released a statement in March 1942 to all Japanese pastors explaining how Protestant churches would aid their congregations. The letter explained details about storing belongings and transferring church property titles but also emphatically stated what the church would not be doing: "We do not have the capital or the land to set up Christian colonies in the mid-West." Smith reassured Nikkei that church representatives who had visited the camps vouched that basic needs would be met, if accompanied by "plenty of wind and dust." He explained that outside pastors had already been assigned to preach during the early weeks of camps, so Nikkei pastors need not worry about that task. The final bullet point read, "TRUST IN THE LORD." The message that followed scolded Nikkei pastors: "Some [of you] are running around like chickens with their heads cut off. Keep calm. . . . War is terrible and you should be thankful it will not be worse for you. Let us as Christians keep our heads, cooperate with the authorities, and believe that all things work for good to those who love God."[59]

Life in the Japanese ethnic churches proceeded with few alterations after the attack on Pearl Harbor, but the war and preparations for their eviction increasingly occupied parishioners' attention. Nikkei adapted schedules to accommodate evening curfews, but services, holiday celebrations, and revivals occurred as planned until each church's final days. The number of war-related activities such as Red Cross first aid classes increased, as they did in many American churches. As tensions rose, Japanese pastors broadcasted restrictions and information about the pending eviction in weekly worship bulletins. Notices informed congregants of aid programs for Nikkei and referred readers to related articles in national Christian publications. Sermons called for peaceful, Christian behavior and reconciliation with the nation's prejudices.[60]

Sermons with titles such as "Being Christian in Times like These" and "Reweaving Our Lives" appeared more frequently as Nikkei pastors focused on the growing crisis in their community. Pastors encouraged congregants to remain as free of resentment and bitterness as possible, knowing their attitudes would determine their parishioners' quality of life in the coming years. Some framed this impulse within patriotic messages, even citing the gratitude Nikkei owed Americans for bringing Christianity to Japan. Others tried to convince their congregants through pragmatism. The Reverend Royden Susu-Mago stated frankly, "This is the only country we have. . . . Let us not be deceived about Japan. We can never go there and weave ourselves into her pattern of life. . . . We Nisei are too strongly saturated with American democratic ideals. Our thoughts, our language, our feelings and our aspirations are all American, and we have known no other." Susu-Mago warned congregants not to "talk irrationally" about going "back" to Japan, a country most had never visited. He acknowledged the many flaws of America but reminded Nisei of their own imperfect nature and the necessity of forgiveness. Rationales like this might not have been easy to accept, but many did and benefited from the mind-set.[61]

The immense task of fostering hope and positive attitudes led many Christian leaders to use biblical parallels of suffering. Analogies between the incarceration and the trials of Abraham, Moses, and Jesus were found in pre-eviction sermons. The Reverend Sohei Kowta in Wintersberg, California, used Abraham's story, reminding his congregation of the spiritual nature of God's promise: Abraham himself did not see its realization; a thousand years passed before the Israelites flourished. Nikkei pastors like Hideo Hashimoto compared their situation to that of the Babylonian exile. Observing that the Bible "is full of . . . evacuation stories," the Reverend John Yamazaki focused on the "mass evacuation" of the Exodus. He viewed the incarceration as a test in the wilderness. An Issei himself, Yamazaki reminded Nisei that the older Hebrew generation died without seeing the Promised Land. His sermon charged Nisei: "Many of us of the older generation erred in many ways in the past. I do not want our youth to repeat these errors. . . . Even if [Issei] perish in the wilderness and disappear from the picture, they will not fail; the Nisei will find a way to a better and newer world. . . . Why not accept this Evacuation as a test and a great opportunity to prove our faith in Christ and loyalty to our country?" Yamazaki's words bestowed Nisei with a great responsibility. Only they could fulfill their parents' hopes for a prosperous life in this country.[62]

Irritated with such comparisons, Lester Suzuki, a Methodist minister in Los Angeles, pointed out that while God promised Abraham great blessings, the Nikkei community had "no such promise." In reference to Moses, he commented that "ours is a strange exodus," since Nikkei were leaving their homes, not slavery. Suzuki found more useful comparisons in Jesus and early martyrs. Just as Jesus was reviled, Suzuki insisted, "We are reviled." The pastor failed to address the fact that Romans persecuted Christians for standing by their faith, not for their undeniable ethnicity.[63]

Many Japanese American organizations, both religious and secular, encouraged Nikkei to minimize conflict and alleviate tensions by cooperating with the WRA. Suzuki expressed indignation and exasperation with congregants who accepted aid inefficiently or failed to show adequate appreciation for white Americans visiting their church. Referring to a racially mixed church social, Suzuki wrote, "If we are so disinterested as to make a measly showing, then what they do to us is none of their fault."[64] Despite their imminent incarceration, or perhaps because of it, Suzuki wanted his congregants to show their gratitude for aid and fellowship. He quoted 1 Peter, telling his church, "Servants, be subject to your masters with all fear; not only to the good and gentle, but also to the froward."[65] His sermon elaborated that Nikkei must obey the government because God is pleased with those who "suffer for well doing" like Jesus. Suzuki concluded with an affirmation of his faith that God will strengthen them as long as they "increase their Christian zeal in order to maintain what little faith we have."[66] Most Nikkei pastors judged their congregations less harshly but still accepted a degree of responsibility for the situation.

Some pastors shared the attitudes of Quakers, acknowledging the culpability of themselves and their congregants for creating a world where such crimes could occur. The sermon of a Nisei Methodist pastor in Fresno, California, spoke of the community's failure to fulfill its "great mission . . . to be the bridge-builders of the Pacific." He compared the community's indifference, self-centeredness, and sinfulness to Jonah, who went in "the opposite direction" of his "God-given destiny," distracted by personal desire. Because of these failures, he intoned, congregants were partially to blame for the eviction.[67]

Other Nikkei pastors expressed critical judgments of the injustice but reminded people of its spiritual possibilities. Andrew Kuroda, pastor of the Salem Japanese Community Church, wrote a long letter to friends and associates before entering an assembly center in Portland, Oregon. He described the situation broadly but focused on the requirements of Christians in this situation and his "determin[ation] to use this crisis . . . to promote the cause of the Kingdom of God." Many pastors shared his position that "we cannot afford to waste this suffering. We have to make use of this evil to bring good." Similarly, one Nikkei called for his congregation to follow Christ's example and turn its false conviction "into redemptive power."[68]

Kuroda's final comments resonated with criticism made by white Christians, calling the "injuries" of the incarceration "the very essence of Hitlerism we are fighting." He called for Americans to "steadfastly [remain] Christian and militantly [practice] Christian principles . . . to atone a little . . . for this mass injustice." Kuroda urged congregants to follow the government's orders but insisted that guilty white parties atone for their criminal actions. Kuroda sounded less critical in a letter to the local newspaper but did not contradict his statements given to other audiences. He assured the public that he and other residents and citizens of Japanese descent would "whole-heartedly cooperate with the government program of the national defense." Comparing their "sacrifice" to men and women going to the front or working in factories, he cried, "Long live America and democracy!" Although critical of the incarceration, Kuroda accepted it and worked for positive ends. Throughout the war, he carefully framed his views for different audiences. After a few months at Tule Lake, he wryly wrote of this "wonderful opportunity for Christians: . . . Problems [and people] are abundant." Christians "don't have to go around to look" for them. While Kuroda offered encouraging remarks about the possibilities for Christian work in the camps, he simultaneously reminded readers of the moral crisis of the incarceration. Many pastors working in the camps described similar tensions.[69]

Alongside educational institutions, Christian organizations provided some of the few counterpoints to propaganda-saturated media. They consistently defended the loyalty of Nikkei but failed to predict or prepare for the intensity of the approaching conflict. While numerous Protestant leaders believed the incarceration was unjust, the vast majority did not object when the government revoked the civil rights of Nikkei, one by one, after the Pearl Harbor attack. After the government announced its plans for the total incarceration of Nikkei on the Pacific Coast, the limited number of Christian voices warning of the potential negative effects of such plans fell silent until the process was well under way. Once given, few fought the eviction orders. Leaders like Bennett thought it wiser "to give the government the benefit of the doubt so far as motive is concerned."[70] Pastors helped individual families, but mainline groups were not engaged to the extent to which Quakers and Roman Catholics mobilized during the months immediately following the attack on Pearl Harbor.[71]

## Roman Catholic Responses

Aware of rising tensions, Leopold Tibesar, the priest of Seattle's Japanese Catholic parish, wrote an editorial on behalf of people of Japanese ancestry in July 1940. Aimed at a broad public audience, his missive countered negative stereotypes and insisted that Nikkei were loyal residents and citizens of the United States. He encouraged non-Japanese to become acquainted with Nikkei and give them an opportunity to show their patriotism. Born of Luxembourgian immigrants, Tibesar grew up in Illinois with seven siblings, four of whom also took religious vows. He graduated from Catholic University and served as the president of the Catholic Anthropology Society prior to the war. Before coming to Seattle in 1935, he learned Japanese through his work as a Maryknoll missionary in Manchuria and Japan.[72]

Gerald Shaughnessy, the bishop of the Seattle Diocese, wrote a statement to be read in every Catholic church in the city on the Sunday following the Pearl Harbor attack. His message focused on the sin of hatred and emphasized the importance of loving one's neighbors, particularly "our fellow American citizens of Japanese extraction . . . who are no less loyal than others." Tibesar spoke to five hundred delegates at a Holy Names meeting to support the bishop's message and rallied support at a diocesan breakfast for Vincentians on 14 December. The National Catholic Welfare Conference released a statement professing the loyalty of Japanese Americans a week later. *Northwest Catholic Progress*, the Seattle Diocese newspaper, printed articles about the city's Nikkei in nearly every issue leading up to the incarceration. It printed Tibesar's call for parishioners to hire Nikkei unfairly dismissed by their employers and recorded the closure of the Maryknoll school and the Nikkei's departure for Camp Harmony.[73]

Catholic clergy working with Nikkei hoped messages from religious authorities would guide parishioners and priests away from prejudiced attitudes. Their decision to direct statements to parishioners typified Catholic public relations at the time, though the Catholic Charities of the Seattle Diocese also submitted a letter to the Tolan hearings, and Tibesar assisted the Japanese American Citizens League Defense Council's composition of a lengthy loyalty pledge. Within one week of the Pearl Harbor attack, Tibesar also sent notices to the homes of his Nikkei pupils to alleviate their families' concerns about making tuition payments after the federal government had frozen alien bank accounts.[74]

Because of the hierarchy within Roman Catholicism, decisions to speak against the incarceration relied on authorization from bishops and higher authorities. Maryknoll missionaries required permission from their regional bishop and Maryknoll headquarters in Ossining, New York. Bishop James E. Walsh, the father general of Maryknoll, responded with caution when informed of a "lunatic fringe" calling for the removal of Nikkei on the West Coast. While he initially stated that the "only thing we could do is make a local protest," he suggested that Maryknollers do nothing because their efforts "would probably effect nothing." For unclear reasons, Walsh and others in the Maryknoll hierarchy insisted that religious workers on the West Coast "ignore local proposals until they become fact." Prior to consulting the Maryknoll Council, which collectively made final decisions, Walsh was open to the possibility of protesting discriminatory actions to the federal government. But the council, which had no familiarity with Japanese Americans, encouraged Maryknollers on the coast to "do what [they] can for the individuals" but cautioned them not to overlook the "well-grounded fears of Fifth Columnar Activities." The council praised Maryknollers for "protect[ing] [their] little flock from any injustice in witch-hunting" in late January 1942. Fooled by Hearst's fallacious reporting, like most Americans, the council did not want to interfere with what it believed were necessary security precautions.[75]

Before hearing these decisions, Hugh Lavery, the Los Angeles mission's head priest, requested support from the state attorney general after forty Nikkei lost their municipal jobs. Lavery reported that the "public officials always prating about the Bill of Rights and shouting against Hitler" were "turning around and doing the very things here."[76] In March 1942, he requested permission from Maryknoll to petition the attorney general on behalf of a few elderly interned Issei, but Bishop Walsh sent a telegram to stop him from even writing a "letter of complaint."[77] Father Francis Caffrey of the Los Angeles mission similarly wished to speak against the nativist propaganda spewing from the Native Sons and Daughters of the Golden West. He asked, "If there is an opening wedge of the Japanese Americans—who comes next?" Dr. Robbins Barstow of Hartford Seminary and Dr. Remsen Bird of California's Occidental College said that Caffrey would be "ill advised" to mention constitutional rights at that time. Maryknoll authorities agreed with the educational advisors, writing an ardent "<u>NO</u>" in the margins next to Caffrey's request.[78]

Bishop Walsh and the Maryknoll Council feared making statements that might be interpreted as "unpatriotic."[79] Since nativist groups still questioned Catholics' loyalty to the United States, Catholic religious leaders felt particular pressure to support government policy. A history of persecution in America may have caused Catholic leaders to withhold criticism of widely accepted policies.

As pressure grew, the Maryknoll Council became more insistent: "We are completely satisfied that we can do nothing to affect the national policy, the determination of which is entirely within the competence of the civil and military authorities of the country." In a twenty-two-page declaration limited to internal consumption, Maryknoll leaders worked through the Constitution and Declaration of Independence article by article to explicate how the incarceration violated the documents' law and spirit.[80] However, they still insisted their people "make no comment on [its] constitutionality." Father James Drought, Maryknoll's second-in-command, felt they could "do more for the people themselves and for the situation by neither approving nor disapproving the legality of the policy and by working for the constructive benefit of the people concerned." The council decided Maryknollers should stand by their people and "accompany them into . . . exile," hoping that the solidarity would benefit the exiles' "future as Catholics."[81] Drought admitted his unease about this position and encouraged missionaries to fight for their religious rights in camp.[82] Maryknoll's final statement of 27 May 1942 declared that "too impetuous a defense" might "militate against the ultimate and solid welfare" of Nikkei. They hoped to follow the Holy See's policy of "rely[ing] on the inherent decency of human nature to right the wrongs when the human race has returned to reason."[83] Maryknoll leaders rejected several articles written by Tibesar that criticized the government's actions.[84]

As a woman unassociated with the ecclesiastical system, Dorothy Day had the freedom to speak her mind. She bemoaned the injustice in the *Catholic Worker*, writing, "If we did not cry out against this injustice done to them, if we did not try to protest it, we would be failing in two of the works of mercy, which are to visit the prisoner, and to ransom the captive."[85]

Declining to protest the government's decision, Catholic leaders and parishioners sought alternatives to the incarceration. Tibesar, like Maryknoll fathers elsewhere along the coast, developed plans to move his students and their families, four hundred people in all, to Catholic parishes in the Midwest and East. By mid-February, Bishop Walsh instructed Tibesar and Lavery to prepare families to establish a new community in St. Louis. Japanese families met at the Los Angeles Maryknoll School on 3 March to brainstorm alternatives to avoid the mass removal. All Nikkei in attendance preferred to leave as a group preemptively. While some people saw this as a chance to avoid incarceration, many Nikkei associated with the Catholic Church felt confident that the church would take care of their families, in or out of camp. Most Maryknoll students were not Catholic, but the church gave all special consideration. Tibesar did not solicit Nikkei beyond his prewar associations, but Maryknoll headquarters encouraged Tibesar and Lavery to "include as many pagans as possible for evacuation plans." Lavery had asked if "two or three thousand pagans" who had requested to join them could "go with our group," but by late March 1942, nearly seven thousand Los Angeles Nikkei families (23,580 individuals) had registered to be removed with the Maryknollers. Brother Theophane Walsh submitted this composite list to the Tolan Committee.[86]

With such great numbers, Maryknoll leaders realized the impossibility of such an undertaking. No community in the United States could absorb such a large population, and Maryknoll could not locate enough sympathetic regions if they divided Nikkei. Maryknoll lacked the money to support such a project as well. While hopes for this project lingered until April, the WRA ultimately rejected their proposal. On 27 March, Public Proclamation Number 4 banned voluntary evacuation from the coast.[87]

Frustration grew as Maryknollers accepted that they could not carry out a "colonization plan" of their own but realized that the government seemed to have no adequate plan either. An irritated Bishop Walsh wrote, "It is the Government that ordered this measure, so let the Government have all the headaches as it deserves." The Catholic congressman John Tolan increased their alarm when he confided to Father Caffrey that "the government . . . was in no way prepared for an evacuation." Though fairly certain the government would provide a solution, Catholic leaders still worried. Bishop Walsh conceded that the Catholic Church would sponsor a settlement plan if the government failed to provide any accommodations for evicted Nikkei. The mission society reoriented its priorities when plans for the camps solidified and asked the WRA to assign Nikkei associated with Maryknoll to the same camp, where they could continue parish activities. Lieutenant General DeWitt gave them the mistaken impression that they would be moved together to one of the California camp sites.[88]

Before leaving for Bolivia to inaugurate a new mission field for Maryknoll in April 1942, Bishop Walsh proposed a plan to guide Maryknoll assistance to Nikkei living on the Pacific Coast. Given the organization's decades of work in these communities, he felt that Maryknollers had "a unique service to offer [the] Government in this crisis" and vowed to "place at the disposal of the Government our personnel of priests, Brothers and Sisters for the inauguration, maintenance and continuance of human activities in the fields of religion, education, social service and Americanization programs." He believed they could "[minimize] the sufferings" of eviction, decrease "bitterness" among Nisei, and "protect in a large measure our Government and its officials from adverse criticism." Although government agencies repeatedly rejected such "social and spiritual" assistance, individuals including J. Edgar Hoover and army officers offered their gratitude for Maryknollers' support in public relations, registration, and eviction. Brother Philip Morini heard that the government was suspicious of Maryknoll offering to help when only a small number of Nikkei were Catholic. Caffrey confronted WRA officials about this rumor, but the speculation led Drought and others to be cautious and conclude that they should wait for an opportune moment to push their most critical agenda since they might have limited opportunities before the government ceased communication with them. Thus, they withheld most requests until the WRA established more permanent camps.[89]

As occurred among mainline Protestants, Catholic individuals working on the coast expressed outrage at the situation, but national bodies held them back, hesitant to oppose the government at a time of war. The unique Catholic approach sought to resettle Nikkei directly from the coast to communities beyond the restricted military zone, but Maryknoll leaders realized the plan was unfeasible.

## Race and Religion

The general American populace, most of whom identified as Christian, supported the incarceration. Most congregations did not offer aid. Some forcefully opposed aiding people they thought to be the enemy. Without mentioning the situation in America, a retired Episcopal rector in Philadelphia denounced missions to Japan on the basis that members of the race could never become Americans or Christians. He said, "Can you Christianize a Jap? Indeed, can you make an Occidental out of an Oriental? Nay, any more than you can change a leopard's spots."[90] In his mind, Americans had no reason to aid people who would never be allies or Christians. Others offered aid while retaining fundamental racial and national distinctions. Encouraged by her pastor's sermon, a deaconess in Berkeley offered, "I'd be glad to take a Japanese cat, if it will get along all right with my American cat."[91] She wanted to help but still imagined severe distinctions between Japanese and American culture, extending their pervasiveness to include household pets. Presumptions about racial or ethnic attributes affected individual responses as well as church and government policy regarding Nikkei.

Quakers, as evidenced by their prewar letter warning of discrimination, were more attuned to the complexities of racial discord in America. It came to their attention and that of mainline Protestant missionaries when economic factors and white supremacy barred Chinese immigration in 1882. When the Immigration Act of 1924 instituted a quota system effectively excluding people of certain ethnicities, the AFSC formed an Interracial Section to sponsor dialogue and public discussions about race relations with white, Chinese, Japanese, and African Americans. Believing education and interaction could relieve these tensions, the AFSC hired African Americans and young Japanese Americans to share their perspectives and sponsored summer institutes on race relations. But even Clarence Pickett, the AFSC's executive secretary, admitted that this work made only "indirect attacks against the generally accepted pattern of racial segregation in the United States."[92]

The Federal Council of Churches founded the Commission on the Church and Race Relations in 1921 to join white and black Americans, while Protestant mission societies and leaders working toward global peace brought attention to the plights of other racial minorities and negative attitudes toward Asian nations. While Protestants acknowledged race as a vital concern within the Japanese American incarceration, wartime work categorized the issue apart from race relations, which still focused on African Americans. Both threatened domestic harmony and triumph abroad. But some progressive Christian leaders did not consider race to be a foundational problem within American society prior to the 1940s. John Coleman Bennett's *Social Salvation: A Religious Approach to the Problems of Social Change* (1935) failed to mention the issue of race even once.[93]

Bennett, an influential scholar of social ethics teaching at the Pacific School of Religion in Berkeley, California, threw his Nikkei students a going-away party prior to their eviction. His farewell speech expressed common, if complicated, sentiments about racial and national categories. Bennett hesitated to make generalizations about all Japanese, acknowledging that "there is no uniformity among them," but still organized the speech around four qualities he "very often noted among Japanese students." While he praised their warmth of piety, courtesy, toughness, and mysteriousness, all common racial stereotypes, nativists had long used the last three to protest Japanese immigration.[94]

The professor speculated that being "closer to actual conversion" fostered "warmth of piety." His statement alluded to the fact that, unlike most Americans, Christian faith was not taken for granted within Nikkei's culture or families. Since their faith did not stem from generations of tradition, conversion represented a deliberate decision.

Bennett then lauded the students' courtesy, commenting that "the Japanese, unlike American students, realize the extent of the importance of the dignity of the faculty. I fear that next year," he joked, "without this Japanese leaven in our community, there will be an even worse condition among us." While calling for their removal, some Americans criticized Nikkei's peaceful compliance with eviction orders as obsequious submission to authority.

Like many Westerners, Bennett observed "a certain toughness" within Nikkei, explaining that "the Japanese can spend less, eat less and work more than the rest of us. They can sit longer in one spot reading the same book than is the case with Americans." Labor unions argued that physical differences enabled excessive frugality and self-sacrifice, giving Asians an unfair capacity to work longer hours for lower wages. Nativists claimed that following what resembled a respectable Protestant work ethic without a religious foundation would lead to disastrous results. The behavior also supported fears that deceitful Asians used prized American qualities to triumph over American citizens.[95]

Finally, Bennett noted that his Japanese students conveyed "a certain mysteriousness," recalling Westerners' historical fascination with all things foreign and exotic. The mysteriousness Bennett described through anecdotes, however, seemed to stem more from his frustrations with not understanding his students' every move, scholastically or in daily life. Unlike the other three qualities, he did not elevate their mysteriousness as something positive but listed it as yet another differentiating factor. Advocates of the incarceration cited this quality as the reason Nikkei needed to be imprisoned—white people could not tell when a Japanese person was lying. It also led to resistance when church leaders encouraged Nikkei to join predominantly white churches. Parishioners did not think Japanese pastors could minister effectively to white congregations and vice versa.

Bennett's conclusion returned to his initial point that all Japanese are distinct individuals and assured the soon-to-be-evicted that the school would miss them "not because you are Japanese—but because you are yourselves and our friends." He listed the many laws and acts of racial discrimination and segregation for which the school was "ashamed" and pleaded that students "keep free from bitterness." He asked Nikkei to "try to understand us, just as we try to understand you," again referring to their mysterious character and overlooking the fact that his students were American and had grown up in the United States. Knowing that many churches would not accept Nikkei into their congregations, he hoped they would "not be tempted to generalize" those experiences with the "whole Church." Many Americans thought Asians were distinctly different and unlikely to adapt fully to American culture. Bennett seemed to agree but did not condemn that status.

Although Bennett's message was heartfelt and affectionate, he did not affirm his students' identity as Americans. Bennett's categorization excluded Nikkei from the realm of America entirely, despite his demonstrated commitment to preventing harm caused by the incarceration.[96] For Bennett, Nikkei remained entirely "other." The line he drew between Japanese and Americans indicated significant, insurmountable differences. But unlike Americans who called for the eviction, Bennett did not necessarily view these differences negatively. He accepted and welcomed Nikkei and their inherently different character. Perhaps because of this mind-set, he made greater efforts than many other individuals and organizations to ask Nikkei what type of aid they desired.[97] He never presumed to know what was best for them but worked toward agreeable, efficient methods, conscious of generational differences and needs.

Among the dozens of Christian statements made on behalf of Japanese Americans, only two organizations addressed the expressed desires of Nikkei. The Northwest Oriental Evangelization Society and the Fremont Baptist Church included the small phrase "if they [Nikkei] wish" within its recommendations. This simple qualification acknowledged the choices of the imprisoned minority, something rarely seen in the dozens of statements otherwise deciding the fate of tens of thousands of individuals. The text did not represent mere rhetoric; white leaders rarely consulted Nikkei at this or other stages of the incarceration, causing increasing difficulties as the incarceration progressed and national groups planned the minority group's future. This lack of consideration demonstrates the racial hierarchy in churches at this time and the paternalism of many white leaders.

Prior to and after America's entry into the war, the Seattle Council of Churches "congratulate[d]" the Japanese for their "good record" as "law-abiding" neighbors and their "above average . . . good citizenship and observance of the best social usages."[98] They reminded non-Japanese that "most [Nikkei] . . . have . . . demonstrated their loyalty to our country and to the American way of life . . . and are no less a part of these United States than are the rest of us."[99] While well intentioned, the council's statements assumed the subordination of Nikkei within a racial hierarchy. Within this context, only the white establishment had the authority to define who was or was not a good citizen. Numerous editorials expressed similar statements. Church leaders and other sympathizers urged Nikkei to declare their loyalty publicly to help quell the rising animosity against members of their ethnicity. In a critical situation such as this, what else could be done? Bennett's speech from 1942 demonstrated the difficulties surrounding the issues of race and nationality. He had high hopes for Japanese pastors ministering to "[their] people" but did not imagine they would fully join white American society.

Catholic leaders, like Protestants, ranged from compassionate to tolerant to racist. Catholic periodicals regularly confronted the sin of racism, but some California priests still supported mass incarceration. In a June 1942 editorial, Bishop Walsh anonymously expressed his hope that the nation would overturn racial discrimination permanently "so that we might make our [wartime] sacrifices in the name of that true democracy which will bring in the full and equal brotherhood of all races and all men. Our victory would be a milestone for the ages, worth all its terrible costs." Walsh mentioned race in most sermons during this time, but he did not make this statement openly. Bishop Walsh and others in the hierarchy occasionally made unfavorable remarks about the "Oriental" disposition when frustrated, though missionaries working with Japanese rarely expressed such sentiments. All Maryknollers consistently wrote of the "Japanese" when referring to Nisei with American citizenship.[100]

Tibesar's writing on race related directly to the United States and the promise of the Constitution. With a liberal understanding of American exceptionalism, Tibesar believed that "Providence [had] entrusted a sublime destiny to us" and that it was America's duty to hold "its doors . . . wide . . . to all the peoples of the world." He pointed out the fallacy of the notion of one "white race" since a diversity of ethnicities claimed whiteness, just as many sects identified as Protestant. He lamented how dull the nation would become if everyone felt pressured to "conform to the drab monotony of a common cultural world." Embracing this pluralistic reality, Tibesar believed, would benefit world peace and the integrity of America. He scorned the "indifference" of tolerance and insisted Americans aim for the higher standard of the Golden Rule. Thinking back on this time period, Tibesar wrote that the United States cannot "approach the nations of the world . . . and expect to be heard when we ask for universal peace" if we do not first grant all Americans "the right to be what they are by origin—the right to be different." While he wrote this in the context of a postwar world in persistent turmoil, Tibesar's actions suggest he felt similarly in the 1940s.[101]

Many testimonies made for the Tolan Committee based their arguments on questions of race, whether supporting a mass incarceration or not. Speaking for the local AFSC, Floyd Schmoe warned that violating American principles of justice could create a "dangerous fifth column" and aid the Japanese government by affirming a "'Holy War' of race." The Reverend Thompson echoed this statement, arguing that turning these conflicts into a "race war of tinted peoples against the whites" would be "play[ing] into the hands of Japan's propaganda."[102]

The failure of the Tolan Committee hearings mattered little in the end, in part due to national racial stereotypes. President Roosevelt believed that "the mingling of white with oriental blood . . . is harmful to our future citizenship." Beyond economic competition and security risks, Roosevelt felt that Nikkei were "immutably foreign, dangerous," and unassimilable. The general of the Western Defense Command, John De-Witt, who called for the mass incarceration, became known for his succinct statement, "A Jap is a Jap." But other government officials like Secretary of War Henry L. Stimson questioned the precedent a race-based incarceration might set for future race relations in the country. The Tolan Committee concluded, "The fact that in a time of emergency this country was unable to distinguish between the loyalties of many thousands of its citizens . . . calls into question the adequacy of our whole outlook upon the assimilation of foreign groups."[103] Presuming the necessity and virtue of assimilation, the committee questioned its universal applicability.

## Eviction and Life at Camp Harmony

In the late spring of 1942, the Reverend Emery Andrews watched his congregation trickle into Camp Harmony, the temporary assembly center hastily erected on the Western Washington State fairgrounds in Puyallup. On Mother's Day, he entered an empty church. He "sat in the pulpit chair," gazed at the "vacant pews," and "visualized Sunday School boys and girls, teachers, young people, church choir and the various individuals." Born in Nebraska and raised on a farm near Modesto, California, Andrews received his license to preach a year before graduating high school. After training at the Bible Institute of Los Angeles, he married Mary Brooks, returned to school, and worked with Modesto's Italian and Mexican communities for two years. Moving to Seattle to attend the University of Washington for degrees in sociology and education, Andrews was hired by the American Baptist Home Mission Society to lead the Seattle Japanese Baptist Church from 1929 to 1955. The man everyone knew as "Andy" not only dedicated his career to the mission church; he devoted most of his life to Seattle's Nikkei community, Baptists, Buddhists, and nonreligious alike. He organized and led a variety of programs at the ethnic church, including English language classes, basketball tournaments, religious services, and Christian education seminars. For thirty-eight years, he held the position of scoutmaster for the first Nisei Boy Scout troop in Seattle. Unlike many of the white Christians supporting Nikkei, Andrews lacked missionary experience in Japan. When the eviction from the coast became imminent, Andrews and the other pastors of Japanese churches helped their congregants prepare for eviction physically and spiritually and waited with each group at their departure sites.[104]

But before Andrews's congregants moved into the makeshift housing in Puyallup, Nikkei living on Bainbridge Island became the first Japanese American community in the country to enter an incarceration camp. Located across Puget Sound from Seattle, islanders' close proximity to U.S. Navy facilities prompted DeWitt to call for their removal on 24 March 1942, the day he issued Civilian Exclusion Order No. 1, which announced the eviction of all Nikkei from the West Coast and Alaska. Bainbridge residents had six days to sell or lease their farms, store belongings, find homes for pets, bid neighbors farewell, and pack the following, "not exceeding that which [could] be carried by the family or individual":

a. Blankets and linens for each member of the family;
b. Toilet articles for each member of the family;
c. Clothing for each member of the family; [and]
d. Sufficient knives, forks, spoons, plates, bowls, and cups for each member of the family.
e. All items carried will be securely packaged, tied, and plainly marked with the name of the owner and numbered in accordance with instructions received at the Civil Control Office.

While church groups helped other communities pack and move into the camps, the Nikkei on Bainbridge, being the first and having the least amount of warning, received little aid. The AFSC stationed a group of volunteers on the island to act as "observers and errand boys," helping with farm work and conveying legal and financial documents from Seattle to Nikkei confined to the island. On 30 March 1942, friends, neighbors, high school classmates, and curious observers lined the Bainbridge docks to watch Nikkei, one-seventeenth of the island's total population, board the ferry. From there, islanders took a train to the California camp that would become Manzanar incarceration center. Just under a year later, the WRA granted islanders permission to rejoin other Washington Nikkei at Minidoka in Idaho.[105]

A month prior to the incarceration of Bainbridge Island Nikkei, the U.S. government evicted all Nikkei residents of Terminal Island, a fishing village in Los Angeles County. They were not incarcerated but given forty-eight hours to pack, move, and find housing on the mainland. While some stayed with family, a coalition of Buddhists, Baptists, Quakers, Congregationalists, Methodists, and Roman Catholics scrambled to turn fellowship halls, church basements, and Japanese language schools into hostels. Herbert and Madeline Nicholson, Quaker missionaries working at West Los Angeles Methodist Church; Allan Hunter, pastor of Mount Hollywood Congregational Church and the West Coast chairman of the Fellowship of Reconciliation; Esther Rhoads, a Quaker missionary working for the AFSC; and Julius Goldwater, the one white Buddhist priest in America, all of whom would work in and out of the camps throughout the war, joined efforts to care for the refugees of Terminal Island.[106]

Most Nikkei received the first material support from churches during the weeks when the Wartime Civil Control Administration (WCCA), the precursor to the WRA, called for individual neighborhoods to report for removal to the temporary camps. Churches all along the coast stored belongings, found homes for pets, and helped families sell or lease their homes, businesses, and automobiles. Andrews marked a grid onto the Japanese Baptist Church's gymnasium floor; each family could fill one square with their belongings. As they delivered items to the church, they signed an itemized contract with the Washington Baptist Convention that released the church of any liability. In one touching case, a young Japanese man appeared at the door of a Berkeley Congregational Church and asked if they would store "a square box wrapped in . . . white silk." He explained, "These are the ashes of the children and my mother." The pastor quickly consented and removed the box to a secure location.[107]

The WCCA often used church buildings for registration and staging areas where families waited for trucks or trains to transport them to their assigned camp. Women of the church provided sandwiches and drinks, watched children, and stood by to comfort families. Other volunteers drove the elderly to camps directly to ease the difficulties of moving and transferring baggage. Since the army made inadequate preparations for holding and transporting large numbers of people, Nikkei relied on the churches' contributions. On several occasions the army purchased inadequate food and asked local churches to serve light meals.[108]

The WCCA housed most Western Washington and Alaskan Nikkei in the shadow of a large wooden roller coaster at the Puyallup fairgrounds before moving them to Idaho several months later. Throughout April and May, the government summoned Nikkei living in Western Washington to register, leave their homes, and enter Puyallup's Camp Harmony. Non-Nikkei friends, pastors, and teachers came to say their good-byes, and many "wept openly" as the convoy of busses pulled away. On "E-Day," as Monica Itoi called Evacuation, Expulsion, or Eviction Day, she and others were grateful to see her youth minister, Everett Thompson, and Emery Andrews. A photograph of Leopold Tibesar appeared in the *Seattle Times* as he stood at the gates of Camp Harmony to greet Nikkei as they arrived.[109]

As their bus pulled into the Puyallup fairgrounds, Itoi and others observed "an entire block filled with neat rows of low shacks, resembling chicken houses. . . . The bus . . . drove through a wire-fenced gate," and to their dismay, they found themselves "inside the oversized chicken farm." They stood in "ankle deep . . . gray, glutinous mud," waiting for their housing assignment. Monica's family, like Nikkei in every center, stuffed mattresses with straw to cushion their army cots, built furniture from scrap lumber, and stood in long lines for every meal. While most California camps were windy and dusty, incarcerees at Camp Harmony battled the "carnivorous Puyallup mud" until the weather improved in late summer.[110]

Most scholarly works about Japanese American life during the war focus on the ten camps constructed for the duration of the war, but the majority of Nikkei faced the initial trauma of incarceration before that time. Camp organizations, Nikkei leadership, and patterns of daily life formed in the coastal WCCA centers. The WCCA did not provide activities, schools, or adequate employment, but incarcerees and volunteers from the outside quickly organized worship services, Sunday schools, Boy Scout troops, English lessons, lecture series, and even correspondence courses to enable students to finish the school year.

The WCCA's official policy on religious liberty stated, "It is the desire of this office to adhere to the American principle of religious freedom regardless of sect or denomination, race or creed, and to tolerate no discrimination against any religious denomination which the Japanese constituency or group within the Center have requested." The declaration vaguely prohibited services used as a "vehicle to propagandize or incite the members of the center," granting camp directors the power to be lenient or restrictive. Later policies forbade Shinto practices specifically because Japanese officials had formulated a compulsory State Shinto in recent decades to promulgate Japanese nationalism and emperor worship. Generally, authorities allowed incarcerees to "promote religious services," "request . . . Caucasian assistance" from the outside, and transfer Nikkei clergy to other camps if a population lacked a religious leader. At Camp Harmony, the center manager J. J. McGovern granted permission for most religious gatherings but inexplicably rejected Protestants' plans for a vacation Bible school.[111]

Limitations on printed matter also restricted religious liberty. McGovern allowed pastors to speak to groups in Japanese if congregants could not understand English, but religious groups could not print bulletins or other material in Japanese initially. Upon entering camp, officials seized all Japanese print matter that had survived the frequent raids following the bombing of Pearl Harbor. This restriction foiled the plan of white church members who bought out a Nihonmachi bookstore with the intention of starting a camp library with the books. WCCA rules permitted Japanese Bibles, but guards permanently confiscated many. The rule banned all Buddhist texts in Japanese. Since the Department of Justice still held most Buddhist leaders in internment camps, this ruling placed heavy burdens on an already disadvantaged religious group.[112]

Tight security regulations complicated pastoral care. White visitors could enter camps only to hold worship services or meet congregants during official visiting hours in crowded visitation halls. But despite attempts to bar and corral visitors, white pastors of Japanese churches, representatives of the Seattle Council of Churches, and other individuals frequently visited Camp Harmony. Gertrude Apel, the council's general secretary, proudly pledged that "the Church [would] continue to minister to its people no matter where they are, under whatever conditions." One of the first women ordained as a Methodist deacon, Apel trained for the ministry in Chicago and pastored a church in Montana before coming to Washington. In the midst of the Great Depression, Apel became the general secretary of the Washington–Northern Idaho Council of Churches, the first women to lead an ecumenical organization of that size. Many local pastors thought she would fail given the dire financial state and disarray of the council, but Apel's diplomacy and administrative skills cemented its disparate components together. Her commitment to ecumenism and efficiency shaped her work with Japanese Americans.[113]

Apel cooperated with WCCA officials to ensure the greatest possible access for her ministers. She enforced visitation rules at Camp Harmony with passion, requiring all council representatives to sign a strongly worded pledge to obey WCCA rules and not "abuse the privilege of visitation by issuing public criticism of the camps." She warned, "An inspection visit should not be carried on under the guise of religious service."[114] Apel knew camp officials could revoke their visitation privileges at any time. White ministers relinquished their ability to publically protest the quality of life in the camps in favor of maintaining direct contact with their congregants.

The dearth of clergy did not stymie Nisei at Camp Harmony. A Seattle Council of Churches report used a militaristic simile to describe the first week in camp: "Like parachute troops who are fighting almost as soon as their feet hit the ground, the young people in the Puyallup Assembly Center began setting up Sunday School the very day they landed. Working efficiently, they mobilized their forces of experienced teachers, drafted new ones where necessary, adopted graded lessons, [and] secured the supplies necessary."[115] Redolent of the can-do rhetoric of wartime America, this action-filled passage heralded the achievements of Christians galvanized by wartime limitations.

Nikkei volunteers, Issei pastors, and white church leaders soon organized Sunday services and other activities. Six hundred Nikkei attended the Protestant service on 10 May, less than two weeks after the camp opened. Attendance nearly tripled the following week as more people entered camp. White and Nikkei leaders offered additional activities, and by June over 2,500 incarcerees attended a Protestant function each week. The total camp population peaked at 7,390 by late May, so about a third of the camp participated in some Christian activity. Methodist, Baptist, Episcopalian, Presbyterian, and Holiness Issei pastors conducted Sunday worship services, prayer meetings, and weekly Bible study in Japanese. Sunday school, worship, youth fellowship, and a Sunday school teachers' training class also filled the weekly schedule. Catholics attended daily mass offered by Father Tibesar. Nikkei members of Seattle's Legion of

Mary continued to instruct children in catechism and bring them to mass. By late May, the WCCA instructed Christians to direct all questions and concerns via their section chaplains, lay volunteers who reported to Chief Chaplain Tom Kobayashi, a Roman Catholic.[116]

Tsutomu (Tom) Fukuyama, a newly ordained Nisei Baptist, assisted outside clergy with English language activities. Fukuyama's early religious life exemplified the experience of many Nisei converts. Growing up on the strawberry farms of Bainbridge Island, Fukuyama attended a Congregational Sunday school with friends. He lacked "serious" interest in religion, but Seattle Baptist missionaries Florence Rumsey and Esther McCullough made positive impressions on him during their regular visits to the island. A Nisei preacher from Bainbridge led Fukuyama to receive baptism at age fourteen. On schedule to graduate from Berkeley Baptist Divinity School in the spring of 1942, Fukuyama returned to Washington and received an emergency ordination at Seattle's Japanese Baptist Church on 30 April 1942, two weeks before his twenty-fifth birthday, to alleviate the dearth of clergy. Fukuyama preached occasionally at Camp Harmony and busied himself with camp youth groups but lacked ministerial experience and could rarely leave his sector of camp. Given the average age of the second generation, few Nisei were experienced ministers in 1941. Most of the Nikkei who would eventually lead the Japanese American church had not finished school when the war began. Many received hasty ordinations like Fukuyama's.[117]

A fat folder within the Church Council of Greater Seattle archives at the University of Washington holds dozens of letters requesting passes for Andrews, Thompson, Jensen, and other church representatives. Divided into four districts by high barbed wire, the structure of Camp Harmony quadrupled the amount of work required to provide religious programs for all incarcerees. The barriers divided established congregations, so Protestants formed an ecumenical church in each section. On most Sundays, white pastors from Seattle, Tacoma, Puyallup, and Sumner drove to the camps—often without remuneration for their time or gas, a rationed commodity after April 1942. Over the summer, more than fifty different clergy worked with the four new congregations. Most came from Baptist, Methodist, Congregational, Episcopal, and Presbyterian churches, but representatives of evangelical churches also visited. Guests could preach only if invited by incarcerees. Given the complex nature of worship in the camps, incarcerated Christians repeatedly asked outside church workers for help.[118]

Leopold Tibesar moved to Puyallup and ministered to Nikkei Catholics daily during their time at Camp Harmony. He held mass in Area A's mess hall (a converted barn) on the first Sunday of incarceration for "hundreds" of people. Approximately twenty Catholics received communion each day, and one hundred to three hundred attended Sunday services. Seattle's Maryknoll Sisters visited incarcerees and provided occasional religious instruction. Tibesar described the chaos of their worship space, which his parishioners struggled to make "presentable" each morning. Breakfast followed Tibesar's early service, after which Protestants placed a Bible and two candles at one end of the hall to mark the space as their own for the following hour. An official managerial meeting frequently followed lunch, and incarcerees used the mess hall as a dance hall or theater after dinner. Catholic services relocated to similarly ill-suited buildings in later months. Camp authorities initially granted parishioners passes to attend church services in the different sections of camp, but Tibesar still rotated among the sectors for confession and mass as officials intermittently revoked this privilege. Everett Thompson apologized to Tibesar after Protestants abusing the system eventually caused camp officials to revoke all authorizations.[119]

The Seattle Council of Churches called Everett Thompson to act as a full-time minister for incarcerated Protestants. Thompson spoke fluent Japanese, having spent years conducting missionary work in Japan before moving to Seattle. Outside workers trained Nikkei to lead Sunday school and other church activities, but Thompson explained that "young people . . . want Americans, not their parents or the Japanese pastors to teach . . . classes." This desire could have been for English speakers as many Issei ministers did not speak English well, but other reports relay an "eager[ness for] Caucasian preachers" specifically. Since no Nisei pastors lived outside the camps by this time, requesting outside aid meant requesting aid from white Americans, however phrased. In Seattle, white ministers led most Nisei services and youth groups before the war. Within the older California Japanese Christian churches, Nikkei filled most positions, so proportionately fewer white supporters worked in other camps.[120]

Once established, the congregations at Puyallup needed supplies and other basic aid. Individuals and local congregations donated recreational equipment, library books, and Sunday school material for all ages. Seattle churches loaned Bibles, hymnals, choir robes, draperies, and communion sets. Church members persuaded the army to provide trucks to transport three pianos and several pulpits from the Japanese church buildings in Seattle.[121]

White volunteers delivered forgotten items and helped incarcerees finalize business deals. Although the WRA eventually organized an office for this work, it could not address the mountain of concerns, nor did all Nikkei feel comfortable confiding in government officials. Visitors came to see friends, former students, and neighbors. They first met across the camp's chain link barriers and later in large visitation rooms. They delivered care packages of food, entertainment, and household necessities. A church report described how people visited to "perpetuate the old ties and to repudiate the disgrace and ignominy which the high barbed wire symbolized."[122]

Even though church had not been a central part of Monica Itoi's life in Seattle, her autobiography describes the consolation provided by religion at this time. Services under the grandstand at Camp Harmony gradually lifted her depressed, angry attitude about the incarceration. On Sunday, the family "came to an abrupt halt, free from the busy round of activities in which we submerged our feelings. . . . It was a great comfort to see [Thompson] and the many other ministers and church workers. . . . We felt that we were not entirely forgotten. With battered spirits we met in the dimly lighted makeshift room which served as our chapel under the baseball grandstand and after each sermon and prayer, we gained new heart." "Bit by bit," she remembered, "our minister kept on helping us build the foundation for a new outlook." Itoi and others found particular comfort in Psalms and other scripture. Amidst the chaos and uncertainty of the eviction, Itoi began reading the Bible "more slowly and conscientiously . . . finding new meaning and comfort." She wrote, "The room seemed filled with peace and awe, as if walls had been pushed back and we were free." Many incarcerated Christians described such experiences during the war.[123]

This liberating sense of peace led Itoi to believe "this was not the end of our lives . . . but just the beginning." After struggling to attain training and professional employment after high school, Itoi had become "tense and angry . . . about prejudice, real and imaginary." While the eviction represented the greatest transgression, she reflected that "there was little to be gained in bitterness and cynicism. . . . It was more important to examine our own souls, to keep our faith in God and help to build that way of life which we so desired." Christianity provided an impetus to face the crisis and take rational actions to meet her goals instead of becoming bitter, angry, and resentful of her circumstances. Numerous Nikkei felt that their faith—whatever it was—got them through the war. Once Itoi realized the army and WCCA officials would not abuse or threaten them physically, she concluded that "the greatest trial ahead . . . would be of a spiritual nature." Many other incarcerees expressed similar determination.[124]

While Nikkei, outside volunteers, and church employees worked tirelessly to provide necessities and occupy the seemingly endless hours in camp, everyone knew their time in Puyallup was limited. Any programs established at Camp Harmony would have to be approved by a different director and possibly be subjected to different regulations. In the end, fewer restrictions existed in the more permanent incarceration centers.

Incarcerees did not know when or where they would be sent. In June, the camp newspaper confirmed a rumor that everyone incarcerated in Puyallup would be transferred to Tule Lake in California. Nisei from Camp Harmony who had volunteered to construct barracks at Tule Lake were shocked to hear that the WRA planned to transfer the remainder of the camp to Idaho instead. After improving their barrack apartments and acquiring jobs first at Camp Harmony and then Tule Lake, some declined the offer to move yet again, despite separation from close friends and family members. On 12 September 1942, the final trainload of incarcerees left Camp Harmony for Minidoka Relocation Center.[125]

When Monica Itoi imagined her new life in Idaho, she envisioned "sunbaked terrain, dried-up waterholes, runty-looking sagebrush and ugly nests of rattlesnakes," an accurate picture that only left out the unrelenting wind and dust, something she would discover on her first day at Minidoka.[126]

## Conclusion

While some Christian groups provided aid to alleviate the trials of eviction and improve living conditions in the camps, few condemned the incarceration until a later date. The Seattle Council of Churches hinted that the Christian public's apathy might be related to the government's disregard for Nikkei and their civil rights, but unlike Quakers, neither the council nor Catholics ever suggested that Christians or the general American public were guilty or obligated to remedy the situation. The Seattle Council acknowledged that "strenuous pressure" on the government could improve conditions in the camps but decided that "continued visitation and hospitality" was the most important concern.[127] National Roman Catholic leaders directed coastal priests to avoid interfering with the course of events despite their belief that the removal was unconstitutional. Mainline Protestants and Catholics showed reluctance to oppose government decisions during a time of war when "patriotic" fervor ran so high. Both groups argued that they could do more good through other channels. Quakers like Gordon Hirabayashi and Floyd Schmoe acted immediately, supporting legal challenges to the incarceration and transferring college students out of the restricted zone. With less success, Catholics sought avenues to move parishioners to the East before the government placed them in camps. These attitudes foreshadowed the types of social work done on behalf of Japanese Americans during the war. Quakers would seek immediate change for individual Nikkei and work through legal channels for justice. Mainline Protestants would focus on religious worship in the camps and public relations. Roman Catholics met religious needs and resettled their parishioners as quickly as possible.

The responses of Nikkei Christians during the months prior to eviction also prefigured their experiences during the war. Nisei later imitated Gordon Hirabayashi's then singular effort when they resisted the military draft for religious and other reasons. Like Monica Itoi, many found solace in their faith and sought biblical parallels to help explain their situation. Their pastors provided spiritual guidance and tried to retain a sense of normalcy within their churches. Pastors would restructure their worship practices to function within the camps and adapt to material and spatial limitations. Nikkei had to determine the extent to which they would cooperate with government officials and follow the leadership of white outsiders who independently determined the ways in which they would support and guide worship in the camps. Some Nikkei felt wounded by mainline Protestant churches' refusal to fight eviction orders, but others were relieved to see any sympathy from white neighbors and community leaders.

# 2  The Organization of Christian Aid

We cannot all be Harriet Beecher Stowes or Otto [sic] Schindlers. . . .
Tides are turned not only by the words and deeds of historic figures,
but by the quiet and enduring heroism of ordinary people acting in
good conscience.

—Shizue Seigel, *In Good Conscience*

Throughout World War II, national Christian organizations and individual
Christians pooled their resources or worked alone to remedy challenges
created by the incarceration of Japanese Americans. Mainline Protestant
and Roman Catholic churches did not initially fight the incarceration directly but tried to reduce its harms. As Nikkei entered the camps, local pastors and national mainline Protestant leaders prioritized the pastoral needs
of Nikkei Christians by helping them organize and staff churches in the
camps. Once this immediate concern abated, they joined Quaker and Roman Catholic efforts to resettle Nikkei outside of the camps. Creating welcoming communities for Japanese Americans required the transformation
of public opinion. Christians hoped their work in the camps and public
relations campaigns would strengthen the country's Christian foundations
and minimize suffering that could lead to greater dissent. Ecumenical committees formed by the Federal Council of Churches and Home Missions
Council of North America confronted these problems, as did groups commissioned by specific denominations. Individuals and nondenominational
groups with specific aims, such as the American Bible Society and the
YWCA, developed their own approaches to improving life in camp.

This chapter examines the broad scope of programs and services designed and implemented by Christians outside of the camps. Most aid took
one of three forms: supporting worship practices of Japanese Christians,
developing public relations campaigns on their behalf, and providing Nikkei with material aid and services. Some Nikkei gratefully accepted
material aid ranging from scholarships to Christmas presents, but others
saw underlying complexities to these exchanges. Christian leaders saw
an opportunity to improve race relations and national unity.

Compassion and the need to right an injustice motivated Christians to help Nikkei, but larger dreams of global unity also fueled their efforts. Mainline Protestants, Quakers, and Roman Catholics all imagined variations of this goal. Leading theologians like John Bennett, H. Richard Niebuhr, and Reinhold Niebuhr perceived a growing crisis in America and the rest of the world. As Christian Realists, Bennett and Reinhold Niebuhr did not believe humankind could create a utopic social order but thought Christians were obligated to use what they saw as universal Christian ethics to promote peace. Most churches vociferously supported U.S. involvement in World War I, only to watch it create greater disunity throughout the world. This failure and the Great Depression resulted in widespread disillusionment and hopelessness, paving the way for Hitler and other totalitarian regimes to provide scapegoats and salvation. Social trends during the flapper era drew accusations of moral decline. As global conflicts surged in the late 1930s, Niebuhr and others saw World War II as *the* point of crisis—not another link in a chain but the decisive moment of justice. Therefore, turning the moral tide in their favor was crucial. A compilation of Protestant wartime work in 1943 concluded, "If the great struggle against the forces that oppose democracy, freedom and human brotherhood is to be successful, the Church must give a fuller embodiment of those ideals in its own life."[1] In this way, the incarceration became a problem for the churches as well as a challenge to democracy. Many leaders thought a spiritual revival would be the only effective weapon against totalitarianism and domestic divisions.[2] They needed to reform the nation and world through the church.

Mainline Protestant leaders believed the nation's moral direction would not shift if people remained isolated in their traditional congregations divided by denominational, national, and ethnic loyalties, so they founded numerous ecumenical organizations to cooperatively address the needs of society. The YMCA and Christian Endeavor Society grew out of the early Social Gospel in the late nineteenth century, and the Federal Council of Churches formed in 1911. International leaders planned the World Council of Churches in 1937, but the outbreak of World War II delayed its formation until 1948. This ecumenical movement encouraged American Protestant leaders to form interdenominational aid societies to address the needs of Nikkei. When tensions rose between Japan and the United States in early 1941, the FCC, the Foreign Missions Conference, and the Home Missions Council formed the Inter-Council Committee on Japanese Christian Work in the United States to coordinate activities of related ecumenical and denominational organizations.[3] They met the day after Japan bombed Pearl Harbor and commissioned a press release from the FCC.[4] As soon as the government announced plans for a mass incarceration, aid groups formed on an ecumenical basis. The FCC and the Home Missions Council founded the Protestant Church Commission for Japanese Service to coordinate worship in the incarceration camps and the Committee on Resettlement of Japanese Americans. The Home Missions Council also appointed a Committee on Administration of Japanese Work to oversee these groups and the work of member denominations.

American Catholics also believed a united Christendom would unite the world but rarely collaborated with Protestants at this time.[5] Similarly, most Protestant ventures did not extend unity to include Roman Catholics and work with Japanese Americans was no exception. With minimal communication with Protestants, Catholics working with Nikkei remained suspicious and skeptical of Protestant work. Catholics worked for the same central goals though: resettle Nikkei outside of the camps and convince the nation to welcome them. Maryknoll missionaries coordinated Catholic worship in the camps with approval from the dioceses in which the camps were located, but Catholic workers operated independently from one another.

Protestant efforts were not fully united, however. Mainline ecumenists sought coordination with Quakers, but the American Friends Service Committee valued its independence. The AFSC formed the National Japanese American Student Relocation Council free of religious affiliation but integrating additional support for Nikkei into its Seattle, California, and Hawaii branches. While cooperating with ecumenical groups, Congregationalists formed their own Christian Committee for Work with Japanese Evacuees. It directed its greatest efforts toward a national public relations campaign to battle negative attitudes and stereotypes of Nikkei outside of the camp.[6] Other denominations, like the Disciples of Christ, operated resettlement programs through their war services or missions committees.

## Coordinating Worship in the Camps

The formation of churches within the camps offered ecumenists the opportunity to expand their vision of unified Christianity to the congregational level—to build churches free of sectarian divisions. The FCC and the Home Missions Council founded the ecumenical Protestant Church

Commission for Japanese Service to coordinate worship in the incarceration camps, find placements for returning missionaries, and manage financial contributions.[7] The commission hosted monthly meetings throughout the war where denominational representatives and other concerned individuals planned the future of Japanese churches. In the summer of 1942, before most Nikkei moved from WCCA centers to the incarceration camps, commission members and other Protestant leaders decided to support only ecumenical Protestant worship in the camps. In December 1943, nearly fifty representatives of WRA centers, resettlement areas, Protestant denominations, and ecumenical groups decided to integrate Nikkei into predominantly white churches after the war.[8] Participants spoke of prioritizing unity, both religious and racial, at every meeting.

Gordon Chapman, with years of experience as a Presbyterian missionary in Japan, operated the Protestant Commission for Japanese Service from California. The FCC and Home Missions Council charged Chapman with two main duties: assign white and Nikkei pastors to the individual camps and coordinate financial contributions to the camp churches. No one asked Japanese pastors if they desired help from a program like the Protestant Commission, but the Japanese Church Federation of Northern California officially recognized the commission's authority. They relayed their endorsement to the WRA and asked the agency to give Chapman access to incarcerated Christians. A telegram from Nikkei to the FCC professed their satisfaction with his work and asked the council to make Chapman the "official representative for all the Christian Japanese living in the various centers."[9]

While Nikkei pastors initially went where the WRA sent them, the allocation of non-Nikkei ministers was more complicated. The WRA would admit only pastors invited by incarcerees. Unable to dispatch white missionaries to camps independently, Chapman devised a functional system to distribute workers to camps. First, missionaries and other religious leaders wrote Chapman to request camp assignments. He then discussed characteristics of different camps with approved candidates and suggested they visit or correspond with the church board within the desired camp. At the same time, Chapman provided a list of missionary candidates to Nikkei church leaders, who responded with their selections. In essence, Chapman operated as a matchmaker. Each camp's Interfaith and Community Activities Committees and the camp director still had to authorize and issue an official invitation. The process took even longer when

Nikkei pastors disagreed over which candidate to invite. The lengthy procedure postponed the arrival of white volunteers and the initiation of many church programs. Such delays frustrated Nikkei congregants who had requested outside help before moving into the camps. The Christians at Minidoka avoided this delay since so many of Seattle's prewar white pastors moved to Idaho with their congregations. They bypassed Chapman's matchmaking process entirely.[10]

The Protestant Commission relied on the cooperation of dozens of individuals and their willingness to move to desolate locations around the country. Forced to leave their foreign posts, missionaries volunteered through the commission to work at the camps. On 25 August 1942, the Swedish ship *Gripsholm* docked in New York, returning many missionaries who had been working in Asia. Since most spoke Japanese, they could work with both Issei and Nisei. Some missionaries requested specific camps, but most offered to go anywhere they were needed. Retired missionaries who had spent time in Japan also volunteered to move to the camps. One such woman, Laura Bodenhamer, wrote Chapman that she and her husband were "anxious to finish [their] days with these brethren in the Camps." Chapman suggested that volunteers unsuited to the hardships of camp help with urban resettlement. Returning Catholic Maryknoll missionaries met in Los Angeles with Hugh Lavery, who dispersed them to camps, much as Chapman did with Protestant missionaries.[11]

In support of the WRA's policy against evangelism in the camps, Chapman denied applicants exhibiting too great an evangelistic zeal access to the camps. A man named Owen Still, for example, sought "personal work . . . talk[ing] to individuals—especially Buddhist individuals—about the Master." He disapproved of the prohibition barring outside ministers from entering the homes of non-Christians because he believed teaching "one family at a time" led a significant "number of people . . . to give up Buddhism." Chapman denied his request, and Still's name never appeared on the list of available outside workers. Members of the commission agreed with the WRA that explicit evangelism to Buddhists was inappropriate, and Chapman prevented missionaries inclined toward those tactics from entering most camps. Due to the sensitive nature of the situation, Chapman rejected most requests from people unassociated with prewar Japanese missions. Leaders of the Protestant Commission made a point to prove that it was not an evangelistic organization, officially recognizing the rights of Roman Catholics, Buddhists, and anyone else to "enjoy the same privileges" as Protestant incarcerees.[12]

At least one evangelist violated the expectations of the commission, WRA administrators, and incarcerated Nikkei. Gordon Chapman arranged for the Reverend Douglas Noble to drive his mobile Wayside Chapel to six camps and several resettlement communities. Chapman eagerly described the chapel to his brother, Ernest, quoting a newspaper article: "The Wayside Chapel is a caravan outfitted with folding chairs, a portable altar, public address system, phonograph records of religious music, moving picture projector and films, Bibles, and so on. . . . [Noble] is equipped 'to take religious service, Christian pastoral activities, counseling work, boys' and girls' group programs, infant baptism, and church school classes into out-of-the-way places.'" Noble led a busy schedule, conducting six meetings in two days at Manzanar. He reported that six to seven hundred Nikkei attended each of his revival meetings. After a performance, he would return groups of people to their barracks, singing hymns over the mobile chapel's booming public address system as he drove through the camp. By the end of his tour, Noble had addressed nearly five thousand people and given away several thousand religious tracts to Nikkei in and out of the camps. Over sixty individuals made "decisions for Christ and His Way," according to the evangelist.[13]

Noble entertained and persuaded some Nikkei, but his tactics offended others. Minidokans complained that Noble spoke to Nisei as if they were not Americans but rather "Japanese from Japan." A report from Topaz claimed that Noble said he "did not like the Buddhists." Chapman cautioned Noble that whether the reports were "true or not," he should not make such comments. He recommended that Noble "stick to [his] positive Christian message . . . and refrain from all reference to Buddhists." The aural invasion of Noble's "sound truck" broadcasting Christian hymns throughout the camp angered Gila River's project director, L. H. Bennett. He and his staff did not want to "disturb the emotional tenor" of the Nikkei "who look to [them] for guidance and protection in certain matters," and he worried that Noble had offended non-Christians. These incidents demonstrated the risk of allowing evangelists into the camps, even when welcomed by some incarcerees. The Protestant Commission and WRA worked hard to avoid the impression that they were evangelizing to Buddhists but failed at times.[14]

In addition to the duties of assigning clergy to different camps and resettlement locations, it became Chapman's job to field complaints about white and Nikkei ministers causing discord in the camps. In the case of Nikkei clergymen, he could do little but encourage the individuals to resettle. Mark Dawber, executive secretary of the Home Missions Council, gave the matter personal attention and relayed complaints that some white missionaries—and the commission itself—voiced "pro-Japanese attitudes" and fueled support for the emperor by expressing appreciation for Japanese history and culture. Chapman's response noted that the majority of commission members never lived in Japan.[15]

The Protestant Commission also coordinated the financial subsistence of the camp churches. As a government agency, the WRA did not pay the salaries of Nikkei or white pastors within the camps, and incarcerees made miniscule wages, so financial support for the churches had to come from outside sources. Mainline denominations provided salaries for their own pastors and contributed funds to ecumenical relief groups like the Protestant Commission and the Student Relocation Council. Regional church councils and individual congregations also gave money to the commission, trusting Chapman to use it where most needed.[16]

Protestant leaders agreed to follow the WRA's pay schedule to support incarcerated pastors, slashing the ministers' prewar salaries. The WRA did not regulate wages coming from outside of the camp, but Protestant denominations limited salaries to nineteen dollars a month, the maximum WRA wage. Denominational and home missions groups deliberated over this decision for over six months, while several Nikkei pastors went into debt waiting for the religious organizations to agree on a pay scale. Some denominations changed the stipulations of established pension payments to incarcerated retirees as well. Many incarcerated pastors earned slightly over nineteen dollars, since some denominations paid pastors' wives a stipend; others provided an extra clothing allowance; and some supplemented the salaries of ministers with children.[17]

Denominations also disagreed who should support which pastors. Which denomination should pay for clergymen who had been working for a denomination other than their own before the war? Was their previous employer obligated to pay their salaries, or did it fall to the group through which they were ordained? All financial supporters of the Protestant Commission subsidized the salaries of Salvation Army pastors because their denomination's headquarters refused to overlook their requirement that officers support themselves. Many outside leaders wanted Nikkei to contribute to their churches to "heighten their sense of self-respect," but incarcerees could not fully support their clergy on wages capped at nineteen dollars a month. Frustrated with the Salvation Army policy, Chapman repeatedly explained to Colonel Holland French, the field representative for the Western Area of the Salvation Army, that his Nikkei officers were "all doing religious work" and deserved compensation. The denomination contributed to the Protestant Commission but not enough to pay their pastors' salaries.[18]

Because Chapman felt the commission should help Nikkei however possible, his work never focused on the camp churches exclusively. For example, when he realized Issei had few ways to pass the time in camp, he arranged for the commission's cadre of missionaries fluent in Japanese to screen popular Japanese reading material for the WRA. Chapman promised that these men and women's "Americanism [was] beyond question" and that they understood the "necessity for guarding against all subversive activity . . . contrary to American democratic principles." This translation project did not relate to religion, but Chapman offered assistance because he could. Tibesar and other Catholics also offered translation services to the FBI and other agencies. The AFSC's Esther Rhoads petitioned the WRA to allow the continued publication of Japanese language newspapers.[19]

As the war continued, denominations gave less money to the Protestant Commission, and Chapman struggled to retain his authority. His extension of authority increasingly clashed with the desires and duties of white volunteers and other aid groups. He expressed extreme frustration when Howard and Ruth Hannaford decided to relocate from Tule Lake to work for a Japanese ministry program in Chicago. Howard replied that they felt "frozen" in an "intolerable" situation, protesting that the commission "interfered" with their "freedom of action" by trying to direct their employment elsewhere. He questioned the Protestant Commission's right to "control appointments" made by independent entities. Some white missionaries hired through the commission felt badgered and protested that Chapman and the other aid organizations did not respect their autonomy.[20]

Since the commission's main directive was to help structure church leadership for Nikkei, Chapman believed his authority remained with those populations, whether they lived in the camps or outside. Regularly visiting the camps and working with incarcerees personally, he argued that the commission had "the most complete information at its disposal at any given time." He also worried that the ecumenical worship experiment would fail if denominations competed for former incarcerees outside of camp, so he needed to continue ecumenical work with Nikkei after they left. Chapman complained that church "workers seem to be moving in without regard to anyone except those of their own denomination." The commission's publicity campaigns asked for all white churches to welcome Nikkei, but Chapman became frustrated when individual congregations or regional councils acted on this directive independently. He complained that they contacted Nikkei "without uniform reference either to the Home Missions Council or the Protestant Church Commission." Several reports show Chapman straining for control.[21]

Complicating the question of who held ecclesiastical authority over Japanese Christians, the FCC and Home Missions Council formed the Committee on Resettlement of Japanese Americans in October 1942 to work with Nikkei outside of the camp. Since the Protestant Commission aided worship within the camps, ecumenical leaders thought a separate group should work with Nikkei outside. This division of duties seldom worked in practice, and tensions grew as the two groups fought for authority and territory. Both wanted to direct white and Nikkei pastors to specific communities in need of pastoral care, and those pastors, of course, also voiced their opinions. The two organizations settled on a problematic compromise where both groups had to approve the transfer of each pastor, a process that slowed resettlement.[22]

Complaints that Chapman welcomed representatives from marginalized Christian traditions such as the Salvation Army increased tensions further. Mark Dawber and others within the Home Missions Council felt that Chapman was too inclusive and said that the commission could not act as an agent of the Missions Council if nonmembers participated. When asked to dismiss these representatives in December 1942, Chapman and other members of the commission refused and cited their autonomous authority as granted by the FCC, WRA, and Commission on Aliens and Prisoners of War. They noted their role as coordinator for Protestant activities within the camps and concluded that "it would be disastrous to exclude" groups unaffiliated with the Home Missions Council. Outraged by the Home Mission Council's narrow view and its threat to cut the commission's funding, Chairman Frank Herron Smith withdrew the commission's affiliation with the council. By April 1943, tempers settled and the commission reached an "amicable" agreement with the Home Mission Council's Committee on Administration of Japanese Work that "assured . . . more harmonious administrative procedure and relationship in the future." The committee stated its willingness to consider applications from unaffiliated parties but voted a few weeks later to continue withholding funding from the commission and its projects. In 1945, the Home Missions Council committee questioned its relation to the Protestant Commission again. When the commission's board reaffirmed that it was an agent of the council, committee members voted to terminate the organization.[23]

When Mark Dawber alluded to the termination of the Protestant Commission in January 1945 as the camps prepared to close, Nikkei pastors and congregations voiced their continued support for the services provided by the commission. The rumor alarmed a number of Nikkei leaders who relied on the commission's help and did not wish to be directed by a new organization. A Californian Nikkei group sent the Home Missions Council a telegram stating, "We Japanese delegates to the special conference on the future of church work in California ask your body for the fullest support of the Protestant Commission, whose services are keenly needed in this critical period."[24] Nikkei leaders at Arizona's Gila River incarceration camp also asked the FCC to continue supporting the commission's work within the camps and during resettlement. These messages spoke of the commission's "invaluable service" and their "grave misgivings" of any plans to dissolve it. They believed the utmost value of the commission lay in the fact that its constituency of former missionaries could "work . . . as if they were of [the Japanese's] own number, intimately, understandingly, and wholeheartedly," something denominational leaders in the East could never manage.[25] Based in New York, members of the Committee on Resettlement of Japanese Americans drew criticism for their geographic origin and lack of historical relations with Nikkei. Nikkei knew they needed assistance from the outside but wanted it from pastors who knew them personally. The statements from Christian Nikkei strengthened Chapman's argument that the commission's work should continue since he and other members knew the involved party personally.

The Home Missions Council consented to Chapman's compromise of shifting the priorities of the commission rather than disbanding. Chapman instituted a proactive system for scheduling outside preachers and other church workers to fill the growing gaps in leadership within the camp churches and acted as a "liaison agency between center churches" and those outside.[26] The commission also offered incarcerees information sessions and private counseling to prepare for their lives outside of camp. Chapman did not drastically change the commission's earlier programs, but the Home Missions Council's approval reasserted the Protestant Commission's authority in the face of growing participation of other ecumenical and denominational groups.

Mark Dawber expressed regular discontent about the AFSC and its lack of cooperation with the Home Missions Council and other mainline groups as well but had no influence over Quakers' agenda. His entreaties fell on deaf ears because several Quaker leaders thought decentralized efforts would resettle Nikkei more efficiently. Homer Morris, executive secretary of the AFSC's Social Industrial Section, thought denominational representatives would have a greater chance of overturning prejudices at a congregational level. Despite encouragement from mainline representatives, AFSC members only occasionally attended interagency meetings, feeling they were not always worth the expense or effort. Floyd Schmoe thought the AFSC should maintain associations with interdenominational groups in order to fully respond to Nikkei needs in the future, but Quakers lacked interest in worship practices, central foci of these meetings. Others ranted about the competitive fights among mainline leaders. The missionary E. Stanley Jones similarly complained about Dawber's "spiritual possessiveness" of the issue.[27]

Amidst intermittent cooperation, quarrels, and power struggles, leaders of the FCC, Home Missions Council, and Protestant Commission failed to ask the object of their work—Nikkei—if they shared visions of unified worship. A summary of the commission's work written by Gordon Chapman claims that the Protestant Commission consulted leaders of the Japanese Church Federation before calling for ecumenism, but no correspondence or other source corroborates his statement. Internal efforts to merge three Japanese denominational churches in New York prior to the war may have encouraged the notion that Japanese Christians favored ecumenical worship.[28]

The Protestant Commission organized a conference for Nikkei pastors in July 1943, but the majority of conference attendees were white, and Nikkei held subordinate roles.[29] White leaders chaired all sessions, presented all reports, and offered the opening prayer for most sessions. National leaders allowed limited discussion about plans for the Japanese churches' future but upheld the decisions about ecumenism, racial integration, and resettlement made at prior meetings. The conference provided an arena where religious leaders outside of the camps could inform incarcerated Nikkei pastors about the plans they had already made for Japanese American Christianity. White leaders stressed the importance of assimilation at the conference for Nikkei pastors, presumably for the minority's benefit.[30]

Poor communication between outsiders and camp workers exacerbated the challenges of administering worship policies in the camps, and leaders encountered resistance to their plans for Nikkei worship. Many Nikkei had little inclination or intention of following directives made without their consent. In some cases, they agreed with the ultimate aims but were not interested in following plans when they had not been part of the decision-making process. The Reverend Kodama from Heart Mountain Relocation Center and other Nikkei complained that the Protestant organizations planning worship for incarcerees and resettlers asked the opinion of only one Nikkei, Toru Matsumoto. Further, they protested that though Matsumoto sat on the Resettlement Committee, he had not experienced the eviction, incarceration, or resettlement personally.[31] While well versed in American culture and a graduate of Union Theological Seminary, Matsumoto was an Issei who had never lived on the West Coast.[32] Though Congregational leader Clarence Gillett pledged in his conference notes, "Begin to work *with* them," his colleagues acknowledged only that Nikkei wanted to know more details about plans being made for their future.[33] This response suggests that national leaders heard only part of what Nikkei requested; they failed to recognize that Nikkei wanted an active role in making those decisions, not simply to hear more about them. This dissonance reflected most encounters between white outsiders and people, white or Japanese, living at the incarceration camps.

Unconcerned about ecumenism and operating within a stricter hierarchy, Maryknoll officials petitioned local bishops in the late spring of 1942 to retain direction over their prewar parishioners. Leopold Tibesar moved to southern Idaho with his Nikkei congregation, and Hugh Lavery oversaw Catholic work in the nine other camps. Maryknoll supplied as many fathers and brothers as possible and recruited missionaries returning from Asia, but they were still spread too thin. The greatest number of Catholic Nikkei lived in Minidoka and Manzanar, but a local priest drew Maryknoll's attention to the needs of Catholics assigned to other rural camps. Lavery lived near Arizona's Poston incarceration camp but drove across the state—seven hundred miles round trip—to offer mass twice a month at the Gila River camp. Maryknoll brothers worked at several camps, and local priests visited regularly to give communion. With minimal financial support from incarcerated parishioners, priests relied on funds from Maryknoll and the national Bishops' War Emergency and Relief Committee. The latter donated $10,000 to support Catholic religious work in the camps.[34]

## Material Aid and Assistance to Incarcerated Nikkei

The range of aid provided to Nikkei by Christian groups ranged from knitted layettes for new mothers to full scholarships and help with college admissions. Churches on the West Coast or those near the camps donated materials for church altars, while others sent monetary donations. The AFSC tried to alleviate the injustice in every possible way, from donating hundreds of balls of yarn to fighting for Nikkei's right to a college education, employment, and freedom. Protestant organizations with narrower agendas helped in their own way. Groups like the YWCA and YMCA addressed the recreational needs of young people in the camps, while the American Bible Society, various Catholic groups, and seminary libraries addressed literary needs.[35]

Rather than attending to incarcerees' pastoral needs or other religious concerns, the AFSC placed its greatest emphasis on improving the situation of Nikkei as speedily as possible through legal services, resettlement assistance, scholarships, and material provisions. Many individual Quakers also tried to improve public opinion about the incarceration through speeches and editorials. Within the camps, workers like Floyd Schmoe gave lectures and helped incarcerees arrange security clearance and find jobs, housing, and scholarships. Outside the camps, the AFSC arranged the first urban hostels to host resettling Nikkei and worked with civic leaders to ease discriminatory laws. The AFSC placed the greatest efforts on finding alternative university placements for the 3,252 Nikkei students enrolled in West Coast colleges.[36]

The National Japanese American Student Relocation Council, founded by the AFSC with aid from other religious and civil liberty groups, helped students fund and secure admission to schools in the Midwest and East. A group of college administrators including the president of the University of California, Berkeley, complained that they themselves would do the job more efficiently than a religious group, but the WRA rejected their offer. Milton Eisenhower, the first WRA director, asked the AFSC to "accept responsibility" for the thousands of evicted students in May 1942. Numerous Quakers felt uneasy about this cooperation with the government, but AFSC executive secretary Clarence Pickett accepted within a letter protesting the incarceration. He felt such aid was the only way to "atone for the violence that has been done to the constitutional rights of American citizens." AFSC publications clarified this stance whenever discussing student relocation work in hope that the decision would not be interpreted as acceptance of the incarceration. Catholic observers thought government officials hoped the AFSC would assume the government's responsibility and "dig up the dough" to fund the program. The AFSC sought representation from all mainline denominations working with Nikkei and a variety of educational leaders.[37]

The AFSC and other groups had already begun transferring students on an individual basis, but a standardized system increased the likelihood of successful placements and expedited the process of government clearance for students and schools. In the early months of the war, some students went to communities unwilling to accept them, resulting in difficult, sometimes frightening encounters. In one of the worst incidents, the University of Idaho retracted admission to six Nisei in response to complaints from the surrounding community. Fearing a lynch mob, the sheriff placed the two female students under protective custody in the Moscow jail until transportation out of town was arranged. To avoid such encounters, the Student Relocation Council planned to "create receptive attitudes" in addition to locating financial aid and selecting students. WRA leaders hoped these students would smooth transitions for future resettlers.[38]

Raising money to pay tuition and fees for students was perhaps the greatest challenge. Congress limited funds in response to complaints about the government educating the "enemy" while "American boys" joined the military. Many schools offered special scholarships to Nikkei, but students with incarcerated families still struggled to pay room and board. Denominations, individuals, and private foundations gave the Student Relocation Council regular donations through 1946, and incarceration centers raised money for scholarships as well.[39] Baptists, Presbyterians, and the World Student Service Fund (a coalition of the YMCA and YWCA) donated the most scholarship money, over $30,000 each.[40] From July 1942 to June 1946, the Student Relocation Council financially supported 966 Japanese American students. By the end of the war, student relocation programs helped over four thousand incarcerees attend six hundred colleges and universities outside of the restricted zone. Nikkei students received over $270,000 in scholarship money.[41] Pickett wrote of their student relocation work, "Few undertakings have ever been more completely satisfactory to me" because the thousands of students succeeded so well academically and socially.[42]

While the Student Relocation Council attempted to provide equal opportunities for all students, many religiously affiliated colleges accepted only their own adherents, and many churches earmarked their contributions for Christian students. For example, the Methodist Church prioritized Methodist Nikkei attending Methodist schools, then Methodists at non-Methodist colleges, and finally, if funds remained, non-Christians might receive aid. Within denominations that did not discriminate regarding the religious identity of their scholarship recipients, like Presbyterians and Congregationalists, white congregants and pastors voiced concerns that the policy would leave their "own young people . . . inadequately cared for." The Quaker aid worker Herbert Nicholson recalled a Baptist superintendent saying, "We'll take care of the Baptists, and the Quakers can look after the Buddhists." While not all Buddhists felt discriminated against, they comprised only 15 percent of financial aid applicants in 1943. At least one-third of incarcerated Nisei identified as Buddhist. Applicants reporting no affiliation, one-quarter of the total, may have included Buddhists reluctant to identify their faith for fear of discrimination. While not quite 60 percent of college-age Nisei were Christian, they received 60 percent of the aid from the Student Relocation Council. The World Student Service Fund, which offered student aid in times of war, tried to correct this imbalance by prioritizing Buddhists. Churches and denominational colleges, however, gave an unknown amount of money directly to students, the majority of which likely went to Christian Nisei. So while the Student Relocation Council approximated a proportional distribution of financial aid, Christian incarcerees or those with close connections to Christians received a disproportionately large amount of total national aid.[43]

Leopold Tibesar, the Maryknoll father at Minidoka, for example, worked tirelessly to find placements for "his people." While the majority of Nikkei associated with the Seattle Maryknoll School were unbaptized, Tibesar felt assured that the young people would soon make that decision. He did not grant Nikkei Catholic students absolute priority but sent Nisei to Catholic schools and tried to find them housing with Catholic families to support their spiritual discernment. He worked closely with the WRA and his brother Seraphin, who worked at the Franciscan Quincy College in Illinois, to obtain leave clearance for that school and expedite the transfer of students. A Catholic Archbishop's Fund granted tuition support to Catholic and non-Catholic Japanese American applicants outside of the Student Relocation Council.[44]

Catholic leaders criticized the government for granting Protestant organizations responsibility and authority over student relocation and resettlement. Given the Protestant leadership of these programs, Catholics worked alone and found independent solutions for their people. Reflecting his lack of faith in cooperation with non-Catholics, the vicar general of Maryknoll, James Drought, advised Hugh Lavery to work "aggressively on your own." Tibesar, Lavery, and Drought assumed programs like the Student Relocation Council would not help Catholic Nikkei or secure sufficient support outside of camp, so they felt little need to cooperate with such programs.[45]

The constant threat of losing converts if students attended Protestant or secular colleges never left the minds of Catholic leaders. Several Catholic schools offered scholarships to incarcerees, but they were inadequate for the number of Nikkei students. The National Catholic Welfare Conference, the precursor to the U.S. Conference of Catholic Bishops, provided $5,000, and Maryknoll secured low-interest student loans for Nikkei, but Tibesar worried about burdening resettlers with debt at this time. WRA regulations made it expedient to cooperate on a minimal level with the Student Relocation Council. The Bishops' War Emergency and Relief Committee sent the council $500 each year of the war. James T. O'Dowd, the San Francisco superintendent of Catholic schools and the official Catholic liaison to the WRA, controlled aid distribution to Catholic students and coordinated some placements.[46]

National recreation organizations brought their programs to the camps almost immediately. The YMCA and YWCA hired Nikkei to operate clubs or gyms in several centers, the first opening at Manzanar in August 1942. The YWCA visited every camp to advise administrators on the importance of supplying recreational activities for girls and encourage local chapters to visit the camps. The YMCA also hired Nisei Masao Satow to integrate Nikkei into established clubs as they resettled across the country. Like other church groups, the YMCA and YWCA supported integration and public relations programs intended to help Nisei assimilate into white America. Similarly, the director of interracial activities for the Boy Scouts of America visited each center to organize new troops, introduce them to local troops outside the camps, and resurrect troops whose membership from the coast remained intact. The Scouts also sponsored Nikkei adults to attend national leadership conferences during the war. All three groups encouraged activities and exchanges with groups outside of the camps, but the camps' rural locations limited these interactions.[47]

The American Bible Society (ABS), an evangelical publishing group, planned its distribution of Bibles to the camps before the eviction concluded. Members hoped to assign a clergyman to sell Bibles door-to-door in the camps at cost, but the Protestant Commission and the WRA would not allow such evangelistic activities. Instead, the ABS sent Christian literature to every incarceration camp and resettlement community. The Protestant Commission helped the ABS by raising funds from its constituent denominations to supplement the project and enable a larger printing. A special imprint of these editions honored the commission for its assistance. By the end of the war, the ABS had supplied over 15,000 copies of an abridged New Testament in Japanese. Japan held the only printing plates containing the full Japanese language New Testament, and texts in Japanese were difficult to obtain during the war. The ABS's leaders worried that presses in Japan would be damaged by bombing, limiting the postwar production of full Japanese editions. The society also reprinted religious tracts for incarcerated Nikkei, including several written by Japanese Christians.[48]

J. Stillson Judah, a librarian at the Pacific School of Religion in Berkeley, organized a different literary project: a rotating library for incarcerated ministers within the WRA camps. The Protestant Commission and Congregational Committee supported operational costs by paying for postage, while eleven seminaries and many individuals donated or loaned books. Judah tried to accommodate requests from Nikkei ministers, while seminaries added titles of their own choosing. His project complemented goals of the popular Religious Book Week program, a canon Judah most likely referenced when compiling the rotating library inventories.[49]

Nikkei ministers responded to the library program with enthusiasm. Clergy at Heart Mountain assembled library shelves out of apple crates. Many Nikkei expressed appreciation for books on theology, homiletics (sermon writing), biblical interpretation, pastoral care, and Christian fiction. Like other aid programs, Judah's efforts reminded incarcerees that people on the outside were "still . . . try[ing] to practice the ideal of the Fatherhood of God and the brotherhood of man . . . when this world is full of bitterness, hatred and strife."[50]

A commitment to ecumenism affected the library's content and Judah's own attitudes as he acquired books that conflicted with his liberal preferences. He tried to "make each library as representative of all fields of

Christian literature as possible" by finding books that appealed to ministers of all denominational backgrounds. Judah solicited bibliographies of books considered essential for ministry by professors at a variety of seminaries. Judah discovered the extent of ecumenical complexity when he realized that some lists did not share a single title. Through these exchanges, his prejudices against conservative evangelicals lessened. When George Aki, a Nisei pastor in Arkansas, shared his difficulties about conflicting theologies and approaches in his Arkansas camp, Judah cautioned Aki "to be careful before judg[ing people] too quickly." Judah's expanded appreciation of religious diversity affected not only the book collections but ministerial life in the camps as well.[51]

Judah intended his library to address pastoral care and evangelism, and it did so in unexpected ways. Correspondence between Judah and Nikkei pastors concerning new titles, lost books, and exchanges became a conduit for pastoral counseling for incarcerated ministers who had few colleagues with whom to consult or commiserate. Judah responded with specific advice and sent books to meet pastors' particular and immediate needs. When Aki struggled to determine his role in the war, Judah sent several books that he thought might assist Aki's "quest." He believed his library had the power "to weld the new faith into their hearts so that they will become better and stronger Christians."[52]

While many incarcerees benefited from scholarships, recreational support, and libraries, every single incarcerated child received an annual Christmas gift. Designed to boost morale in the camps and raise awareness among white Americans, Protestant leaders sponsored what they marketed as "America's Biggest Christmas Party" each year of the war. While the AFSC, the Protestant Commission, Catholic churches, and various denominations had already begun planning gift programs, the Home Missions Council turned its acts of kindness into a publicity stunt to bring attention to the crisis of incarcerated U.S. citizens. The Home Missions Council matched mainline denominations with incarceration camps and assigned them the duty of providing those children with presents. During the first year, Minidokans received an astonishing 17,000 presents from Christian groups. Floyd Schmoe thought the project's greatest significance was that 50,000 to 75,000 Americans "unaware a year ago of the problems faced by the Japanese in America are now not only aware but sympathetic" to their hardships.[53]

Churches gave small gifts, but the act reassured Nikkei that free Americans had not forgotten them. Typical of many recollections, a former

Rohwer incarceree said, "Just when I thought everybody out there hated us, I get this present and it restored my faith in mankind again."[54] That impression was a primary goal of large and small Christian projects. Outside aid workers hoped people understood that the Christmas program was not just "a kindly gesture to provide holiday cheer" but a chance to assure incarcerees of the "continuity" of their "friendship and concern."[55] Some people outside of camp extended the benefits of the gift program by attaching names and addresses to presents, requesting a pen pal. Tad Fujita, an incarceree at Utah's Topaz incarceration center, corresponded with a woman from Massachusetts until her death in the 1970s after she sent his son a pocket knife at Christmas.[56] These connections built bridges between their cultures and helped repair rifts caused by the incarceration. Some incarcerees saw the gifts as proof of the goodness of America. Tom Fukuyama of the Minidoka church wrote, "The number of gifts shows that the heart of America is essentially warm and the vociferous race mongers constitute only a small minority."[57] Just as the kindness shown by church members during the eviction strengthened Nikkei, many incarcerees appreciated small tokens from the outside and more significant aid, such as scholarships. Long after the war, a Sansei wrote of the necessity of small acts, "Tides are turned . . . by the quiet and enduring heroism of ordinary people acting in good conscience."[58] The FCC and Home Missions Council presented their work with incarcerees as the united will of American Christians, but many objected. Numerous churches outside the camps refused to support the Christmas project out of a belief that the liberal leaders were "comforting the enemy."[59]

## Local Church Involvement

The degree, type, and frequency of interaction between Christians in the incarceration camps and those from nearby churches and ecumenical organizations varied widely. At Heart Mountain, local churches served coffee and gave a "warm welcome" to incarcerees as they arrived. The Colorado Council of Churches delegation visited Granada to survey the needs and services of the church and wider camp. Replicating a successful open house among over one hundred Protestant and Catholic leaders at Minidoka, Nikkei pastors in several camps sought to introduce themselves to their new neighbors. These events established relations that continued throughout the war. Choirs from camp churches visited area churches, and local pastors gave guest sermons. At Minidoka, Leopold

Tibesar facilitated joint meetings with the Boise Legion of Mary and Jerome's Holy Name members. While some outside churches initiated contact with incarcerees, they usually offered aid or fellowship, not evangelism. Attendance at denominational conferences and hosting denominational superiors challenged the artificial ecumenism of camp.[60]

The Protestant Commission encouraged liaisons between camps and local churches but had little control over the content of these exchanges. Regional religious influences crept into Arkansas's Jerome and Rohwer incarceration camps despite efforts to restrict evangelism. Expressing enthusiastic evangelistic intentions, white Arkansan religious leaders participated in camp church services and other religious activities to a much greater degree than local clergy in other regions of the country.

Arkansas Christians saw the incarceration as a test of their faith and commitment to the gospel. The president of the Executive Board of Arkansas Southern Baptists announced that God had "brought to our very doors the greatest opportunity for . . . winning to Christ those of pagan faith we have ever witnessed." Baptist T. L. Harris called for white Christians to embrace these unique conditions for evangelism. Since missionaries could not reach non-Christians abroad during the war, God's "great plan of evangelism," Harris concluded, had delivered unconverted souls to their doorstep. Knowing that "providence [had] placed . . . thousands of Japanese . . . within [their] borders" only "temporarily," churches and individuals in Arkansas mobilized evangelistic efforts. Evangelists pinned their hopes on the younger generation who they thought was "ready to accept the salvation of our Saviour" (and could communicate more easily with monolingual Arkansans). The editors of regional denominational journals like the *Arkansas Baptist* urged clergy to visit the camps, meet the Christians there, and help bring others to Christ. The state's Episcopalian publication reminded readers of their "great Christian duty and privilege" to welcome these "visitors." This interest was not, of course, universal. Gordon Chapman struggled to gain the cooperation of a local Presbyterian minister who believed incarcerees were dangerous.[61]

The Little Rock Council of Protestant Ministers sent a pastor to preach at the camps every month, and other pastors came independently, including Congregationalists, Free Methodists, Presbyterians, Salvation Army officers, Episcopalians, and a local Catholic priest.[62] Protestant pastors in McGehee, the town closest to Rohwer, also urged locals to take a neighborly, "American Christian" approach to supporting religious activities in the camps.[63] The comments of Arkansas's mainline Protestants suggest they lacked the missionary zeal of Southern Baptists, but they still visited the camps in great numbers.

Heightened interest in the newcomers overcame obstacles that reduced interaction in other states. Located about a twenty-five-minute drive from one another, Rohwer and Jerome were situated in a rural area like most WRA sites. On today's highways, the trip from Little Rock, the home of many visiting preachers, takes two hours, but others came from Fayetteville—nearly five hours away. Given the limitations of tire and gas rationing and poor roads, preachers sacrificed considerable time and material resources to travel to these distant camps.[64] They made these sacrifices despite the state's severe poverty and other great needs. With the significant exception that Nikkei had limited freedom of movement, the incarcerees had a higher quality of life than many of their new neighbors. Their superior health care, education, and nutrition drew the ire of many Arkansans.

Evangelistic Southern Baptists should not have been allowed to enter the camps according to WRA rules; they lacked a prewar history with the camps' incarcerees. In addition to their exceptional enthusiasm, three factors contributed to the prominence of local Christians. First, a dearth of clergy stalled the foundation of Rohwer's ecumenical church for three months. Camp administrators and local clergymen and laity preached and led services to fill this void. Mainline missionaries were less willing to relocate to Arkansas, so Rohwer and Jerome lacked their support and moderating influence as well. Second, the borders of Jerome and Rohwer were "highly permeable," permitting Arkansan preachers to enter of their own accord.[65] Outsiders in Arkansas could initiate their ministries without invitation, based on personal interest or denominational encouragement.[66] Third, the racial politics of the South also may have encouraged the work of outsiders.

Lacking historical conflicts and competition with Nikkei and the intense racialization that promoted discrimination in the West, southerners deemed Nikkei "white" within the South's largely binary racial system. Many southerners insisted everyone treat Nikkei well specifically because they were not black in order to reinforce that structure. Southerners instructed Nikkei to use "white" facilities and refused to give them the most laborious types of employment. Jason Morgan Ward explained that southerners considered those jobs—digging ditches and picking cotton—to be "black" jobs, causing many farmers to refuse to give them to Nikkei. In addition to the potential confusion of a group working at both "black" and "white" jobs, people worried that incarcerees would demand higher wages and establish a precedent for minority advancement. This categorization meant that Nikkei interacted with white Arkansans on a more equal level than they did with whites elsewhere. Historian John Howard argued that the shared identity of "not black" united white Arkansans and Nikkei incarcerees. Boundaries dissolved further in a macabre minstrel show at Jerome that starred "Caucasians and non-Caucasians, islanders and mainlanders" together on stage—all in blackface. This act allied white, Hawaiian, and Japanese Americans in opposition to African Americans.[67]

All of these factors contributed to stronger bonds between incarcerees and locals than those witnessed in western camps. Photographs, camp newspapers, and correspondence show that Boy Scouts, Girl Scouts, and YMCA members within the camp either merged with chapters on the outside or cosponsored camping trips, summer camps, and leadership retreats around the state.[68] Young incarcerees attended club meetings and events outside of camp, but white children and adults also met inside the camps.[69] Aside from camp sports teams competing with outside leagues and choirs performing at local churches, this level of interaction occurred infrequently elsewhere. That white Arkansan parents allowed their children to interact with Nikkei makes a significant statement. But while church bulletins and administrative records show that evangelical leaders established a strong presence in camp, they did not succeed in winning any more converts than did Protestants in western camps.

## Changing Public Opinion

Galen Fisher, chairman of the American Principles and Fair Play Committee, insisted that a "persistent and long term" public relations campaign must be implemented throughout the nation, both publicly and within congregations, to improve public opinion about resettlement. Raymond Booth of the AFSC Pasadena branch agreed that churches could more successfully resettle Nikkei if the Christians of America fully understood the associated social problems. Aid workers believed that resettlement would fail without a full "conversion of public opinion." Mainline Protestants began coordinating these efforts during the summer of 1942 and developed a systematic approach to public relations regarding the situation that fall. Quiet during the evictions and initial incarceration, mainline Protestants felt they should become "more aggressive as far as public opinion was concerned" by fall 1942 and dedicated resources to meet that objective. An exception, the Committee on Resettlement of Japanese Americans, still felt public relations campaigns would "arouse the country unnecessarily" and might "get communities excited over a 'Japanese invasion.'" They recommended waiting until early 1943. A few religious leaders like Methodist E. D. Kohlstadt still worried that publicizing resettlement in mid-1944 would "put Eastern communities on the defensive." Many, if not most, American Christians still harbored unsympathetic and hostile attitudes toward Nikkei and believed they were a threat to national security. Trying to slip Nikkei in under the radar might have worked, but the majority of people working with incarcerees prioritized the greater goal of overturning racism nationally.[70]

Protestant public relations efforts took three major forms: combating race prejudice and discrimination through print media, educating and encouraging sympathetic actions from Americans at the congregational level, and disputing negative portrayals of Nikkei in the media. Led by Clarence Gillett, the Congregational Christian Committee for Work with Japanese Evacuees wrote the largest number of pamphlets for its own congregants and the general public. The committee first targeted its own congregants with a multifaceted public relations campaign in the spring of 1942 and then worked to reduce the prejudices of all Americans. The Congregational campaign included a supplement to *Social Action*, the denomination's social justice publication, articles in the *Missionary Herald*, personalized letters to ministers around the country, and brochures to inform the public about the incarceration, related relief work, and the fallacies of common racial stereotypes. Incarcerees expressed their gratitude to groups like the Congregational Committee that worked to "overcome unthinking prejudice and bring about fair-minded public sentiment." The Fellowship of Reconciliation, the AFSC, the Pacific Coast Committee on American Principles and Fair Play, and smaller groups developed public relations material as well.[71]

The pamphlets, magazine articles, denominational bulletins, and editorials in secular newspapers used a variety of approaches to improve America's opinion of Japanese Americans. Many arguments mentioned Christianity's role within the nation, such as the Colorado Council of Churches's reference to the "genuine Christianity" that "undergird[s]" American democracy.[72] Other publications avoided religious rhetoric and appealed to democratic responsibilities and scientific studies of racism. Many included personal stories and quotations from West Coast religious and educational leaders who knew Japanese Americans personally. Still others used photographs and cartoons to persuade readers of the loyalty of Japanese Americans. Reprints from secular sources like *Reader's Digest* expanded their literature further.[73] Public relations material avoided direct criticism of the government, focusing on compassion, democracy, and the responsibilities of Christian citizens.

Many pamphlets used the rhetoric of Americanism, which blended values of "true Christianity" with those of "true America." "A Touchstone of Democracy," published by the Council for Social Action of the Congregational Christian Churches in June 1942, used this language, instructing readers, "It is our responsibility as citizens to help [Nikkei] keep their faith in democracy. It is the responsibility of the Church to help them keep their faith in God." Within this publication, John Bennett "condemn[ed] . . . the public . . . for accepting" the incarceration "with complacency" and called for America's atonement. He declared that the fate of Nikkei "will be a major test of integrity of the Christian churches and of the realities of democracy." To Bennett, the obligations of Christianity and democracy were complementary: both required Christian citizens to support Nikkei. Even secular newspapers argued that Nikkei should be welcomed back into communities on the basis of America's Christian foundation. In Montana's *Billings Gazette*, Sam Nagata mentioned the obligation to protect the nation's human rights granted by "Divine Providence." Allan Hunter and Quaker missionaries Gurney and Elizabeth Binford compiled Nikkei sermons given just before their incarceration for a unique publication, "The Sunday Before." Never intended for a public audience, the sermons portray the raw suffering and fortitude of Japanese Americans.[74]

The American Baptist Home Mission Society reminded readers what "Democracy Demands" of its citizens in relation to American Nikkei (Figure 2). Specifically, it demanded that "papers speak up for it" and "people practice it." To demonstrate this message, the publication contained supportive excerpts from newspapers across the country and photographs of Nikkei "practicing" democracy. Most quotations refer to citizens' responsibility as Americans, while the photographs depicted children playing football and Japanese American engineers, teachers, grocers, university students, doctors, and soldiers. The glossy pamphlet implies that Nikkei are democratic Americans worth helping and worth having in American communities. Using Ansel Adams's strategy from his photography exhibit and book about Manzanar incarcerees, *Born Free and Equal*, the photographs prompted viewers to imagine these people working and living normal lives rather than thinking of their abnormal,

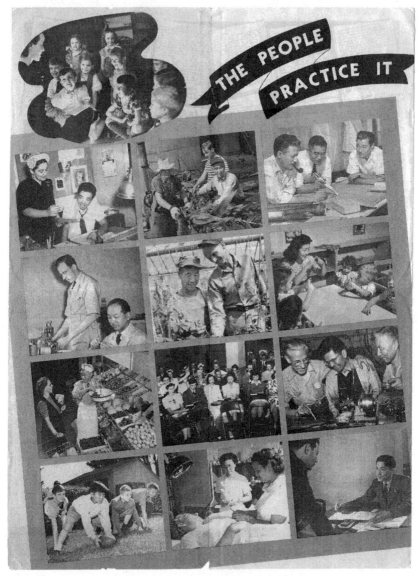

FIGURE 2 "Democracy Demands," American Baptist Home Mission Society, 1944. Source: Japanese American Relocation Collection, Occidental College Special Collections and College Archives.

criminalized lives behind barbed wire. The images showed readers that Nikkei were normal citizens just like them. Other pamphlets, like "A Touchstone of Democracy," describe Nikkei's exemplary American values and accomplishments, such as their perseverance through hardship. Contributors called Nikkei within and outside of the camps "colonists" and pioneers," tying their experiences to those of iconic early Americans. An article by Galen Fisher compared a Japanese American community in Utah to "a modern Joseph Smith—minus the Book of Mormon." This was perhaps a risky metaphor given negative sentiments about Mormons, but it names a figure entrenched in an American narrative. Comparing Nikkei to Christian American pioneers diminished their foreignness as well.[75]

Catholic speeches and publications also used democracy to battle the issue. Tibesar wrote of Americans' obligation to "implement and enforce" the rights endowed by the Constitution lest they abandon the Golden Rule and lose those privileges for themselves. "Now it is time for us to act," he declared, "We must dare to be as big as our religious and civic convictions and idealistic professions—dare to be as American as the Constitution and as Christian as Christ."[76]

Some Christian efforts addressed the general problem of racism with science. In hope of dispelling racial misunderstandings, a group of religious leaders and anthropologists composed and distributed a Public Affairs booklet entitled "The Races of Mankind" in 1943.[77] Through conversational explanations of racial theory and comic illustrations, anthropologists Ruth Benedict and Gene Weltfish differentiated between physical racial characteristics and nationality, noting the singular origin of humankind described in Genesis and proven by science (Figure 3). Explaining that nonphysical characteristics stem from a person's upbringing, the text distinguishes learned behavior from biological traits. The booklet addresses misinformation propagated by Nazi propaganda, clarifying that Aryan and Jewish are not racial designations. It describes the roots of prejudice in an approachable, unconfrontational, and uncondescending manner, but the War Department and United Service Organizations banned it for provoking "racial antagonism."[78]

The Presbyterian Church (U.S.A.) missions board released a pamphlet containing anecdotes of Asian minorities succeeding with help from people of other races. These pamphlets complemented books promoted through the National Conference of Christians and Jews (NCCJ) Religious Book Week, a program that encouraged spiritual edification through reading. During the early 1940s, Catholic, Protestant, and Jewish committee

FIGURE 3 "The Races of Mankind," by Ruth Benedict and Gene Weltfish. Source: Author's Collection.

THE PEOPLES OF THE EARTH ARE ONE FAMILY.

members selected several Jewish histories, as well as *Race against Man* (1939), *Man's Most Dangerous Myth: The Fallacy of Race* (1942), and *The Race Question and the Negro* (1943). These books used biological science, sociology, and anthropology to show the falsities underlying race prejudices. As Matthew Hedstrom demonstrated in *The Rise of Liberal Religion*, the NCCJ hoped for more than public education; the committee hoped its selections would meet the greater good of strengthening the United States by breaking down barriers and unifying its citizens.[79]

American Catholics used existing secular and religious periodicals to profess the loyalty of Nikkei and voice support for resettlement. Tibesar, Lavery, and others regularly described life in the camps, reminded readers of Nikkei's loyalty, and promoted Christian charity in Maryknoll's *The Field Afar* and the national Catholic newspaper, *Our Sunday Visitor*. *Commonweal*, a Catholic lay publication, devoted an entire issue to the incarceration in March 1944. Tibesar became the most prolific contributor with his critiques of the incarceration. Since he required permission to publish his work, he sent all articles to Maryknoll headquarters before submitting them to newspapers or magazines. While Maryknoll rejected several on the grounds of being too inflammatory or critical of the United States, it reprinted others by the thousands for the AFSC and Protestant Commission to distribute. The WRA requested permission to reprint one of Tibesar's articles. The *Seattle Times* received nearly one hundred favorable letters in response to his article about the loyalty of Nikkei at Minidoka, "Are Japanese Getting a Fair Break?" Released on 14 November 1943, the article cited the Four Freedoms and warned of the danger if Americans did not establish friendly relations with Asian nationals.[80]

Congregations responded positively to these publications. Pastors in resettlement areas, denominational boards, regional ecumenical councils, and the leaders of social action and women's organizations received pamphlets and copies of magazine articles from the Protestant Commission, the Congregational Committee, the AFSC, and other groups. Churches requested educational material and pamphlets to use in vacation Bible schools and Sunday school. As Nikkei began returning to the coast in 1945, the Congregational Committee expanded its educational campaign, sending material to around five hundred California public school principals and librarians to ease the adjustment of new students. After receiving "widespread and cordial" feedback from recipients, it planned another mailing at the beginning of the 1946 school year. Pamphlets and magazine articles sought to dispel prejudices and increase unity within the country, much like programs for ecumenical and interracial worship.[81]

The Congregational Committee encouraged Social Action groups and the Congregational youth organization Pilgrim Fellowship to help with its public relations campaign. At a national meeting of the Pilgrim Fellowship, leaders resolved to "express . . . fellowship and unity" with Nikkei Christians in light of the "national failure to fulfill . . . Christian convictions and democratic principles." In addition to extending fellowship to resettled Nikkei and sending material donations to incarcerees, the fellowship tried to educate the public. Its public statement condemned the "intolerant public" who "fanned the flames of racial antagonism because of lack of understanding, vested interests [and] false patriotism." Members hoped their efforts would increase "tolerance and friendliness which will make it safe for government authorities to release Japanese." Other youth groups, like the World Student Christian Federation, made similar efforts to educate the public and offer hope and friendship to incarcerated young people.[82]

Speaking tours expressed the same messages as the pamphlets but tied the message to a relatable individual. Father Tibesar began addressing religious and civic groups in southern Idaho in October 1942. He accepted many invitations to help settle the "controversy [raging] outside camp among the whites who can't quite make up their minds to trust our people to be as American as their birth in this country suggests." He spoke at Catholic societies, Rotary clubs, women's civic clubs, and various state conventions. He continued this work after his move to Chicago in January 1945 when his messages shifted from Nikkei loyalty to broader issues of democracy and racial pluralism. Tibesar impressed upon Chicago's Catholic Youth Organization that the "ideals of the Catholic Church were embodied in the Constitution." Uniting their obligations as Catholics and Americans, he explained that the promise of the United States could not be "realized or endure" without "strength of religion." He juxtaposed the ideals of democracy and Christianity with totalitarianism and racism, placing racial discrimination in direct opposition to America's destiny and God's will. As the war progressed and Communist threats grew, Tibesar, in the vein of FDR, bound Christianity and democracy tighter, going so far as to claim that "democracy . . . divorced of its Christian meaning would be useless" and could not survive.[83]

Recognizing that Nikkei speakers often had a greater effect on audiences than white men and women speaking for or about them, the Congregational Committee, the AFSC, FOR, and other groups urged former incarcerees to give talks in their new communities and hired a few Nisei for national speaking tours. Financially supported by the Congregational Committee, Setsuko Matsunaga spoke to dozens of groups around the country, including organizations like Lions Clubs and the American Legion that typically supported the incarceration. Under the auspices of the YMCA, American Baptist Home Mission Society, and FCC, Jobu Yasumura traveled the country to promote resettlement efforts. The Episcopal priest Daisuke Kitagawa visited churches and civic groups to "present the camp story and the church angle." A women's auxiliary club felt that there would be "complete understanding" if more people like him would educate Americans around the country. The group pledged financial support and prayed for the "courageous . . . women of Minidoka" after hearing Kitagawa speak.[84]

The Fellowship of Reconciliation hired Perry Saito, a conscientious objector from Aberdeen, Washington, studying for the Methodist ministry, to speak with service groups, chapters of FOR, and student groups in the

Midwest and New England. Saito told audiences about his family's patriotism and devotion to "American principles," explaining, "We are not complaining one bit [about the incarceration] because we are Americans. If the American soldiers can battle with bullets, we can afford to battle with mosquitoes. We are not complaining because of the physical hardships. All we want is to be recognized as Americans. . . . You can be American even though you have a face that looks like an enemy." He told Lions Clubs how his father learned English by memorizing the Gettysburg Address. Like many people, Saito's concepts of Christianity and Americanism overlapped significantly, and he described his work in religious terms. He considered his sermons and speeches about racial equality an attempt to "Christianize other areas of human relations." But since pacifism garnered criticism during the war, some Christians did not believe his patriotic claims. The FBI followed Saito's actions, interviewing children at summer camps where he spoke and pastors with whom he worked. A Congregational minister suspicious of Saito's descriptions of camp life described him to the FBI as "subversive" and claimed Saito would "commit acts against the United States if he had a chance to do so."[85]

The speaking tours may have made a positive impact overall, but they also stirred a negative response from groups that resisted Nikkei rights. The Teamsters union criticized religious groups for sending Nisei speakers into "important war production centers of the Midwest." Their international newsletter claimed that "secretly hostile Japs . . . hoodwinked" FOR and the Reformed Church into organizing and funding such tours, allowing Japanese spies to organize Nikkei industrial workers. The article proposed that Nikkei leaving the incarceration camps planned to "infiltrate labor unions and establish a new espionage system . . . to prepare for the next Pearl Harbor." But Nikkei no longer posed the only threat. The minority had "ingratiated themselves into unsuspecting religious denominations" in an attempt to fuel support for a "Christian peace" that would "leave Japan strong enough" to destroy the United States and Christianity itself. The author of this Teamster article believed that protecting Christianity meant fighting the false "Christian peace" described by mainline Christians of the time. He felt threatened by free Nikkei but also the new global peace lauded by liberal Protestants. As liberal public relations campaigns spread across the country, conflicts between the beliefs of progressive Christian leaders and those of average American Christians became increasingly obvious.[86]

## Confronting Injustice

While only a few small Christian groups definitively condemned the incarceration during the early months of 1942, criticism grew once the Federal Council of Churches announced its intention to cooperate with the resettlement program. The Presbyterian Synod of California denounced the incarceration without hedging its accusation in late October 1942. The synod used direct language to claim that the incarceration policy "involved racial discrimination" and a "suspension of the constitutional rights." It called for the return of Nikkei to the West Coast in July 1944. The National Inter-Collegiate Christian Council was "ashamed at the ease with which certain economic and political pressure groups . . . so drastically changed the lives of this great number of people." A Methodist missionary organization pledged to "Christianize attitudes toward racial minorities" in response to the incarceration. It voiced concern not only for the nation but for the "future of the World Mission and that new and better Order in which, under God's providence, we are to have our part."[87]

Religious leaders entered the political arena to support Nikkei and other minority groups by 1943. Church groups like the Sacramento Council of Churches wrote letters protesting legislation that would have canceled the U.S. citizenship of Japanese Americans. The Church Federation of Los Angeles and the Southern California Council of Churches justified racial equality on the grounds that "in violating Christian principles, one violates the spiritual basis of western civilization and of democracy itself." They warned of "historical repercussions" of the "racial warfare" such legislation implied. When labor unions and nativist politicians placed anti-alien land laws on ballots once more, a number of religious groups leapt into action, forming lobby groups and petitions to bar their success. Colorado Congregationalists helped defeat an anti-alien land law in 1944, and the Congregational Committee campaigned against California's alien land laws in the fall of 1946. While churches resisted new legislation, they refrained from calling for a return to the coast until 1944, believing it might increase anti-Japanese sentiments on the coast.[88]

The AFSC, the Seattle Council of Churches, and many Christian groups in California began supporting the return of Nikkei to the coast in early 1944. Seattle's AFSC office petitioned Friends to write to the president to request an end to the incarceration, but recommended people not incite congressmen by drawing attention to the issue. The Seattle Council of Churches passed a resolution calling for the "return of loyal Americans of Japanese ancestry . . . at such time as . . . there is no further military necessity." While the statement implied there had been military cause for the incarceration, a possibility the council had rejected privately in 1942, it supported the return of Seattle's Nikkei. Furthermore, the following month, the general secretary of the Seattle Council of Churches, Gertrude Apel, argued that "to ask some Americans of Japanese ancestry to serve in the armed forces and confine others, of unquestioned loyalty, to restricted areas seems wholly inconsistent." The council promised to assist the state government's plans to integrate Nisei into "normal community life." Council leaders and the Quaker activist Arthur Barnett condemned Washington governor Arthur B. Langlie's attitude and ignorant equation of Japanese Americans with the Axis power. The Christians reminded him and the public yet again that no Nikkei had been "charged with an overt act against the government."[89]

By the fall of 1944, California church groups, including the Roman Catholic Interracial Council of Los Angeles, denounced the incarceration without reservation, condemning the "un-American, unconstitutional and un-Christian" motives that continued to fuel such "Nazi" policies in the United States. The Reverend Aaron Heist of the First Methodist Church in Santa Maria accused President Roosevelt of continuing the incarceration for political gain. Denominational groups including the Methodist General Conference, the General Assembly of the Presbyterian Church (U.S.A.), the Northern Baptist Convention, and the Congregational Christian General Council also released statements in mid-1944 supporting the return of Japanese Americans to the Pacific Coast.[90]

While Catholic leaders agreed that Nikkei should be allowed to return, some refrained from lobbying for policy change because they believed Nikkei could build better lives elsewhere in the country. Tibesar repeatedly told his superiors, "Japanese return to the Coast in any number is out of the question—no housing, etc." He had advised incarcerees to sell rather than lease businesses when they left in 1942. By the end of 1943, he consented that property owners might be able to return "in time" but thought it would "be a mistake to try to get too many back there." Seattle's Bishop Gerald Shaughnessy agreed that "public sentiment [was] increasingly against them." While Protestant churches called for Nikkei to be allowed back to the coast, Tibesar and some other Catholics refused to speak for it.[91]

Some of the most successful public relations campaigns focused on the sacrifices of Nikkei soldiers, but even they were not protected from discrimination. When the American Legion Post Number 22 in Hood River, Oregon, erased the names of sixteen local Nikkei soldiers from a war memorial in November 1944, newspapers across the country recorded indignation and disgust. Over three hundred servicemen wrote to the *Hood River News*; only one applauded the post's action. Local Methodist pastor W. Sherman Burgoyne and the Hood River Ministerial Association led the charge to amend the monument with support from the ACLU, the National Association for the Advancement of Colored People, the Portland Council of Churches, Friends of the American Way, and the Committee on American Principles and Fair Play. Within five months, the post begrudgingly returned fifteen of the names to the monument. (One soldier had since been dishonorably discharged.) Despite this apparent success, several families left Burgoyne's church, and his wife worried that they would be "beaten up or run out of town any moment." Three years later, just after receiving the Thomas Jefferson Award for advancing democracy, Burgoyne was reassigned to a remote church one-fifth the size of his former post. He was one of many pastors who failed to sell his sense of justice and compassion to his own congregants.[92]

In addition to writing letters and distributing petitions protesting discriminatory legislation, a number of West Coast pastors spoke to their congregations about these political issues. Some paired pragmatism with religious arguments explaining why Americans must support Nikkei. A sermon given by Albert Day in Pasadena, California, argued that God loves people of every race equally and that racist acts and thoughts distance Christians from God. After methodically addressing each practical concern and argument against the freedom of Nikkei, Day quoted a Methodist bishop who said, "You may have race prejudice if you want it; you may have Jesus Christ if you want Him. You can't have both."[93] These men believed racism and Christianity, as well as racism and Americanism, were incompatible. Day's sermon also reflects the growing recognition of wider racial discrimination and the place of Nikkei within it. Messages focusing on Nikkei shifted to encompass all minorities.

While pastors and regional groups increasingly defended Nikkei rights, mainline Protestants' public relations campaign also required combating prejudices from a defensive position, attempting to correct negative stereotypes in the media. Clarence Gillett corresponded with the editors of newspapers and magazines, clarifying or correcting facts about the incarceration and defending the loyalty of Japanese Americans. In many cases, journalists simply did not know the facts. Both *Time* magazine and the *Los Angeles Times* responded to Gillett's letters with gratitude for correcting their reports. When addressing falsities in the media, Gillett did not refer to religious justifications or his position as a minister, choosing to fight public battles with simple logic. When describing the work of the Congregational Committee, his letters never mentioned Christian or humanitarian motivations, only pragmatic logic. Perhaps he thought this approach provided the strongest argument, or he did not want people to think his close relationships with Japanese Americans or optimistic, naive Christian sentiments influenced his position.[94]

Opponents of Nikkei returning to the coast scoffed at preachers' oratory of brotherly love, labeling the pastors as naive or even insincere. A citizens' petition in Orange County, California, accused religious groups of "defeating the very thing they are asking for"—peace—because the return of Nikkei to the coast would cause mob violence. A columnist for the *Japanese Exclusion League Journal* presumed pastors would be displeased if their children married Japanese Americans. Floyd Schmoe proudly responded that his daughter Esther did marry a Japanese American, the Quaker activist Gordon Hirabayashi. His public statement described the absurdity of racial distinctions.[95]

Many religious leaders responded to common prejudices by correcting rumors about Nikkei or the camps. Father Tibesar wrote a detailed article from Minidoka for the *Seattle Times*, describing loyal, American incarcerees and the substandard living conditions within the camps. Similarly, the Denver and Colorado Councils of Churches released a flier with the heading, "Hate Is Moral Poison: The Church Answers Propaganda against Americans of Japanese Ancestry with These Facts." The word "hate" is printed in fallen, cracked, three-dimensional block letters; smoke curls upward to show the destruction caused by hate and allude to the fires of hell. The councils' pamphlet refuted rumors of sabotage and preferential treatment in the centers and warned against detrimental discrimination. The Colorado Council also planned "counterpropaganda" to fight a racist radio show.[96]

Protestant leaders combated negative depictions of Nikkei in popular culture as well, recognizing its power to influence both children and adults. Racist views flourished within popular entertainment, reinforcing stereotypes that characterized people of Japanese ancestry as a deceitful population mindlessly following their sacred emperor. While the American Protestant community could not prevent such depictions from entering the public's consciousness, they published articles and distributed

pamphlets to dispel misrepresentations and criticized the producers and publishers of such material. Bernard Waring, chair of the AFSC's Social Industrial Section, asked Twentieth Century Fox to end screenings of *Little Tokyo, U.S.A.* in 1942 because its "racial hatred and prejudice" exacerbated racial divisions in the country. Playing on fears of sabotage, the film's publicity material pledged the veracity of its story about a Los Angeles German–Japanese spy ring. Upon receiving letters from Quakers objecting to the anti-Japanese American depictions in the 1943 Superman series "The Sneer Strikes," Homer Morris, executive secretary of the AFSC's Social Industrial Section, wrote the McClure Syndicate to criticize the "misrepresentation of a whole people." While visiting an incarceration center, Clark Kent, with his x-ray vision, sees Nikkei plotting an escape, uses Superman's "amazing muscular control" to reshape his face to look Japanese, and infiltrates their ranks. Worried about the "millions of children who read Superman," Morris cited the lack of sabotage and good record of Nikkei in the United States. McClure's managing editor, Albert Leman, replied that one frame of the cartoon "specifically mentions loyal Americans of Japanese descent" but defended his choice to address possible enemy Nikkei outside of the incarceration centers. Morris's correspondence, complaints from the Office of War Information and the WRA, and pleas from the Reverend Royden Susu-Mago, an incarcerated minister, may have influenced the final frame of the series (Figure 4). In it, Superman faces the reader and intones, "It should be remembered that most Japanese-Americans are loyal citizens[.] Many are in combat units of our armed forces, and others are working in war factories. According to government statements not one act of sabotage was perpetrated in Hawaii or territorial U.S. by a Japanese-American." This may have been a concession to critiques from religious leaders and government officials.[97]

A *Little Joe* comic strip drew the ire of Emery Andrews, the pastor of Seattle's Japanese Baptist Church, when it revealed anxiety about sending Christmas gifts to incarcerees and outright fear of Japanese Americans. The cartoon depicts a white housewife sending a tall pile of presents to an incarceration camp against the warnings of a ranch hand, a mustached man wearing a large cowboy hat. The woman wears an apron, and a small child trails after her in each cell. She instructs the man, "You take these gifts to those poor Japs—right now! And don't forget—tell them merry Christmas!" Even the kind woman calls them "Japs," acknowledging the pervasive nature of that slur. The man grumbles but returns to the house with a return gift from incarcerees. Expecting treachery, he opens the package from a distance with a long string. Sure enough, the package explodes. The naive woman learns her lesson and shouts, "Oh-h-h! Those awful, inhuman beasts! They tried to kill us!" The man concludes, "Yep—I still claim Japs jest don't understand kindness."[98]

Not only does this comic exhibit appalling prejudice against Nikkei, it mocks mainline Protestantism and clergy, embodied as a simple woman, for being so gullible and distracted as to be organizing Christmas presents for a dangerous people. The comic's author, Robert Leffingwell, suggested that any attempt to treat Nikkei as human beings was a wasted effort. Furthermore, it told readers that any contact with or proximity to incarcerees could be life threatening. This seems to be the source of anxiety over the gift giving—that it encouraged contact with Nikkei, a group so cruel that they "grinned a lot" when presenting the gift-wrapped explosive, showing glee at the imminent disaster. Leffingwell depicted them as something other than human, unworthy of America's trust.

Andrews opened his retort to Leffingwell, "You aren't funny." He described Japanese Americans who proportionately bought more war bonds, donated more to the Red Cross, and volunteered for the armed forces in greater numbers than any other ethnic group. He concluded, "If you only knew what happened in the relocation centers this Christmas and Christmas last year, you would make a public apology for the ignorance portrayed in your 'funny' strip." Andrews's extensive paper collection at the University of Washington includes no response to this letter. Like Gillett and other activists, Andrews worked ceaselessly to educate others and eradicate prejudices.[99]

Protestant leaders struggled with their decision to make official resolutions about social issues like the incarceration while knowing the "rank and file" in their churches disagreed. Some feared that forcing a viewpoint that many saw as political—not religious—could "antagonize" people, decreasing the likelihood that congregations would support the issue. A member of the Protestant Commission "pointed out that excessive publicity is sometimes harmful, and the quieter methods preferable." Acknowledging that point, the commission decided to avoid the subject of first-generation Japanese. Issei could resettle east of the exclusion zone, too, but mainline Protestant leaders did not want to push their case further than necessary, deciding it would be "bad publicity" to mention that fact publicly. Some leaders hoped to approach sympathetic Christians without alerting people opposing their cause.[100]

This problem involved the pulpit as well as the pews. Nearly a third of representatives attending the regional Episcopal Church convention in Western Washington voted against supporting the return.[101] A California paper published the anti-Japanese views of a local Southern Baptist pastor.[102] Many more white pastors balked when asked to help Nikkei. After sending an enthusiastic letter to the Seattle Council of Churches, the executive secretary of the church council in Buffalo, New York withdrew his support when Seattle pastors responded positively. He described the proposition of hosting Seattle Nikkei as a "serious spiritual challenge" and stated that not contemplating the matter would be "craven and unworthy," but apparently contemplation was adequate. He decided that the physical, political, and financial risks to himself, his family, and the Buffalo Council were too great and declined to help any Japanese Americans.[103] Despite lingering notions of a social gospel and a firm belief that "Jesus would indict the churches as well as the legislators" for their "racial antipathies" and lack of "true Christian attitudes," many pastors hesitated to push unpopular views upon their congregants.[104] Some even submitted to their congregants' demands to bar Nikkei from church buildings.[105] Elesha Coffman observed this dissonance between the agenda of mainline Protestant leaders and the attitudes of many congregants and pastors, noting that reality never equaled Protestant rhetoric because "mainline leaders too seldom glanced over their shoulders to see if anyone was following."[106] Church workers seeking placements for resettlers faced this gaping trench daily, but national leaders working from New York offices seldom fathomed the extent of that dissonance.

## Conclusion

Ecumenical organizations successfully provided material goods, educational material, and support for resettlement throughout the war. Gordon Chapman's work within the Protestant Commission demonstrated the practicality of consolidating resources and decision-making powers when tackling a challenge as large as this one. Total efficacy would have been greatly reduced if each denomination had dealt with every problem associated with the incarceration independently. Mainline Protestants around the world were becoming increasingly interested in this type of ecumenical cooperation in the 1930s and 1940s, and such organizations expanded exponentially after World War II. Initially conceived to reduce conflict among denominations, the Protestant Commission's success demonstrated the benefits of ecumenical organizations.

Christian work became more pluralistic but grew on a shaky foundation. When Chapman welcomed—and demanded—the inclusion of all denominations and worked on behalf of marginalized and uncooperative groups like the Salvation Army, he faced opposition from Mark Dawber and the Home Missions Council. Disagreements about power and pluralism hindered their work. Though they worked for the same general goals, mainline Protestants, Quakers, and Catholics did not always work together fluidly. Catholics rarely collaborated with any other group, and AFSC workers scorned the squabbling of mainline Protestants. Quakers and some mainline Protestants, however, assisted Buddhists. In Hawaii, Quaker aid workers Gilbert and Minnie Bowles saved the Buddhist Shinshu Kyokai Mission from closure.[107] The Committee on Resettlement of Japanese Americans worked with the WRA to help Buddhists retain tax-exempt status on their California temples.[108] The Congregational Council of Social Action offered the Buddhist Churches of America $5,000 to support their ministry programs for resettlers, prioritizing resettlement over evangelism.[109] But even staunch ecumenists like Gordon Chapman felt conflicted when acting fairly to all meant "neglect[ing] duties to [his] own denomination."[110] He reported to the WRA that "competent investigators have testified that our cooperative achievement has been the most significant Christian unity project in a generation."[111]

Conscious of the unseen elements within such exchanges, a number of non-Christians worried that accepting aid from Christian organizations would obligate them to attend church or be subjected to other forms of evangelization.[112] They did not wish to be indebted to Christians in this way. Mark Osteen described this indebtedness as the Godfather Paradigm, where favors increase the prestige of the giver and obligate recipients to an unstated vow or future debt.[113] In the case of incarcerees, this debt might involve an obligation not to speak against the inaction of the churches and instead applaud the aid, however small. And most Nikkei did wait for decades before publically criticizing the churches. The public nature of the churches' support demanded that Nikkei respond with gratitude, and the lack of aid from other sources amplified the gravity of Christian support. If anyone was looking for a savior in this situation, Christian churches were the lone candidate. While some Nikkei eventually disparaged the insufficient resistance and support from churches, others only saw the kindness, whatever its magnitude.

Marcel Mauss, an anthropologist who laid foundational theory about gift economies, explained, "It is not individuals but collectivities that impose obligations of exchange and contract upon each other."[114] Aid strengthened preexisting bonds between Protestant Nikkei and national churches, while also solidifying the churches' power and domination within a stratified racial hierarchy. Receiving aid reaffirmed the Japanese Americans' lower social status and their sense of obligation to the outside churches.

Christian leaders worried that church workers would lose sight of the spiritual mission amidst their seemingly secular work. Aside from efforts to direct worship practices and supply Christian reading material, most aid had no obvious connection to the church. In a phenomenon within mainline Protestantism noted by historians David Hollinger, Matthew Hedstrom, and Elesha Coffman, Christian activism looked increasingly secular as the twentieth century progressed. Quakers, Catholics, and mainline Protestants all expressed concern about the ramifications of secularization and reminded their workers of the Christian motivations and goals of their efforts. Raymond Booth encouraged Friends to remember their primary task of "interpreting the way of Christ in mundane affairs." He warned that losing sight of this orientation would turn the AFSC into "simply another social work organization." As Hollinger and historian Bettye Collier-Thomas argue, secular social justice work was an extension of Christian commitments, not alternatives to them.[115]

**Building Churches behind Barbed Wire**

· · · · · · · · · · · · · · · · · · · · · · · · · · · · · · · · · · · · · · · · · · · · · · · · · · ·

> The right of freedom of religious worship in relocation centers is
> recognized and shall be respected.
> —WRA Administrative Instruction Number 32

A violent dust storm welcomed Monica Itoi and her family to southern
Idaho's Minidoka incarceration camp in August 1942. Before finding their
assigned barrack, "sand filled [their] mouths and nostrils and stung [their]
faces and hands like a thousand darting needles. . . . Hanging on" to her
father's and brother's jackets, "gasping and blinded," they tumbled
through a mess hall door. "Dust poured in through the cracks like smoke."
Just as quickly as the storm began, the sky cleared, leaving no trace of
the storm but howling children, stinging eyes, and "thick layers of dust
covering the dining tables and benches, . . . filling teacups and bowls."[1]
A year later, the *Minidoka Irrigator* described how "fiendish folds of
[a] savage dust storm . . . wrapped around" the new arrivals.[2] This was
the Itois' new home.

The hastily built center was not completed when Seattleites arrived
in the early fall of 1942. Plumbing for public showers and toilets did not
function, and the War Relocation Authority failed to install stoves before
mid-December. As the agency completed construction, the scattered
clumps of buildings began to resemble a functional, if spartan and
regimented, town. The camp's 950 acres eventually held thirty-six resi-
dential blocks, administrative buildings, a compound for military police,
warehouses, staff housing, a hospital, two fire stations, a cemetery, an
auditorium, the *Minidoka Irrigator* newspaper office, two elementary
schools, a high school, two watch repair shops, two dry cleaners, two barber shops, a beauty parlor, and eight stores. For recreation, incarcerees
built a gym, Japanese gardens, thirteen baseball fields, several play-
grounds, an improvised ice skating rink, and, after a boy drowned while
swimming in irrigation canals, two swimming holes. Eight guard towers
and, for part of the war, barbed wire surrounded the camp. Each residen-
tial block contained twelve barracks, a mess hall, a recreation hall, laundry

facilities, and communal lavatories and showers. Open toilets and showers without partitions horrified teenagers and the elderly alike. The barracks, constructed of wooden frames covered in tar paper, baked in the heat of summer and allowed cold winds to enter throughout the winter. The WRA assigned each family a partitionless room furnished only with army cots. Skilled Nikkei built furniture out of scavenged materials, hung curtains to fashion minimal privacy, and crafted ornaments to make the rooms into homes. They did what little they could to fill holes in the floor and cracks in the thin walls, but it proved impossible to block dust and winter snow from seeping into their makeshift homes. Hurried construction tore up the acreage loaned by the Bureau of Land Reclamation, exacerbating the dust problem. Housing blocks, school classes, and individuals grew victory gardens to stabilize the earth and supplement their meals, many of which came from cans. The WRA paid incarcerees to farm larger fields and raise hogs and chickens.[3]

Nikkei settled into routines, working or attending school. Monica Itoi's father took a position as an internal security guard, while she worked with her sister at the camp hospital. Incarcerees received between twelve and nineteen dollars a month, while employees of all other ethnicities earned seven or more times as much for the same job. The latter slept in furnished, finished apartments and dined on superior food. Many Nikkei left camp temporarily to harvest local sugar beet crops. Within the camp, incarcerees competed in sporting events, took art classes, sang in choirs, attended dances, and tried to build normal lives. A number of men and women, young and old, used their abundant free hours to attend church services and learn more about religion, whether Buddhism or Christianity. Some sought consolation or an explanation for the injustice, while others, curious or bored, now had time to delve into the subject.

This chapter leaves the tidy conference rooms and cluttered offices on the East and West Coasts where national leaders planned aid and worship structures for Nikkei, moving to the bare, shoddy, and dust-filled barracks where Nikkei organized their churches. They started from scratch, building pews and altars, organizing and allocating donations, and arranging for the transport of supplies from their prewar churches. White religious workers obtained entry passes from camp administrators and found housing in nearby towns. In addition to the challenges of guiding their congregants in an incarceration center, Nikkei and white church workers implemented instructions from the Protestant Commission for Japanese Service to define and form what was for most of them a new type of church. Outside church leaders and some incarcerees revered the concept of ecumenism, but no one agreed what ecumenical worship should look like or how pastors of different denominations and theologies would lead an ecumenical church. This chapter focuses on the white and Nikkei pastors who struggled to perform basic pastoral duties, raise camp morale, and arrange jobs for incarcerees east of the exclusion zone. The demand for immediate care within the camps competed with efforts to resettle Nikkei outside of camp as quickly as possible.

## War Relocation Authority Policies on Religion

Amidst a criminal disregard for Nikkei's civil rights, the U.S. government attempted to "enforce" religious liberty in the incarceration centers. Administrative Instruction Number 32, the WRA's policy on religion in the incarceration centers, expanded the model of religious freedom established for the temporary assembly centers.[4] The latter banned religious services used as a "vehicle to propagandize or incite" incarcerees, but Instruction 32 eliminated this loophole for restriction.[5] Against the advice of attorney Philip Glick and Chief of Community Services John Provinse, WRA director Dillon Myer also agreed to a policy that omitted an explicit ban on State Shinto or emperor worship. Japan currently claimed that Shinto was not a religion and classified it apart from Buddhism and Christianity.[6] Following this example, the WRA could declare absolute religious liberty by categorizing Shinto as something other than religion. In any case, camp directors always had ultimate veto power, even if a clause to that effect was omitted from the final draft of Instruction 32.[7] Camp directors were generally permissive. They allowed adherents of Japanese new religious movements like Seicho-no-Ie to meet and practice within the camps, assuring WRA authorities that the group had "no political significance."[8]

Religious liberty played a defining role in WRA propaganda to incarcerees and other Americans. Newsreels of the camps showed Nikkei at worship, in part to show the extent of democratic rights within the camps but also to enhance public perceptions of Nikkei, emphasizing their Christian values and behavior. As resettlement became the agency's primary objective, films like *A Challenge to Democracy*, produced by the WRA and the Offices of War Information and Strategic Services, qualified incarcerees' freedom of religion. The narrator assured viewers that aside from "State Shinto involving emperor worship, there is no restriction of religion in camp."[9] Despite the hypocrisy of a race-based incarceration during a war against ideologies of racial supremacy, freedom of religion remained one of Roosevelt's Four Freedoms. The president believed that "protecting religious faith and the freedom of worship were . . . essential prerequisites for democracy . . . a source of virtue and community spirit . . . that . . . encouraged a sense of responsibility to the welfare of others."[10] A similar attitude may have influenced Director Myer and the officials who monitored the camps.

But while not overtly restricting the three main religious bodies—Buddhism, Catholicism, and Protestantism—a self-monitoring system gave incarcerees the power to regulate one another. A Committee on Religion had studied policy options for religion in the camps during the late summer of 1942. Buddhist and Christian leaders submitted their opinions, as did administrators working in the camps.[11] The WRA followed the Committee on Religion's recommendation to form an interfaith council within each camp to "decide all questions affecting religious conduct within the center." The committee hoped interfaith councils, alongside Nikkei community councils, would suppress "pseudo cults" by deciding "whether there was a sufficiently large constituency within the relocation areas to justify establishment of such religious organizations." The interfaith councils would also bar groups with "no other purpose than proselytizing."[12] A Community Activities Committee that oversaw camp recreation had to approve religious events or new hires within the camp churches as well. Granting free worship with one hand, the WRA constructed an innocuous-sounding apparatus for limiting worship with the other. Nikkei committees could censor religion within the camp, though no evidence suggests they did.

Gordon Chapman of the Protestant Church Commission and other Christian leaders working with Nikkei objected to granting any council such authority and asked the WRA to revise Instruction 32 accordingly.[13] Catholics expressed the greatest concerns with the process. Requiring incarcerees to choose leaders was not an extreme policy for Protestant laity who regularly participate in the election or rejection of their ministers, but Catholic parishioners have no such authority. Only bishops and archbishops can assign priests to parishes. While some priests considered the WRA precaution "a wise rule" to prevent "horde[s] of evangelists descending upon" camps and recommended incarcerees work within that system to request priests, most refused to cooperate on principle.[14] In a statement contradictory to a Catholic, the WRA's first director, Milton

Eisenhower, explained to Bishop James Walsh of the Maryknoll Missionaries, "It is our intention to administer the wartime relocation projects as self-governing, democratic communities insofar as circumstances will permit. In keeping with that intention and traditional American principles of religious freedom, we propose that the residents themselves shall decide what religious services and functions are required and who shall conduct them."[15] Maryknoll's Thomas Kiernan countered that "the Catholic pastor alone is the judge of the nature and scope of religious services."[16] Despite these complaints, Myer rejected proposed amendments to Instruction 32.

WRA administrators also called for ecumenical Protestant and Buddhist churches at the request of the Federal Council of Churches and the Home Missions Council of North America. They wanted one Buddhist, one Protestant, and one Catholic church at each camp. Not everyone liked this idea, and the rule interfered with the religious liberty of sectarian religionists, creating numerous practical problems. The Committee on Religion recommended that "the cornerstone of religious worship within the centers should be a continuation" of prewar practices, but few Nikkei worshiped in ecumenical churches before the war. In the end, the WRA did not enforce ecumenism. They allowed Pure Land Buddhists and Episcopalians to break away from the main churches, but leaders within the ecumenical churches pressured them to assimilate.[17]

Director Myer, several camp directors, and a few mainline Protestant leaders still worried about the lack of support and resources for Buddhists.[18] Religious leaders at Minidoka circumvented Idaho education laws that incorporated religious teachings within the public school system to avoid forcing Christian teachings on the camp's many non-Christians.[19] The WRA prioritized questions about religious liberty to a degree that Guy Robertson, the director of Heart Mountain incarceration center, asked Director Myer directly about the legitimacy of a Buddhist holiday. Incarcerees had requested a day off for the celebration of Buddha's birth, pointing out its similarity to Christmas. Robertson disapproved since the Buddhists lived in a "Christian nation." Myer rejected the proposal on the grounds that Buddhist-majority countries do not proclaim federal holidays on that day.[20]

Two policies within Instruction 32 regulated the use of state property and resources by religious groups in an attempt to distinguish the work of the government from that of the church. First, Nikkei pastors could not be paid a salary by a federal agency but could accept one from outside sources. Unlike the U.S. military, the WRA would not provide chaplains for their wards. This rule drew extensive debate and critique from camp employees and religious workers. In many cases, Nikkei pastors doubled as morale officers and social workers, deserving, in the minds of several camp directors, a government salary. John Powell, the assistant director of Poston, a camp in Arizona, argued against the rule on the very grounds of religious liberty. Since pastors functioned as community activities leaders, a salaried position in the camps, withholding salaries "punished" clergy for being religious. He noted that several camps funded clergy under the guise of social workers or education directors anyway, so authorizing salaries to clergy would eliminate the need for such deception. Manzanar's director, for example, placed Nikkei pastors on the Community Welfare Department payroll. The incarcerated Presbyterian minister Sohei Kowta submitted a similar request on behalf of Poston's Inter-Religious Council. John Provinse admitted that the current system privileged Christians, since only they could obtain outside support. Congregants could not afford to support their own clergy on limited camp salaries. On the other side, Elmer Shirrell, the director of Tule Lake incarceration camp, supported the policy, arguing that paying pastors would violate their religious liberty because it opened the possibility for the government to influence the pastors' messages.[21]

Second, the WRA would not provide housing for white religious workers unless they worked for the project in a separate position. This clause limited the number of white clergy members who could work at the camps because few could find housing near the rural camp sites. The several small towns near Minidoka contributed to the camp's relatively large number of white church volunteers. Shirrell argued that white pastors should not be permitted regular access to the camps at all. Catholics argued that while Protestant and Buddhist incarcerees could access Nikkei religious leaders in camp, no Japanese American Catholic priest existed to serve that function. Finding WRA housing restrictions inconvenient and unreasonable, Seattle's Japanese Catholic parish priest Leopold Tibesar "squatted" in a camp barrack at Minidoka. The camp director Harry Stafford bent rules and allowed him two rooms that served as his bedroom, office, chapel, library, and social center. Though never officially authorized, Stafford told Tibesar he could stay as long as no one objected.[22] No one did. Tibesar's experience shows that camp directors had the latitude to bypass regulations in many cases, but he was the only white religious worker to live for an extended period in a camp without other WRA employment.

Beyond Instruction 32 and its pledges to preserve religious liberty and retain a separation of church and state, the WRA banned proselytization by white church workers in cooperation with mainline Protestants from the Federal Council of Churches and the Home Missions Council. The agency permitted occasional revivals led by renowned missionaries like E. Stanley Jones and Kirby Page but billed them as voluntary events for Christians—not efforts to convert non-Christians. The meetings drew high Christian participation and do not seem to have disrupted camp life. More fervent evangelists occasionally slipped in, but camp directors and white pastors generally respected the policy. Nikkei pastors could freely evangelize to fellow incarcerees.

John Howard claimed that "the WRA relied on religious organizing, revivals, and other modes of Protestant evangelism to shape the identity and conduct of their wards," but his research, limited to the Arkansas camps, may have been skewed by Southern evangelical attitudes that did not represent experiences in the rest of the country. He offered no evidence to support his claim that "officials advocated conversion" or invited missionaries to "win over the majority Buddhist population." Much evidence to the contrary can be found, as described in the previous chapter.[23]

Catholics revolted against the ban on evangelism, citing recent Supreme Court trials that recognized religious organizations' right to evangelize. Thomas Kiernan also invoked the WRA's theoretical intention to re-create life similar to the prewar experiences of Nikkei, which included a "normal opportunity for . . . evangelization." He protested, "The most potent form of Americanization among these Japanese in America has been Catholic and Protestant proselytization," contending that the Pearl Harbor attack would not have occurred if Christian missions in Japan had been more successful.[24] The WRA met Catholic objections with silence but did not interfere with Catholic work in the camps.

Catholics also worried about religious education, as they hoped to continue their parochial schools within the camps. Despite a rule permitting such work, the venture was not feasible. Maryknoll offered to pay and house accredited instructors and provide teaching supplies, but incarcerees could not fund the construction of school buildings while receiving substandard pay. The WRA refused to construct buildings for Catholic schools or group all Nikkei Catholics in one camp. Since Maryknoll leaders believed incarcerees should be relocated outside of the camps as expediently as possible, they deemed investing in schools at multiple camps impractical.[25]

News of a contraception clinic opening in Poston alarmed several priests. They dropped the matter after a few months but not before checking Arizona law and investigating whether Nikkei requested or desired such provisions. Contraception violates Catholic religious law, but Maryknollers seemed more concerned that the clinic was an ill-disguised attempt to reduce birth rates in order to diminish the Nikkei population.[26]

Catholics felt particularly maligned by WRA policy, noting Protestant assumptions underlying camp regulations. Diaries and correspondence reveal the threat Catholic leaders perceived from Protestant workers and government officials. They accused the agency of granting freedom of worship to Protestants and perhaps Buddhists but not Catholics. In a meeting with E. R. Fryer, the WRA regional director in San Francisco, Kiernan "explained that [they] could not and would not accept Protestant or secular definitions of religious freedom, freedom of worship, religious programs, etc. [They] were prepared to take [their] minimum demands to the highest authority in the land if necessary; . . . the Church as well as the Japanese internees had rights in this matter." Though not officially contesting the incarceration, Catholics would fight for their constitutional rights to religious liberty. Moreover, they encouraged incarcerees to fight for these rights. Drought advised, "To be obedient to the Government is one thing. To be a complacent rabbit for the Protestant organizations is a very different thing." The secretary general of Maryknoll summarized his perception of the situation: "We Catholics have gotten little in this country except that for which we valiantly fought and this may be another occasion for us to challenge the despotic politicians who have created this situation." Recognizing the power of Protestants in the WRA administration, however, Maryknoll officials recommended that Catholic workers remain "clear of political consequences and implications" to protect their access to Nikkei. No anti-Catholic rhetoric exists in the WRA's surviving correspondence or meeting records. WRA officials seem to have been operating under sincere, if ignorant, efforts to preserve religious liberties and prevent unwanted evangelism. The hierarchical structure of the Catholic Church and the lack of Nikkei priests conflicted with the WRA's plans for religious liberty, but the ecumenical Buddhist and Protestant churches similarly disrupted prewar worship.[27]

## The Foundation of Camp Churches

The first Protestant meetings in each incarceration camp varied, but most produced similar ecumenical structures, constitutions, and activity schedules. Worship services almost always began on the first Sunday incarcerees spent in camp. Local clergy or members of the camp administration led services if no Nikkei pastors were available. As Nikkei ministers arrived over the course of weeks or months, they debated and reassessed the ideal form and style of Christian worship. Until a critical mass of clergymen arrived (no women held the topmost positions), worship styles and religious activities varied as different ministers asserted their leadership. By the time white church volunteers arrived months later, Nikkei pastors had already established their basic approach to ecumenism and designed the churches' leadership structures. White missionaries and ethnic church pastors filled positions as needed, but few took significant leadership roles.

The formation of the Tule Lake Union Church typified the way in which Nikkei pastors established churches in the incarceration camp. A group of young Christians requested a local pastor to deliver a sermon for their first Sunday in camp. The first resident minister, Andrew Kuroda, arrived the following week. An English-speaking Issei, Kuroda had led the Salem Japanese Community Church in Oregon until his eviction. On the second Sunday in Tule Lake, Kuroda led a morning worship service, organized a Sunday school, and arranged for an outside lecturer to engage fifty young people that evening. He immediately began planning a unified Protestant Church that resembled the church he led in Salem. As additional pastors arrived, some wished to retain the cohesion of their prewar congregations apart from other Protestants, while others demanded divisions along denominational lines; still others favored Kuroda's ecumenical approach. By the end of July 1942, the last large group of incarcerees arrived, bringing Tule Lake's population to 15,000. All now shared their views on the composition of the church. Not long after, Tulean clergymen christened the Tule Lake Union Church, an ecumenical church consolidating all Protestant leaders and adherents in the camp. Several months later, Howard and Ruth Hannaford, retired Presbyterian missionaries from Japan, volunteered to work at the church, commuting from a nearby town.[28]

Minidoka's pastors had a slight advantage over Tuleans because most had collaborated at the Puyallup assembly center. A few weeks before the first incarcerees left for Idaho in August 1942, Protestant leaders from

Camp Harmony and the greater Seattle area began planning the Minidoka church. They decided how to structure worship, considering denominational churches, united churches, and federated churches before deciding on the last.[29] Records do not indicate how much pressure non-Nikkei leaders exerted at this meeting, if any. Suspecting Tom Fukuyama would be the only Nisei minister within this large community, Nikkei pastors asked the Protestant Commission to send additional church workers, "preferably returned missionaries from Japan," to work with Nisei and other young people.[30] This request was a formality, since five white Protestant workers from Seattle already planned to follow their congregations to Idaho. The city's Nikkei pastors continued making compromises and adjustments during the first months at Minidoka, adapting to the WRA's rules, finding worship space, meeting clergy arriving from the Portland Assembly Center, and welcoming their white pastors in the late fall of 1942.

Managing space within the camp was the first challenge for incarcerated religious leaders. While camps remained at maximum capacity for the first six to eight months, space was at a premium. The WRA approved plans for a uniform house of worship to be shared by all groups, but schools and other buildings took precedent.[31] By the time the WRA could have built the promised worship halls, attention had turned to resettlement and empty barracks became available. Gila River was one of the only camps to benefit from a WRA-built church.[32] The Protestant Commission also envisioned constructing churches in each camp but realized the impracticality of spending sparse resources on structures that would be used for only a few years.[33] Religious groups initially shared public buildings with different groups throughout the week. Some of the first visitors from the outside complained that Nikkei had to worship in recreation halls with insufficient furniture or in smelly, noisy mess halls.[34] WRA administrators soon assigned community groups, including religious organizations, spaces to share. This allowed the Minidoka Federated Church to cease its peripatetic existence and begin meeting in the same recreation halls consistently. But since they shared the spaces with a variety of groups, church workers had to remove altars and other equipment after each meeting.[35] Workers built cupboards in these shared buildings to store hymnals and altar accouterments, but discontent still arose when groups did not clean the space.[36] An Issei pastor felt that the intermittent sanctuary was "almost impossible to beautify or dignify."[37] When the first Episcopal bishop visited Minidoka, Alaskan Abe Hagewara

FIGURE 5 Leopold Tibesar's living quarters and the Minidoka Catholic Church, September 1943. Source: National Archives and Records Administration Collection, Densho Digital Archives.

"borrow[ed]" lumber from a construction site to build kneeling benches. Caught in the act, he described how congregants wanted to "create a little of a church setting" in the "shell" of a recreation center. Camp authorities made Hagewara return the lumber after services.[38]

Shared public space did not provide the privacy necessary for pastoral care or permanent altars where individuals could worship privately. Transitioning from chairing the Japanese Church Federation in Seattle to leading the Protestant Church Council at Minidoka, the Issei Congregational pastor Nao Kodaira found the initial lack of private chambers for study or pastoral counseling nearly unbearable.[39] Without an office, he had few alternatives to working in his bachelor dormitory. While Kodaira and Minidoka's other pastors never received individual offices, camp administrators allocated two apartments each for the Federated Church, the Catholic Church, and the Buddhist Church in 1943.[40] As Figure 5 shows, their rooms were located in the same tar paper-covered barracks in which Nikkei lived.[41]

Sympathetic camp administrators also found spaces where Roman Catholics, Episcopalians, and Buddhists could erect permanent altars

FIGURE 6 First Communion class, Minidoka Catholic Church, September 1943. Source: National Archives and Records Administration Collection, Densho Digital Archives.

where adherents could offer devotions at any time of day. Tibesar draped a cloth over the altar while using his chapel for social gatherings. Mr. Takeda, a man under instruction for baptism, constructed a tabernacle, and Mrs. Nakagawa sewed its curtains and antependium (Figure 6). Tibesar held mass there every morning for around twenty Catholic Nikkei. Sunday services for two hundred or more had to be held in recreation halls. Catholics did their best to beautify the exposed beams and unfinished wooden walls by installing icons around the altar and pinning holy cards near the communal bookshelves. The altar held a scroll containing the names of every soldier from Minidoka. For Christmas, another incarceree, Mr. Shimizu, carved a nativity crib out of sagebrush. At the daily Catholic mass, Tibesar lighted a candle and prayed for enlisted Catholic and non-Catholic Minidokans.[42]

In their barracks, Catholic incarcerees also constructed "beautiful little altars" containing statues of Mary, crucifixes, and flowers. Tibesar observed that some "family altars are things of beauty made of sage-brush wood" from the desert surrounding Minidoka. Exhibitions at the Smithsonian's Renwick Gallery and the Japanese American National Museum have featured intricate Buddhist shrines constructed in the camps as well. After a barrack of single men constructed a rock garden outside their building, one of the Catholic residents added a statue of Mary to transform the site into "the first Grotto of Our Lady of Minidoka." It commemorated a similar grotto constructed and financed by the community at the Seattle Maryknoll mission.[43]

Kenneth Helphand compared this to other "defiant gardens" built in wartime spaces. Creating Japanese-style rock gardens expressed cultural identity and changed the physical landscape. Jane E. Dusselier argues that art, including the construction of personal gardens, provided a unique space within which Nikkei could express freedoms denied to them in reality. Beauty, a necessity of life and a value particularly prized in Japanese culture, was a scare commodity in incarceration camps. Through the creation, maintenance, and enjoyment of religious or secular art and gardens, Nikkei asserted their cultural heritage, enhanced their physical environment, and improved their mental well-being. The grotto at Minidoka connected Nikkei Catholics to their home in Seattle as well as their home within the church. Incarcerees took ownership and control of space within their confinement, sanctifying space inside and outside of the churches and barracks.[44]

Minidokan Episcopalians constructed an elaborate altar where Joseph Kitagawa held daily services in remembrance of church members who died in the war. Icons and scripture adorned the walls, and skilled church members constructed an elaborate candelabra to optimize use of the small space. A dark curtain draped the back wall, establishing a backdrop for a small, ornate cross.[45] Christians filled cracks in the church walls to keep out the dust and sewed curtains to cover the thin windows. One might say these incarcerees made the best of a bad situation, which is true, but creating sacred space within an incarceration camp also asserted their religious identity and independence from the subjection outside the thin church walls.

Leaders and members of the Federated Church left their worship spaces relatively spartan. The church occasionally displayed flowers, a precious commodity in the desert, or a U.S. flag, but its empty walls resembled the plainness found in their prewar churches. This mimics the austere nature of many Protestant churches, which are frequently devoid of ornamentation and images. The contrast between the ornate Episcopal shrine and the plain ecumenical Protestant church denoted one of the difficulties of merging churches with different worship styles.

## Defining Ecumenism

After locating worship space and familiarizing themselves with the WRA's regulations and plans for an interfaith council, Protestant pastors tried to agree on a definition of ecumenism. Internationally, ecumenists hoped to build a truer, stronger Christianity through union but generally stopped short of abandoning denominational worship. Nikkei pastors who believed in the strength of this ideal approached the creation of an ecumenical church differently than those who simply understood that Baptists and Methodists and Presbyterians would meet together in the same building each Sunday. Andrew Kuroda and Tom Fukuyama both advocated unified, ecumenical churches in their camps, but each envisioned different goals, approaches, and realities.

Believing in the grander goals of ecumenism that inspired the implementation of this structure by outside leaders, Kuroda took a systematic, intentional approach to ecumenism. Having worked within such an organization before the war, he brought knowledge and experience to the Tule Lake Union Church. More than other pastors, his approach emphasized how commonalities among worship practices formed the "common heritage of Christendom" through "unity in the purpose, significance and historical relationship" of devotional acts. Kuroda encouraged his colleagues to study an ecumenical worship service based on a comprehensive analysis of Protestant hymnals and liturgies. The service utilized core elements found within many denominations.[46]

Kuroda tried to enlighten his congregation as well as his fellow pastors. He knew young incarcerees lacked "denominational consciousness" out of indifference rather than intent. He called for an ecumenical education program, so Christians would embrace the beauty of common truths among Protestants and see their moral power within society. While most people saw the ecumenical camp churches purely as a wartime experiment—and chairman of the Protestant Commission Frank Herron Smith admitted as much in a sermon to the Poston Christian Church—the optimistic Kuroda hoped Tulean Christians would spread these viewpoints within their churches after the war. Kuroda asked new members not to choose a denomination until or if it became necessary outside. Few, if any, other camp churches devoted time to discussing ecumenism with congregants. Kuroda wanted congregants to know that their church's ecumenical design was not a decision made out of convenience but rather an intentional opportunity to experiment with a sacred, true manifestation of Christianity. Kuroda embodied the manifestation of what the Federal Council of Churches, the Home Missions Council, and the Protestant Commission desired for pastors in the camps.[47]

The young Baptist pastor Tom Fukuyama valued ecumenism but took a more casual approach than Kuroda. He joked about how "liberal" he must appear to outsiders for speaking at churches of all denominations. After speaking at several Methodist churches in the area, he wrote to his fiancée, "Tom could be a good Methodist! Anyway, he's far from the orthodox Baptist." This attitude surprised local church leaders, who did not expect him to speak at non-Baptist churches or attend their regional conferences. This perspective fit his admiration for the sentiment, "A Christian is one who is at home anyplace in the world." Fukuyama felt as comfortable in other pulpits as he did preaching in a Baptist church but still thought in terms of sectarian divisions. His understanding of ecumenism reflects the reality of ecumenical worship in the camps. Most Nikkei pastors thought of ecumenism as a finite action rather than an ideal to work toward. Their observations and disagreements focused on the visible manifestations of ecumenical worship: Is everyone worshiping in the same building at the same time? Without an established connection with the ideal of ecumenism, other Nikkei pastors rejected the ideology or lacked training to confront its practical challenges.[48]

Defining ecumenical Protestantism required incarcerees to agree on a definition of Protestantism. These decisions dictated who qualified as a church member and who would be considered a member of the camps' clergy. Since mainline Protestants outnumbered other Protestants in the camps, they defined ecumenism. As a result, the ecumenical churches' hierarchy, structure, and worship styles resembled those of mainline Protestantism. Some policies inadvertently marginalized denominations, but mainline Nikkei clergy also designed structures to exclude certain worship styles or beliefs.

Several Nikkei church councils wrote constitutions to outline their churches' beliefs, doctrine, and practices to manage foreseeable conflicts. At their request, Gordon Chapman used Poston's constitution to create a generic document he believed could be used by any Protestant church. Pastors needed only to write their church's name in the provided spaces. While no evidence indicates that any camp churches used this exact constitution, it formed a useful template from which to work. The document declared that church membership would consist of "persons who are already members of the Christian churches," a phrase inviting broad interpretations. The "required . . . confessions of faith" read as follows:

a. I believe in God the Almighty, who is the creator and Father of mankind.
b. I believe in Jesus Christ as the Son of the living God and as the Saviour of mankind.
c. I believe in the Holy Spirit.
d. I believe in the Holy Catholic Church (Universal).
e. I believe in the Bible as the Canon of the Church and standard of our faith.

These beliefs resembled the fundamental doctrine of all mainline denominations represented in the camps. The stated purpose of the church, "to proclaim the Gospel of Christ and to realize the Kingdom of God among mankind," was open to interpretation. The gospel could be interpreted in any manner, and the kingdom could be literal or metaphorical, in heaven or on earth. Intentionally vague phrases throughout the rest of the constitution allowed for different sacraments and interpretation of ritual. Church members could define the significance of communion individually and choose their own form of baptism. Such openness avoided the disputes over membership and communion that occurred in some camps. Wyoming's Heart Mountain's original constitution limited membership to baptized Christians, which barred Salvation Army members and Quakers, who do not perform baptisms. It also barred members refusing to drop their denominational affiliations. To "keep peace and harmony," Heart Mountain's pastors liberalized these membership requirements. Jerome's Community Christian Church required baptism for membership but permitted an exception for Salvation Army members.[49]

New converts posed one of the greatest challenges to fostering ecumenical Protestant identities. They presented problems inherent to a temporary ecumenical church. When converts left camp, what church should they attend? If a person joined an ecumenical church and had never belonged to anything else, what denomination would he or she be? While they could always change affiliations later, converts had to choose baptism by immersion, as occurs within Baptist, Free Methodist, and most Holiness churches, or a sprinkling of water, as in Episcopalian, Presbyterian, and other Protestant churches. Or they might wish to abstain, following beliefs of the Salvation Army or Quakers. For Easter services, when many people received baptism, camps chose one method for the sake of ceremony and a show of unity. Sohei Kowta reported that converts who preferred a different method would be rebaptized later.[50] As young people started families in the camps, doctrinal differences determined when they would baptize their children—as infants or adults. Baptism means different things within different denominations and occurs at different times with different degrees of preparation. Kuroda hoped converts would choose no denomination, but these differences made his ideal untenable. All camp pastors agreed that the eventual choice of denominational affiliation rested with the individual.

While pastors willingly compromised to delineate church membership, defining clergy was contentious. Mainline pastors had to work closely with accepted clergy and entrust them with their congregants. With guidance from the Protestant Commission, pastors in the camps decided that a man must be ordained or officially recognized by a denomination to join a camp's board of clergy. Though not a requirement, they hoped candidates also had seminary training.[51]

Practically speaking, the Protestant Commission required a definition by which to judge clergy, since it organized the ministers' salaries. The commission lacked funds to support all people who met their qualifications, let alone those who did not. If a denomination refused to pay a pastor, as in the case of the Salvation Army, the commission tried to raise funds for the individual. The guideline provided the commission with a systematic way to turn away lay Nikkei within the camp who wished to serve within the church. By March 1943, outside religious organizations provided salaries for 107 Protestant ministers in the ten incarceration centers.[52]

Intentionally or not, this policy discriminated against certain Christian denominations. It excluded Christians lacking a hierarchy similar to that found in mainline Protestantism. Members of Mukyōkai, which used only lay leaders, could not join the ecumenical clergy. Not only did these Christians lack formal religious training, they had no denominational board to consult. Members of Mukyōkai and other lay-oriented Christians volunteered as Sunday school teachers, choir directors, or youth leaders but rarely influenced the structural formation of the camp congregations or worship services.

Defining the boundaries and role of ecumenical churches gave mainline pastors the power to block certain types of Christianity from practicing in the camps, shaping the substance and appearance of ecumenism. The mainline ministers at Tanforan Assembly Center in California denied a Holiness Nikkei access to the pulpit and rejected the denomination's proposal of a rotational preaching system.[53] Many mainline Protestants disapproved of the boisterous worship they associated with Holiness and Pentecostal Protestants. "The excesses . . . and abnormal conduct" of a group of exuberant Issei at Manzanar "greatly disturbed" Henry Bovenkerk, a Presbyterian missionary. He could not "believe that such demonstrations [were] helpful either to the Christians individually or to the influence of the church in this community." This concern for the camp's church and evangelistic capacity helps explain the responses of mainline Protestants at Tanforan. Voting to "keep the group unified as possible" meant removing undesirable worship styles. Many pastors feared that "revivalistic" worship would damage their churches. Bovenkerk and the pastors at Tanforan did not believe emotive, evangelistic preaching "represent[ed] . . . the American Christian Church," nor could it be a positive influence within the community.[54] Such pronouncements were not uncommon. Even Minidoka's Tom Fukuyama, usually generous and open to different styles of worship, confided to his fiancée, "Golly, Betty, I react against old time evangelistic hymns and shoddy worship service. You must help me to have more sympathy and kindness to methods and ideologies which are contrary to mine. I feel like a heretic tonight!"[55] The letter did not clarify if he felt like a heretic for disapproving of or participating in such services. In the end, "ecumenical" services in every camp resembled those of Baptists, Presbyterians, and Methodists. Leaders did not welcome contributions that highlighted the diversity within Protestantism. Mainline Protestants claimed unity by preserving the practices they saw as normative.

But the ecumenical experiment still expanded Christians' definitions of Christianity, whether they approved of inclusivity or not. The experiences of Holiness groups in the camps demonstrate how ambiguous definitions of ecumenism permitted a range of acceptance and discrimination within the ecumenical churches. Pentecostal pastors and Salvation Army officers usually sat on the board of ministers since their theology and clerical structures did not differ greatly from mainline Protestantism. At Minidoka, a Nikkei Holiness pastor from Seattle acted with equal authority alongside Baptist, Methodist, Presbyterian, and Episcopalian leaders.[56] While it is unknown whether mainline pastors welcomed him with open arms, he shared equal responsibilities for preaching and leading services.

Toward the end of the war, correspondence about Holiness members revealed positive insights. Chapman expressed his pleasure "with the fine attitude . . . demonstrated again and again by . . . Holiness ministers" in the camps. He said that they "have not only cooperated heartily with the community churches in the various relocation centers, but in most cases have been recognized as true leaders by Christians of all denominations." He praised individuals' "deep spiritual influence" and noted how one evangelical had become "a tower of strength" at Topaz, the camp in Utah.[57] These comments are notable because such behavior was expected and assumed of mainline pastors, who rarely received such singular praise, despite comparable achievements.

## Ecumenism at Minidoka

Levels of denominational independence fluctuated at Minidoka as pastors learned how to implement ecumenism at a congregational level. Pastors eased their congregants into the new structure by holding periodic "reunion services" for prewar congregations. Members enjoyed the familiar companionship of prewar church groups, but most welcomed members of other denominations when prompted. Margaret Peppers, a white Episcopal deaconess from Seattle, opened her Ladies' Aid Society to all Issei women at the suggestion of Methodist Everett Thompson. Choir members from the different prewar churches similarly united.[58] Episcopalians, however, increasingly met independently from the Federated Church. Other religious groups, like the Seventh Day Adventists, rarely joined other Protestants for religious activities.[59]

In addition to weekly ecumenical meetings for young people, Protestant leaders organized an ecumenical vacation Bible school. Gordon Chapman collaborated with WRA officials to encourage all camp churches to sponsor vacation schools. Minidoka's administrators and pastors invited Buddhist and Roman Catholic leaders to teach separate courses as well. With few recreational options, most Minidokan parents chose to send their children to the religious summer school. Catholics followed the curriculum of the Seattle Maryknoll School, while classes for Protestants used "standard" interdenominational texts. Since the reading material presented only one narrative, ministers relied on Sunday school teachers to introduce a wider range of biblical interpretations and denominational traditions. Perhaps in an attempt to avoid conflict, leaders designed classes that would allow teachers to avoid denominationally contentious material.

Protestant high school students chose among sessions such as the "Life and Teachings of Jesus," "Modern Christian Heroes," the "Christian Roots of American Democracy," and more introspective topics, such as "On Being a Real Person."[60] Church leaders offered elementary students a similar range of topics, including Christian poetry and early Christian history. At the conclusion of the two-week summer school, Protestant and Catholic graduates pledged their allegiance to the United States, a Christian flag, and the Bible at a graduation ceremony. Buddhists arranged a separate ceremony.[61]

Adults and children also attended denominational summer camps around the country. Some camps required no payment while others gave half scholarships to incarcerees. Experimental ecumenical camps inside the church and denominational camps outside reflected the artificial structure of religious life in camp.[62]

Unlike recreational activities that could ostensibly avoid challenging Protestant unity, doctrinal, theological, and liturgical differences forced Protestants to make compromises. Episcopalians faced the most severe challenge. While Anglican law permits adherents to participate in Eucharist services led by non-Anglicans, the church teaches that its own consecration of the host serves a greater purpose. In a space between Catholic transubstantiation, in which the bread and wine turn into the literal body and blood of Christ, and the symbolic reenactment of the Last Supper conducted by most Protestant churches, Anglicans believe in consubstantiation, where the Real Presence of Christ unites with the bread and wine. Since only an Anglican priest can affect that transformation, Episcopal incarcerees required the presence of their own clergy and met separately for communion in every camp. Bishop Charles Reifsnider, the man appointed to coordinate incarcerated Episcopalians, insisted they retain this autonomy.[63]

Differences in biblical interpretation also encouraged Episcopalians to break away from the ecumenical church. After visiting Minidoka on behalf of the Episcopal diocese of Oregon, Jane Chase reported that Episcopal children were absorbing information contrary to Episcopal teachings. She examined the workbooks of "puzzled" Sunday school children and found "they were good Baptist material with a most literal interpretation of Genesis." One question asked, " 'Why does the serpent crawl on his belly?' and students were supposed to explain it as a curse of God." Conversely, a different observer deemed a Nikkei pastor excessively liberal for "calling attention to the inaccuracies and exaggerations of the

New Testament" during Bible study classes. Bemoaning the students' eventual need to "unlearn most [of the material] someday," Chase noted that Deaconess Peppers planned to teach separate lessons for Episcopalians but cautioned that it might confuse the children further. Many Episcopalians ultimately found the adaptation to ecumenism too problematic.[64]

Minidoka's customary casual worship style may have exacerbated conflicts with Episcopalians accustomed to formal liturgies. Since Baptist and Methodist pastors predominated at Minidoka, services generally followed those denominational styles. In addition to following a precise order of services, Episcopal clerics wear different robes, incorporate incense and processions into services, and adorn the sanctuary with more images than other mainline Protestants. Episcopalians already worshiped at their own shrine at Minidoka.

The frequency of separate Episcopal meetings at Minidoka increased after Reifsnider and the Episcopal bishop of Idaho visited Minidoka in November 1942. The camp's resident Episcopal priest, Joseph Kitagawa, eventually offered full church services apart from the ecumenical church. He made efforts to avoid scheduling their denominational services and Sunday school meetings at the same time as those offered by the Federated Church, but few congregants attended both meetings. Episcopalians at most camps followed a similar process of divergence.[65]

Episcopalians at Minidoka may never have been interested in an ecumenical program, though most evidence to this effect comes from sources outside of the camp's Episcopal church. Chase observed, "The Methodists and Baptists are all enthused over forming a Federated Church and quite resent our even having our own Communion Service. . . . Equally of course our people don't like it." The resentment she sensed may not have been widespread, but it likely existed. Everett Thompson, the Methodist pastor from Seattle, complained that Episcopalians lacked commitment to the ecumenical project and "instinctively" prioritized their separate church over unified efforts. He considered them to be the "most thorny problem" in the church, believing they imagined or wanted "a federation of churches rather than a Federated Church." Thompson refrained from criticizing Kitagawa, however, and suggested that hierarchical pressures compelled the priest to arrange separate services. When the Episcopal bishop of Idaho led services with the Reverends Shoji and Kitagawa on Christmas 1943, they met at the same time as the ecumenical Christmas service. The bishop's presence acknowledged that the denomination had not forgotten Episcopal incarcerees, but it also suggests that they, or at least this bishop, had little interest in the camp's experimental ecumenism. A history of Japanese American Episcopalians written decades after the war supports Thompson's charge of disinterest by failing to mention the existence of Protestant ecumenism within the camps.[66]

Some pastors had no interest in ecumenism. They were happy with their denominations and saw no reason to leave them. While most federated churches incorporated Salvation Army officers, Adjutant Tozo Abe led separate, well-attended meetings at Heart Mountain from October 1942 to the end of the war. Two other officers helped him plan services and evangelize to incarcerees with no religious affiliation. Like Kitagawa, Abe held meetings at an early hour so his congregants could also attend the ecumenical church. Few did so.[67]

Several camps supported autonomous Seventh Day Adventist congregations that never attempted full union with ecumenical groups. Some Adventists joined the latter, however, perhaps due to their denomination's shortage of clergy in the camps. The Idaho Conference of Adventists hired William Hiroshima as a pastor for the twenty Adventist Minidokans, but camp authorities and the interfaith council never formally recognized the group. Hiroshima bicycled around camp to lead weekly meetings and Bible study groups. Only Colorado's Granada incarceration camp listed an Adventist pastor within the Federated Church. This minister, George Kiyabu, held Adventist prayer meetings on Wednesday evenings, youth fellowship on Fridays, and Sabbath school and services on Saturdays in addition to preaching in the ecumenical church on Sundays. Through these efforts, Kiyabu educated non-Adventists about his religion. Granada's ecumenical church newsletter listed Adventist meetings and events, unlike those of other camps. At camps with fewer members, Adventists met for informal Bible study, and a local pastor occasionally conducted services. Despite their small numbers, Adventists held occasional evangelistic meetings in camp, including one at Heart Mountain that attracted eight hundred attendees. At least fifty Nikkei converted to Adventism in the camps, and dozens more joined the church while attending Adventist colleges in the East that welcomed Nikkei students.[68]

The pronounced division between generations posed an even greater challenge to the spirit of ecumenism. Leaders attempted to facilitate cooperation between the Issei and Nisei with little success. In addition to language barriers, the groups favored different styles of worship, different theologies, and different activities. Issei typically preferred a more conservative interpretation of the Bible. Some Nisei complained that Issei planned too many "Japanese programs," which should be discouraged in order to "promote more distinctly American programs." Protestant Nisei sponsored social events that welcomed non-Christians, while Issei met for Bible study and prayer. Aside from obligatory cooperation on holidays, the two groups rarely interacted.[69]

A disagreement over the presence of charismatic missionaries exacerbated Minidoka's generational rift and tested the interfaith committee's willingness to regulate religion in the camps. Marie Juergensen, an Assemblies of God missionary, and Miss Johnson, a former Nazarene pastor from Washington, visited Minidoka and "won the approval" of the Reverend Kodaira, who, on behalf of the Issei Council, requested that the WRA approve the women's continued work in the camp. The Nisei Council opposed this decision on the grounds that the two women had no former members within the camp, a prerequisite of the WRA's policy on outside religious workers. The subtext of their stand, however, related to Nisei's negative opinions about Pentecostalism, despite Juergensen's insistence that she and her denomination fully supported ecumenical work. She promised that her organization was "absolutely free from what is usually termed 'Pentecostal.'" Gordon Chapman, who knew Juergensen in Japan, confirmed that she was "quiet and well-behaved" and explained that even though Assemblies of God identified as Pentecostal, they "did not seem to be particularly noisy . . . and seem to be doing a good work." When the two generational councils at Minidoka met, their debate "produced more heat than light," as Everett Thompson described it, and leaders could not reach an amiable conclusion. Juergensen and Johnson joined the missionary staff at Minidoka.[70]

## Assessment of Ecumenical Worship

Notifications for religious services in camp newspapers, oral interviews, and the personal papers of Andrew Kuroda and Paul Nagano, a young Baptist pastor at Poston, suggest that the ecumenical experiences of white and Nikkei pastors working at Minidoka incarceration camp resembled those in other incarceration camps. Many Christians hoped to inculcate an ecumenical spirit—and reality—among incarcerated Protestants, but the everyday demands of ministering to a people in a critical situation took precedence. Many lay incarcerees mentioned the ecumenical nature of the camp churches in postwar oral histories and memoirs, but few expressed opinions or offered details on the topic. The lack of comments suggests that the ecumenical structure may not have made a large impression on congregants or that incarcerees accepted it along with the many other differences between life in and out of camp. As Kuroda suggested, indifference was likely at fault, though some congregants described ecumenism as something they were "forced to have." Kenji Okuda, a Seattle Fellowship of Reconciliation member, derided ministers for the hypocrisy of defining doctrine for an "all-embracing church." He felt that their false attempt caused even greater division.[71]

Official publications lauded the smooth way church leaders and members blended their desires for a unified church. The Protestant Commission released a statement commending assembly center churches for their "spirit of cooperation and unity." While many incarcerated pastors and white church workers cooperated, their private statements attest that the endeavor did not go smoothly. Kodaira acknowledged that it may have looked like "harmonized cooperation," but pastors encountered "many troubles." Calling for cooperation, he continued, is "very easy, but in reality it is very hard to organize one strong interdenominational church." Both Everett Thompson and Emery Andrews echoed this sentiment, acknowledging the challenge of changing people's "set habits" and the continual negotiations required of a unified program. Leopold Tibesar's observation that "no one seems to rightly understand" how to run an ecumenical church shows that their disorganization was evident from the outside.[72]

Privately, even the Protestant Commission's director Gordon Chapman admitted that it took "several months to convince most of the Japanese and some of the denominations that a united work would be best." After four months in camp, denominational groups still met regularly for social hours or prayer despite attending ecumenical Sunday services. Some religious leaders claimed that Nisei "on the whole glory in this new Federated Church," while Issei only accepted it begrudgingly.[73]

White religious leaders expressed a range of judgments on the camps' ecumenical arrangement. Working with incarcerees at Camp Harmony, Charles Warren, a Congregational missionary from Seattle, "believe[d] it [would] be a great opportunity lost if . . . work continued on a denominational basis." He "most heartily" favored "union work in religion." Emery Andrews thought ecumenism "worthwhile" and did not protest this arrangement or interfere with the organization of the Federated Church at Minidoka but expressed many frustrations with it. He reported to his supervisor in the American Baptist Home Mission Society, "This church federation business is the 'bunk.' Things move so slowly, one does not feel like pushing. It is almost impossible to plan and work freely as one could in [his] own church . . . because there are so many checks and limitations." Andrews preached and met with congregants regularly but distanced himself from the organization of ecumenical services.[74]

The experiment backfired in some cases and strengthened denominational ties. After the war, the prolific preacher Jitsuo Morikawa said, "Ecumenism has deepened rather than weakened my sense of denominational identity. I have never felt lured or seduced to join other denominations; and I rejoiced with those who have remained loyal and steadfast in the face of every provocation. . . . I have always been proud of being an American Baptist and . . . proud to represent American Baptists in ecumenical circles."[75] Morikawa viewed the ecumenical experiment as a test of faith that complemented the larger test of Christian faith during the incarceration. He respected interdenominational work but not if it came at the expense of denominational identity. Toru Matsumoto of the Home Missions Council later described the efforts made and experiences gained by laity and clergy as "praiseworthy" and "valuable" but thought that "church life without a denominational basis was not normal." For normalcy's sake, he believed denominational worship must be resumed; ecumenical unification could function only as a "necessary stop-gap."[76] While few congregants recorded their impressions of ecumenical worship in the camps, one Issei remarked at the time that he was "starved for meaty Presbyterian sermons."[77] Some laypeople clearly noticed the changes.

Tom Fukuyama enjoyed the opportunity to work with members of all Protestant denominations and frequently cited these experiences as a benefit of the incarceration.[78] But while he held ecumenism in high regard, he never exhibited the passion of ministers like Andrew Kuroda. To Fukuyama, who still thought in terms of sectarian divisions, ecumenism simply meant people from different denominations working together.

Other pastors regarded the experiment a success. After the war, Paul Nagano said that the "wonderful thing about the . . . incarceration was that we became one." Failing to mention denominationally minded religious leaders, he stated that "we weren't thinking in terms of denominational groups. . . . We all worked together, not denominationally."

Similarly a former missionary in Arkansas wrote of the "joy of taking communion together, where all are one in Christ Jesus, with no distinction," though she acknowledged that the experience could not be "understood by those who have never had nor desired such an experience." She rejoiced at seeing a "Baptist minister hold the bowl of water for the Presbyterian." Despite some resistance, the ecumenical experiment met with definite success by some accounts.[79]

## Duties of the Camp Churches

Regardless of disagreements over doctrine and practice, the camp churches had unique roles to fulfill. After a year in Idaho, the Federated Church at Minidoka defined its three primary aims: "assistance in personal problems, aid in relocation, and the development of Christian faith and character."[80] Many Nikkei too proud to approach the Social Welfare Division, too distrustful to ask the WRA for assistance, or unwilling to divulge their personal problems to strangers shared their concerns with pastors or female missionaries. The Federated Church organized a social services committee to counsel incarcerees and help meet physical needs.[81] Items relating to resettlement appeared in church bulletins regularly, and church-sponsored lectures broached the topic in all camps. Resettlement efforts met a practical need and directed the attention of incarcerees toward their future beyond the barbed wire. Stressing the church's first two aims, leaders advertised their open door policy: "For those of you who haven't discovered this haven, we extend you an invitation to visit us. The Church exists to help people. It is assisting in the relocation of family units and students. It will do anything humanly possible to assist people."[82] Church leaders emphasized that they would help anyone who asked, Christian or non-Christian.

WRA officials depended on the churches to help with disciplinary and morale problems within the camps. Religious leaders regularly met with camp officials to discuss morale and help mediate disputes between incarcerees and administrators.[83] The WRA staff at several camps asked Christian leaders to manage juvenile disciplinary problems. A white teacher observed this practice at Minidoka: "I had only one discipline problem, and I didn't blame him one bit. He had a right to be as angry as he was. Between Father Kitagawa and Father Tibbisart [sic], they took care of the situation, and he became a very well-adjusted young man. It worked out very well."[84] Camp administrators recognized the stress caused by the incarceration and hesitated to inflict unwarranted punishment, worried that a further limitation of rights would intensify problems. Some administrators may have referred troublesome youth to Christian clergy in hope of their conversion or Americanization, but pastors were also the closest thing they had to counselors or social workers.

Minidoka's Federated Church ended its list of aims with the development of Christian faith. Although white church workers and many young Japanese pastors spent time meeting social needs, they did not overlook spiritual counseling or evangelism. The greatest challenge for some ministers was to keep their congregants—and themselves—from losing faith in the face of such uncertainty. Their tactics resembled activities on any church calendar—skits, dances, Bible study, prayer meetings, and choirs. When asked in an interview how ministers kept the spirits of their congregation up, Paul Nagano recollected a chorus book he and friends compiled, *101 Choruses*. For him, "hymns of assurance and joy" were "very therapeutic. . . . It meant so much . . . to have that very naïve and simple faith in God in a time of uneasy, unknown future."[85] Congregants in all camps enjoyed musical distractions, and churches held regular "singspiration" gatherings to lift one another's spirits.

Within their preaching and pastoral counseling, some ministers retained metaphors used in the months prior to incarceration. Daisuke Kitagawa, the brother of Minidoka's Joseph Kitagawa, felt that he preached the best sermons of his life during this time, as people were more receptive and worshiped with greater sincerity. He later wrote that he and the incarcerated congregation "shared the awesome sense of standing before the Judgment Seat."[86] The bond created by common difficulties increased solidarity within the Japanese Christian community and encouraged creative theologies among congregants and pastors.

Paul Nagano invoked the story of the Israelites wandering in the wilderness to describe the experiences of the Japanese American incarceration. He identified with the experience of aimless, unproductive wandering for an uncertain period of time in an environment quite similar to the wilderness described in the Book of Exodus. Just as God prevented the Israelites from establishing a stable community for forty years in the desert, the incarceration put the lives of all Nikkei on hold, halting the progress of individuals and communities. Jitsuo Morikawa, another pastor at Poston, and several white church workers made a similar parallel, using the theme "A Home in the Wilderness." They expanded the metaphor to include Jesus's temptation in the wilderness and spoke of the incarceration as their cross to bear. Decades after the war, Nagano extended the metaphor, claiming that the incarceration "identified and set them apart as a people," just as the wilderness experience did for the Israelites.[87]

Daisuke Kitagawa utilized a different aspect of the same story, quoting the Israelites' complaints in the wilderness. The liberated Israelites moaned, "Would that we had died by the hand of the Lord in the land of Egypt, when we sat by the fleshpots and ate bread to the full" (Exodus 16:3).[88] Speaking to Nisei leaving the camps, he employed this passage to warn them not to look back to the security of camp, but to face the challenges of resettlement, knowing they would be tested many times before rebuilding a secure life. This metaphor identified the camps with slavery in Egypt, an inevitably worse, if safer, fate than freedom. Methodist Frank Herron Smith invoked Abraham's story to stress the importance of trusting and following God.[89]

While Nagano, Morikawa, Kitagawa, and Smith described the incarceration and resettlement as a trial, Tom Fukuyama focused on its benefits. He frequently meditated on a verse from Esther, "Who knoweth whether thou art not come to the kingdom for such a time as this?" Fukuyama knew he received "abnormal" training at Minidoka, but he embraced the challenges. He agreed with a young incarceree that the "Christian attitude of brotherliness is the only effective way of bringing about a permanent world peace. No political, economic, or social reform can match the deep, sincere, and non-prejudiced mind with which Christians are bridging the gaps of misunderstanding among people." Fukuyama tried to show how the incarceration united Protestants. The model could be replicated within other groups.[90]

Religious leaders also reminded incarcerees that their difficulties paled in comparison to those of many people around the world. The Protestant Commission reminded Nikkei ministers in 1943 that their "affliction has been light . . . in comparison with what the Christian clergy and laity of Europe and parts of Asia have had to suffer."[91] Hachiro Yuasa, the future president of Japan's International Christian University, told Minidokans that they were "lolling in idleness and luxury compared to people in wartime Japan . . . and not suffering from the war yet."[92] He disagreed with people who saw a spiritual benefit to their sacrifices. Chapman and Yuasa did not want to instill guilt but hoped to encourage congregants to view their situation from a different perspective. In a private letter to Andrews and his wife, Fukuyama expressed gratitude for the Minidokans' "extremely privileged" experience when considering the struggles of "the Burmese in India, the Chinese in far West China, [and] millions of war prisoners separated from their loved ones throughout the world." While he regretted that some incarcerees could not "see anything but release from the boundaries of our Center," he argued that "we should be grateful for life, a great degree of freedom and liberty, sympathetic authorities, and the possibilities for creative growth right here in Minidoka."[93] A number of incarcerees shared Fukuyama's attitude and looked for positive experiences within the incarceration.

Father Tibesar rarely discussed the incarceration explicitly in his Sunday sermons or midweek lessons but attempted to strengthen incarcerees' resolve through their faith. Characteristic of this approach, he did not suggest camp-related ideas to orient Catholics' Lenten sacrifice in 1943, nor did he diminish the necessity of sacrifice at a time when they had lost so much already. But his Lenten messages still provided his incarcerated parishioners succor. On the fourth Wednesday of Lent, his lesson, "The Presence of God," opened with a story about the faith of a Catholic martyr locked in the Tower of London who indelibly scratched "Jesus keepeth me company" into the stone wall of his cell. Tibesar explained that only God's grace kept people from losing their sanity during lonely, monotonous years of imprisonment. Just as a mother cannot forget her child, Tibesar promised that God would not forget any individual and was always present "in . . . the classroom or office, in the midst of the clank and clatter of machinery in a factory, in the barracks, on the battlefield, on the sea." This message may have resonated with Nikkei who feared God had abandoned them. A sermon on "fair weather Catholics" and Peter's denial of Christ chided believers who abandoned God in times of stress. Here Tibesar spoke of the necessity to keep one's faith and religious practices in the close quarters of camp barracks, regardless of the "scoffer's sneer" that might mock a Catholic kneeling in prayer.[94]

Besides the day-to-day activities of camp churches, Christian leaders held occasional revivals or other special events to encourage believers and attract others. Prior to their first Easter at Minidoka, pastors of the Federated Church sponsored a (Christian) Religious Emphasis Week, which became an annual event featuring local speakers of many denominations. Nearly a hundred people reportedly gave a confession of faith that Easter. After a year at Minidoka, the Federal Council of Churches helped leaders organize a National Christian Mission with speakers from around the country. Membership training classes for Issei and Nisei followed such events to accommodate new members acquired during the week. Emery Andrews took those who desired baptism by immersion to the First Baptist Church in Twin Falls. The ecumenical church also held baptismal services in nearby Jerome to connect with additional communities. Fukuyama recorded that the Federated Church baptized 103 young people at Minidoka, half of whom came from non-Christian backgrounds. A number of Nikkei requested baptism soon after leaving camp as well. The Catholic Church at Minidoka baptized forty-one new members during the war.[95]

Despite Christians continuously leaving camp, Catholic and Protestant church membership remained steady.[96] Fukuyama remarked that he knew less than half of the Nisei congregation by the fall of 1944 because many Buddhists had joined and some Christians began attending the camp church for the first time.[97] Nagano joked that the ministers had a "captive audience," drawing many people toward Christianity's "wonderful message of the Savior."[98] The truth within his joke was the fact that many incarcerees began attending church as a way to occupy their time.[99] Given the "uncertainty and oppression" in their lives, Nagano thought emphasizing the concept of a savior resulted in a "tremendous response, and . . . [a] lot of them became Christians."[100] As casual visitors bonded with church members and listened to the gospel, many converted. Had they converted due to a perceived pressure from evangelists, the WRA, or other sources, it might be assumed that most conversions would have occurred earlier in the war, but many incarcerees who attended church in the camps did not officially convert until resettlement or after the war.[101]

Father Tibesar showed great reluctance to baptize incarcerees because he hoped the sacrament would provide a foundation for a relationship with a parish outside of camp when catechumens resettled.[102] He also understood the nebulous pressures that may be influencing incarcerees' decision in this "unsettled" time and hoped to avoid insincere conversions.[103] Delaying baptism also protected the Catholic Church and new Catholics from criticism by outsiders who might "discount the merit" of such choices.[104] Tibesar explained this philosophy in nearly every diary entry and reiterated it to his superiors, perhaps in defense of what he perceived to be low conversion rates. When Thomas Kiernan, a Maryknoll official, surveyed the camps, he observed that Tibesar prioritized the needs of his own parish over efforts to influence non-Catholics.[105]

Catholics at Manzanar operated with different priorities and baptized many Nikkei during the war. The two incarcerated Nikkei nuns and a large population of Catholics shaped the atmosphere of Manzanar's parish. Jeanne Houston's classic autobiography, *Farewell to Manzanar*, chronicles her infatuation with Catholicism as a child in the camp. She secretly attended catechism classes led by the nuns until her father forbade it. Commenting on the notable increase in church attendance, Brother Theophane recorded that "we believe that these people are sincere in their interest . . . and are not coming out of gratitude for what Maryknoll has done for them. . . . Many have remarked . . . that they realize now that the Catholic Church is sincere in its disinterested humane work; that we are working solely for the good of the people themselves, and not for that which we might get out of it." Under the authority of Father Leo Steinbach, 246 incarcerees received baptism and 8 left Manzanar to train for the Catholic vocations.[106]

The Catholic Church did not "extend . . . more than ordinary effort toward" evangelism, despite its earlier complaints that barring proselytization violated the U.S. Constitution.[107] Tibesar noted that he did not advertise services or special events, in part because he thought that an ostentatious approach would discourage attendance. Publicity for Protestant Christmas events contributed to his perception of their "awful panning."[108] While eschewing self-promotion, he gratefully accepted "items of publicity" for events like Catholic participation in interfaith memorial services. Tibesar recorded that these events helped Catholics "hold [their] own against the constant stream of publicity given to distinguished Protestant visitors."[109] Protestant workers "flooded" Minidoka, he lamented, insisting, "We aren't afraid of them but they do get into one's hair."[110]

The Buddhist community's response to Christian evangelism is difficult to discern because unofficial censorship and pressures in the camp limited dissenters from speaking against camp policies and camp life. John Howard mentioned that some young Buddhists felt "uncomfortable" during a weeklong Christian mission, but the young men chose to attend events.[111] That is not to say that no pressure to appear Christian existed, but it would be difficult to argue that incarcerated Buddhists experienced substantially greater pressures to convert than they would have outside of the camps. Buddhist churches in the camps gained members for many of the same reasons as did Christian churches: incarcerees attended out of boredom or took advantage of greater free time to learn about the religion.

Buddhism provided solace in a time of crisis and confirmed one's identity as a Japanese American just as Christianity did for others.

What pressure to convert that did exist came from Nikkei pastors. Church newsletters and bulletins occasionally encouraged members to "bring a friend to church" and warned of the "lost opportunities" to evangelize.[112] The Reverend Thomas Machida at Minidoka expressed his eagerness to evangelize "not only among the christians, but also heathern [sic] people."[113] The Reverend George Aki in Arkansas expended efforts to convert Buddhists in particular. He bragged about the number of children from Buddhist families he had baptized, noting, "We are slowly swinging the Buddhists toward us."[114] Presumably he would have been making these same efforts had the incarceration not occurred. Some Buddhists may have felt that being Christian would make them seem more American at a time when the nation questioned their loyalty, but the WRA and most Nikkei and white pastors discouraged targeting evangelism at them.

### White Church Workers at Minidoka

Numerous white religious workers moved to towns near the camps to provide pastoral and material support. Nine such people from Seattle followed their flocks to southern Idaho: Emery Andrews, Nora Bowman, Ethel Hempstead, Marie Juergensen, Gladys Kaiser, Esther McCullough, Margaret Peppers, Everett Thompson, and Leopold Tibesar. Mary Andrews and Zora Thompson accompanied their husbands, and Andrews brought their three youngest children. In addition to the comfort of retaining their prewar leaders, incarcerees in many camps benefited from the experience of American missionaries forced to leave Japan and its occupied territories. These men and women spoke fluent Japanese and had worked with Japanese communities for years in both Japan and the United States. Many incarcerees appreciated their unique perspective, though some complained that the missionaries' experience led them to treat incarcerees like Japanese, not Americans.[115] Some returned missionaries smoothed relations among Nikkei ministers and fostered a "cooperative spirit" between Protestant and Buddhist churches in the camps.[116] Incarcerees and WRA staff usually welcomed these missionaries.[117]

Maryknoll's primary directive was to show solidarity with Nikkei by going with them to camp. Recalling their visits to Camp Harmony, Seattle Maryknoll Sister Regina wrote, "I was happy and pleased to go. I loved the people and felt very keenly the grave injustice being done to them. I guess I thought that by sharing their life with its grave inconveniences, poor food, extremes of heat and cold, sandstorms, etc. would somehow convince them that there were those who loved and trusted them." Numerous Catholic Nikkei appreciated the sacrifice of religious workers who lived in camp, particularly Sisters Susanna and Bernadette, two Nikkei sisters who chose to go to Manzanar rather than return to Maryknoll headquarters in New York. They sympathized with the sisters' sacrifice of wearing heavy wool habits in the extreme heat. Volunteers built a private space in the shower room to spare the sisters the indignity of communal showering. Mary Ichino, a Nisei incarcerated at Manzanar, considered it "a sacrifice to God" that showed their "total dedication to good work."[118]

Nikkei added white leaders to the rotation of preachers, appointing them to chair committees, organize Sunday schools, and lead choirs. In addition to pastoral duties, white church workers performed countless tasks that Nikkei could not address. They spent the war attending meetings with other church leaders, visiting incarcerated congregants, arranging for the resettlement of Nikkei farther east, and traveling back and forth to the coast to keep an eye on church buildings and congregants' properties. Nikkei who leased their West Coast houses or businesses had little recourse when renters refused to pay or left the premises. Since they could not manage these concerns from camp, many asked white pastors to find renters for their properties, detailing the exact amount to charge if renters wished the house to be furnished or not. The pastors would then store or remove furniture from storage accordingly.[119]

More often than other pastors at Minidoka, the Reverend Andrews traveled between Idaho and Seattle, running these errands in his reliable "Blue Box." Once Nikkei began leaving Minidoka, Andrews drove incarcerees' cars from Seattle to Idaho, so families could "drive off on their own power" to new jobs and homes. He retrieved not only furniture and cars but specific household items from warehouses, "pots of soil from the old place back home," or "a couple of bottles of shoyu from [a] basement." He escorted incarcerees to Seattle for the burial of family members, once driving two incarcerated members of the Salvation Army whom he had never met to Seattle and back, interring the body of a Nikkei he had not known, and performing a funeral service. Like many other religious workers, Andrews visited other incarceration camps and met with resettled Nikkei all around the country.[120]

A meticulous record keeper, Andrews determined that he traveled 151,413 miles, wrote 3,538 letters, and attended 644 meetings, in addition to the religious duties of performing forty-nine weddings, baptizing seventy-nine young people, and conducting 104 services during the war. Andrews's superiors, WRA staff, and incarcerees commended his "unselfish service and splendid ministry." His superior in the American Baptist Home Mission Society, John Thomas, wrote, "I know of no other member of our staff that would be better able to service in this way than you." They also relayed compliments they received on his behalf. One heard that Andrews "meant more to the people than any other one worker" and was "the ideal Christian missionary, able to allow others the credit while [he] did the work." Outside workers who remained at the camps also logged long hours. A returned missionary at Manzanar noted that he worked twelve to fourteen hours a day on average.[121]

Swamped with incarcerees asking him to resolve their myriad problems, Father Tibesar wrestled over the meaning of "priests' work." "Since when is sweet charity not a priest's work?" he replied to his own concerns. He described the monotony of his days, "Nor do the tasks . . . vary a great deal from day to day, week to week and month to month and we might add, from year to year. . . . Our work is quite confining of late." Receiving little support, Tibesar became frustrated and depressed by mid-1943. Concluding a rambling summary of five months of work, he lamented, "Well, this didn't turn out to be a diary. . . . Nothing ever happens out here anyway." He wrote of his loneliness to Maryknoll superiors who tried to encourage him. Tibesar projected a much improved outlook in letters and diaries after reading their supportive, sympathetic response and redoubled his efforts to release Nikkei from the monotony of camp.[122]

Protestant and Catholic workers all labored to resettle Nikkei outside of the camps and connect them with job opportunities. This challenge required several steps. A family in Ohio, for example, who learned about resettlement programs at church might write to their denomination's headquarters, offering to sponsor a family or individual by providing housing or employment. The church would notify pastors like Andrews and Tibesar who worked in the camps to select an appropriate incarceree for the position or advertise the position in church bulletins. Tibesar coordinated placements for Maryknollers with great success. He focused his attention on moving families, the largest challenge to resettlement. He counseled them before leaving camp and regularly corresponded with them and their sponsors, leading to fewer complaints and a higher success rate than other resettlers. WRA director Dillon Myer and Minidoka's camp director, Harry Stafford, visited Tibesar's quarters in October 1943 to praise his success in relocating families. Tibesar boasted to his brother and Maryknoll superiors that Myer goaded Stafford by noting that Tibesar had sent out more families from Minidoka than the WRA. Tibesar recorded that he sent 250 Minidokans out of camp between April 1943 and April 1944. He credited his success to various Catholic leaders outside, particularly Father McCormick in Detroit. Since he encouraged Nikkei to wait until their release for baptism, finding Catholic-friendly placements was essential. He cautioned his brother that the Hirabayashi family was "not Catholic as yet, but all will be so if I can place them right. . . . No sense in our educating people and then letting Protestants run away with them."[123]

The WRA required leave applicants to provide a list of non-Nikkei references, and hopeful resettlers frequently listed their prewar pastors. Thompson, Andrews, and others received hundreds of these requests during the war, as did Maryknoll sisters in Seattle and Los Angeles.[124] Some incarcerees joked about the formality, asking pastors to assure the government that they were not "a spy, saboteur, secret agent, or member of the Black Dragon Society," while others apologized for not asking before providing their names, trusting clergymen to vouch for their loyalty.[125] Some had not been in contact for several years but knew their former pastors would help.[126] Andrews wrote over eight hundred character recommendations during the war.[127] Christian pastors also petitioned for the release of Issei still interned in Department of Justice camps.[128]

The households of Andrews, Thompson, McCullough, and others in nearby Twin Falls served as lodging houses, tea parlors, and wedding chapels throughout the war. In a typical week, Minidoka's administrators issued shopping passes to three or four hundred incarcerees. Another dozen left camp for church activities, Boy Scout outings, or weddings.[129] Military police or camp administrators drove Nikkei to town and picked them up at an appointed time, leaving them to conduct business without escorts. Nora Bowman, Gladys Kaiser, and Ethel Hempstead advertised their "Haven of Rest" in the *Irrigator*, urging incarcerees to "rest and refresh themselves" while visiting Twin Falls.[130] Incarcerees shopping in town would drop by to discuss a problem or simply to enjoy the comfort of a normal home. White religious workers hosted monthly gatherings for Nikkei who resettled locally.[131] On more than one occasion, youth groups of sixty or more descended on a pastor's house during outings.[132] While most baptisms and weddings took place at Minidoka, many Christian couples chose the more intimate and less institutional setting of a pastor's home. Attendees got to leave camp, spend time in a real home, and receive special foods and other treats.

Monica Itoi's brother, Henry, and his fiancée, Minnie, held their wedding ceremony in the Thompsons' small apartment with family and close friends, followed by a reception at camp. This arrangement resembled many Minidokan Protestant weddings, though a few arranged ceremonies at local churches. Rushing to wed before Henry shipped out, Minnie's and Henry's families planned the ceremony in less than a week. The couple acquired a marriage license and wedding dress in Twin Falls the day after their engagement. Minnie "made up her mind to have a full-blown civilized wedding, camp or no camp." In fact, the bride felt more restricted by her impression of being "way out in the wilderness" of Idaho than being incarcerated. When she discovered the department stores had no veils in stock, Minnie fashioned one complete with "an orange-blossom design" out of "a dozen baby pearl necklaces, wire and yards of netting." Monica felt assured that her future sister-in-law "could have willed even the most scraggly clumps of sagebrush to bloom calla lilies and orchids to adorn the wedding altar . . . if she had had the slightest inclination." The wedding notice in the *Irrigator* noted that the "sister of the groom was organist," but this element also took some improvisation. The couple insisted on having music during the ceremony, so they acquired a battered portable organ. But it was so uncontrollably, blaringly loud that Monica's brother forced her to play the wedding march from the confines of a small bathroom while seated on the toilet. Of course, the couple's march from the kitchen to the living room lasted only a few steps, so they quickly silenced her. Trapped in the bathroom, Monica missed the entire ceremony, but her younger sister said the "music sounded as if it were floating right down from heaven!"[133]

While the Itoi wedding was a cheerful, comical celebration, continually hosting such events in one's home grew tiresome. Since Andrews traveled often, the primary responsibility of attending to visitors fell to his wife, a dutiful, if not always willing, partner. Mary Andrews kept house, raised three children, and hosted between 150 and 270 Nikkei visitors per month. Over the course of the incarceration, the Andrews family hosted 7,202 visitors at their Twin Falls house. Although Emery Andrews referred to "our" house, his correspondence and reports never incorporated anecdotes about or even oblique references to Mary or his children, despite the tremendous work required of her and the difficulties they all encountered due to their association with the camp. Local restaurants and stores occasionally refused to serve the family, and classmates taunted the Andrews children at the public school. After refusing to serve Andrews and disgusted by his presence in town, a café owner purchased their rental home in Twin Falls and evicted the family. They found a larger home to rent with little difficulty. Mary worked closely with the Japanese women, and they appreciated her presence. She ran errands for them in Twin Falls, helped in the nursery, and acted as a witness when Andrews officiated weddings. When he did not respond quickly enough, incarcerees wrote Mary in the hope that she could intervene or explain when he would be available.[134]

Mary Andrews's situation was not unique; the wives of other missionaries also supported the camp churches. Zora Thompson directed a choir, advised the youth program with Fukuyama, and even preached occasionally.[135] Like Mary and other missionary women, she entertained at her Twin Falls home and helped with Sunday school. Church hiring committees of this time typically expected a pastor's wife to work for the church full-time but did not officially acknowledge her contributions monetarily. Employment documents and activity reports seldom mentioned the wives' presence in camp. Former missionary couples worked at the camps and resettlement hostels throughout the war, but the appointment and arrangements were always made for and by the man. An exception, Thompson regularly mentioned Zora and spoke of "our" desires or plans. In a letter expressing their desire to move to Idaho, he included her opinions and stated that he was "speaking for a team." He reminded organizational leaders that she "has been just about as busy as I at this task without getting any publicity or title or recognition" (or pay).[136] Ministers occasionally wrote of "their" concerns, but more often than not, they did not mention their wives or families at all.

Single white female church workers took prominent roles within the ecumenical churches. Margaret Peppers led several programs at Minidoka, but few primary records written by Peppers exist. After spending ten years as a missionary in the Philippines, she worked in rural communities for the Diocese of Olympia, Washington. After moving to Idaho for the duration of the war, the mission board assigned her to work with Navajo in Arizona.[137] Her peers and superiors regarded her highly.[138] Esther McCullough, a missionary who had worked at the Seattle Japanese Baptist Church's women's mission, Fujin Home, acted as the advisor to a girls' mission study group at Minidoka and chaired the social services committee. Her scrapbooks document the years before and after the war, but McCullough did not preserve memories of life at Minidoka.[139] Tibesar regretted not making more efforts to include Seattle's Maryknoll sisters in his work at Minidoka. Decades later, he wrote, "I still owe a big apology to the Maryknoll Sisters for not having asked them to share my apostolate in Idaho."[140] When they received funds to work at the camp for a few months during the summer of 1943, he realized how much he needed their assistance.[141]

Wives and single women living in or near the incarceration camps endured difficult conditions and sacrificed years of their lives to aid Japanese Americans, but their stories remain obscure. Their names appear on church bulletins and in the occasional letter, but their lives are largely invisible within the public memory and public records of the incarceration. Personal records and correspondence of female teachers survived, and female incarcerees like Monica Sone and Jeanne Houston published memoirs and kept journals during the war.[142] Oral histories have also recorded the voices of incarcerated women and, to a lesser extent, those of white women who volunteered or worked at the camps. The exact roles of Nora Bowman, Ethel Hempstead, Marie Juergensen, and Gladys Kaiser, all of whom worked at Minidoka, are unclear, but they forsook their urban lives to move to Idaho and devote years to the Japanese American community.

## Conclusion

Government agencies such as the WCCA and WRA made considerable efforts to maintain freedom of religion in the incarceration camps. Scholarship has increasingly shown that the WRA tried to minimize the violation of Nikkei rights in several ways.[143] But their policies presumed a Protestant church structure in which individual lay people have an authoritative voice in the organization of their church. While Catholic pleas to change such rules fell on deaf ears, individual camp directors allowed priests to work in the camps with few restrictions. The official policy of religious freedom and the complicity of white Protestant missionaries and camp administrators to ban evangelism—as shown in private correspondence, church records, and camp newspapers—proves that the WRA was not colluding with Christian leaders to convert the Japanese American population or otherwise interfere with their religious liberty, as previously assumed. Attempting to eradicate evangelism and protect incarcerees from outsiders, however, contradicted their commitment to religious liberty on a certain level. Catholic leaders were right to cite Supreme Court trials that guaranteed the right to evangelize. Enforcing this freedom turned out to be quite tricky, as did agreeing on a proper separation of church and state.

Ecumenism dictated by outside church authorities constrained freedom of religious expression more than any WRA policy. While in practice incarcerees could form independent worship groups, guidelines from the WRA suggested otherwise, and Protestant leaders pressured Nikkei to stay within the bounds of the camps' ecumenical churches. The strain of incarceration and anxiety about following regulations reduced the likelihood that pastors or congregants would rebel against the given structure. Dumped in a foreign environment, people may have been more likely to accept the altered structure of familiar institutions. Accepting the idea of ecumenical churches, however, rarely resulted in uniform practices. Pastors tried to overcome the practical stumbling blocks of doctrine, ritual, and clerical boundaries, but mainline Nikkei pastors had a preconceived notion of what American Protestantism should look like, and they formed ecumenical churches to fit that vision. This resulted in the censorship of charismatic Christians in some camps, reflecting widespread prejudices within mainline Protestantism. Privileging churches that mimicked the structural organization of mainline Protestantism also shaped the ecumenical churches.

This structural exclusion may have contributed to Mukyōkai's demise in the United States. Without ordained clergy, they had little influence within the ecumenical Protestant churches. The confusion and trauma of the incarceration ultimately obliterated that religious group in the United States. As the war dispersed members, individuals lost the community essential to their religious life. Most members joined other Protestant churches wherever they settled after the war.

Two predominant problems stalled the success of ecumenism in the camps: irreconcilable doctrinal differences and inefficient decision-making constraints. The former should have come as no surprise, as disputes over communion, baptism, and biblical interpretation are primary reasons why so many denominations exist within Protestantism. Constant changes in leadership exacerbated the latter, but pastors suggested that the inefficiencies were inherent to ecumenism, where every decision or activity must be discussed at length, compromises forged at every step.

But despite, or perhaps because of, the fractures that manifested within the federated churches, the pastoral needs of most incarcerated Christians seem to have been met. A dearth of leadership limited the churches' capabilities, but ecumenism was not to blame. Pastors received floods of requests from Nikkei. While white leaders bore the burden of facilitating the logistics of resettlement—finding jobs, schools, scholarships, housing, and social support for incarcerees—both white and Nikkei pastors supported efforts to sustain morale within and beyond the church. WRA administrators relied heavily on Catholic and Protestant leaders to help with disciplinary management and morale. Incarcerated Christians expressed appreciation for their churches in memoirs, oral histories, and correspondence.

# 4 Experiences of Christianity in the Camps

. . . . . . . . . . . . . . . . . . . . . . . . . . . . . . . . . . . . . . . .

"How many of you can truthfully say that the past year in the
relocation center has been the most glorious in your life?" With
upraised hands and radiant faces, a group of fifty young people
responded unanimously.

—Paul Nagano, *Streams in the Desert*

Nikkei experienced a total lack of privacy in the camps. Incarcerees were
packed into overcrowded barracks, eating every meal at long tables in a
mess hall and seeing the same people day in and day out. Every small
event or unusual behavior was observed by dozens, if not hundreds, of
fellow incarcerees. Outside of school and work, churches, sports teams,
and social clubs organized Nikkei's routine and filled their copious
free time. These activities buoyed the attitudes of some, but this public life
made others feel alone. Nikkei parents and WRA employees lamented the
destruction of family life in the camps: children ran wild, men no longer
provided for their family, and young men and women started new independent lives outside of camp. White and Nikkei leaders worried that the
dispirited young people remaining in camp would lose all creative energy
and motivation for life, trapped in this tedious, disheartening existence.

The startling blunt declaration of this chapter's epigraph describes an
occurrence at a midweek Protestant youth service at Arizona's Poston incarceration camp. How could anyone rejoice about living in a miserable
desert camp? Bundled in oversized, military-issue pea coats and long
underwear distributed by the WRA or sweltering in mail-ordered summer
dresses in the shack that comprised their church, did the young people
sincerely believe these years were the best of their lives? Had a sermon
by their youth leader raised them to heights of religious fervor where they
would agree with anything he said? Had God inspired them, or had the
incarceration fractured their concept of reality?

This chapter seeks to answer these questions and others through an
exploration of Christian life in the camps. Beyond the organization of
ecumenical churches and far from the dictates of white leaders outside

of the camps, it opens church doors to reveal what Christian life was like for the average Nikkei layperson. What role did religion play in their everyday lives? Social theorist Michel de Certeau argues that everyday pursuits cannot be separated from their particular circumstances. The ordinary adopts conflicting characteristics on South Pacific isles, during the Blitz in London, within Nazi concentration camps, and in suburban American homes. Extraordinary circumstances still beget everyday life. People create unique aesthetics, ethics, and "struggle[s] for life" in every cultural or circumstantial network.[1]

The chapter's first section considers the acceptance of Christianity in the camps. Most non-Christians tolerated and attended social events sponsored by Christian churches, but others physically threatened Nikkei pastors and congregants. These Nikkei accused Christians of betraying their fellow incarcerees and Japanese heritage. The next section examines the unusual challenges incarcerated Christians faced because of the war itself. What challenges did life on the home front pose when the home front was enclosed in barbed wire? Americans lauded the cooperation of Catholics, Protestants, and Jews during World War II, but "Tri-Faith America" in the camps consisted of Catholics, Protestants, and Buddhists. War-related ceremonies like induction banquets and memorial services became unique interfaith collaborations. Speakers explained how the values of Catholics, Protestants, and Buddhists allied with American ideals and extolled religionists' capacity for patriotic union. Pacifist incarcerees struggled to express their patriotism while refusing to fight. The chapter's final section returns to the Poston youth introduced above to examine lay Christian organizations and the formation of lived theologies that helped laity make sense of the incarceration. Lay communities and faith helped many Christian Nikkei make the best of their difficult situation, but some religious groups also pressured incarcerees to express positive attitudes about camp life.

## Acceptance of Christianity in the Camps

Evidence from Minidoka and other camps shows that many non-Christians benefited from the community fostered by Christmas celebrations and events sponsored by Christian groups. During the first weeks of camp, Protestant youth meetings often drew more attendees than any other activity. Nikkei sociologists living and working in the camps speculated that the popularity of such groups stemmed from the nonreligious themes of most meetings.[2] Many committed Buddhists and other non-Christians felt comfortable attending Christian youth activities because they contained minimal sermonizing, prayer, or Bible study. Attendees discussed pragmatic issues like resettlement, college admissions, and the question of marrying while incarcerated.[3] At Tanforan, a California assembly center, the Christian youth group hosted meetings to discuss how to improve the camp.[4] The Nisei pastor Tom Fukuyama held forums on current issues that attracted up to 350 Minidokans, including many non-Christians.[5] Fukuyama focused on being a positive role model for all incarcerees, not just Christians.[6] Christian youth groups also sponsored dances, record concerts, and "singspiration" gatherings where participants would sing religious and nonreligious songs. Many youth groups prioritized the needs of the community over evangelism. The Student Christian Association at Tule Lake even considered dropping "Christian" from its name in order to make non-Christians feel more welcome.[7] Incarcerees attended these youth events for the social interactions that broke up the monotony of camp life as well as for Christian fellowship.

Christians and non-Christians mixed within youth groups, celebrated secularized Christian holidays together, and cooperated in interfaith memorial services in most camps, but this harmony did not exist everywhere. Some Nikkei identified Christianity with the nation that incarcerated them and felt that conversion betrayed Nikkei solidarity. Camps that expressed the greatest distrust and resentment toward the WRA and U.S. government did not welcome Christianity or Christian leaders. A sociologist at Tule Lake observed that Christians seemed "to always have . . . a higher social status" in the camps and were "more Americanized."[8] That perception may have fueled animosity from non-Christians. Some Buddhists resented the fact that the FBI interned many Buddhist priests after 7 December but detained few Christian clergymen.[9] The American public and government assumed greater loyalty from Christians, believing they had broken religious ties with Japan and were more Americanized. Government officials institutionalized this belief by granting Christian incarcerees a higher loyalty rating than Buddhists.[10] When tensions rose in the camps, this association made Christians a target for abuse from resentful incarcerees.

Angry incarcerees ostracized and verbally abused congregants but reserved most physical violence for clergymen and Nikkei working with the WRA. Incarcerees attacked newspaper editors, cooperative store managers, and Japanese American Citizens League representatives as well as

Protestant ministers. Congregants volunteered to protect their pastors when camp security failed to prevent attacks. A few "very husky . . . weightlifters" volunteered to be bodyguards for the Baptist pastor Paul Nagano at Poston "just in case anybody would attack [him] for being more . . . sympathetic." These "fine Christian fellows" escorted him through the camp. After a serious beating by a masked individual with a lead pipe, the WRA transferred Topaz's Reverend Taro Goto to Denver. His colleague, the Reverend Shigeo Shimada, greatly appreciated the church member who guarded his barrack.[11]

On 6 March 1943, two incarcerees at Arkansas's Jerome incarceration center approached the Issei Episcopal priest John Yamazaki and announced, "Reverend Yamazaki, we came here to beat you, so take off your glasses and hat and put them on this tree stump."[12] Purportedly beaten for translating documents for the WRA, Yamazaki was hospitalized for a month before camp administrators sent him directly to Chicago.[13] He wrote a poem about the event:

When I received the blow I felt
As my own child hitting me
For they were of my own kind.
Each blow reminded me of God's will
Who taught me of our own lack of suffering.[14]

While attackers felt betrayed by the priest's cooperation with camp administrators, the rift in their community pained Yamazaki and other Christian leaders. Soon after the attack, a fellow incarceree, the Christian artist Henry Sugimoto, painted Yamazaki "in clerical collar, in a striking crucifixion pose, blood all over his face and midsection" (Figure 7).[15] Two additional crosses formed by signposts and telephone poles further emphasize Yamazaki's posture, identifying a parallel between the innocent suffering of Jesus and that of Yamazaki. The painting shows the priest's Bible, hat, and glasses strewn on the ground, contrary to Yamazaki's account. Sugimoto chose not to change this element of the painting after Yamazaki told him of the "respectful" decorum of his attackers.[16] The scattered objects reflected the incivility and disorder of camp life and the Nikkei community.

Animosity toward Christians rose when white and Nikkei clergy members helped translate the government's controversial 1943 questionnaire that marked incarcerees as loyal or disloyal. In line with the president's decision to allow Nikkei to enter the military and the agency's desire to

FIGURE 7 "Reverend Yamazaki was Beaten in Camp Jerome," Henry Sugimoto, 1943. Source: Japanese American National Museum (Gift of Madeleine Sugimoto and Naomi Tagawa).

expedite resettlement, the WRA instructed all incarcerees over the age of seventeen to complete a so-called loyalty questionnaire. Eric Muller's study of the government's loyalty tests demonstrated that they revealed more about the administrative agencies that wrote the questions and designed its ramifications than it did about the Nikkei themselves. No government official successfully determined a definition of loyalty, and the actions of Nikkei played nearly no role in the resultant assessment.[17] In the most contentious version of the questionnaire, two questions were particularly problematic:

27) Are you willing to serve in the armed forces of the United States on combat duty, whenever ordered?
28) Will you swear unqualified allegiance to the United States of America and faithfully defend the United States from any or all attack by foreign or domestic forces, and forswear any form of allegiance or obedience to the Japanese emperor, or any other foreign government, power, or organization?

Confusion arose immediately as incarcerees did not know what the effects of their answers would be. Did answering "yes" to number 27 volunteer oneself for the armed forces? Would Issei become stateless people if they answered "yes" to number 28, since they were ineligible for U.S. citizenship? Or was that question intended to trick Nisei into admitting they formerly had an allegiance to the Japanese Empire? Would incarcerees who answered "no" to both questions be deported to Japan or lose their U.S. citizenship?

Answering these two questions divided families and left the government with no clear determination of loyalty. Some people answered "no-no" to avoid segregation and separation from family members after it became known that those who answered in this way would be sent to Tule Lake. This camp would hold only incarcerees deemed disloyal by the government. Incarcerees already at Tule Lake, who might have otherwise answered "yes-yes," gave negative responses to avoid another forced move.

Like many others, the Reverend Emery Andrews thought the WRA's policy of segregation "sound[ed] very fine" but recognized that it "cause[d] a lot of grief . . . in practice."[18] Most people understood the ambivalent nature of the questionnaire results. Camp workers saw the fallibility of the segregation plan and did not deem segregants a security risk or un-American. Administrators and incarcerees at Minidoka held a campwide farewell dinner for segregants leaving for Tule Lake, suggesting that many people—including WRA employees—held no stigma against segregants.[19] Lester Suzuki, an incarcerated minister at Granada incarceration center, clarified such impressions in a letter to his congregation and white associates. Suzuki called the categorization of "loyal" and "disloyal" Nikkei a "misnomer" because people answered "no" on the controversial questions for a wide variety of reasons. To reconcile this incongruity, he used the word "segregatees" to describe individuals marked disloyal by the government survey.[20]

After the segregation, individuals pleaded with ministers to intercede with the WRA for their release from Tule Lake. One case exemplified the disorder of segregation: a WRA administrator told a pair of Nisei siblings that they would be separated permanently from their father, who had been interned as a "disloyal alien," if they did not renounce their American citizenship. After doing so, the Department of Justice released their father, but they were trapped at Tule Lake, fearing imminent deportation.[21]

As the WRA segregated Nikkei answering "no-no" at Tule Lake in the fall of 1943, the camp became a dangerous place for Christians. The camp's environment changed dramatically as administrators increased security measures and built a stockade, essentially a jail within a jail. Violence rose within the camp, and resentment grew between the Nikkei and WRA administrators. The Japanese American Citizens League denounced "no-no boys," some of whom harassed members of the league for "collaborating" with their jailers. Leaders of pro-Japan gangs distributed lists of Tuleans considered to be sympathetic to camp authorities to ensure incarcerees did not elect them as block representatives. Many church members feared associating with Nikkei pastors and white missionaries. Gangs of Kibei (Nisei educated in Japan) roamed the camp, "tormenting" and "intimidating" everyone "they judged to be pro-American" and "brand[ed] them traitors."[22] They threw garbage in front of the Tulean Episcopal priest Daisuke Kitagawa, saying, "Dogs should eat this."[23] Antagonists saw Nikkei Christians as collaborators with the WRA and called them dogs or *inu*, Japanese slang for spy or traitor. A false rumor about Kitagawa's superb fencing skills may have spared him physical abuse, but church members still patrolled his block each night.[24] The ecumenist Andrew Kuroda was not so lucky. Angry incarcerees evaded the congregants guarding Kuroda's barracks and beat him. The WRA expedited the transfers of Kuroda and his guards after the incident.[25]

These confrontations at Tule Lake and the difficulties encountered by church members who associated with Nikkei or white pastors made Christian ministry nearly impossible. Kuroda, Kitagawa, and the Hannafords, white Presbyterian missionaries working at Tule Lake, left as segregation neared its completion. Kitagawa wrote, "It's categorically impossible for me or for any other person to stay on after segregation to do church work." Not only could they do more effective work outside or in other camps, Kitagawa recognized that his "position may be entirely misunderstood so that [his] presence and activities may do more harm than good." His work drew unwanted attention to the camp's Christians. Howard Hannaford felt "relieved and glad" when the WRA moved Kitagawa "safely out."[26]

By the end of September 1943, almost the entire Protestant congregation of Tule Lake had been relocated to other camps. Hannaford described the camp as "grow[ing] stranger and stranger" as "few people whom we know remain in it and by the end of next week those few will be practically vanished from sight."[27] By November, he felt that their mere "presence . . . at a church service . . . tends to be a hindrance rather than a help" at this "sadly changed place."[28] Gordon Chapman of the Protestant Commission, WRA administrators, and the Hannafords' superiors in the Presbyterian Board of National Missions did not understand the severity of the situation and asked the couple to stay, incorrectly believing that the couple would be "more effective . . . than the Japanese pastors."[29] The Hannafords knew they needed to leave and notified the Protestant Commission that they would look for a new post.[30]

Tule Lake's strong Protestant church almost collapsed when most members and pastors left. Hannaford estimated that between 100 and 150 Christians remained or had arrived at the camp once transfers were complete. They had only one pastor, the Issei Baptist Shozo Hashimoto from Minidoka. Attendance of thirty or forty contrasted with the hundreds who attended when the ecumenical church first opened. Only about a third of the camp's Christians attended services due to the severe stigma now attached to their religion. Young people met at the high school to hide their interest in Christianity from their families and other Tuleans. At least one Christian Tulean joined the Buddhist church, but she returned to a Protestant church after leaving camp. Many Christians felt intimidated and isolated from fellow incarcerees.[31]

Despite these challenges or perhaps because of them, one Tulean convert considered this period "the greatest harvest of [her] lifetime" because the suffering, doubt, isolation, and vast amount of free time led her to become "more serious, more deeply involved with the Bible." Shigeko Fu-kuye's identification as a Christian, occasional church attendance, and association with white Christians led non-Christian Tuleans to call her an *inu*. They shouted "Bow-Wow . . . when [she] passed by their door." Tuleans did not threaten the older single woman physically. She explained that God and her Bible study gave her the "strength to . . . withstand all kinds of difficult situations" even though she was the only Christian in her housing block. Decades later, Fukuye spoke of the kindness of WRA employees and Nikkei pastors more than the taunts.[32]

The Tulean church never reached its presegregation level of member-ship but grew persistently after the segregation was completed. Gordon Chapman preached to three hundred incarcerees at the camp's 1944 Eas-ter service, noting that the church "seems to be finding its strength." By that summer, enough young people were participating that Hashimoto re-quested the aid of seminary students to help with vacation Bible school. When Douglas Noble and his Wayside Chapel stopped at Tule Lake in the spring of 1945, five people made commitments at the conclusion of his main service. Chapman noted that Buddhists caused fewer problems by mid-1944, since they did not "assert themselves" on Easter even though it coincided with Hana Matsuri, a Buddhist holiday. At some other camps that year, however, Buddhist and Christian incarcerees collaborated for a joint service.[33]

Although Chapman singled out Buddhists, the conflicts at Tule Lake and elsewhere did not consist of one religion set against another. Some of the troublemakers were Buddhist, but many were not, nor were all the victims Christian. Disruptive gangs criticized Christianity's association with America more than its theology. They attacked not as Buddhists but as members of the Japanese community. Christian Nikkei's relationships with white Americans might have been enough to draw accusations.

Minidokans never experienced such violence. A number of outsiders familiar with the incarceration centers considered Minidoka to be the "good" camp. James Sakoda, a Nisei sociologist transferred from Tule Lake to Minidoka, described the latter as a "mild place peopled by mild people who did not resort to violence."[34] After visiting several camps, Gordon Hirabayashi also commented on the "quiet, submissive" nature of Minidoka as compared with the turbulent, "very resentful and hostile attitude" at Tule Lake.[35]

American Friends Service Committee workers, newspaper reporters, and WRA administrators marshaled quantitative and qualitative evidence to substantiate Minidoka's good reputation. They claimed that Nikkei from Washington were more loyal to the United States and more amicable and assimilated than Nikkei from the rest of the country. Ninety-one percent of Minidokans answered that they would serve in the U.S. military as opposed to the national average of 72 percent.[36] The WRA segregated relatively few Minidokans at Tule Lake. The large number of Christians at Minidoka also strengthened its reputation, as did its number of army volunteers. While the camp held only 7 percent of all Nisei eligible for service, a quarter of Nikkei army volunteers came from Minidoka. Fewer strikes and no riots occurred at Minidoka.[37]

Hirabayashi offered a sensible explanation why conditions at Minidoka seemed better than elsewhere. He saw a "marked correlation" between prewar experiences and behavior in camp, noting that "resentment and bitterness were the largest where mistreatment was the greatest." The large number of Nisei military volunteers from Hawaii, where Japanese were more accepted, supported his hypothesis. Hirabayashi proclaimed simply, "Human beings like to be treated humanely." He thought the differences in behavior directly related to the status of the community before the war. Seattle's populace did not accept Nikkei fully, but the minority's general circumstances were better than elsewhere on the coast. Holding less hostility toward the U.S. government and perhaps white people in general, most Seattle Nikkei cooperated willingly and made the best of their situation. The AFSC's Floyd Schmoe concurred with Hirabayashi's rationale.[38]

Most Christian leaders understood the faulty nature of the loyalty questionnaire but believed in its spirit and made efforts to separate Christians from possible negative influences. While their public relations generally painted a picture of Nikkei's total loyalty, they stressed the divergence in order to secure Nikkei transfers to Minidoka. The WRA sent most Nikkei from Western Washington to Minidoka, but smaller groups went to Manzanar and Tule Lake. Supported by Emery Andrews, Walt Woodward of the *Bainbridge Review,* and others, Nikkei from Bainbridge Island requested transfers in letters to the WRA, members of Congress, and other outside contacts. They missed family, friends, and fellow church members, and many disliked the atmosphere of the California camps. Washingtonians and Californians quarreled, and teenagers got into physical fights.[39] Andrews lamented how Californians "ostracized" the group from Bainbridge despite the latter group's "endeavor[s] to . . . cooperate." He thought their different "cultural background, democratic ideas . . .

and Caucasian contacts" caused friction.[40] True or not, white and Nikkei observers alike concluded that the greater assimilation of Nikkei from Washington increased tension since they were "much more advanced in . . . American ideas" than Californian Nikkei.[41]

Several people warned that the association with Californians would reverse the assimilation process and result in the Washingtonians' eventual rejection of the United States. A few white leaders claimed that the Bainbridge group would "revert" back to Japanese habits and customs. Whether people familiar with the group believed this or merely used it as an excuse to persuade WRA officials is unclear. But even after the war, a former incarceree described the incompatibility of mixing (Washington) apples with (California) lemons, twisting the proverb of a bad apple spoiling the bunch.[42] In March 1943, the WRA complied with Washingtonians' requests, and about forty families from Bainbridge arrived at Minidoka.[43] While this move occurred before segregation, the decision followed the same belief that assimilated Nikkei should be separated from "bad apples." The involvement of Christian Nikkei and their white pastors likely bolstered their case.

## Christian Nikkei and the War

Amidst the wretched conditions of camp life, Nikkei still had to face the war and life on the home front. Like many Americans, they deliberated the morality of war, but their loss of rights complicated their acceptance of the military draft and caused difficulties for Nikkei pacifists. Like other Americans, they attended memorial services for fallen soldiers, but incarcerated clergymen developed interfaith ceremonies to accommodate the religiously diverse camp populations. Like many Christian Americans, they adjusted to new leadership structures in their churches as pastors joined the military chaplaincy, but the incarceration camp churches faced additional drains as pastors and lay leaders joined the military and resettled outside of the camps.

Though many Nisei were already serving in the U.S. military and Issei had fought for the country during World War I, the military rejected Nikkei who volunteered immediately after the attack on Pearl Harbor. Approximately one year later, Roosevelt commissioned the 442nd, a segregated unit for Nikkei. Nisei began receiving draft notices in February 1944, and nearly three hundred young Nisei went to prison for refusing induction. While Eric Muller's *Free to Die for Their Country: The Story* of the *Japanese American Draft Resisters in World War II* analyzes the political motivation to resist, other Nisei declined to serve on pacifist and religious grounds. One Minidokan explained simply, "I cannot fight and uphold the principles laid down in the Bible."[44] However, because so many Japanese Americans, including many loyal citizens, protested the draft for political reasons, the government granted conscientious objector status to few Nikkei. Unless an applicant held membership within a historic peace church, like the Quaker or Mennonite churches, they could rarely obtain conscientious objector status.

Perry Saito, the Nisei pacifist who led speaking tours for the Fellowship of Reconciliation, felt as if "he were forsaking the entire Japanese populace here in America," since people would blame his draft resistance on "[him] as a Japanese and not as a Christian."[45] He qualified an answer on the loyalty questionnaire accordingly: "Due to my religious beliefs, . . . I could not bear arms for any force, whether it be for this nation or any other. . . . Insofar as I do not have to bear arms, I do swear allegiance to the United States of America."[46] His personal correspondence reflected a sense of shame or embarrassment when revealing this status to friends. He admitted to his closest Nisei friend, "You probably don't know it, but I am a conscientious objector," suggesting his feelings had been a secret for some time.[47] Saito remarked that "most people will probably say I am opposed to war because we are at war with Japan, but that isn't true. . . . I am most certainly a true American, but I consider myself also a true Christian."[48] He regretted that his religious beliefs conflicted with a standard expression of patriotism and knew people would misinterpret his actions.

Gordon Hirabayashi, the Seattle Quaker who had challenged the curfew and incarceration, also refused to serve, directing his energy toward the foundation of an interracial faith organization in Spokane, Washington and working for the American Friends Service Committee to resettle incarcerees. Through race reconciliation, Hirabayashi's center worked toward the same global goals sought by other Christians: remove "the causes of war, and other social evils, and social disease." Since he chose not to fight against fascism in a physically combative manner, he hoped that he could make an alternative contribution by forming "foundations for peace and freedom."[49] He based his opposition to fighting on racial injustices as well as pacifist beliefs. His resolve strengthened after receiving the loyalty questionnaire, which he refused to answer on the basis of its racist presumptions. He saw it as "unChristian, undemocratic [and] unAmerican."[50] The act of conscription itself violated freedom of person and freedom of religion in his mind. While the draft board seemed to ignore his repudiation of the questionnaire, they did not overlook his refusal to appear for a physical.[51] After defending himself in a Spokane court by explaining the particulars of his Quaker faith, the judge pronounced that Hirabayashi's notion of conscience was not religious but a "purely personal philosophy . . . evolved through [his] own thinking."[52] Both Floyd Schmoe and Homer Morris of the AFSC submitted letters in his defense, but the judge sentenced Hirabayashi to one year at McNeil Island Penitentiary.[53] Even membership in a peace church could not always overcome the assumption that Nisei refusing to fight were neglecting their patriotic duties.

White and Nikkei pastors counseled young congregants and their families as they struggled over the choice to enlist, but not all supported draft resisters. A Methodist pastor encouraged members of his Nisei youth group to "do your duty to God [by joining the army], and show them that we niseis [sic] are true Americans!!" Saito thought he should have said, "Do your duty to God, and show them that we niseis are true CHRISTIANS."[54]

While the question of Nisei in the military caused discord, it increased solidarity among the volunteers' families. A tri-faith union of Buddhists, Catholics, and Protestants manifested in visual performances and speeches that heralded their common "devotion for America." At a series of banquets honoring army volunteers in March 1943, the Issei Kinya Okajima gave an inclusive speech that equated traditional values of Buddhism and Japan—wisdom, benevolence, bravery, and honor—with those of Christianity and America. He praised Issei parents for raising their children in such a manner that they would choose to make this "supreme sacrifice" to their nation. Okajima attempted to reach every member of his wide audience, giving each generation of Buddhists and Christians a way to frame their united goal. The speech closed with a prayer for "the glory of America which is founded upon the rock of justice, liberty and equality which can never be removed by any power under the sun," an irony surely noted by incarcerated citizens. The *Minidoka Irrigator* reported that 1,200 people attended the banquets and heard Okajima's speech. Interfaith efforts only went so far, however. At one induction ceremony, the Minidoka Parent-Soldier Association presented each recruit with a Christian Bible.[55]

Evoking the sentiments expressed in Okajima's speech, every camp held interfaith memorial services. Catholic, Buddhist, and Protestant

FIGURE 8 Memorial service, Minidoka Incarceration Center, August 1944.
Source: Bain Family Collection, Densho Digital Archives.

leaders collaborated with WRA staff, the Community Activities Committee, and the Parent-Soldier Association to develop liturgies, design altar pieces, and write programs.[56] Every few months a memorial at Minidoka honored the sacrifices of young soldiers who had died recently. Services were held at the outdoor amphitheater, exposed to hot, dusty wind (Figure 8), or in the unfinished school gymnasium (Figure 9).[57] Dressed in their best clothes, large crowds of Nikkei sat on folding chairs donated by West Coast churches.

The memorial services for Minidokan soldiers expressed a patriotism blended with ritualistic and rhetorical elements of Buddhism and Christianity. At each service, Catholic, Buddhist, and Protestant leaders sat on a low stage alongside camp administrators and other participants. Surviving photographs and newspaper reports suggest that leaders did not display religious symbols at Minidoka's services. The stage usually held flowers, a U.S. flag, and occasionally urns holding the soldiers' remains.[58] Religious leaders may have felt uncomfortable assembling religious icons together or found the challenge of visually balancing the representation of multiple traditions too difficult. Perhaps they decided

FIGURE 9 Memorial service, Minidoka Incarceration Center, 1944. Source: Hatate Collection, Wing Luke Museum of the Asian Pacific American Experience.

that competing religious symbols would distract from the central patriotic message. The immense flag would have overshadowed any religious objects.

Components of the interfaith programs varied little: between patriotic songs and speeches, representatives of each religion—Protestant, Catholic, and Buddhist—offered prayers, delivered sermons or other religious messages, and read scripture. A Buddhist invocation and the "Star-Spangled Banner" opened the third memorial service at Minidoka, honoring the lives of ten soldiers from the camp. Incarcerees also sang the "Niseis' Stars and Stripes," a revision of the traditional patriotic hymn that dramatically opens:

> In Old Glory's stripes of Red
> Now flows, the Nisei blood.
> In struggles great they fought and bled
> Stemming the enemy flood.[59]

The song emphasized the absolute loyalty of some Nisei and their willingness to sacrifice their lives for America. A speech in Japanese and messages from WRA director Myer and the Minidoka camp director followed. Speakers praised recruits for proving the loyalty of Nikkei and helping save America from its enemies. After military guards presented flags to the soldiers' families, Minidoka's Catholic priest Leopold Tibesar offered a benediction, and Boy Scout buglers closed each ceremony with "Taps."[60] Standing in front of a large U.S. flag at Minidoka's fourth memorial service, honoring twelve fallen men, WRA administrator George Townsend closed his message by saying, "Lord Buddha taught that to every good deed there is an equal result, and the lives given up by these brave men will benefit those of you left behind. The founder of the Christian religion said, 'Greater love hath no man than this, that he lay down his life for his friends.'"[61] Like Okajima, Townsend spoke to both religious groups, highlighting the different ways each religion values sacrifice. Programs at other camps varied slightly from those at Minidoka. At Rohwer, for example, representatives of bereaved families offered incense following the Buddhist prayer.[62] Most camps carefully balanced elements of Buddhism, Catholicism, and Protestantism.

Funeral services for individual soldiers incorporated religious iconography and additional rituals. At one such funeral (Figure 10), the U.S. flag hung to the side and slightly behind the central white cross set against a black cloth.[63] Since this funeral took place in a low-ceilinged mess hall, where the flag already hung amidst the entrenched smell of American and Japanese food, the only alternative may have been to place the makeshift altar directly in front of the flag. Someone constructed a large wreath in patriotic stars and stripes for the service as well. The family chose to prioritize Christian faith but did not eliminate the patriotic sentiments for which their son died. The sight of a mess hall table and otherwise spartan surroundings highlight the difficulties of organizing the essential performances of everyday life in camp.

Religious holidays offered another opportunity to foster camp unity, and community leaders secularized elements to attract wider participation. Christians acknowledged the benefits of uniting incarcerees and wanted to share Christmas's good cheer for the sake of morale, but it meant sacrificing religious elements of the holiday. Everett Thompson, the Methodist pastor, explained, "The Buddhists are sharing in these [Christmas] plans, and of course it is a bit difficult to have the kind of a celebration that Christians would like without displeasing the Buddhists. Because this is a community wide affair, we are endeavoring to do this, and various kinds of compromise[s] are being worked out."[64] Indeed, a group of Buddhists founded Minidoka's annual dining hall decoration competition and expressed indignation at the suggestion that Chris-

FIGURE 10 Funeral for Nisei soldier, Minidoka Incarceration Center. Source: National Archives and Records Administration, Densho Digital Archives.

tians could outperform Buddhists in their celebration of the holiday. While campwide Christmas events generally omitted commemoration of Jesus's birth, a large number of non-Christians still attended Protestant and Catholic religious services. The aspects of Christmas celebrated most widely at Minidoka related to patriotism, community, and joy, though they included subtle elements of dissent as well.[65]

Buddhists at Minidoka invited the entire camp to celebrate Obon with them.[66] Some non-Buddhists began to view Bon Odori as a nonreligious cultural practice just as many non-Christians saw Christmas as an American holiday rather than a Christian one.[67] In prewar urban areas, nonadherents would have witnessed the celebrations of other groups, such as Bon Odori festivals that filled city streets or Christmas celebrations in public schools and shopping centers, but few individuals participated in both. In the confined living spaces of camp, however, these occasions drew observers and participants of all faiths. These instances model how the incarceration and the performance of religion within the camps affected incarcerees' knowledge of and attitudes toward different religions. After the war, Japanese Americans united for cultural celebrations that integrated pieces of American, Christian, and Buddhist traditions to form a unique communal ethnic identity.

As occurred in military camps, the absence of private space in incarceration camps forced dialogue and cooperation with people unfamiliar with different traditions. One of the clearest examples of the effects of the interfaith memorial services and religious diversity in the camps can be found in the journal of Minidoka's school superintendent. He wrote, "The students in one of the elementary school classes had a pet turtle. It died recently. A group of the students buried the turtle outside the schoolroom door. A cross was erected at the head of the grave. A grave marker was made with the inscription, 'Here Lies Tony the Turtle. He Came To Us on March 1, 1945 and Died May 2, 1945.' The students then placed slices of oranges and bits of candy on the grave. At different times the teacher noticed them lightly sprinkling water on the grave and chanting. The children were using both the Christian and Buddhist burial services."[68] By May 1945, these children had spent a significant part of their lives growing up in the incarceration camps. They likely had attended interfaith memorial services and funerals that used the rituals they later reenacted for their pet turtle. Had the incarceration never occurred, these young Buddhists and Christians would have been less familiar with the traditions of both religions nor inclined to combine them. Buddhists met down the hall from Protestants during summer school, and teachers caught students sneaking into friends' classrooms, regardless of their own affiliation.[69] Camp life gave children a more intimate view of different religions than they might have encountered on the West Coast.

One might assume that progressive Christian leaders would have supported these interfaith endeavors in hope that they would foster domestic and global harmony, but they generally did not. National Protestant ecumenical groups did not oppose interfaith events but did not encourage them either. From their perspective, liberal Christianity—or at least the newly conceived Judeo-Christian tradition—provided the foundation for a peaceful world order, not pluralism. Father Leopold Tibesar appreciated the publicity ceremonies garnered.[70] Despite being the smallest of the three main religious groups, Catholics received attention equal to that of Buddhists and Protestants, a value also recognized by Catholic leaders collaborating with Protestants and Jews outside of camp.[71] But when the Quaker Floyd Schmoe invited Tibesar and Maryknoll sisters to speak at a 1944 interfaith conference on minority problems in Seattle, Tibesar had to persuade local bishops and Maryknoll headquarters for permission to participate.[72] Tibesar delivered the opening speech, "Universal Aspects of Our American Heritage," and made remarks on the incarceration.[73] Maryknoll Sister Mary Lawrence appeared on the program to discuss her experiences working with minorities, but Maryknoll headquarters discouraged her participation on the grounds that the American Friends Service Committee, the primary sponsor, was "a bed of hot potatoes."[74] The Maryknoll hierarchy generally discouraged interfaith activities and instructed Maryknollers working in the camps to "keep an eye on" Protestants, adding, "Let the burden of your work be direct action for the people."[75] Everett Thompson proposed collaborative activities to Tibesar several times, but the Catholic priest did not encourage cooperation.[76]

Numerous Christian and Buddhist leaders working within the camps saw the benefit of interfaith ventures. Tom Fukuyama attempted to design an interfaith creed that could be used in the schools, but Minidoka's other religious leaders showed limited interest.[77] Buddhist groups at several camps invited Christian speakers to their gatherings to reduce possible tensions and model cooperation and open-mindedness to their congregations.[78] Interfaith youth councils held joint discussions attended by members of all three religions.[79] High school baccalaureate ceremonies combined Buddhist, Catholic, and Protestant elements in a way similar to the memorial services.[80] For Fukuyama and others, the interfaith works suggested a brighter future, but interfaith cooperation among incarcerees and camp workers beyond public performances remained rare. As with ecumenical worship, many religious leaders felt that interfaith work required unacceptable accommodations.

Progressive religious leaders outside the camps popularized the notion that American values and way of life developed from a Judeo-Christian foundation. Anti-Semitism and anti-Catholicism diminished as soldiers of different faiths mixed in military camps and on the battlefield.[81] Fighting for a common cause strengthened the unity and tolerance lauded by government propaganda and the National Conference of Christians and Jews. Concerned that the nationalistic and ethnocentric rhetoric from Europe would spread to the United States, the U.S. Office of Education produced a radio series heralding diversity and tolerance in 1938–39 entitled "Americans All . . . Immigrants All."[82] The NCCJ's "Tolerance Trios" of Catholic, Protestant, and Jewish clergymen crisscrossed the nation to promote the bonds between their faiths.[83]

This popular pluralism related to camaraderie among Protestants, Catholics, and Jews but not alliances between Christians and Buddhists.

NCCJ leaders deliberately excluded other faiths from their pluralist messages. But incarcerated Nikkei of all faiths championed their role within national unity, contradicting popular opinions that labeled Nikkei—whether Christian or Buddhist—as the major exception to the pluralistic rule. Buddhist, Catholic, and Protestant clergy formed their own Tolerance Trios in incarceration centers, standing side-by-side to honor the sacrifices of Nikkei soldiers. Organizers in the camps may not have been familiar with the NCCJ's program, but they demonstrated the same message visually and rhetorically. The camps' combination of faith traditions was not the only characteristic distinguishing them from popular pluralism. The NCCJ consciously limited its pluralism to religious, not racial unity. The organization sacrificed racial equality for its cause, performing for segregated crowds and sponsoring only white Tolerance Trios. William Randolph Hearst's invented holiday, "I Am an American Day," celebrated the nation's ethnic diversity while pointedly omitting Japanese Americans. Emily Roxworthy argues that the "nationalistic self-righteousness" encouraged by Hearst's spectacles gave white Americans the "moral high ground that justified prejudice" against minorities, particularly Nikkei. Exclusion within a garb of inclusivity intensified racial and religious discrimination, but white and Nikkei Buddhist and Christian clergy stood together within the barbed wire of incarceration centers.[84]

As Nikkei entered the army, they confronted the exclusion of Buddhist chaplains. Buddhist clergy could not join the U.S. military chaplaincy until several decades after World War II. The Nisei chaplain George Aki convinced his commanding officer at Camp Shelby, where the army stationed most stateside Nikkei, to allow Buddhist clergy from the nearby Arkansas incarceration camps to visit regularly and offer services.[85] Buddhists on the front had no access to a Buddhist priest. The U.S. chaplaincy institutionalized the nation's tri-faith identity as Catholic, Protestant, and Jewish chaplains worked together and ministered to one another's adherents.

With mixed feelings, several Nikkei Christians joined the military chaplaincy. Paul Nagano and his wife, Florence, left Poston for Bethel Theological Seminary in St. Paul, Minnesota, the day after their wedding. He planned to obtain the seminary degree required of army chaplains. Of this decision, Nagano wrote, "I can still remember walking alone across the fire-break in the evening making my way quietly and soberly to the recruiting office and registering my intent. That was a truly lonely and soul-wrenching commitment. . . . I would ordinarily be a conscientious objector—but as I thought of other Japanese Americans, many who were my dearest friends, volunteering and their need for spiritual strength, I was moved to make this decision."[86] Though the chaplaincy is a non-combat station, the idea of joining a military force still bothered many pacifists.

Emery Andrews volunteered for the army chaplaincy for similar reasons a few weeks after the formation of the 442nd. Though he may have considered chaplaincy earlier, a former congregant, Ernie Yamamoto, told him of the segregated unit's critical need for chaplains. The young man thought "a firm and unwavering conviction in Jesus Christ" would help soldiers struggling to determine just actions. When faced with the dilemma of killing people in battle, the soldier recognized his need for a moral guide.[87] Andrews could not have overlooked the urgency of Yamamoto's plea, which lamented his unit's lack of a chaplain and the difficulty and expense of attending services off base. Andrews volunteered on the condition that he would not displace a Nisei chaplain, and the army concluded that they did not need his services.[88] Though disappointed, Andrews recognized that he could accomplish more by meeting the numerous needs of incarcerated Nikkei.[89] Tibesar also volunteered to offer his services, but Maryknoll leaders asked their priests to refrain from military service. Bishop Walsh hoped the army would not hire chaplains who had specialized in missionary work, since their presence would exacerbate perceptions of the troops' foreignness.[90]

As more volunteers went overseas, their families sought pastoral care. Fukuyama reached out to the wives of soldiers, some of whom were expecting their first children, but could only "touch but a fraction" of them. Andrews observed that the war is "distressing enough to people in ordinary life, but to people confined it is much more so." Rarely hindered by his poor Japanese language skills, Andrews "wish[ed he] could speak Japanese" when conducting services for Issei mothers who had lost their sons in battle. The war stretched the already thin supply of pastoral resources.[91]

The rising number of people leaving for school or employment outside the camps "sharply crippled" ecumenical churches' personnel resources further.[92] Everett Thompson explained that their "work [was] upset . . . almost every time some new person secured a permanent release from the project."[93] The most motivated individuals with the greatest leadership skills resettled first, leaving gaps within church leadership that could not be filled. Two-thirds of Minidoka's Sunday school teachers left camp by June 1943—more than two years before the camp closed. Nearly all of the young people's church council members were gone by then as well. Younger, less experienced people filled the positions.[94] By December 1944, only 15 percent of Minidoka's male Nisei Christians remained in camp. One-third of Issei Christian men had departed, as well as nearly three-quarters of male Kibei Christians. Fewer women of all generations resettled, though two-thirds of Nisei Christian women left Minidoka before the close of 1944.[95] Many camps lost Nikkei pastors who believed they could better serve the community from the outside.[96] Lay leadership in other American churches shifted as members left for the military or war industry work but did not suffer the continual losses that incarceration camps incurred through resettlement.

As more Nikkei left the camps, the responsibilities of remaining pastors grew. Because Nisei left in greater numbers than the first generation, the ecumenical churches were frequently left with primarily Issei clergy. A sizable number of school-age Nikkei remained, however, since most incarcerees did not leave camp until after high school graduation. Minidoka's Nisei congregation did not shrink substantially until the final year of the war because new members from Christian and non-Christian families joined the Federated Church.[97] White pastors filled some gaps left by Nisei clergy who resettled or joined the army chaplaincy, but white missionaries also left to prepare for their return to Japan.[98] By 1945, the Manzanar church was staffed largely by white pastors visiting for the day or weekend.[99] Although Minidoka's church suffered less because of its large number of pastors from Seattle, its leaders still struggled to sustain basic programs for the duration.

The war still affected the daily lives of Japanese American Christians isolated in rural camps. Their incarceration complicated the draft, memorial services, and the sustainability of their churches. Amidst a flurry of patriotism and growing support for America as a tri-faith nation, Nikkei Christians configured a more pluralistic view of America that embraced enemy aliens without diminishing their cultural or religious traditions and values. They exceeded the capacity of free Americans to manifest the nation's ideals of equality and unity by radically allying the values of Buddhism and Japan with American Christianity. They expanded racial and religious definitions of American identity in ways that would not be accepted throughout the nation for decades.

## Community and Faith

While draft resisters and incarcerees creating new forms of American pluralism confronted their incarceration through action, a greater number of Christians resisted through meaning-making. The lived theologies of incarcerated laity show us how Christians reshaped the narrative of their experience to place themselves at the center of the story. They rejected official explanations and emphasized their own capacity to build community and imagine positive effects of their incarceration. Lived theology entails adopting biblical, theological, and historical models to fit a lived reality. Nikkei Christians possessed and enacted Christian tropes of sacrifice and redemption amidst their experience of incarceration.

Incarcerated Christians drew two primary benefits from their religion: solidarity and fellowship from religious communities and strength from their faith in God's will. Ritual and other manifestations of Christianity played a significant role in many incarcerees' lives, but contemporary records and oral histories mention the roles of community and faith more frequently and with more fervor than any other aspect of the religion.[100] Resurrected prewar Christian groups in and outside of the camp churches fostered a sense of normalcy and continuity with their former lives. Like the prewar ethnic churches, religious organizations in the camps provided a place for Nikkei leadership and autonomy apart from systemic discrimination.

Within weeks of landing in camp, lay Christians began reassembling their prewar church clubs and societies. Groups that remained largely intact after removal hit the ground running. Members of Seattle's St. Vincent's Society charged themselves with sustaining morale at Minidoka incarceration center and formed a welcoming committee to help new arrivals move into the barracks.[101] Choirs formed to enhance Sunday services. With extra free time, religious groups met more frequently than they had before their incarceration.[102] Christian youth groups exemplified the importance of community formation. (For the purpose of this discussion, "youth" and "young people" refer to upper elementary- to college-age incarcerees.) Having few options for entertainment, many incarcerees participated in church groups and religious organizations like the Christian Endeavor Society, one of the first evangelical youth organizations in America, and Hi-Y, a high school club associated with the YMCA and YWCA. These groups required interdenominational cooperation, but young people organized other clubs ecumenically without direction from authorities as well.

White and Nisei pastors led youth groups in some camps, but Nikkei who had participated in Protestant youth conferences in California led the strongest, most active groups.[103] Armed with leadership skills from prewar endeavors, these young people consulted advisors but worked autonomously and developed their own forms of Christian life. Their groups met independently from the camps' main ecumenical Protestant churches for worship, prayer, Bible study, sports, dances, and other social events. This structure strengthened bonds among young people and exacerbated the rift between generations in the larger community. A large camp with active Christian youth, Poston contained twelve ecumenical Protestant youth groups divided by age, four chapters of the Christian Endeavor Society, and an active YWCA.[104] Young Postonites, with the assistance of adult pastors, held an eight-day conference and revival in the spring of 1943 that attracted nine hundred attendees per night. At the final service, 175 Nikkei reportedly answered the altar call to dedicate their lives to Christ.[105] The wartime experiences of young Postonites reflect the diverse range of responses to the incarceration among Nikkei Christians.

The Poston Junior Church's yearbook, *Desert Echoes*, shows the importance of community within the lives of incarcerees.[106] The book chronicles the social activities of nine- to fifteen-year-old Protestants during their first year in camp. Photographs of sporting events, singspiration gatherings, graduation parties, field days, and Christmas celebrations fill the pages. The high ratio of social activities to devotional meetings suggests the importance of social bonds within the community. Replicating prewar activities enabled some Nisei to retain the notion that they were still normal American teenagers. With the exception of introductory pieces by adult advisors and four short essays on religion, a reader might not realize that the book came from a religious community. *Desert Echoes* resembles a typical school yearbook, showing the centrality of social activities in the lives of young Christians. Poston's middle and high schools produced independent yearbooks, so its presence heralds the unique status of their Christian community.

The religious testimonies of Junior Church members emphasize communal aspects of Christianity—fellowship, church attendance, and learning about Jesus with others. The editors of *Desert Echoes* included compositions from an essay contest, "One Year with God in Poston," that reveal how individuals envisioned Christian community. The essays begin with testimonies of conversion. Straightforward, uniform language describes the "unforgettable day" when each young person "accepted Christ . . . as [their] personal Saviour" and articulates how this conversion changed their sense of community and relationships with others. Margaret Murakami wrote of working hard to be "a real testimony for the Lord" by being a good friend. David Shimomura wrote that for him becoming an "everyday Christian" meant trying to keep the Ten Commandments all week long and learning to keep his temper. Shared social experiences taught members of the Junior Church how to cooperate, build good character, and appreciate one another's fellowship. Community was essential for incarcerees, particularly young people torn from prewar social networks. As young Christians resettled outside of the camps, many expressed their longing for this solidarity.

Some Nikkei claimed that the incarceration fostered unique fellowship, something greater than that found outside the camps. Paul Nagano, a pastor and youth advisor at Poston, explained, "The common experience of injustice, suffering and deprivation brought people together in a spiritual fellowship of genuine mutuality and oneness. Differences and status were eliminated as everyone was suffering a common predicament. There is a true *koinonia* (deep fellowship of love) in suffering together. In this sense, the camp life was an unforgettable experience of joy and fellowship."[107] Nagano described this communion fifty years after his release from camp, giving the ideas and memory time to percolate within his psyche. Nagano's bright memory of camp fellowship may have grown over time, as the pain of the indignity faded, but his attitude long after the war resembles comments made by incarcerees during their confinement. In the summer of 1942, an Issei at a Montana Department of Justice camp said, "The group esprit de corp[s] and the cooperation and willingness to live harmoniously was something very inspiring and beautiful to see. It was truly a rich experience and anyone who lived through the grand feeling of real love and harmonious relations will thank the Almighty for giving them the chance to experience it."[108] Poston Endeavor member Lloyd Wake described how "lives . . . changed" through bonds of fellowship.[109] Incarcerees of all ages in camps across the country generated communities that fueled positive experiences.

Many incarcerees associated fellowship with faith, the other primary component of Christianity in the camps. Christian Endeavor Societies united spiritual development and religious education with community.

Several Japanese Endeavor chapters had thrived on the West Coast before the war. Sharing the views of many liberal Christians of the time, Endeavor founder Francis E. Clark believed that communication among international groups would reinforce the belief that "all nations should be friends, under the government of Jesus Christ."[110] Limiting membership through strict rules and a lack of recreational activities, these groups of committed Christians focused on personal development. Regular testimonies and self-criticism sessions filled weekly meetings of Poston's Endeavor Societies that focused on a variety of religious topics, including missions, prayer, church history, and the "Trials and Tribulations of a Christian."[111] Members arranged occasional social gatherings, but organization rules stated that they must be "strictly limited to the active, associate, and honorary members," to prevent insincere or casual participation.[112] Unlike the Poston Junior Church and other youth groups, the Endeavor Society did not seek inclusivity, though it was vigorously ecumenical by design. The rosters of Poston's Junior Church and the Endeavor Society reveal that several incarcerees belonged to both groups, perhaps meeting needs for both relaxed fellowship and religious contemplation. The Junior Church's events drew ten times more attendees than gatherings hosted by the Endeavor Society.[113]

Many of Poston's young people expressed a response heard throughout the camps—gratitude that God helped them bear the "trials and oppression" of camp life—but others thanked God *for* the incarceration. Members of the Poston III Endeavor Society (the Endeavor chapter in the camp's third sector) assembled their personal revelations in a testimonial booklet, *Streams in the Desert*. Three-fourths of the testimonies refer to the authors' confinement. These brief compositions written by society members exemplify the group's spiritual focus and express a representative range of theological responses to the incarceration. Several reflect the positive sentiment expressed in this chapter's epigraph. Endeavor members offered several reasons for their gratitude for the incarceration, including strength, perspective, contentment, and a deeper understanding of Jesus's trials.[114]

A few Endeavor members thanked God for the incarceration because it led them to Jesus or strengthened their faith. One high schooler wrote that she "wouldn't exchange the last six months of [her] life for all the 14 previous years" because she converted to Christianity in the camp.[115] A Nisei testified that he lost faith upon entering the camp but later thought camp was "the best place in the world." He believed "the Lord wanted" him at Poston because he came to "know the Lord and accept Him as [his] Savior" there.[116] Another described how the incarceration "tempered" his faith, which could now withstand even greater challenges.[117] A youth pastor at a different Arizona camp used the same metallurgical metaphor, believing his congregants left camp with a "firmer and sounder faith in God."[118] Sadaichi Asai, the Junior Church advisor in Poston I, agreed that the incarceration would mold "noble characters qualified to meet the uncertain difficulties ahead."[119] These Christians believed that retaining religious faith while undergoing difficulties and injustices would strengthen a person's character and faith. After resettling outside of camp, a Christian man confessed, "Truthfully speaking, this was the first time I really needed Christ, somebody to guide me and see me through. I found him and he helped me."[120] These religious experiences permanently changed the lives of many.

Numerous Christians found peace and contentment through submission to what they understood to be God's plan. By focusing on his trust in God and his faith that he would be given "the power to . . . overcome sufferings and hardships," Yoshisada Kayai recalled that "being confined physically in the barbed wires" gave him "spiritual freedom." He explained, "I thought that I really experienced the freedom which was given to me by God, and I felt that it was the most important thing we can have."[121] The incarceration did not make him more pious or "ritualistic," as he said, but rather content to follow the destiny God planned for him. In 1943, Bob Okazaki projected a sunny outlook when he wrote, "As long as I am one of God's children, I'm as content as one of Carnation's cows. I'm not mad at anybody—even Roosevelt."[122] Requesting a character recommendation from his white pastor, Okazaki may have exaggerated this attitude. Tok Hirashima, one of the contributors to *Streams in the Desert*, recounted how Jesus "showers countless blessings upon me daily, filling me with peace and joy." Another Endeavor member, Tayeko Kitahata, wrote simply, "Yes, there is peace— real peace and certainty—in my heart and in my mind and a satisfying reality of Christ, which nothing in the world can take away." Poston's Reverend Sohei Kowta exaggerated this phenomenon, comparing the discontented non-Christians with his parishioners, who were "sincerely thankful for their life in the Center."[123] Numerous incarcerees expressed similar feelings that they were no longer "resentful for being pushed into camp, not bitter, nor discouraged, but happy, strengthened . . . through Christ."[124]

These lived theologies stem from a long tradition that incarcerees would have absorbed from sermons, hymns, and Christian literature before the war. From the inception of their religion, Christians have placed a special value on suffering, interpreting it variously as a test, an opportunity to emulate the suffering of Jesus and Christian martyrs, a punishment, or a method of purification.[125] A number of Nikkei pastors made analogies between their plight and Jesus's trials, and some congregants expressed their appreciation to have the opportunity to "know the true meaning of Christ's suffering."[126] Masakazu Konatsu, a member of the Poston III church, expressed that sentiment after a year of incarceration. An Endeavor member invoked the related notion that "God must bring torrents of tribulations upon us in order to wash out our impurities. Then, after the storm is over, we are pure and clean, ready for the Master's use."[127] This incarceree believed in the redemptive value of his experience. In these ways, Christian beliefs equipped incarcerees with the theological tools to craft explanations for the injustice and develop strategies to appreciate its benefits. Anointing their suffering enabled incarcerees to "live" their theology. Meaning-making was not an observable action, but this intentional belief enabled incarcerees to determine their experience of the incarceration.

Many incarcerees struggled with the incarceration, however, and their religious communities did not always welcome dark perspectives. In addition to losing material goods and freedom, many Nikkei felt betrayed by their country. Others felt abandoned by their churches, which did not speak against the injustice. Members and leaders of Christian fellowship groups pressured Christians to exhibit positive attitudes and resist inclinations to express dissatisfaction or anger. Christian groups at several camps performed a play heralding the importance of retaining a positive Christian attitude. *The End We Seek*, written by Mary Nakahara, a Nisei incarcerated in Arkansas, follows the downfall of resentful, disillusioned incarcerees and the triumph of optimistic Christian Nisei. Acknowledging the destructive powers of the incarceration, the narrator within Nakahara's play concludes, "We do not have to step out of this center to reach that outside. Spiritually, if there is understanding of the present situation, love for country and fellowship, faith and hope in God, and a desire to hold on to the Christian way of life, then, there is not a borderline. There is no barrier."[128] This message urged incarcerees to channel the strength of their community, patriotism, and religious faith to accept their current circumstances, resettle outside of the camps if possible, and live positive, productive lives. Nakahara rejected the play's accommodating approach after the war.[129]

This pressure to cultivate positive attitudes surely contributed to the fifty young people mentioned in this chapter's epigraph who agreed that their first year in camp was the "most glorious" year of their lives. Pressure to conform and the Christian Endeavor's practice of self-criticism may have contributed to the sentiments expressed in George Takaoka's contribution to *Streams in the Desert*: "As I continue to live in Poston and see Christians living in testimony to our Lord, I feel I am increasingly unworthy to walk in the name of my Savior. . . . Self-examination has served only to reveal the pauperish state of my spiritual existence." While many contributors to the testimonial booklet mentioned faltering or not living up to Christ's demands, only Takaoka failed to conclude with joy in God's forgiveness. The inclusion of this less positive testimony suggests that editors did not strictly censor submissions, but peer pressure and the traditional form of the testimony genre garnered predominantly positive responses.

Other Christians retained their faith but struggled to see anything positive about the incarceration. A poem from Heart Mountain exemplifies this attitude:

Father, you have wronged me grievously
I know not why you punish me
For sins not done or reasons known
You have caused me misery.
But through this all I look on you
As child would look on parents true
With tenderness come mingling in
The anguish and Bitter tears;
My heart still beats with loyalty
For you are my Father, I know no other.[130]

A traditional lament, this poem invokes universal frustration with seemingly meaningless suffering. Other Nikkei Christians alluded to the first verses of Psalms 137, in which Israelites expressed their despair in exile and inability to rejoice or sing songs of praise.[131] Few surviving testimonies recall Job's trials, but incarcerees invoked the theme of innocent suffering as both sorrowful and redemptive. Alice Kono, a young laywoman living in Utah, warned that the Israelites' "lack of faith" in the wilderness resulted in their "utter destruction."[132] All but two Israelites from the Exodus perished in the wilderness as punishment for their doubt, and Nikkei could fail similarly without trust in God. These Christian tropes, common throughout Christian history, would have been familiar to churchgoing Nikkei from scripture and sermons. Facing personal and community trials, Nikkei embodied parallel traditions.

The editors of *Desert Echoes* showed readers the resilience of their members but never painted a glossy picture of life in camp. Much of the text seems to be written tongue in cheek. Even the Junior Church's advisors refrained from exclusively positive messages. Kowta wrote of his determination to "make this new community an ideal one" but also confessed that he had been "disillusioned in many things and in many ways." *Desert Echoes* closes with a list of senior wills, pledging, "We . . . without a tear nor a sign, shall leave, when the time finally does come, our beloved Poston, with its wealth of dust, mosquitoes, too much heat and scorpions to whomever is dumb enough to take it." This conclusion lends a shade of sarcasm to the annual's foreword: "May this yearbook help echo the sweet memories of the desert life." While Junior Church members projected a generally positive attitude in their annual, they did not thank God or anyone else for the experience.

Neither *Desert Echoes* nor *Streams in the Desert* appears to have been circulated beyond their immediate youth groups and advisors. Private jokes fill the former, and the latter designates its purpose as a "sacred promise" to God and one another to live their testimonies. Youth editors and their advisors printed a small number of each book. No evidence suggests that WRA administrators received copies, and officials rarely censored or oversaw the publication of English language church materials.

Positive sentiments about the incarceration can be difficult to comprehend, but they demonstrate the intense role Christianity played in some incarcerees' lives. Anthropologist Michael Jackson offers a helpful model to explain how subjected groups and individuals use storytelling as a way to "subvert the power of the original event to determine one's experience" of it. Further, he argues that sharing these stories can reduce the shame and isolation caused by a traumatic event.[133] Jackson analyzed narratives produced long after the precipitating event, but constructing a narrative of their incarceration in *Desert Echoes* and writing testimonies for *Streams in the Desert* may have benefited incarcerees similarly. The forums provided opportunities to express personal interpretations of events.[134] The memory books empowered incarcerated Christians to represent their experiences in a way that showcased their agency and personal growth. They mobilized their experiences of Christianity—both social and theological—to construct a narrative about their own actions and those of God, not a story about what was being done to them. The WRA and U.S. government are conspicuously absent from Nikkei Christians' wartime testimonies. The state and its officials are not depicted as racist perpetrators, misguided, ignorant people, or neutral agents; they simply are not part of the story.

Many things affected the faith of incarcerees, and many factors influenced the articulation of that faith within the Poston annual and testimony booklet. This understanding corroborates Hannah Arendt's view that storytelling is never purely a social or personal project; political and public interests complicate the construction of every narrative.[135] While young Postonite authors compiled their projects as mementos for themselves and their advisors, many things could have affected the content of these works, including a desire to represent how they wanted to remember the incarceration. Following the forms of specific genres also shaped the final products. A yearbook is designed to celebrate the experiences of a group, not lament life's limitations, bemoan routine, or protest injustice. Likewise, Christian Endeavor members followed a practiced form of testimony that praises God and concludes on a positive note. One could argue that the genres predetermined the positive content, but this overlooks incarcerees' exceptional circumstances and the notable derivations from expected messages.

Using the Pearl Harbor attack as an example, Daphne Desser points out the difficulties of trying to make meaning from a "meaningless" traumatic event. She argues that pressure to move beyond the event leads many people to accept dominant public understandings of the crisis at the time, particularly in cases of national trauma.[136] Government propaganda and some church leaders pressured incarcerees to foment positive attitudes, but Poston's young people reconfigured their stories rather than accept national understandings of the legitimacy of the incarceration. Some incarcerees may have internalized newsreels' explanations for the incarceration—that it was their necessary wartime sacrifice and it protected them from racist mobs—but expressions of these politicized rationales are absent from contemporary records, memoirs, and oral histories, Christian or otherwise. Christians devised theologies to transform their experience in positive ways but did not invoke public excuses for the injustice.

Faith compelled other individuals to stand against the injustice of the incarceration. Gary Okihiro and David K. Yoo argue that Christianity and Buddhism fueled resistance by strengthening ethnic solidarity.[137] Gordon Hirabayashi and other pacifists fought the government on the basis of religious convictions, and incarcerated Protestants echoed that rhetoric. A sermonette from Poston demanded that Christians "turn the tide" and stand against injustice. The author wrote, "Apathy is a greater sin than blasphemy. Better to make blunders in trying to correct an evil, than sit back and wonder why it could not have been done a difference way."[138] The piece argued against complacency and resignation.

Alternatively, historian John Howard interpreted positive Christian statements about the incarceration as "a theology of resignation more than resistance" and implied that individuals were waiting to be delivered from their misery.[139] Brian Hayashi cited sermons that "sidestep[ped]" criticism to argue that religious leaders dissuaded people from participating in politics and resistance.[140] Indeed, white pastors and incarcerees, Christians and non-Christians, frequently invoked the Japanese saying *shikata ga nai*: it can't be helped.[141] They urged one another to accept the incarceration in order to make the best of their situation. Not until the institution of the draft did notable numbers of Japanese Americans refuse to comply with government orders. But resistance occurred in more subtle ways. Testimonies and sermons show incarcerees actively creating community and developing ways to cope with the trauma of the incarceration and camp life. They may not have resisted eviction orders in the spring of 1942, but many Nikkei successfully resisted the government's narrative and the ease with which they could have succumbed to the misery of incarceration.

The dissonance between this understanding and Howard's view may rest in differing definitions of resistance. James Scott's often debated thesis claims that researchers must look beyond traditional, active forms of resistance to see how oppressed people shape safer, subtler styles of resistance.[142] Fashioning alternative narratives that place themselves as the protagonist is a form of resistance in itself by rejecting mainstream propaganda. Michel Foucault might contend that identifying your oppressor's action as your own is the manifest proof that you have succumbed to the oppressor's will, but Michel de Certeau argues for the need to examine how groups "resist being reduced" to this understanding of discipline. Nikkei Christians' lived theologies created a "network of anti-discipline."[143] Both the annual and testimonial booklet from

Poston exhibit how religion empowered Nikkei to take control of their situation and write their own history.

The testimonies of young people at Poston echoed the range of sentiments expressed by young and old Christian Nikkei around the country. That one group chose to commemorate the social world it constructed in camp while another catalogued religious experiences from the time attests to the diversity of lay Christian experiences within the incarceration camps. Pastors and congregants at all camps spoke during the war and later about the benefits of faith and religious communities in camp and the ways in which the incarceration strengthened both their belief in God and the solidarity of their ethnic and religious communities. Whether religious adherence gave them hope, provided a distraction and a caring community, or put suffering in perspective, religious belief and practice—whether Buddhist or Christian—helped many incarcerees endure their incarceration and loss of rights.

## Conclusion

Whether through action or meaning-making, incarcerated Christians attempted to remain true to the United States and their religious faith. Lectures, discussion series, and more contemplative meditation and prayer sessions provided a place for young Christians and non-Christians to consider their circumstances and devise practical approaches to resolving or reconciling their incarceration. While many non-Christians participated in secular activities sponsored by Christian groups, others opposed all Christian pursuits and leadership as collaboration with their incarcerators. Protestants, Catholics, and Buddhists worked together as people of faith to acknowledge civic events, diversifying the popularized unity found outside of camp racially and religiously. Lay religious groups helped many incarcerees endure their current situation, and Christians of all ages developed empowering testimonies that framed their experience not as victimization but as an opportunity for constructive growth as individuals and people of faith. But lay communities and prevalent lived theologies also pressured incarcerees to visibly manifest positive Christian lives. Narratives faltered under pressure to display optimism at times, but individual piety strengthened many incarcerees. These manifestations of Christianity in the incarceration camps demonstrate how incarcerated or otherwise subjected people utilize their faith for productive ends.

# 5 The End of Japanese Ethnic Churches?

· · · · · · · · · · · · · · · · · · · · · · · · · · · · · · · · · · · · · · · · · · · ·

> It is just as tragic to invite a Negro or a Japanese into a fellowship
> simply because he is Negro or Japanese as it is to restrict him on
> those grounds. The basis for true fellowship is on the grounds of
> common interest and personal quality.
>
> —Gordon Hirabayashi, June 1944

Progressive church leaders who had refrained from opposing the incarceration publicly seized the opportunity to hasten its demise by 1943. Many saw a possibility to reduce national racial tensions if they could disperse Nikkei throughout the country. They saw the reentrance of Nikkei into American society as *the* opportunity to eliminate the segregation of Japanese Americans. The Federal Council of Churches "dare[d] not refuse" the challenge of reintegrating incarcerees within American life.[1] Religious workers strategized how to shape the best possible future for America and Japanese American Christians as Nikkei struggled to reestablish their interrupted lives by entering new schools, moving to new cities, and recovering businesses on the West Coast. Publicly acknowledging the societal harms caused by the incarceration, progressive Protestants and Catholics worked to resettle Nikkei outside of the camps to reinstate their civil rights as soon as possible. Mainline Protestants focused on eliminating ethnic urban enclaves and segregated ethnic churches, while Catholics and Quakers more frequently recognized the need for solidarity and fellowship within the ethnic group. Nikkei pastors were divided. They saw the practical and religious advantages to integration but harbored concerns for their congregants and their own job security. Most white church employees and many Nikkei worked with the underlying assumption that "public opinion demands [assimilation] for the sake of national unity."[2] Church leaders believed their greatest contribution to assimilation efforts would be to abolish ethnic churches in the postwar period.

The WRA began pressuring incarcerees to leave the camps only a few months after forcing Nikkei to enter them.[3] The agency encouraged resettlement during the war to alleviate the difficulty of closing the camps, save operational expenses, and minimize the detrimental effects of camp life. WRA employees thought opportunities for resettlement would raise morale in the camps, but they had the opposite effect. Administrators gradually reduced support for community activities to encourage people to leave. Less than a year after the camps opened, Baptist pastor Emery Andrews observed that the "WRA is making it as hard as possible for people to stay in camp."[4] Despite many success stories, unhappy reports also trickled in from the outside, and some resettlers returned to camp. Nikkei became hesitant to leave the camps' security and minimal comfort. Pressure to resettle grew in 1945 when the government reopened the West Coast to Nikkei and made plans to close the centers. Many families had lost homes, farms, or businesses and had little to recover. Few had financial resources after years of extremely low pay. Many older Issei felt that they could not rebuild their lives yet again, but the reality of the camps' imminent closure pressed upon them.

Since entire congregations were evicted from their hometowns, the pastors of most Japanese ethnic churches leased or sold their buildings to ecumenical or denominational groups to be used as needed until the community's return. This gave denominational leaders, the Home Missions Council of North America, and the FCC an opportunity to eliminate ethnic Japanese churches permanently. In cooperation with the government's policy of dispersed integration and assimilation, these organizations refused to return properties after the war and instructed Japanese Americans to join predominantly white churches.

The government had increasingly taken charge of the nation's social welfare during the New Deal, but with the advent of World War II, U.S. government officials turned to the churches for help and asked them to share the burden of difficulties related to the incarceration.[5] At a 24 September 1942 meeting with the FCC, Home Missions Council, and other church representatives, WRA official Thomas W. Holland rationalized that clergy should "take the lead" in national resettlement programs since they are "idealists" and have "the ears of millions of people."[6] Among other tasks, they charged the AFSC and the FCC with supporting the resettlement of Nikkei leaving the camps during the war and transferring college students to schools in the interior. This cooperation revealed the close relationship between churches and U.S. government in civil affairs but belies the unease government officials felt about granting religious groups such authority and responsibility and the tension

Christians felt about cooperating with state agencies perpetrating an injustice.

## "The Future of Japanese in American Churches"

American church leaders determined a course of action for postwar religious work with Nikkei at a series of interdenominational conferences in 1943. At the end of the year, Nikkei and white pastors, Presbyterian, Congregational, Baptist, Methodist, and Episcopalian representatives, and members of the Protestant Church Commission and the Home Missions Council's Committee on Administration of Japanese Work gathered in Denver for the Conference of Leaders of Japanese Christian Work to determine the "Future of Japanese in American Churches."[7]

Efforts to increase national and Protestant unity motivated debates about restructuring Japanese worship, and leaders argued over the best way to foster unity. Should Protestants continue emphasizing ecumenism or work for a different type of unity? Since Nikkei of different denominations worshiped together in the incarceration camps, some church authorities reasoned that continuing this ecumenical pattern would be best. They valued "decreas[ing] denominational consciousness" even if participants did not "agree in all things." Despite evidence to the contrary, a number of outside leaders argued that ecumenical churches were "more ideal and effective" because they were "more Christian." They believed such Japanese churches could serve as a model for other American churches that would see "the value of union." Harold Jensen, president of the Seattle Council of Churches and pastor of Seattle's First Baptist Church, initially prioritized ecumenism over racial integration and encouraged returning Nisei to "avoid doing anything which would reestablish the old denominational pattern." When the tide turned toward racial integration, Jensen reoriented his priorities.[8]

Many people opposed forming ecumenical churches because of the problems encountered in the incarceration camps. Work was "slow, inefficient and confusing," and many groups refused to participate fully. Opponents also worried about financial support, since denominational resources would not be available to Nikkei if they worshiped in interdenominational churches. This practical concern may have been the driving force behind the decision to forsake ecumenism, since financing the camp churches had been a constant struggle. Enforcing ecumenical worship for one ethnic group was impractical within a global church divided by denomination. Consolidating Nikkei and white church members would reduce costs for every denomination.[9]

Participants voiced pragmatic and theological arguments explaining how racially integrated worship would benefit the nation and church. Pragmatically, white and Nikkei leaders believed that integrating churches would help the recently incarcerated rejoin American society more easily and reduce the racial divisions that contributed to the "misunderstanding and suspicion which helped to produce the evacuation." If white congregants worshiped alongside Nikkei, pastors hoped prejudices would diminish and tolerance would expand to the workplace and outer community. Additionally, the elimination of segregated churches, like the elimination of ethnic urban communities, would fortify America's future by erasing evidence perceived by outsiders to be resistance to joining American life.[10]

Theologically, many Protestants believed racial integration would be a step toward a "full[er] . . . realization" of true Christianity. They thought an integrated church would more closely resemble the church envisioned by Jesus two thousand years earlier. Belief that American Christians would lead the global community to a new, peaceful world order reinforced such sentiments. Some Protestants worried that these grand ideas would fail if America and its churches could not improve domestic race relations. Some Denver conference participants argued that bringing Japanese into predominantly white churches could "stimulate higher Christian ideals in the Caucasian churches" and the Japanese community. Accepting and becoming acquainted with one another would make them better Christians and better people.[11]

These arguments for integrated worship led to harsh criticism of those who favored segregation. Some Protestant leaders saw a direct correlation between the extent of an individual's Americanization and his or her willingness to attend an integrated church. Just as outsiders viewed the existence of urban Nikkei communities as a rejection of American society, some people saw ethnic churches as a rejection of America's promise as a cultural melting pot. While concepts of cultural pluralism and unity through diversity increased during the 1940s, many Americans still imagined a more homogenous union. Since others viewed segregated churches as a corruption or rejection of "normal" Christian worship, refusing to attend an established, predominantly white church could label an individual anti-Christian as well as anti-American. People of different races and ethnicities called predominantly white churches or communities "regular" or "normal," creating a value system in which ethnic organizations were inferior and foreign. By November 1945, a few white church leaders began describing what they hoped would become integrated churches as "nonracial" or "intercultural," acknowledging Caucasian as a race, not just a description of normativity. This attempt to deracialize or diversify their religious institutions failed, however, and most people continued to speak exclusively, urging Nikkei to join "our Caucasian churches."[12]

On the other side, some Denver conference participants worried that non-Christian Nikkei would be less likely to join predominantly white churches, thereby hampering evangelistic efforts. Integrationists countered that ethnic churches only appeared to aid evangelism "at the moment" because conversion into an ethnic church would hobble the process of joining interracial churches later on. These leaders wanted to introduce converts to "true Christianity," which could not be found in a segregated church.[13]

Ordained Nikkei posed another challenge to integrating America's churches. The Reverend Kobei Takeda led a discussion in Denver about the "Nisei ministerial problem" and encouraged churches to recruit Nikkei pastors as they left the incarceration camps. Churches welcomed guest sermons by Nikkei but questioned their ability to bring new non-Japanese members to the church and offer effective pastoral care to white congregants. Many Issei pastors did not wish to minister within predominantly white churches even if one did call them. Members of the Protestant Commission considered sending the "surplus" of Issei ministers to Japan, but few wanted to go abroad and several missions boards opposed the idea as well. "Issei ministers are more or less useless now," Toru Matsumoto pronounced to the American Baptist Home Mission Society. An Issei himself, if an exceptionally assimilated young one, Matsumoto thought that "it would be a good and kind idea to put them on the retirement list with adequate pension." Segregated churches seemed to be the only possibility for their employment.[14]

Disagreements among Nikkei pastors surfaced outside of the Denver conference. The Reverend Mihara from Minidoka argued, "Christian forces must stand united as never before . . . in light of the [world's] pressing problems." He described segregated worship as "disastrous" for Nikkei and claimed that most Minidokans wanted to join "regular [white] denominational churches." Others testified that Minidokans felt otherwise. Some Nikkei pastors seemed to consider their ethnic churches to be aberrant, subordinate Christian institutions. An Issei Christian leader reportedly remarked, "In years to come we will see the good of it all, we shall be really a part of America and not only a part of a Japanese community in America." A pastor at Arkansas's Rohwer incarceration camp, Joseph Fukushima, expressed similar feelings, believing that segregated worship would be detrimental to the postwar world. He wrote that Nikkei must accept their responsibilities as "builders for tomorrow." But other Protestant leaders at Rohwer thought integration was "impossible," declaring that "there will be Japanese churches as long as there are Japanese people in America." Issei ministers at Wyoming's Heart Mountain incarceration camp favored ethnic ecumenical churches after the war. A number of Nikkei agreed with white leaders that integration would lead to "normal" American Christian lives, while others felt uncomfortable in a segregated church after living a more integrated life in the East during the war.[15]

These statements show that the sides of this debate were not racially homogenous; the struggle was not Japanese Christians versus white Christians. Numerous white leaders working in the camps thought that ethnic churches needed to exist for pragmatic and ideological reasons, and some Nikkei pastors believed that the formation of a peaceful church, nation, and world required integration. The conflict was not purely a racial struggle for power or authority, but racial inequalities affected how Christians negotiated the disagreement. Despite having operated independent, self-sufficient churches before the war, white leaders ruled that Nikkei pastors would do so no longer.

Racial stereotypes supported the intelligence and capabilities of Japanese people, but the majority of white Americans did not consider the minority to be social equals. Many white missionaries still thought in paternalistic terms though they had ceded control of most Japanese churches in the United States before the war. The Protestant Commission believed that Nisei's "high degree of ability to integrate . . . into American society . . . fully justified" the policy. They admitted that integration would require "special effort, courage and self-sacrifice" but felt it was for the Nikkei's own good and the good of the nation. An informal committee at the Denver conference noted confusing contradictions: "Programs for evacuees must be satisfying to the evacuees," but "there has been too much emphasis on what the Nisei want." As occurred throughout the war, national Protestant leaders made decisions based on long-term goals for national unity and American Protestantism. Ultimately, the majority of participants and observers at the conference voted to integrate the churches. While it is unclear who participated in this vote, an equal number of Nikkei and white church workers served as official delegates. White observers outnumbered Nikkei observers by seven. While this may have tilted the vote in favor of integration, race did not fully determine its outcome.[16]

The majority of Denver conference participants concluded, "Integration must not only be the ultimate ideal; . . . it should become the immediate ideal as well." Believing the most Christian option was a church united by racial diversity, leaders christened it the "most ideal and the most practical." Member churches and ecumenical organizations affiliated with the Home Missions Council and the Protestant Church Commission received a policy statement after the December 1943 meeting and again on 18 January 1945 when Nikkei began returning to the West Coast. The document encouraged white pastors across the country to invite Nikkei into their churches and instructed regional authorities to prevent Christians from establishing or reopening ethnically segregated churches. It would be an exaggeration to say that most American congregations welcomed Nikkei, but regional ecumenical groups across the country worked for this end.[17]

This statement and the meeting minutes from Denver suggest a consensus on the plan to eliminate Japanese ethnic churches, but United Methodists disagreed, as did many Nikkei and white individuals. While Methodists agreed to send Nikkei to predominantly white churches east of the Rockies, they never consented to the elimination of ethnic churches on the West Coast. Moreover, church leaders never consulted the predominantly white congregations that Nikkei were to join. Several vigorously opposed worshiping alongside people they saw as the enemy, and many felt little compulsion to welcome Nikkei, let alone evangelize to others.[18]

Maryknoll held similar motivations. Bishop James Walsh explained, "It is time now for these good people to settle down in their local parishes." Echoing Protestant perspectives, he acknowledged that it would require "a lot of hard problems for our good Japanese," but "this period of transition can be made providential . . . if it is used to wean them away from the separatism of our former . . . mission to an incorporation in the normal stream of American life." While they expected this to be a simple matter, overcrowded parochial schools could not or would not accept returning Nikkei children. Others disagreed with integration because the

Catholic Church had separate missions for African Americans, Chinese, and Mexicans. Why should the Japanese be singled out?[19]

## Resettlement

Integrating churches was part of an expansive plan to incorporate Japanese Americans into communities throughout the country. President Roosevelt favored "a gradual release program designed to scatter" the ethnic community. To "[avoid] public outcry," he hoped to "distribute" Nikkei systematically, sending one or two families to each county of the country.[20] Howard K. Beale, a director of the Student Relocation Council, shared the sentiments of government officials and many national church leaders, stating, "This whole process of mass evacuation may possibly bring good, if the Japanese are scattered throughout the country—no more 'Little Tokyos.'"[21] Prewar ethnic enclaves, usually enforced by racial housing restrictions, had drawn resentment from white residents who assumed that immigrants did not wish to mix with other Americans. Progressive leaders hoped the elimination of visible segregation would remove that social barrier.

Mainline Protestant leaders fully endorsed the government's integration efforts. The Protestant Church Commission for Japanese Service supported wide distribution as a "sounder social policy" than resettling Nikkei in groups because it would "maintain the American character of citizens, aid in the Americanization of non-citizens, and foster good morale." Such rhetoric echoed concerns that the ethnically homogenous nature of camp life would hinder or even reverse assimilation. In many people's eyes, immigrants and their descendants could not become true Americans if they primarily associated with one another.[22]

Many Christian activists immediately seized responsibility for resettlement. Catholics, Quakers, and Congregationalists had already tried to move as many coastal Nikkei as possible before their forced exile. Some church leaders felt this responsibility was unavoidable, having little to no confidence that the government could resettle Nikkei. In April 1942, Clarence Gillett, the executive secretary of the Congregational Christian Committee for Work with Japanese Evacuees, wrote, "There is no doubt in my mind but that the seeking of places for relocating Japanese and Nisei in small groups, is one of the best things that we can do."[23] In July 1942, E. Stanley Jones, a Methodist missionary working closely with the AFSC, proposed that the government "turn over the Japanese . . . to us [the AFSC] for settlement across the country." He envisioned the AFSC administering the project while the FCC encouraged churches to participate. Clarence Pickett, executive secretary of the AFSC, felt this was not realistic; Gordon Chapman and others did not want Friends leading the project.[24] Jones insisted they focus on resettlement and began the first constructive national debates about resettling all Nikkei. At the time, most Nikkei still occupied the temporary assembly centers, but Jones urged Quakers and mainline Protestants to organize mass resettlement plans. Numerous individuals were planning such ventures but lacked a unified approach. Jones acknowledged these difficulties but advised that it would be better to fail than "succeed in doing nothing."[25]

Christian leaders prioritized resettlement for different reasons. Some considered it to be a social aid project while others emphasized civic justice and its theological necessity. They agreed with the WRA that the incarceration's aftermath would be extremely difficult and recognized the need for public support. In March 1943, the FCC voted that "the program of resettlement . . . deserves the wholehearted support and cooperation of the Protestant churches in America." They added that Japanese Americans "should be accorded the same privileges and freedom as are the rights of other Americans." Two months later, a brochure issued by the Committee on Resettlement of Japanese Americans combined Christian and patriotic duties by describing resettlement as a "concrete Christian enterprise which is at the same time democratic and, in the best sense of the term, American." It explained that Christians have a "special responsibility" to alleviate the incarceration. The Presbyterian Board of National Missions warned of the incarceration's immense "Christian implications."[26]

The Reverend Daisuke Kitagawa, who later became an active leader in the World Council of Churches, spoke of resettlement as "primarily a religious duty and not a political movement." Tolerating the mere existence of the camps, he insisted, was "an inexcusable sin on the part of the Christians" because confinement destroyed "the dignity of home or sacredness of family life" and dampened motivation to develop "constructive" lives. He believed that such "complacency" could "not be tolerated . . . from the Christian standpoint." Echoing the Social Gospel, Kitagawa explained that the incarceration harmed all Christians by implicating them in its sin.[27]

The churches encouraged all incarcerees, not just Christians, to resettle in 1943 and 1944. Aid workers like the AFSC's Floyd Schmoe gave presentations and offered private counseling to incarcerees, advising them of opportunities outside. Christian youth groups held discussions and panel forums on the topic. The Congregational Committee designed two fliers to alleviate fears of the life outside the camps. One directed Nisei "How to Be Happy 'Outside' "; the other, "Why Leave?" was in Japanese for Issei.[28] Both omitted discussions of religion. Church staff filled newsletters with stories of successful resettlement and news from men in the army, as did camp newspapers. Reprinted letters from resettlers described unexpected homesickness for camp but almost always ended with a positive statement about life on the outside and a call for others to follow them out.[29] They saved less positive stories for private correspondence but still rarely complained.

A number of white and Nikkei pastors toured the nation to estimate the potential of various regions to serve as resettlement communities. Schmoe made a film of different resettlement communities during a scouting mission to excite incarcerees about life outside.[30] The Arkansas pastor George Aki and his wife, Misaki, traveled to Chicago and St. Louis in the summer of 1943, reporting to their congregation in Jerome incarceration center that the former city was a "sad place for Japanese" despite the good jobs. He encouraged congregants to relocate to St. Louis, a "much more friendly city" inhabited by "better people."[31] Father Leopold Tibesar described the success of Nikkei in Spokane, Washington, but cautioned that an increasing number of hotels and restaurants refused to serve them.[32] As people moved out of the camps, pastors wrote letters of introduction to local churches and helped former congregants transfer church memberships.[33] Tibesar, Emery Andrews, Everett Thompson, and other missionaries working in the camps would ask local clergymen to visit resettlers and help them adapt to their new community. Likewise, ministers on the outside wrote camp pastors for referral letters when resettlers wished to join their churches.[34] Recognizing the benefits of this process, the chief of the WRA's Community Management Division requested that all clergy adopt the practice.[35]

Christian Nisei eager to leave camp asked their prewar ministers for help finding jobs and housing. Many incarcerees willingly took menial positions in order to leave camp. One young woman wrote, "I must have some kind of an employment out in East. Now, Mr. Andrews, I am asking for your help. I know you must know some people living out in Chicago where I can get a job even as a house girl. I would appreciate it a lot if you would see what you can do for me. I know I would be much happier working like that than living here." Incarcerees trusted church leaders to find them more suitable employment than they might obtain through the WRA's limited programs. White pastors attempted to place non-Christians as well, but many host families and churches wanted only Christians. And despite efforts to screen hosts, some sponsors saw resettlement as a "golden opportunity to obtain slave labor at bargain prices, . . . kid[ding] themselves that they are performing a big charity in taking in such people." The failure of white Americans to see the missionary possibilities in supporting non-Catholic resettlers disappointed Fathers Tibesar and Lavery.[36]

Catholic workers in and out of the camps prioritized resettlement. Maryknoll's James Drought worried that the insular ethnic colonies organized in the camps would breed resentment from other Americans and harm the nation's international reputation. Understanding that allies and enemies monitored America's actions, the author and former Presbyterian missionary Pearl S. Buck recommended Maryknoll prioritize resettlement. She hoped every Christian community would take responsibility for a few families to "give a living proof of the reality of our democracy and of our Christianity."[37]

While Catholic attempts to move Nikkei to the interior during the spring of 1942 failed, Tibesar never abandoned plans to organize Nikkei Catholic colonies. After Maryknoll discouraged Tibesar's idea to move people onto land in southern Idaho, he mobilized his family members to survey land and seek employment for Nikkei near his home town of Quincy, Illinois. He considered the quality of farm land and the time needed for Nikkei to adopt farming methods for new crops and obtain equipment, as well as the temperament of locals. He ordered soil analyses and promised locals that Nikkei would extend the region's limited irrigation systems. Plans to establish a community in Quincy never came to fruition, however, as negative responses from locals slowed the project in April 1943. Additionally, since the government discouraged group resettlement, they would not provide funds to support such a venture. Individual students and families still entered Quincy with assistance from Tibesar's brother, Seraphin Tibesar.[38]

Leopold Tibesar wanted to find "Catholic environment[s]" for his people for several reasons. First, he hoped that increased toleration would strengthen American Catholicism by taking a "stand on Catholic grounds and defend these people in their Catholic rights . . . whether we like their color—or noses—or not." Second, he believed parishioners would welcome Nikkei if their priests and bishops steadfastly supported resettlement. Third, Tibesar worried that unbaptized Nikkei might lose their interest in Catholicism.[39]

After surveying cities for resettlement possibilities in the summer of 1944, Tibesar recommended that Maryknoll assign someone to coordinate resettlement from outside of the camps. Volunteering for the position, Tibesar made plans to leave Minidoka for Chicago. Only fifty Catholics remained at the camp by the fall of 1944 when Hugh Lavery sent Clement Boesflug to minister to their needs until the camp's closure. Tibesar's new duties included finding jobs and housing for incarcerees, meeting with local priests to garner support for resettlers, helping resettlers join their new parish churches and parochial schools, coordinating social and religious gatherings for resettled Nikkei, and hearing confessions of non-English speakers in the region. The Catholic Youth Organization worked with Tibesar and Brother Theophane Walsh to open a community center for Nikkei in Chicago. An exceptional social activist, the city's bishop Bernard Shiel helped fund the venture because he supported its goals and considered it an archdiocesan affair. Nearly one hundred Nisei attended its open house in April 1945, and a "steady trickle" later visited to ask questions or socialize with other Catholics.[40]

While Nikkei encountered fewer restrictions in the Midwest and East than they had on the West Coast, racial discrimination still limited their access to public services and housing on many occasions. To alleviate that concern in Chicago, the AFSC contacted nearly one hundred of the city's physicians, surgeons, dentists, and optometrists to establish reliable contacts for resettlers. When crematoriums or cemeteries refused to accept Nikkei bodies, AFSC representatives lodged complaints and helped families obtain alternative services. The AFSC sought to eliminate housing and employment discrimination throughout the country.[41]

Urban hostels were perhaps the most beneficial form of aid provided by religious groups. The WRA initially required incarcerees to secure housing and employment or acceptance to a school before leaving the camps, but incarcerees and potential employers found this arrangement untenable. Quakers developed the idea of operating hostels where Nikkei could live while finding employment and permanent housing. The WRA agreed to this plan and soon pressured American churches to use all available property as hostels for resettling or returning Nikkei. A short hostel stay became a primary way for Nikkei to leave the camps. Quakers, the Brethren, and mainline denominations opened hostels throughout the country.[42]

Ralph and Mary Smeltzer, previously teachers at Manzanar incarceration center, developed one of the first hostels under the auspices of the Church of the Brethren Service Commission in Chicago. It opened in March 1943 and set a precedent for similar operations. Hostels functioned as community living spaces where resettlers paid minimal fees, usually a dollar a day, for room and board. They helped with chores, such as gardening and cooking. Hostelers stayed for a week and a half on average before securing permanent employment and housing. Most hostels housed around thirty people at a time, though some had room for up to one hundred Nikkei. Since each hostel had a limited capacity, incarcerees had to apply for admission. Hostel operators judged applicants on their potential for employment but also considered their character as described by white pastors or camp administrators. Accepted Nikkei received detailed travel instructions with their invitation, advising them where to sit on the train, who to look for at the station, and what to eat on the journey. Some hostels required Nikkei to attend group discussions about re-acclimating to life outside of the camps.[43]

The WRA and church workers gave resettlers strict advice for their new lives. Both encouraged Nikkei to make "hakujin" (white) friends, live inconspicuously, and "learn to 'take it': Do not let discrimination and persecution bother you and do not get a martyr complex. . . . Do not fight back." Some aid workers warned Nikkei that they must be exemplary neighbors even if mistreated. While hostel operators and other outsiders involved in the resettlement process informed resettlers of their rights, they also reminded Nikkei that their actions "directly affect those who come after" them. People labeled Nikkei who quit or changed their jobs "six week Japs," suggesting the unreliability of resettlers. Nikkei were warned not to do anything that would harm the reputation of Japanese Americans or damage their fragile public acceptance.[44]

The resettlement program relied on the successful assimilation and good nature of the first arrivals. When Monica Itoi left Minidoka, the director of the local WRA Employment Office warned her that quitting her job would give Nisei "a reputation as poor risks." Despite repeated clashes with her employer, she worried that he might "go around telling everybody Nisei aren't any good" if she left. Fortunately, a college scholarship allowed her to leave his employment gracefully. While this placed unfair and even hazardous pressure on Nikkei, Itoi's concern was merited by the level of discrimination against returnees. A woman in Iowa told Clarence Gillett of the Congregational Committee that her friends were interested in hosting Nisei but would not consent before seeing "what kind of a girl" came to her house. The WRA publicized photographs like Figure 11, which shows Monica Itoi entering a church in Indianapolis, to show successful assimilation.[45]

Despite these challenges, many Nikkei assembled satisfying lives outside of the camps. Monica Itoi's friend Matsuko found a job and a host family in Chicago through church workers and wrote that "for the first time in her life . . . she was breathing free and easy . . . and no longer felt self-conscious about her Oriental face." Itoi's siblings and sister-in-law also had positive experiences as they left Minidoka for work outside. Itoi took their advice, and the Reverend Everett Thompson introduced her to Dr. and Mrs. John Richardson, former missionaries to China who lived in a Chicago suburb. The couple welcomed her into their family and found her a receptionist job. A number of host families in the Midwest anxiously awaited the arrival of former incarcerees. One woman bought a new Easter outfit for the Nisei girl coming to work in her home. She and her friends wanted to begin "making up to her for the humiliation of camp life." Others wrote to the incarcerated parents of young Nisei to express their excitement and reassure them of their children's happiness. Thomas Sasaki expressed his deep gratitude to Tibesar for helping him leave camp and then finding good placements for his parents and younger sisters in Detroit. Upon being drafted, he felt confident that his family was well settled and happy in their new lives.[46]

College students resettled most successfully. Monica Itoi's host family arranged a work-study scholarship for her through a former missionary colleague who now worked as the president of Hanover College, a Presbyterian liberal arts school in Indiana. She lived with a minister's widow near campus. Itoi made friends with American and international classmates, and many campus organizations welcomed Itoi and the other three Nisei on campus. Though national rules barred her from sorority membership, the officers and faculty advisor of one such group apologized to Itoi personally and pledged their friendship. Sororities at some other schools, including the University of Pennsylvania, did initiate Nikkei. Nisei joined student governments, sports teams, and clubs. Kenji Okuda became the first Nisei elected as Oberlin College's student body president, and classmates of a Nisei in Texas voted her "Most Charming Girl."[47]

FIGURE 11 Monica Itoi (right) attending church in Indianapolis, August 1943.
Source: WRA Photograph Collection, Bancroft Library, University of California,
Berkeley.

The rapid influx of Nikkei to popular resettlement areas made some people uneasy about public gatherings of Japanese Americans. The largest number of Nikkei moved to Chicago. While only 390 people of Japanese descent lived in that city in 1940, 15,000 to 20,000 resided there by the end of 1946. The population of free Nikkei in Colorado grew by 9,000 over the course of the war, though 5,500 soon returned to the West Coast. Utah saw a similar fluctuation in its number of Nikkei.[48] Nisei worried about public opinion and feared reprisal. Sue Aromura, a Nisei in Ann Arbor, Michigan, noted her surprise at meeting "so many Hunt [Minidokan] Nisei . . . in such a small college town." She felt "quite conspicuous" and asked Andrews if he did not think it was "a bit overpopulated for such a small community."[49] In areas like these, integrationists could not keep Nikkei from meeting and spending time with one another.

But many Nikkei felt lonesome as they adjusted to regular life and coped with racial stigmas. Andrews regularly visited resettled Minidokans because many were "lonely and [did] not feel at home."[50] Bob Kiino, a teenager in Kalamazoo, Michigan, wrote his former camp teacher about his struggles to find a Nisei girl to date.[51] Kiino enjoyed the company of many white friends, but he did not consider dating white girls. Tibesar noted the endemic loneliness of resettlers who were "treated well" but missed family and friends back in camp. A student in St. Louis admitted she was "considering marriage 'to end it all.'"[52] The intense loneliness felt by many resettled Nikkei could not be overcome without their lifelong friends, who happened to be Japanese. But as people flooded out of the camps, those remaining described the "lonesomeness of camp life."[53] Memoirs and oral histories show that, for incarcarees, leaving camp and rebuilding their lives were frequently more challenging than the incarceration itself.[54]

Some Nikkei pastors disapproved of the mainline churches' unwavering support for the WRA's resettlement program. While they did not want to encourage resistance, the pastors did not believe religious leaders should bring "such controversial problems" into the church. They feared morale would drop lower if religious leaders pressured incarcerees to resettle.[55] George Rundquist, executive secretary of the Committee on Resettlement of Japanese Americans, reported that incarcerees were "sick of discussing the matter" by 1944.[56] Nikkei at Minidoka asked Floyd Schmoe to speak about Quaker beliefs instead of the scheduled lecture on resettlement.[57] Incarceree Akira Kikuchi requested that the churches focus on spiritual needs, since the churches' aid looked like cooperation with the government.[58] Tom Fukuyama reserved most of his criticism for the WRA, suspicious of its broader program. He wrote, "The cold sociological interest of some of the WRA personnel sickens me. All they want to see is a high rate of relocation without consideration of the human problems involved. Wonder[ing] how lone individuals in far off places feel," he questioned whether outsiders should "admire" resettlement. He felt that "human sentiment and bonds of fellowship [were] sacred" and must be respected, regardless of race or political pressure.[59] While he shared these doubts with his fiancée, his articles for Minidoka's Federated Church newsletter predicted that the eviction would have "a beneficial effect . . . in the long run as people migrated Eastward and really become a part of a greater America."[60] Most Nikkei and white pastors supported resettlement.

The way in which the government and mainline Protestant leaders wanted Nikkei to resettle complicated the matter further. Gillett recognized that resettlement was "as much an obligation on the part of the Japanese who goes out as on the Caucasian who welcomes him." Government officials and Protestant aid workers shared this understanding and instructed Nikkei to avoid one another after leaving camp to foster social integration. In addition to restricting the formation of Nikkei churches, Protestant aid societies advised Nikkei to "avoid Nisei dances and Nisei churches" and not "cling only to Nisei friends." Expressing a common view among older Japanese, a Methodist Issei called the government's attempt to destroy their communities a tragedy, saying "he would rather stay [in camp] with friends and die with them." After the government took virtually everything else away from them, Issei depended on "Japanese community, their friends and associates, and their common cultural background." Loss of community and a desire to return directly to the coast led many Issei to remain in the camps until forced out. The majority returned to the coast after the camps closed in 1945.[61]

Most white Quakers and Catholics approved of dispersion in principle, but neither group pressured Nikkei to comply nor made efforts to spread resettlers to new areas. Both Floyd Schmoe and Leopold Tibesar spoke vehemently against the effects of dispersed resettlement. Schmoe's November 1944 treatise "Dispersal No Solution" argued that "the unjust policy of wide dispersal . . . denies opportunity, comfort, and peace of mind to the unhappy victim." He desired a wider distribution of the population and interracial marriage but thought they must happen naturally. Schmoe believed Midwest and East Coast leaders had a skewed vision of the situation because they met only successful resettlers who had integrated into broader society. Young people could manage the challenge, but he knew dispersion would cause "tragic and unnecessary hardship" for the thousands still in camp. AFSC workers were critical "not of [voluntary] segregation itself, but of the injustices and inequities inevitably arising from it." Institutional records reveal a concern for the "vicious circle" by which discrimination causes a minority group to become more insular, which in turn "invite[s] further discrimination." They worried about the problems caused by segregated communities but sought to change public sentiment rather than minority groups themselves. Increasing public acceptance, they hoped, would naturally create more diverse, integrated communities.[62]

Catholic leaders eventually recommended the integration of parishes on the coast but tried to resettle incarcerees in groups to sustain community ties. Tibesar continually attempted to organize group resettlement. Despite frequent discouragement from the WRA, local bishops, and Maryknoll, he persistently tried to relocate his people as a group. When the WRA announced its dispersal plans, he wrote to Bishop Walsh, "I look upon this as unnatural and cruel and a slap at the Japanese people. . . . I feel then that the Japanese should not accept this scattering of their people without protest since to do so would be to admit they are not worthy of trust nor of their civil rights as citizens."[63] He blamed Protestants for developing the plan. Maryknoll leaders did not discourage small groups from resettling together but considered Tibesar's hopes for resettling hundreds together unreasonable given the political situation. Irritated with Maryknoll's decision to "be realists and handle the situation with all its prejudices as we find it," Tibesar continued to work toward group resettlement.[64]

Despite their best efforts, churches could not solve the immense problem of resettling 120,000 individuals. Struggling to meet the needs of Nikkei returning to the West Coast, participants of the National Conference of Japanese Americans wrote to President Truman in November 1945 to request that the government address its "peculiar responsibility" for these problems.[65] Leopold Tibesar asked Maryknoll to place pressure on the government to fulfill its obligations. He hoped they would fight for resettlement on religious grounds as he felt that "our national democratic ideals are Christian ideals and should be defended as such."[66] Tibesar speculated that the "crystallizing of Camp opinion against [resettlement]" came from a "lack of confidence" in the government and frustrations that it "does not understand them or their problems."[67] The churches' efforts to resettle incarcerees provided an essential service for the U.S. government but could not overcome the lack of housing and jobs.

## Worship in Resettlement Communities

The success of integrated worship relied on support from Nikkei pastors. If they held their own meetings, Nikkei would have little reason to frequent predominantly white churches. The Chicago Council of Churches decreased this possibility by employing Nikkei ministers to strengthen ties with the ethnic community. This secured support from pro-integration Nikkei ministers who felt "purposely . . . left out" elsewhere. The Chicago Council hoped its program would make resettlers feel more welcome. Receiving a joint invitation from a Nikkei pastor and a white church member secured the interest of more resettlers than an invitation from the latter alone, and Nikkei counselors facilitated the transition of newcomers into their new churches. About half of the Nisei Christians in Chicago joined established churches during the war, making the city's integration program one of the most successful in the country. A number of Nikkei pastors still hosted segregated fellowship meetings and worship services, however, drawing Nikkei away from local white churches. The Chicago Council only hired Nikkei from denominations that supported their ministry financially, which narrowed the breadth of integration. Employed clergymen complained that churches called them to positions of "semisecular" social work only, not Christian ministry. The First Baptist Church of Chicago, a notable exception, called Jitsuo Morikawa despite the opposition of many congregants. Morikawa won their favor and soon invited African Americans to expand the church's diversity further.[68]

Integration frequently failed due to a lack of organization. While strong regional ecumenical organizations led efforts in the nation's largest cities, pastors in smaller locales like Columbus, Kansas City, and Denver lacked coordination.[69] The situation in Colorado, which Gordon Chapman called the "happy hunting grounds of every group," presented particular problems. White Protestant leaders in the area seem to have been under the impression that each denomination would be assigned a different region of the state in which to evangelize to Nikkei.[70] In June 1943, Chapman reported, "There is a good deal of mutual treading on each other's toes already."[71] This disorganization resulted in the formation of ethnic churches. Colorado pastors requested a white missionary in 1944, complaining that the Japanese pastor in the area failed to adequately integrate his congregants. They seemed unaware that the FCC had assigned them that task.[72]

The history of discrimination in the American West also hindered integration. Several white pastors in Colorado and eastern Washington would not allow resettlers to use their buildings, let alone join their congregations. Church members acted "hostile" to Japanese Americans in those regions.[73] After visiting resettlers around the country in the fall of 1943, Minidoka's Tom Fukuyama expressed displeasure about the "Little Tokyo" forming in Denver but complimented Nikkei on their successful integration in the Midwest and East, where he felt the possibilities for integration were greater.[74]

## The Return

Rumors of lifting the West Coast restrictions began circulating in early 1944, but Roosevelt withheld the announcement until securing his reelection. On 17 December 1944, Public Proclamation 21 rescinded the exclusion orders for most Japanese Americans and Japanese nationals living in the United States. Within an hour of Roosevelt's announcement, church councils on the West Coast began calling for congregations to support returning Nikkei.

Nikkei welcomed this news, but few knew how to proceed. Most had lost their homes, farms, and jobs. Was it even safe to return to the West Coast? Emery Andrews repeatedly stated that Nikkei did not know where to go or how to get there. Most were "bewildered and uncertain what to do. . . . Many outside of camp lack security and have feelings of frustration."[75] A few Nikkei pastors made plans to return to the coast quickly and be "pioneers" for their congregants.[76] Pastors selected willing families to "act as guinea pigs" by returning to communities with "serious opposition" to Nikkei.[77] Andrews began driving carloads of released families from Idaho to Seattle soon after the government lifted the restrictions. By mid-February 1945, only 150 Nikkei had returned to Seattle, but that number grew to 700 by July and approximately 1,500 by September.[78] The prewar population of Seattle Nikkei had approached 7,000. The majority of Nikkei returned to the Pacific Coast by mid-1947.[79]

Many Christian leaders on the West Coast had petitioned for the return of Nikkei for over a year, but the responses of coastal residents ranged from happiness to hostility. Reports of welcoming neighbors raised hopes, but boycotts, vandalism, storefronts reading "No Japs Allowed," severe unemployment, and housing shortages barraged Nikkei as well. Most discrimination was not violent, but vandals destroyed or stole around a quarter of the property left behind by Seattle's Nikkei.[80]

Members of Seattle's Remember Pearl Harbor League spoke vociferously against the return, aiming attacks at both Nikkei and the white church members who supported them. Principally, they cited the "menace" Nikkei posed "at the very time armed forces . . . are at death grips with the most dangerous foe in the history of our nation." Japanese invasion no longer threatened the coast, but some Americans feared retribution from Japanese living in the United States. In an open letter to all church groups, the league asked, "Are you good ministers unmindful of the menace these Japs you are pleading for will be when they see our valiant soldiers invade to destroy the only nation to whom these Japanese-Americans are loyal? Surely, you gentlemen of the cloth, know that every Japanese-American you seem to favor has been indoctrinated with sadistic philosophy emperor worship." The league carefully avoided questioning the patriotism of Seattle ministers but placed doubt on the religious leaders' perception of the situation. It portrayed pastors as well meaning but dangerously "misguided."[81]

The Seattle pastor U. G. Murphy submitted a sharp response. His editorial compared members of the league to Southern slave owners, Hitler, and the pharaoh of Exodus, reminding readers of the disasters that befell these perpetrators of racial discrimination and subjugation. Murphy's public response typified the new outspoken defense of Japanese Americans among church leaders. Murphy also scolded the league for "attempting to belittle the Church."[82] While Seattleites were divided in their feelings about Nikkei returning to their homes, ecumenical organizations and most mainline Protestant churches fully supported Nikkei's rights.[83]

Nikkei faced greater problems outside of Seattle, where belligerent "patriots" destroyed property and refused to sell Nikkei insurance, business licenses, or fishing permits, all of which led banks to decline their loan applications.[84] Despite the existence of twenty-three hostels in Los Angeles alone, religious and nonreligious humanitarian groups could not support the thousands of Nikkei "dumped," as Clarence Gillett described it, into Southern California.[85] He explained that the WRA opened six emergency camps in the fall of 1945, subjecting 1,500 former incarcerees "to a plan of psychological intimidation and terrorism."[86] This conduct ruined the WRA's remarkably good reputation. In May 1946, Nikkei remaining in these temporary camps—over half of the original group—were removed to a run-down, unsanitary trailer camp. Over three-fourths of the trailers lacked electricity and running water. The County Bureau of Public Assistance had to bring mobile kitchen units to feed the hundreds of Nikkei.[87] With the support of the Congregational Committee, Gillett coordinated relief efforts with the ACLU, the AFSC, and regional and national welfare agencies, all of which tried to tackle the overwhelming task of restoring civil rights to a population that had lost everything and been displaced for years. Religious groups petitioned the WRA, President Truman, and other officials to take responsibility for incarcerees with little success.[88]

Emery Andrews composed a prescient list of the general and specific needs of Seattle's Nikkei community: conversion of the Seattle Japanese Baptist Church into a temporary hostel, a business agent to secure jobs and negotiate potential boycotts, an increase in pastoral visitations, special fellowship meetings, and people to drive Nikkei to and from church "until they are actually a part of that church."[89] The Protestant Church Commission, the AFSC, and other Christian groups shared Andrews's first priority, the organization of hostels.[90] Most Nikkei had lost their homes and had nowhere to go. Hundreds of Seattle Nikkei of all religious backgrounds found temporary shelter at hostels in what had been the prewar Episcopalian, Methodist, and Congregational Japanese churches and a center operated by the AFSC. Returning Seattleites still needed more space but avoided the Los Angeles housing crisis.[91]

A number of Christian organizations coalesced to help Seattle's returnees. The Christian Friends for Racial Equality worked through political and educational channels to reduce racial discrimination in hiring practices.[92] Floyd Schmoe and Andrews created the Japanese-American Relocation Project Work Camp, an interracial group of student volunteers.[93] University of Washington students ran a weekly Saturday Work Party that helped Nikkei reopen their businesses.[94] The AFSC continued to help Nikkei as well; their members cultivated fields, moved belongings, and scrubbed racist graffiti from houses and storefronts.[95] For a full year after their release from the incarceration camps, Nikkei in Seattle could not sell their produce on the open market because the Teamsters union refused to haul their crops. Aid workers distributed and sold the harvest from Nikkei farms, returning the profits to the farmers at the end of the day.[96]

Maryknoll's Father John Walsh, who had taken charge of the Seattle mission when Tibesar left in 1942, dealt with the problems of returning Catholics as best he could. Since the Seattle Maryknoll church had remained open for Filipino and Chinese Americans during the war, Nikkei could rejoin their prewar parish immediately. Most Nikkei affiliated with Maryknoll had resettled in the Midwest earlier in the war, so they returned to Seattle slowly. The first to return found jobs in Catholic institutions, but by July 1945, Walsh wrote, "We are doing what we can for them and . . . that seems to be precious little if anything!" He visited the federal employment agency on behalf of returnees only to learn that the agency was doing its best, but employers refused to interview Nikkei or rejected them at first sight. Seattle's bishop Gerald Shaughnessy also helped Maryknollers find job placements. Housing shortages posed a greater problem than jobs so Walsh went house hunting himself. Laws capped rents but not sale prices, so landlords would refuse to rent to Nikkei but offer exorbitant sale prices. Maryknoll sisters negotiated challenges when the staff of a Seattle health care center threatened to quit if Nikkei moved on site. Walsh considered turning the former school building into temporary housing, but plans never got off the ground.[97]

In April 1945, the Seattle Council of Churches formed the United Church Ministry to Returning Japanese (UCM) to coordinate social outreach and integrate Nikkei Protestants into the city's established white churches. The group helped Nikkei open and reactivate bank accounts, locate housing and jobs, and move belongings out of storage. The council also initiated a "Newcomer" program through which church workers visited returning families to welcome them back to the community and refer them to a local church of their denominational preference.[98] Aware that not all congregations would accept Nikkei, the council asked "select" area ministers to accept Nikkei into their churches.[99]

The policies and rhetoric of the Seattle Council of Churches enthusiastically supported the rules about integrated worship instituted in Denver. The ecumenical organization's leaders voted unanimously to integrate "the Japanese people into regular, established denominational churches" in 1943 and again on 19 February 1945. The council discussed the possibility that its plans might conflict with the wishes of Nikkei but concluded that a "return to the old pattern" would "be hard to justify." Echoing Roosevelt's hope to reassimilate Nikkei by diluting their visible solidarity, the Seattle Council urged churches to "do everything we can . . . to assimilate these people in the *normal* community life by tying them to . . . *regular* churches" (emphasis added). Their notions of progress shone when speaking of the alternative: "reverting" to the "re-establishment" of ethnic churches. They saw a unique opportunity to "build anew" and "practice the principles and ideals for which Christianity stands."[100] Seattle Council members sounded empowered and invigorated in the face of this challenge, a chance to improve the church and secular society by creating what they understood to be a truer form of Christianity and "a new religious pattern in race relations." Gertrude Apel, the general secretary of the Seattle Council of Churches, expounded on the connection between racial tolerance and world peace in her 1945 annual report for the Washington State Council of Churches.[101] The Seattle Council believed the realization of her goals would benefit the nation and world, not just the church.

As a provision for potential discord, the Seattle Council of Churches established a moratorium on their decision to integrate churches. They planned to reevaluate the process on 1 May 1946 but would not change course until then. Following the Denver guidelines, the Seattle Council and other regional groups allowed Issei to form ecumenical, segregated, Japanese language churches and arranged for Issei pastors to direct their activities.[102] Other church councils along the coast ratified similar policies.[103]

The Seattle Council did not emulate Chicago's practice of employing Nikkei pastors but formed a Nisei steering committee to obtain their opinions. Steering committee members occasionally attended council meetings but usually expressed opinions through their white advisors. The precise transmission and influence of those messages is uncertain. In November 1945, the United Church Ministry pledged not to launch additional programs without the "definite approval" of the steering committee, suggesting that this had not always been the case. The UCM hoped this would decrease the "lack of unity and . . . sense of conflict" that had characterized Nisei programs.[104] However, the desires of Nikkei who wanted to reopen their former churches did not overpower the council until the latter lost all hope for integrated worship.

According to white representatives from each denomination, not every Japanese Protestant group in Seattle wished to re-form their denominational church at this time, but none wanted to join existing congregations. Congregational Nisei desired an interdenominational ethnic group led by a Nisei pastor. Methodists wanted a united service only if all denominations participated. Episcopalians preferred ethnic denominational churches united under a separate organization, essentially a Japanese Council of Churches. Presbyterians were reportedly "satisfied" but reserved the right to separate later.[105] The Baptists' desire for independence disappointed some groups, since it ended hopes for an ecumenical Japanese church. Notably, no group wished to follow the Council of Churches's plan to assimilate into established congregations; all wanted some form of a segregated church. Only a small number of individuals joined and remained in predominantly white churches.

When Nisei Baptists brought their desires for segregated fellowship to the UCM's attention in July 1945, they were overruled and dismissed. Andrews supported their plea by reporting that only twenty-five Nisei in Seattle attended "regular [white] churches." UCM members admitted that "it might be easier" to allow Nisei to worship together but believed it would be "detrimental to the group . . . in the long run." This sentiment echoed arguments made years earlier in Denver, where integrationists had cautioned that "the segregated church should not be perpetuated as a *practical* solution to an unfortunate historical practice." The UCM acknowledged the immediate challenges for Nisei, but council members overwhelmed petitioners by calling for everyone's "influence and support" in integrating youth. Harold Jensen persuaded the Baptists to "cooperate fully" with integration efforts "after considerable discussion." White organizers feared that a segregated fellowship group would detract from the "desired assimilation program." They saw universal benefits to integration but knew that, given the option, most Nisei would choose a segregated group over the current scheme.[106]

While the Seattle Council of Churches insisted that any group was "perfectly free" to establish its own church, the council and local churches controlled most Japanese church properties. At the time of the eviction, most Japanese churches on the coast had been signed over or "sold" to denominational or regional Christian groups for "the sum of $1.00," leaving Nikkei with no legal recourse to regain their buildings. Japanese congregations had to trust these groups "to do what [was] right with the property and to return it to the church if, and when, the congregation [was] able to return."[107] At the time, the transaction seemed sensible in case the government impounded Japanese Americans' property. The arrangement also allowed the buildings to be used for wartime purposes during the Nikkei's absence.[108] The Washington Baptist Convention gave the Seattle Council of Churches authority over the Japanese Baptist Church (JBC) until the May 1946 moratorium for Seattle's experimental integration. The Baptist Convention assured Nikkei that this was in their best interests and falsely claimed that Japanese Christian groups would retain their "utmost freedom in . . . Christian activities."[109] Similarly, the Seattle Council insisted that Nikkei could do as they liked but also cited the 1 May deadline after which point Nikkei "would be free to make their decisions."[110] Their contradictory messages frustrated ethnic church supporters. Practically speaking, Japanese ethnic congregations could not restore their churches without consent from the groups that held their deeds.[111]

Nisei eventually ignored the UCM's rules, and the steering committee formed the ecumenical Young People's Fellowship in the final months of 1945. While non-Japanese attended some functions, the Fellowship was a Nikkei club. Its composition and agenda resembled youth groups within the camps that invited guest speakers and intermittently held socials with local youth groups outside of camp. Between 60 and 125 Nisei, including several Buddhists and other non-Christians, gathered in churches around the city each week for three hours of singing, worship, and social activities. Leaders devoted one hour to music and worship, while participants socialized for two hours.[112] In December 1945, the young people went caroling and made Christmas gift baskets for the recently returned.[113] Ruth Mayasaka, a former Seattleite who resettled in Philadelphia, expressed what seems to have been a common sentiment. She complimented the "friendliness and kindness of Caucasians" but gushed about the fun had at Nisei social gatherings. She knew Protestant leaders discouraged Nikkei from attending segregated events but "realize[d] Niseis [sic] need[ed] social contacts and relaxation."[114]

The ways in which Nisei and white Protestants joined for worship in Seattle hindered the likelihood of integration. In the fall of 1945, members of the Young People's Fellowship attended Woodland Park Presbyterian, University Temple, University Baptist, and the Renton Baptist Church. Attending a different church each week reduced Nisei's ability to become part of an established congregation. The churches announced their presence and asked them to speak about life in the camps. While these churches literally welcomed Nisei, such events did not create any sense of normalcy or routine. Donald Toriumi observed that "Nisei do not respond" to such "elaborate . . . special events," and white church members thought that the minority group was not interested.[115] Being singled out made some Nikkei uncomfortable. The Quaker activist Gordon Hirabayashi astutely observed, "It is just as tragic to invite a Negro or a Japanese into a fellowship simply because he is Negro or Japanese as it is to restrict him on those grounds. The basis for true fellowship is on the grounds of common interest and personal quality."[116] Churches asked Nikkei to join not as individuals but as representatives of their ethnicity.

Most Nikkei expressed their opinion of the integration program through their actions: the vast majority simply stopped attending church regularly. Many visited white churches once or twice, but few joined these congregations. The low average age of the second generation at the time of the war meant that few Nisei had experience leading a congregation, let alone leading a social movement against local authorities in 1945. The war had interrupted the seminary training of the ethnic group's Nisei pastors. Moreover, the majority of socially active, motivated Nikkei had left the camps earlier in the war, moving to colleges or work in the East. Having established lives there, few immediately returned to the West Coast. Many others were not yet discharged from the army. Only elderly Issei pastors returned to Seattle immediately, so inexperienced laity led the city's youth groups. Thus, white pastors led most efforts to reestablish coastal Nikkei churches.

## Reopening Seattle's Japanese Ethnic Churches

Ethnic churches re-formed as integrationists relented and immediate needs overwhelmed desires for integration. By October 1945, Presbyterian Nikkei began holding separate services and opened a Sunday school in Seattle. Japanese Episcopalians also began meeting independently for Sunday services. Under the authority of Frank Herron Smith, the director of Japanese Methodist missions in California, a Nikkei pastor prepared to reopen Seattle's Japanese Methodist church in the spring of 1945, but the Seattle Council of Churches "immediately registered strong protests" and stalled his activities. The Japanese Baptist Church confronted the same problem. Neither group attained independence until mid-1946.[117]

In July 1945, Japanese Baptists refused a request to relinquish their parsonage, the only building they still held. Irritated with this outcome, Harold Jensen complained that the council might need to rethink its "entire hostel program" because of their "unwillingness." The UCM and the American Baptist Home Mission Society (ABHMS) had resisted Andrews's plans to convert rooms in the JBC into temporary living spaces that March. Andrews repeated this entreaty in every report to his superiors for months, but the Mission Society never permitted him to use the JBC as a hostel. With some bitterness and resignation, Jensen wrote to a Japanese pastor at Minidoka, "somehow the spirit of God was present and will continue to . . . direct the actions of the entire group so as to advance His cause." Jensen may have assumed "His cause" was the council's program to integrate churches.[118]

In the summer of 1945, Fujin Home, a Baptist society for Japanese women, reopened after "much deliberation." The Seattle Council returned this building relatively quickly because Nikkei Baptist pastors agreed to use the building for ecumenical Japanese language ministry to Issei. However, Nikkei refused to submit to the council and local Baptist authorities' request to remove the home's Baptist affiliation. The wife of a Japanese Baptist pastor had opened Fujin Home in 1904 to aid Japanese women, most of whom were not Christian. The facility provided resources and temporary homes for immigrant women, including many picture brides, as they adjusted to life in the United States. After the war, Fujin Home provided housing for returning Nikkei and organized gatherings for the "spiritual welfare" of Issei.[119]

Baptist missionary Esther McCullough operated the home after her return from southern Idaho. The Seattle Church Council emphatically ruled that she be under its administration, but her priorities clashed with those of the UCM. She pledged, "As I understand it, the [Nisei] Steering Committee is to steer us and I, personally, will go wherever they tell us to go."[120] While the Seattle Council did not contradict her, leaders doubted her commitment to the integration program for Christian "progress." Harold Jensen and others thought that McCullough could not be "objective in [her] thinking" after being "so close to the Japanese people and suffering so much with them."[121] Hinting at this distrust, they ordered that "Miss Esther McCullough . . . shall in every way cooperate with the Hostel Committee of the Council of Churches . . . and follow [its] rulings."[122] Their comment that McCullough lacked objectivity because of her close relationship with Nikkei became a frequent trope among combatants. Just as political leaders and other outsiders felt that the missionaries' contact with Nikkei tainted their perception of national security risks, regional and national leaders felt that the experiences of white religious workers in the camps hindered their perception of the goals of the global church.

A number of white congregants in Seattle supported the rights of returning Nikkei to reopen their churches, agreeing with Minidoka's former workers. Mainline representatives from the Japanese Women's Home Board wrote an unsympathetic letter to the Council of Churches. They criticized the council for not supporting Nikkei efforts to "build their own church physically and spiritually" before proposing major changes like integration and giving Nikkei cause to mistrust their few supporters. Mrs. F. R. Leach, a member of the Board, also sent a personal letter to Harold Jensen, expressing her disgust with the way things had been handled:

> Dear Dr. Jensen,
> If as much thought and trouble had been taken in helping and not hindering our returning Japanese Baptists, of welcoming them and not making them feel they had also been betrayed by the Church, and if a real Christian hand of fellowship had been given to their fine American pastor and consecrated missionaries, and the church had been helped onto its feet again, there would not be the unhappy situation which exists.
> I hang my head in shame.

Both letters reflected divisions within Seattle churches and further demonstrated that race did not define sides of the debate.[123]

White and Nikkei pastors fought with denominational and regional boards while trying to minster to their scattered congregants. Emery Andrews attempted to minister to the Nikkei community but avoided actions that might be perceived as re-forming an ethnic church. Andrews could not reopen the JBC without authorization from his denominational superiors, due to its status as a mission church chartered by the ABHMS. Andrews remained on its payroll despite the absence of a church. The Mission Society recognized the need for continued support even if it did not want a formal Baptist mission to Nikkei. Andrews did not lack for work; he made pastoral house calls to nearly three hundred Nikkei each month following his return to Seattle. In response to continual difficulties, Andrews insisted to his superiors, "[The churches] need to be opened NOW. . . . The people in camp have been betrayed by so many people—the government, some WRA employees, so-called friends who promised to keep their things but stole them instead—that they have had only their church to sustain their hope. For the past three months it has been when? when? when? is the church and the [Fujin] Home going to be opened. If those buildings are sold or are not opened, it will be the last straw. The church, the one thing they have confidence [in], will have failed them. The Bud[d]hist group and other groups are going ahead, but no word from the church." Andrews's distress could not be hidden. After moving his family to the desert for three years to support Seattle's Nikkei community, the ABHMS and the Seattle Council of Churches now tied his hands. He sounded helpless and increasingly angry.[124]

While authorities thought integration into established churches would result in the rapid assimilation of Nikkei into the larger society, Andrews saw their plan disintegrating. His fear that the program would cause Nisei to leave the church and end effective evangelism to the community became a reality. Andrews reported that "many niseis [sic] are bitter and resentful because the church has not been open, and have now lost interest." When a group of sixty-five young Christians and Buddhists attempted to organize their own Sunday fellowship meetings, the Seattle Council of Churches "objected to their meeting together . . . and the group as a potential Christian influence was lost." Andrews worried that many of these people would be impossible to reach in the future due to their disenchantment and anger with the church. "I have stalled so long that I have lost the confidence of many people," he confessed. "We knew that relocation and resettlement would bring more headaches and more problems than the evacuation, but no one dreamed that on top of all those problems, there would be all this quibbling, discussions and delay over our churches." The integration plan also obstructed his ability to baptize new Nikkei converts. Segregated congregations in the suburbs thrived, reaching people uninterested before the war because the jurisdiction of the Council of Churches did not extend beyond the city limits at this time.[125]

Members of the council accused Andrews of deliberately sabotaging plans for integration and trying to revive the JBC. For over a year, Andrews and Gertrude Apel exchanged ardent correspondence about their conflicting plans for Japanese Americans in Seattle and their differing perceptions of the current situation. Apel ranted in council meetings, telling area leaders that Andrews could not be trusted, "refuses to be a gentleman," and was "out to defeat any united program." She relayed her suspicions to Andrews's superiors within the ABHMS and questioned their choice to "retain a man" who may "seriously jeopardize, if not . . . wreck entirely, a constructive Christian program." Her accusations ranged from secretly reopening the Japanese Baptist Church to not attending church every Sunday and refusing to return phone calls.[126]

Andrews defended his work and blamed conflicts on miscommunication and an excess of bureaucracy. "I don't know what kind of a game has been going on or who is responsible, but it is certainly unfair and unjust," he protested. "If the Council has made a mistake, why do a lot of false accusations have to be laid against me, because I have refused to betray our own people?" He complied with UCM guidelines to drive Nikkei to different denominations each Sunday and declined to speak at the Young People's Fellowship meetings. Lincoln Wadsworth of the ABHMS rebuked Andrews, however, for denying "Nisei the benefits they may receive if [he would] help them accept" integration. They felt he was in a unique position to aid the integration program but refused. Andrews's indignation and frustrations stewed through the winter of 1945–46 before he decided to take further action.[127]

In addition to concerns about the spiritual lives of Nikkei, discontent and rising charges of delinquency among Nikkei youth demanded attention. A December 1945 survey of Nisei ages seventeen to twenty-two showed that their recreational, religious, and economic needs were not being met. Analysts called for the organization of a "Nisei dominant intercultural church," a community recreational center, employment services, housing assistance, and an improved communication system to inform Nisei about available activities. The Seattle Council of Churches accepted these results but made no immediate changes. Even when integration was clearly failing, members of the Seattle Council of Churches agreed to "eventually" expand the program to include other racial groups. This never occurred.[128]

Andrews thought that the JBC could have become a center of Nisei social life if it had opened earlier. He lamented that public dances attended by hundreds of Nisei had become their primary social outlet instead. Andrews bemoaned that the many Nisei soldiers coming through Seattle "congregated in colored taverns and places of cheap amusements" because they felt unwelcome in white establishments and "no wholesome place" existed. Nikkei mothers requested that the kindergarten be reopened as well. "Mothers," Andrews dramatically wrote, "whose husbands were killed, whose husbands are still in service, whose husbands have not been able to get jobs because of prejudice" needed the churches' support. For these reasons and others, Andrews vowed to reopen his church for the thousands of Nikkei in Seattle.[129]

By the end of March 1946, Andrews began preparing to reopen the JBC, regardless of his authority to do so. He wrote, "I am so tired of these people being used as guinea pigs to try out some idealistic theory of integration, and I can no longer stand on the sidelines and watch the Nisei go down. After May 1st I am going to break my handcuffs. If the Home Mission Society will back me, well and good. But if not, then, I am going on my

FIGURE 12 Seattle Japanese Baptist Church reopening, 21 April 1946.
Source: Densho Digital Archives.

own." Former members of the JBC had voted to reopen the church "with the Nisei taking full responsibility, backed and helped by the Issei." Andrews's community newsletter reported that only 22 of the 116 Baptist Nisei in Seattle had joined churches, despite having returned more than a year earlier. Andrews pointedly quoted Milton Evans's 1911 speech at the Northern Baptist Convention: "The one demand we Baptists make of our fellow men, the one gift of grace we seek from God is the opportunity to become in Christ free members in free churches in free lands." Andrews did not see how the possible benefits of integration outweighed removing Baptists' autonomy.[130]

With the 1 May deadline approaching, Seattle's mainline Protestant leaders asked the city's Nikkei to "determine their future policy." The following Sunday, 21 April 1946, Seattle's Japanese Baptist congregation proudly posed for a photograph in front of their reopened church (Figure 12). They met together for worship and fellowship after four long years.[131]

Similar stories occurred all along the West Coast. The Congregational Committee worked toward integration with little success. In September

1946, the committee reasserted that the churches should do "every-thing possible" to make Japanese Americans "an active part in the group life . . . in Caucasian" churches but accepted that Nikkei needed "a sense of security and freedom which in many cases can only be achieved by membership and activities in Nisei groups." The committee periodi-cally cautioned Congregational leaders to "be on guard that we do not over step Christian and democratic relations in our efforts to promote integration."[132]

Integrationists labeled Shigeo Shimada and Frank Herron Smith "trou-blemakers" for their insistent demands to reopen the Japanese Method-ist Church in San Francisco.[133] Smith urged Japanese Christians to resist the notion that their churches are "a stigma on Methodism."[134] Ralph Mayberry, the former executive secretary of the Los Angeles Baptist City Mission Society, also spoke for Nikkei and was disturbed that denomina-tions would require Nikkei to "lose [their] identity to help the others'" cause. He rejected the idea that Nikkei should relinquish their right to self-determination. Using a potent metaphor in a 1968 sermon, Mayberry said, "They must have the privilege to determine for themselves what they were, and what they wanted to be, and what they would be. And so I say, with some emotion, I have too large an investment in this whole ethnic idea to be a theorist of the popular type and surrender my friends or any group to the gas chamber of anonymity and oblivion."[135] After meeting the immediate needs of Seattle's JBC, Andrews's rhetoric shifted to support Mayberry's emphasis on Nikkei rights and leadership.

Seattle's Catholic Nikkei returned immediately to their ethnic parish, but it closed at the end of 1953, and their school never reopened. The wife of James Sakamoto, one of the leaders of Seattle's Catholic Nisei commu-nity, said that despite the retention of the church, returning Nikkei were disappointed that Maryknoll had closed the school. Local parochial schools resisted admitting "Orientals" and could refuse non-Catholics. Non-Catholic families associated with Maryknoll had no alternative but public school. Working mothers could not rely on Maryknoll for nursery care as they had before the war. Since Buddhists and Protestants eventu-ally opened kindergartens, Catholics sent their children there out of ne-cessity. Many lost their trust in Maryknoll, but others retained their allegiance. As an old woman, Mary Ichino remembered that Maryknoll still felt like the safest place after leaving camp. She recalled that Maryknoll "was where . . . you felt like you were at home. . . . It was a good, safe, friendly place." Catholic leaders lamented that fewer Nikkei

Catholics attended mass after the parish's closure, but the number of Japanese involved in the parish's activities had already decreased by then.[136]

The Maryknoll struggle in Los Angeles more closely resembled the tensions among Seattle's Baptists but had a very different ending. Parishioners became disillusioned when Maryknoll authorities in New York refused to reopen the church or school. Bishop Walsh wrote, "Cardinal in this plan is the duty of persuading the Japanese people to accept it for their own good." Prejudice tinted his complaint that "nobody likes something hard even when it is for his own good and least of all the Oriental." He insisted that "Maryknoll is ready and anxious to give help, . . . but we cannot advocate something that will do them harm in the long run just in order to please them now." Walsh became increasingly irritated with the situation as more people asked him to reopen the mission. In the margins of a letter from Hugh Lavery he wrote, "Why doesn't someone tell the Japanese to open their eyes to what they are getting into by returning to the Coast—and to decide either to take what it involves or stay away from the place?" Walsh consented to a temporary hostel, but Lavery failed to find an appropriate building.[137]

Maryknoll's decision disappointed Catholic Nikkei and the white priests who worked with them. In Los Angeles, where Maryknoll closed the mission and sold several buildings, Nikkei felt "neglected" and "let down." Nikkei Catholics still living at Manzanar petitioned Maryknoll to reopen their mission center and school. Minnie Ono wrote, "Please do not abandon us after you have been so good to us. One may think that Japanese can integrate with the Caucasian but they cannot because their race is yellow and not white. . . . Many Caucasians do not wish to have us mingle in their society." Father Leo Steinbach, who worked with Catholics at Manzanar, also petitioned Maryknoll to reopen the Los Angeles Center. He worried, "After converting so many people . . . turning them loose without giving them proper attention does not seem to be right." He argued that ethnic groups naturally "clique to themselves," and the church had no right to interfere with that desire. He also noted that the "harvest [was] ripe" after the defeat of Japan and cautioned Maryknoll not to "let the Protestants reap the harvest we have sown."[138]

Distressed, Lavery worried about the many non-Catholics associated with Maryknoll, especially after hearing of a prejudiced Maryknoll priest in San Juan who refused to support returnees. Lavery complained that the man "seems to take the attitude that to take care of his Catholics is all that God demands of him" rather than "fighting for the rights of any down trodden minority, black, white or yellow." Bishop Walsh blamed this resistance on misled parishioners and excused the priest, concluding, "A good pastor cannot ride rough shod over [his parishioners'] sensibilities."[139]

## Conclusion

Seattle's Japanese Baptist Church still stands today and supports a thriving, active church life.[140] It became self-supporting in 1955 and is now a member of the Church Council of Greater Seattle, formerly known as the Seattle Council of Churches. Due to Frank Herron Smith's efforts, only two prewar Japanese Methodist churches failed to reopen.[141] Japanese Congregational, Presbyterian, Episcopalian, Methodist, and evangelical churches also maintain active congregations in Seattle, while additional Japanese ethnic churches thrive in New York, Detroit, Chicago, St. Louis, Denver, Portland, throughout California and Hawaii, and elsewhere.[142] As Japanese churches regained their place within Christian communities, their story became a symbol of unity despite their segregation. A report on the Seattle Japanese Presbyterian Church noted its revival in March 1947 without mentioning the status of worship during the immediate postwar years. It concluded that the church is "a unit of good will, a center of Christian fellowship, where enmities of nations separated by war may be blotted out by the forgiving grace of Christ."[143]

Some Nikkei congregations never re-formed after the war. Seattle's Japanese Holiness Church, always one of the smaller congregations, did not survive, though a number of Japanese Holiness groups re-formed in California. While segregated Salvation Army posts along the coast prospered prior to the war, the denomination forbade Japanese congregations to re-form. At least one ordained Japanese officer left the Salvation Army as a result of these changes.[144]

Two successful experiments in interracial worship that occurred in the West in 1944 shed light on the failed battle for integration. The Nisei Quaker Gordon Hirabayashi organized an ecumenical, interracial Fellowship Center in Spokane, Washington, and the African American theologian Howard Thurman and Presbyterian Alfred Fisk founded the Church for the Fellowship of All Peoples, the nation's first intentionally integrated, interfaith (though largely Protestant) church in San Francisco. Like leaders passionate about the integration of Japanese Americans,

Thurman believed that "American Christianity has betrayed the religion of Jesus almost beyond redemption" through its racially segregated worship.[145]

Two factors explain why these groups succeeded when integration failed nationally. First, they coalesced with interracial worship as a primary goal, so changes were not pushed on uninterested congregants. Because all participants had a similar agenda, they eliminated "superficial" or "patronizing" activities like interracial teas. Second, the leadership of each group was interracial and they met in buildings unaffiliated with any participants, so no group felt like a guest of the other. Since Hirabayashi's center was not a formal church, Christians could partake in activities without abandoning their established congregations. Hirabayashi stressed the importance of individual choice and agency within the organization. Similarly, Thurman emphasized the necessity of "two freed spirits" for a privileged and an underprivileged person to love one another and worship together." Seattle Protestants lacked the unifying goals of these two groups. Nisei had been told what was best for them, as had white parishioners, many of whom adamantly disliked the notion of integration.[146]

Predominantly white churches invited Nikkei, who were not considered to be their social equals, to join their churches. Even if all else was equal and both groups voluntarily chose integration, Nikkei still would have been entering another group's sacred space without their usual leaders or authority. The recent experiences of Nikkei fostered little trust in white authority figures. No possibility existed for equal exchange or communion. Dreams of racial unity proved ephemeral as few Japanese Americans found homes in predominantly white churches. After losing basic freedoms during the war, many Nikkei wanted a space where they could control the environment and escape the constant challenges of discrimination. The lived theologies grounded in suffering and survival that developed during incarceration also clashed with Christian life on the outside, distancing Nikkei from their white coreligionists. Most often, integration efforts left Nisei without a religious community or pastoral guidance until their ethnic churches re-formed a year or two after the war. Donald Toriumi pointed out the "impractical and unrealistic" nature of "trying to force the Japanese Americans into doing something which many of the other racial groups have been *unable* to do in the past 50, 75, and 100 years."[147] Liberal Protestants did not attempt to force the integration of any other racial or ethnic minority.

Restricting the ethnic churches made Nikkei recognize their value and fight for their reestablishment. When outsiders challenged the status quo, Nikkei appreciated the benefits and pleasure of segregated worship. Fifty years later, the Baptist theologian Paul Nagano explained that these needs have not changed and Nikkei still resist joining predominantly white churches because "they don't feel at home in the larger [integrated] group in the sense that they become the victims of a paternalism." They are invited to join but not lead. He continued, "They would prefer to be with the Japanese group [because] they're more involved in it."[148] Having worshiped and led religious groups independently before and during the war, Nikkei did not want to join another group's organization. The failure to integrate churches ultimately strengthened ethnic congregations and clarified their arguments for segregated worship.

Many leaders in the 1940s held high hopes that dispersed resettlement and integrated churches would decrease national racial tensions, but others noted the shaky ethical premise of a plan for racial equality that required the subordination of a minority group. Tibesar saw resettlement as a success since it "created a new Japanese image for the American people" in the Midwest who had known only Hearst's caricatures previously.[149] But agendas intending to achieve racial equality by restricting the agency of racial minorities were doomed to fail. Seattle's Protestant leaders saw that racially mixed congregations did not meet the spiritual or social needs of the city's Nikkei population. A small percentage of Nikkei joined predominantly white churches after the war, but Protestant authorities' attempts to integrate Japanese and white churches failed. Leaders called for unity and inclusion but disagreed what that meant—an invitation for outsiders to assimilate into white society or an acceptance and encouragement of pluralism, be it racial, cultural, or institutional. Attempts to enforce new worship structures challenged preconceptions about the viability and desirability of united worship, revealing shifting understandings of race and diversity within mid-twentieth-century liberal Protestantism. Negotiating the independence of an ethnic minority in the churches illuminated imbalances of power within American Protestantism.

# Epilogue

. . . . . . . . . . . . . . . . . . . . . . . . . . . . . . . . . . . . . . . . . . . .

The Japanese problem compel[led] the church to face other minority
problems.

—Executive Secretary Mark Dawber, Home Missions Council of
  North America

Christian efforts to confront the incarceration of Japanese Americans revealed shifting attitudes about diversity within American Christianity,
the role of race in America, and the limits to which religious institutions
will comply with unjust government policy. Progressive Christian leaders addressed systematic and personal discrimination that rent the United
States. Only Quakers and a few individuals actively opposed the incarceration from its inception. Joined by Roman Catholics and mainline Protestants, who eventually lobbied for its end, they organized campaigns to
alleviate the crisis, educate white parishioners, and minister to incarcerated Christians. Japanese Americans responded to the incarceration and
the mixed responses of churches by forming new theologies and negotiating compliance with directives made on their behalf.

This epilogue describes how the incarceration inspired broader
civil rights activism in several individuals, shifted the status of Nikkei in
American churches, and catalyzed the development of Asian American
theology.

## Civil Rights Activism

In the final year of the war, religious workers involved with Nikkei aid
programs expanded their agendas to consider all minorities. Expanding
on sentiments expressed in this chapter's epigraph, Leopold Tibesar wrote
that incarceration led the entire nation to gain a "deeper consciousness
of the stress and strain of minority group relations within our own United
States."[1] In October 1941, prior to the attack on Pearl Harbor, Mark Dawber
and members of the Inter-Council Committee on Japanese Christian

Work in the United States had broached the possibility of inviting African Americans to the committee's Goodwill Dinner with Nikkei, but their motive was partially financial. Someone had suggested that the FCC Race Relations Commission might fund their work if they expanded their definition of race and appeared open to collaboration.[2] These fleeting considerations dissipated after 7 December, though Seattle Fellowship of Reconciliation member Kenji Okuda requested that Bayard Rustin, other African Americans, or "any other minority group" speak in the camps so Nikkei would understand the spectrum of race issues in America and be inspired by the work of others.[3] Recognition of the complexity of race in America rose toward the end of the war. Missionaries previously devoted to Asian populations saw the wider scope of race relations as they helped Nikkei move into black neighborhoods during and after the war. The Congregational Committee changed its name to the Congregational Committee for Christian Democracy and reorganized its approach to serve "people as human beings rather than as members of particular races or groups."[4] In April 1945, the FCC asked George Rundquist, head of the Committee on Resettlement, to expand his work by representing the FCC Race Relations Department on the West Coast.[5] Floyd Schmoe organized a conference in Seattle to discuss the problems of all minorities.[6] Esther Rhoads and the Pasadena chapter of the AFSC developed a summer camp with the intention of introducing refugees, Nikkei, other minorities, and white Americans to one another. She and others tried to diversify the AFSC's hierarchy with minimal success.[7]

The incarceration also inspired Christian race relations committees to expand their focus beyond African Americans. Aid workers concluded that working for justice as a universal objective was preferable to focusing on a particular disadvantaged group. Publications like *The Races of Mankind* contributed to this goal, and religious leaders like Gordon Chapman and Clarence Gillett made concerted efforts to encompass other types of advocacy. Their poster campaigns and a booth at the Second Southern California Industrial Exposition in 1945 encouraged better race relations and tolerance.[8] Churches and the WRA sought to avoid isolating Nikkei as an outlying minority group and increasingly shaped their public education efforts to integrate all minorities.[9] The AFSC's new race relations program went a step further by changing its name to the Community Relations Committee in recognition that racial differences are social fabrications, not inherent characteristics.[10]

Progressive Christians increasingly opposed unjust government policies aimed toward Nikkei. Denominational representatives and the associate general secretary of the Federal Council of Churches, Roswell Barnes, lobbied Congress to extend naturalization rights to all immigrants and to pass an Evacuee Claims Bill that would reimburse Nikkei for some of their financial losses. Christian groups on the West Coast joined the FCC's successful efforts to prevent the deportation of Nikkei who had renounced their American citizenship during the war. Christian leaders like Episcopalian bishop Henry Knox Sherrill worked with the President's Committee on Civil Rights, which, among other recommendations, advised Truman to grant restitution to former incarcerees for financial losses and endow Asian immigrants with naturalization rights. Christian organizations throughout the country, though most strongly in the West, campaigned against anti-alien land laws and for reparations in the 1940s. Agencies of the FCC, home and foreign missions councils, and the American Committee of the recently formed World Council of Churches recommended liberal immigration quotas and policies for postwar relations with Japan.[11]

The incarceration of Japanese Americans inspired numerous Nikkei Christians to begin civil rights activism after the war. Three Nisei ministers in San Francisco, Nick Iyoya, James Nakamura, and Lloyd Wake, turned their attention to African Americans after the war with the belief that fighting for anyone's rights and freedoms made them "better Americans." A member of Poston's youth groups, Wake eventually led "covenant" ceremonies between same-sex couples at his United Methodist church in the Tenderloin District. Mary Nakahara, who had written the accommodationist play *The End We Seek* in Jerome incarceration center, changed her name to Yuri Kochiyama and joined the Black Power movement in Harlem. After completing his seminary training, Tom Fukuyama and his new wife, Betty, directed the Brotherhood Home in Denver, building intercultural programs and leading an attempt to desegregate the YMCA's swimming pool. The interracial couple met when Betty volunteered at Minidoka's vacation Bible school. After returning to Seattle in the 1960s, the Fukuyamas continued civil rights activism and joined Vietnam War protests, earning criticism from their parishioners.[12]

Amidst Perry Saito's wartime speaking tours on behalf of Japanese Americans, he collaborated with civil rights leaders James Farmer and Bayard Rustin to develop models of nonviolent civil disobedience that would become standard practices in the struggle for African American rights. Through FOR, Rustin had helped protect the property of Japanese Americans during the war. The activists' 1943 sit-ins and boycotts in the Midwest tested methods of nonviolence protest. Saito engaged churches by posting lists of local businesses that supported equal rights on church bulletin boards and congratulating shopkeepers from the pulpit for their "democratic and Christian practice." During the Korean and Vietnam conflicts, Saito led antiwar rallies through his church. He also testified before the U.S. Commission on Wartime Relocation and Internment of Civilians alongside other Christians and presented supporting resolutions from the General Conference of the United Methodist Church.[13]

White church workers also expanded their outlook, several providing relief in Japan. Ralph and Mary Smeltzer, who operated Brethren hostels in Chicago and New York, became prominent civil rights leaders in the South and protested nuclear testing. Mary joined the Peace Corps, worked as a host at the World Friendship Center in Hiroshima, and served as the Brethren's delegate at the World Council of Churches Assembly in 1983. George Rundquist of the Committee on Resettlement of Japanese Americans served as the executive director of the New York Civil Liberties Union for fourteen years, bringing cases such as *Engel v. Vitale* to the Supreme Court. Esther Rhoads, a Quaker missionary who worked for the Student Relocation Council and the AFSC, became the latter's representative for the Licensed Agencies for Relief in Asia. She also tutored the crown prince and other members of the Japanese imperial family.[14] Herbert Nicholson, a Quaker missionary who spent the war meeting the needs of Nikkei, worked with Heifers for Relief after the war. Nicknamed "Uncle Goat," he ferried goats from the United States to Japan and worked with his wife in both nations' tuberculosis sanatoriums and leprosariums.[15]

As Christian institutions and individuals entered new areas of activism, church workers increasingly left religious organizations for nonreligious service groups. Nationwide interest in supporting democracy and fair play had boomed during the war, providing an endless demand for social activism outside of the church. Raymond Booth, for example, who had taken a job with the WRA to meet the same resettlement objectives for which he had worked in the AFSC, began directing the Los Angeles Council of Civic Unity. Many church workers joined or formed regional councils on civic unity and race relations in response to rising racial tensions during and after the war. The South Pasadena Council for Civic

Unity reported that over five hundred councils for such work formed in the United States during the war. While representatives from religious organizations composed the bulk of their membership, the agendas of religious activists looked increasingly secular from an institutional perspective. Religious ideologies may have inspired their work, but the limited religious rhetoric of Christian aid organizations for Japanese Americans diminished even further in nonreligiously affiliated race relations committees.

Following this trend, Floyd Schmoe left the AFSC when it refused to sponsor his efforts to build homes for atomic bomb victims in Japan. Through his own fundraising, he founded Houses for Hiroshima and built thirty-two homes in Hiroshima and Nagasaki with assistance from Emery Andrews and others (Figure 13). He organized Houses for Korea through the United Nations Korean Rehabilitation Agency following the Korean War and Wells for Egypt in 1957 at the request of Gordon Hirabayashi, then working at American University in Cairo. Like Raymond Booth, Schmoe found that he could seek the same goals, perhaps more productively, by working in secular organizations. Progressive congregations, regional church councils, and national ecumenical and denominational organizations also collaborated more frequently with activists outside of the church following the war.[16]

## Nikkei, American Christianity, and Asian American Theology

As an increasing number of people left religious organizations to pursue social activism outside of the church, Japanese American Christians asserted themselves within denominations and ecumenical organizations. The failed integration of white and Nikkei churches fortified Nikkei Protestant solidarity. Members of Japanese ethnic churches discovered the unique value of their congregations when authorities took them away. The challenge enabled Nikkei to articulate why that type of worship was beneficial and enjoyable. Many Nikkei craved affirmation from the solidarity created through common experience. At segregated churches, they did not need to explain their experiences of incarceration or of being a visible minority because everyone understood. Justin Haruyama described this as "Tsukemono theology." Tsukemono are Japanese-style pickled vegetables and an essential component of Japanese meals, but one that someone might hesitate to bring to a potluck at a predominantly non-Japanese gathering. Tsukemono theology asserts that parishioners cannot

FIGURE 13 Floyd Schmoe building homes with Houses for Hiroshima. Source: *Chugoku Shimbun.*

establish "a true dialogue with God" if they do not feel comfortable revealing their true selves. Haruyama wrote, "It is wholesome to be honest with ourselves and simply be what we are." A seminary scholarship in Haruyama's name supports the "uniqueness and special religious needs of the Japanese churches."[17]

Andrew Otani's history of Japanese Episcopal churches concluded, "Blood is thicker than water"; Japanese Americans could be "better Christians" within segregated congregations. Otani agreed with the Reverend Alfred Akamatsu's opinion that "each . . . ethnic group ought to make a contribution to the United States with the culture which their ancestors had brought into this country." Nisei leaders sought to strengthen American churches and the nation by leading their own churches and contributing their unique perspective. William Shinto, Roy I. Sano, Lloyd Wake, and many non-Japanese Asian Americans used similar rhetoric, though Wake eventually became a pastor at Glide Memorial, a countercultural, interracial church in San Francisco.[18]

Striving for true pluralism, where people "respect and affirm each other," Paul Nagano believed Japanese Americans must first "take pride in who [they] are and . . . really feel good about . . . [their own] background" before they can respect the diversity of others.[19] He used the story of Moses upholding his "ethnic heritage" by leading the Israelites out of Egypt to suggest that God wanted his people to celebrate their ethnicity.[20] Nagano increasingly called for Nikkei to assert pride in their ethnic identity and quit accepting their role as the "silent minority."[21] Once people reached that understanding and established "a level playing field," society would have "genuine community." Without this dignity, he believed that a "dichotomy of superior and inferior" would result in their culture being "swallowed up and absorbed by the dominant group" or they would become "an ingrown, self-supported group" that could find security only "in being with [their] own."[22]

After reestablishing their ethnic congregations, Nikkei Christian leaders turned to other sectors in which they were excluded by the white Christian establishment. When the American Baptist Foreign Mission Society barred Nisei ministers from serving in Japan, Paul Nagano founded the Japanese Evangelical Missionary Society (JEMS) to send the unique skills and perspectives of Japanese American pastors to the Japanese mission field. Initially meeting in Nagano's California home, JEMS expanded its work to university campuses and became an influential institution in the Asian American identity movement.[23]

Fighting a related problem, Emery Andrews petitioned white American Baptists to call Nisei ministers to their churches. He staunchly supported Nikkei's right to operate their own churches but also hoped predominantly white congregations would welcome Nikkei pastors. Since so few Baptist churches hired Nikkei pastors, Nisei graduates of American Baptist seminaries worked for other denominations. Perry Saito waited years for ordination in the United Methodist church because he lacked a parish invitation. Black churches, however, welcomed numerous Nikkei, including Seattle's Tom Fukuyama.[24]

Acknowledging that Nikkei could influence denominational policy only "by the good graces or paternal gestures" of the white majority, most Protestant denominations agreed to establish ethnic caucuses within their hierarchical structures to give minorities a voice in their own futures and that of the denomination. Perry Saito helped organize the National Federation of Asian American United Methodists in 1971, which was soon followed by the formation of Asian American United Presbyterian, American Baptist, Episcopalian, and United Church of Christ caucuses. Former Postonite Roy Sano emphasized that these special interest groups did not splinter churches but rather manifested the true universality of the Christian message.[25]

Former incarcerees called for pan-Asian unity to consolidate power and address their unique concerns.[26] In 1972, a group of Asian American Christians formed the Asian American Center for Theology and Strategies. The pan-ethnic organization offered workshops and seminars to Asian American church leaders to expand their collective "political, economic, social, cultural, and spiritual liberation."[27]

Ethnic churches predated and complemented Yellow Power movements of the 1970s. At the annual meeting of the Council of Japanese American Churches in 1975, Congregational leader and former incarceree Teruo Kawata confirmed the roots of this resilience and fortitude in the incarceration camps' religious life.[28] Nikkei theologian Fumitaka Matsuoka states that Japanese American religious life cannot be understood apart from a cosmology shaped by the incarceration.[29] The incarceration and its unusual worship styles inspired many Japanese Americans to become pastors and heavily influenced their formative professional years. Novel approaches to ministry during the war, including the ecumenical and integration experiments, accelerated the construction of new theologies. Though many pastors disliked the Protestant ecumenical worship program, they learned a great deal from the collaboration. While Japanese

American Christians constitute a small minority within Asian American Christianity today, they heavily influenced the first wave of Asian American theology in the 1960s and 1970s.[30]

Former Postonites Jitsuo Morikawa and Paul Nagano became prominent theologians. In his 1986 sermon "Toward an Asian-American Theology," Morikawa explained how Japanese Americans' "experience of rejection and collective incarceration" showed them "the extravagance of God's grace, that even pain, suffering and injustice He often transforms into blessing." This rhetoric echoed almost verbatim the theologies developed in camp that predated the international and domestic rise of liberation theology. Like many incarcerated Christians, Morikawa believed God had used the injustice for positive ends by teaching incarcerees how to identify with "that vast community of people in this land and around the world who live in chronic and unending suffering and deprivation." Morikawa emphasized, however, that this theology was viable for any person faced with the "pervasive anxiety of weakness and powerlessness" in society.[31] Paul Nagano developed the concept further after concluding that his marginality within America was a "permanent predicament."[32] This "theology of marginality" was later embraced and expanded by Korean and Vietnamese American theologians.[33]

Speaking for the future of American Christianity, Paul Nagano wrote that the church must "mean the humanness of the minorities as well as the majority—the majority freed from their peculiar arrogance and the minorities freed to be what God has meant them to be as persons." Nagano argued that Asian American churches can not only play a vital role in changing America but move the world toward what he called the New Community, a variation on the new world order envisioned by liberal Protestants in the 1940s. In Nagano's New Community, Asian Americans and their struggles would help America find its soul as a people and support Western Christianity's struggle to find authenticity in the world.[34]

## Conclusion

Nikkei and white leaders offered mixed assessments of Christian responses to the incarceration of Japanese Americans. Many felt disappointed by the churches' failure to do more but appreciated that Christian groups did anything at all. A review conducted by Marshall Sumida and Paul Nagano concluded that the churches "for the most part, acquiesced to the government's decision [to incarcerate Nikkei] despite convictions of justice, equality and human rights."[35] An FCC report agreed that the churches were "not wholly successful" and could have done more.[36] Floyd Schmoe gave the churches a similarly poor appraisal: "The non-Japanese churches, on the whole, fell far short of their opportunity and responsibility, both in the attempt to prevent the tragedy of relocation and in helping to heal the wounds that resulted from it."[37] A number of Christian Nikkei felt "deserted" and "suspicious" after Christian organizations did not initially speak against the incarceration and closed their ethnic churches.[38] Paul Nagano and others saw the incarceration as a lost opportunity "for the church to reveal its true nature and mission under God."[39]

A large portion of Nikkei's latter-day accounts cite gratitude for what the aid signified—the existence of allies in America and assurance that the nation had not forgotten them. While appreciating the material support, Nikkei still wondered, "Where was the church when an innocent and powerless minority were forcibly removed from their homes?" But those same individuals affirmed that "without the church, many of us would be indeed lost!" While few people spoke against the incarceration on behalf of American churches, hundreds of people, if not thousands, provided small but meaningful comfort through words, donations, and deeds that sustained many Nikkei's faith in humanity and Christianity.[40]

Ultimately, most progressive Christians chose social ministry over social action, though some attempted both. All people working for or within Nikkei communities recognized the need for the former, but few answered calls for the latter. Many responses fell between these extremes, such as the substantial efforts to shift public opinion. The incarceration created a desperate need for both aid and activism.

Canadian Christians made similar decisions, though the need for basic aid was even greater. The Canadian government immediately seized fishing boats and eventually all other property of Nikkei on the coast. Japanese Canadians were forced from their homes earlier than Japanese Americans, and the Canadian government divided most families, assigning men to labor camps while women struggled to meet the basic needs of their children in deserted mining towns. The Canadian government did not build camps with schools, dining halls, or recreational activities, nor did it allow Nikkei to return to the West Coast until April 1949. Religious workers and other activists tried to provide schooling, food, and clothing in addition to spiritual guidance. They worked to improve public opinion of Nikkei and protested the forced "repatriation" of thousands of Japanese Canadians, many of whom had never before visited Japan. Canadian ex-

FIGURE 14 Emery E. Andrews receiving Order of the Sacred Treasure, 1970.
Source: Author's Collection.

periments with ecumenical worship and postwar integration of churches
met with similarly limited success.[41]

Japan and local communities showed their gratitude to white church
workers. The Japanese emperor bestowed the Order of the Sacred Treasure on Esther Rhoads, Floyd Schmoe, Leopold Tibesar, Hugh Lavery, and
Emery Andrews (Figure 14).[42] Schmoe also received the Hiroshima Peace
Center's Peace Award, a special proclamation from Washington governor
Mike Lowry, and a Nobel Prize nomination from Congressman Jim Mc-
Dermott. Schmoe used the money from his Hiroshima prize to complete
construction of the Seattle Peace Park. Seattle's Japanese Baptist congregation continually showed its love and appreciation for Andrews. Three
months before his death in 1976, the JBC held a testimonial dinner where
seven hundred people recognized Andrews's immense contributions to
their community.[43]

Andrews's extreme devotion to Seattle's Nikkei community cost him
his family. When they returned to Seattle in 1945, Mary announced her
intention to divorce him. Emery Brooks Andrews, their youngest child,

is understandably proud of his father's accomplishments but has publicly stated his disappointment that they were not closer. He explained to one interviewer, "I think my father had a huge amount of love and commitment to give, but it wasn't to his family, it was to the [Nikkei] community." Brooks confessed that most of the family only begrudgingly accepted Andrews's commitments and priorities. Andrews's "mild case of pastoral workaholism" became a "full-blown obsession" during the war. The Reverend Andrews continued to advocate for the independence and authority of Nikkei pastors and retired from full-time work in 1955 to allow the church to call a Nisei pastor. Paul Nagano assumed the position of senior pastor of the JBC in 1971.[44]

While Quakers, Roman Catholics, and mainline Protestants worked toward the same ultimate goals of peace and unity, their responses to the incarceration demonstrated their differing approaches and worldviews. Acting on his Quaker beliefs, Gordon Hirabayashi challenged the incarceration directly, refusing to comply with unjust government orders. The AFSC devoted resources toward alleviating and righting the political injustice through legal support, material aid, and other assistance, doing whatever possible to improve the physical circumstances of Nikkei. The AFSC's pragmatic approach faced the realities of the political climate and challenged flaws within America's society and political system rather than trying to work around them. Friends fought within the system to create positive social change while alleviating the harm caused by its current problems. Unwilling to confront the government at a time of war, Catholics prioritized solidarity with Nikkei communities and resettled them as quickly as possible. Distrustful of Protestant aid programs, they worked independently, cooperating with government agencies as needed. Mainline Protestants focused energy on building stronger Christian foundations on which a moral society could be established, in addition to offering material support. Rather than directly confront the injustice at the beginning of the war, they opted to strengthen fellowship and faith. They believed unity at the congregational level would resonate throughout society. Protestants tackled stereotypes through print media and speaking tours, trying to reduce widespread racial prejudices. When white leaders failed to permanently dissolve ethnic enclaves, they slowly recognized that predominantly white churches no longer defined American Christian worship. As powers within American Christianity reconciled a more pluralistic reality within the church, effects spilled into national political arenas and activists began fighting other discriminatory laws.

Asian American theologies developed in the wake of integration efforts support a pluralism that values individual identity and diversity rather than homogeneity. The mixed results of worship experiments, increasing awareness of pervasive racial injustice, and the advent of the Cold War gradually led mainline Protestants to expand their definition of unity to include pluralist representations of Christianity as imagined by different sects and ethnic groups. The development of Asian American theology helped define this new pluralism and the ways in which individuals must understand themselves and others for it to succeed.

# Notes

## Abbreviations to Notes

| | |
|---|---|
| ABHMS | American Baptist Home Mission Society |
| AFSC | American Friends Service Committee Archives |
| CCGS | Church Council of Greater Seattle Records, Accession No. 1368-7 (UW Collection) |
| CSI | College of Southern Idaho |
| DDA | Densho Digital Archives |
| FCC | Federal Council of Churches of Christ in America |
| FOR | Fellowship of Reconciliation |
| GTU | Graduate Theological Union Archives, Berkeley, California |
| HC | Haverford College, Special Collections |
| JAA | Japanese-American Assistance (AFSC Archives Collection) |
| JAER | Japanese American Evacuation and Resettlement Records, BANC MSS 67/14 c (UCB Collection) |
| JANM | Japanese American National Museum |
| JAR | Japanese American Relocation Collection (OC Collection) |
| JARP | Japanese American Research Project (UCLA Collection 2010) |
| MFBD | Maryknoll Fathers and Brothers Diaries (MMA Collection) |
| MMA | Maryknoll Mission Archives |
| NARA | National Archives and Records Administration |
| NCWC | National Catholic Welfare Conference |
| NWCP | *Northwest Catholic Progress* |
| OC | Special Collections Department, Occidental College, Mary Norton Clapp Library |
| PACTS | (Pacific and) Asian American Center for Theology and Strategies |
| PCC | Protestant Church Commission for Japanese Service |
| PHS | Presbyterian Historical Society |
| PNW | Pacific Northwest Regional |
| QU | Quincy University, Brenner Library, Tibesar Japanese Collection |
| SIS-JAR | Social Industrial Section–Japanese American Relocation (AFSC Archives Collection) |
| UA | University of Arkansas Libraries, Special Collections |
| UCB | University of California, Berkeley, Bancroft Library |
| UCLA | University of California, Los Angeles, Charles E. Young Research Library, Department of Special Collections |

UCM    (Seattle) United Church Ministry to Returning Japanese
UW    University of Washington Libraries
WRA    War Relocation Authority

## Introduction

1. Government officials spoke of "evacuating" Japanese from the coast and placing them in "relocation centers," though President Roosevelt and others also described the detention facilities as "concentration camps." "Internment" refers to the legal detention of enemy aliens, which also occurred. These terms fail to convey the reality of the government's unconstitutional act. I write of the "removal" or "eviction" of Japanese from the coast to "incarceration centers" or "camps." I concede that calling the sites "camps" can mislead as well, but I leave the task of challenging that term to others. For a summary of the scholarly debate about this terminology, see Roger Daniels, "Words Do Matter: A Note on Inappropriate Terminology and the Incarceration of the Japanese Americans," in *Nikkei in the Pacific Northwest: Japanese Americans and Japanese Canadians in the Twentieth Century,* ed. Louis Fiset and Gail Nomura (Seattle: University of Washington Press, 2005), 190–214.

2. Monica Sone recorded this autobiographical information in *Nisei Daughter* (Boston: Little, Brown, 1953). The National Archives and Records Administration's Japanese-American Internee Data File (RG 210) suggests that Seizo Itoi worked in the United States for eleven years before purchasing the hotel.

3. U.S. Congress, 100th Congress, 2nd Session, H.R. 442, *An Act to Implement Recommendations of the Commission on Wartime Relocation and Internment of Civilians,* Public Law 100-383, 10 Aug. 1988.

4. Recent scholarship filling this dearth includes Shana Bernstein, *Bridges of Reform: Interracial Civil Rights Activism in Twentieth-Century Los Angeles* (Oxford: Oxford University Press, 2011); Mark Brilliant, *The Color of America Has Changed: How Racial Diversity Shaped Civil Rights Reform in California, 1941–1978* (Oxford: Oxford University Press, 2010); Derek Chang, *Citizens of a Christian Nation: Evangelical Missions and the Problems of Race in the Nineteenth Century* (Philadelphia: University of Pennsylvania Press, 2010); Scott Kurashige, *The Shifting Grounds of Race: Black and Japanese Americans in the Making of Multiethnic Los Angeles* (Princeton, N.J.: Princeton University Press, 2008); and Joshua Paddison, *American Heathens: Religion, Race, and Reconstruction in California* (Berkeley: University of California Press, 2012).

5. Jacquelyn Dowd Hall, "The Long Civil Rights Movement and the Political Uses of the Past," *Journal of American History* 91 (Mar. 2005): 1233–63.

6. Duncan Williams's work has begun to introduce the experiences of incarcerated Buddhists: "Camp Dharma: Japanese-American Buddhist Identity and the Internment Experience of World War II," in *Westward Dharma: Buddhism beyond*

*Asia*, ed. Charles S. Prebish and Martin Baumann (Berkeley: University of California Press, 2002), 191–200; "Complex Loyalties: Issei Buddhist Ministers during the Wartime Incarceration," *Pacific World: Journal of the Institute of Buddhist Studies* 3 (Fall 2003): 255–74; and "From Pearl Harbor to 9/11," in *A Nation of Religions: The Politics of Pluralism in Multireligious America*, ed. Stephen Prothero (Chapel Hill: University of North Carolina Press, 2006), 63–78. His forthcoming book, tentatively titled *Camp Dharma: Buddhism and the World War Two Incarceration of Japanese Americans*, will be a great contribution to the field. See also Susan Davis, "Mountain of Compassion: Dharma in American Internment Camps," *Tricycle: The Buddhist Review*, Summer 1993, 46–51.

7. For an overview of the incarceration, see Greg Robinson, *A Tragedy of Democracy: Japanese Confinement in North America* (New York: Columbia University Press, 2009). Studies about outside responses to the incarceration include Allan Austin, *From Concentration Camp to Campus: Japanese American Students and World War II* (Champaign: University of Illinois Press, 2004); Austin, *Quaker Brotherhood: Interracial Activism and the American Friends Service Committee, 1917–1950* (Urbana: University of Illinois Press, 2012); Stephanie Bangarth, *Voices Raised in Protest: Defending North American Citizens of Japanese Ancestry, 1942–49* (Vancouver: University of British Columbia Press, 2008); Douglas M. Dye, "For the Sake of Seattle's Soul: The Seattle Council of Churches, the Nikkei Community, and World War II," *Pacific Northwest Quarterly* 93 (Summer 2002): 127–36; Ellen M. Eisenberg, *The First to Cry Down Injustice? Western Jews and Japanese Removal during WWII* (Lanham, MD.: Rowman & Littlefield, 2008); Robert Shaffer, "Cracks in the Consensus: Defending the Rights of Japanese Americans during World War II," *Radical History Review* 72 (Fall 1998): 84–120; and Shaffer, "Opposition to Internment: Defending Japanese American Rights during World War II," *Historian* 61 (Spring 1999): 597–619.

8. For a review of this work, see Philip Q. Yang and Starlita Smith, "Trends in Black-White Church Integration," *Ethnic Studies Review* 32 (Summer 2009): 1–29. For two excellent exceptions, see Gerardo Marti, *Worship across the Racial Divide: Religious Music and the Multiracial Congregation* (Oxford: Oxford University Press, 2012); and Brad Christerson, Korie L. Edwards, and Michael O. Emerson, *Against All Odds: The Struggle for Racial Integration in Religious Organizations* (New York: New York University Press, 2005). A special 2008 issue of the *Journal for the Scientific Study of Religion* (47, no. 1) also considered this greater diversity.

9. Hollinger, *After Cloven Tongues of Fire: Protestant Liberalism in Modern American History* (Princeton, N.J.: Princeton University Press, 2013); Hedstrom, *The Rise of Liberal Religion: Book Culture and American Spirituality in the Twentieth Century* (New York: Oxford University Press, 2012); Coffman, *The Christian Century and the Rise of the Protestant Mainline* (New York: Oxford University Press, 2013).

10. The few studies that mention religious practices rely on Lester Suzuki's *Ministry in the Assembly and Relocation Centers of World War II* (Berkeley, Calif.: Yardbird Press, 1979). Suzuki based his research on personal experiences as an incarcerated minister, camp newspapers, and sociological data collected in the camps. The book contains no analysis. Toru Matsumoto's *Beyond Prejudice: A Story of the Church and Japanese Americans* (New York: Friendship Press, 1946) is also more valuable as a primary source. Intended to support missionary efforts in postwar Japan, Matsumoto records the "tireless efforts" of Christian aid to Japanese Americans. More rigorous scholarship on religion in the incarceration can be found in John Howard, *Concentration Camps on the Home Front: Japanese Americans in the House of Jim Crow* (Chicago: University of Chicago Press, 2008); Gary Okihiro, "Religion and Resistance in America's Concentration Camps," *Phylon* 45 (Third Quarter 1981): 220–33; and David K. Yoo, *Growing Up Nisei: Race, Generation, and Culture among Japanese Americans of California, 1924–49* (Urbana: University of Illinois Press, 2000). Madeline Duntley's articles on Seattle's ethnic churches consider effects of the incarceration; see, in particular, "Confucianism, Internationalism, Patriotism and Protestantism: The Ecclesiological Matrix of Japanese Christian Activists in Japan and the U.S. Diaspora," in *Ecumenical Ecclesiology: Unity, Diversity and Otherness in a Fragmented World*, ed. Gesa Elsbeth Thiessen (New York: T&T Clark, 2009), 223–38.

11. Excellent recent studies include Jasmine Alinder, *Moving Images: Photography and the Japanese American Incarceration* (Urbana: University of Illinois Press, 2009); Elena Tajima Creef, *Imaging Japanese America: The Visual Construction of Citizenship, Nation, and the Body* (New York: New York University Press, 2004); Stephen S. Fugita and Marilyn Fernandez, *Altered Lives, Enduring Community: Japanese Americans Remember Their World War II Incarceration* (Seattle: University of Washington Press, 2004); Eric Muller, *Free to Die for Their Country: The Story of the Japanese American Draft Resisters in World War II* (Chicago: University of Chicago Press, 2001); and Alice Yang Murray, *Historical Memories of the Japanese American Internment and the Struggle for Redress* (Stanford, Calif.: Stanford University Press, 2008).

12. Kurashige, "Unexpected Views of the Internment," in *Colors of Confinement*, ed. Eric Muller (Chapel Hill: University of North Carolina Press, 2012), 105.

13. Kevin Schultz treats the subject in *Tri-Faith America: How Catholics and Jews Held Postwar America to Its Protestant Promise* (Oxford: Oxford University Press, 2011), as do Ray H. Abrams, *Preachers Present Arms: The Role of the American Churches and Clergy in World War I and II, with Some Observations on the War in Vietnam* (Scottsdale, Penn.: Herald Press, 1969); Donald F. Crosby, *Battlefield Chaplains: Catholic Priests in World War II* (Lawrence: University of Kansas, 1994); William Issel, *For Both Cross and Flag: Catholic Action, Anti-Catholicism, and National Security Politics in World War II San Francisco* (Philadelphia: Temple University Press, 2010); Alan Robinson, *Chaplains at War: The Role of Clergymen during World War II* (London: Tauris Academic Studies, 2008); and Gerald Law-

son Sittser, *A Cautious Patriotism: The American Churches and the Second World War* (Chapel Hill: University of North Carolina Press, 1997).

14. G. Kurt Pielher, "The Free Exercise of Religion: Religion and New Deal Liberalism at War," and Ronit Stahl, "Between Race and Religion: The Army's Approach to African American and Japanese American Chaplains during World War II" (papers presented at the American Historical Association annual meeting, Washington, D.C., 3 Jan. 2014).

15. Louis Fiset, *Camp Harmony: Seattle's Japanese Americans and the Puyallup Assembly Center* (Urbana: University of Illinois Press, 2009), 11–12.

16. Just prior to the eviction, the U.S. Department of Agriculture reported that Japanese farmers grew 90 percent or more of California's peppers, celery, and strawberries and over half of the snap beans, artichokes, cauliflower, cucumbers, spinach, and tomatoes. Constituting only 2 percent of the California population, Nikkei supplied 10 percent of the state's agriculture income by 1920. U.S. Department of the Interior and War Agency Liquidation Unit, *People in Motion: The Postwar Adjustment of the Evacuated Japanese Americans* (Washington, D.C.: Dept. of the Interior, 1947), 60; Ronald Takaki, *Strangers from a Different Shore: A History of Asian Americans, Updated and Revised* (Boston: Little, Brown, 1998), 191.

17. This number does not reflect the greater number of Japanese who immigrated to Hawaii. Roger Daniels, *Prisoners Without Trial: Japanese Americans in World War II* (New York: Hill and Wang, 1993), 8.

18. Fiset, *Camp Harmony*, 4.

19. Toyotomi Morimoto, *Japanese Americans and Cultural Continuity: Maintaining Language and Heritage* (New York: Garland, 1997), 24.

20. Maryknoll missionaries operated schools in Seattle and Los Angeles; the Fathers of the Society of the Divine Word ran a Japanese Catholic school in San Francisco. For the five years preceding the incarceration, Sisters of the Holy Name operated the St. Paul Miki School for prekindergarten to second-grade Nikkei in Portland, Oregon. Lillian A. Pereyra, "The Catholic Church and Portland's Japanese: The Untimely St. Paul Miki School Project," *Oregon Historical Quarterly* 94 (Winter 1993/1994): 399–434; Fugita and Fernandez, *Altered Lives*, 26.

21. J. P. Swift, Los Angeles Mission Diary, Supplement to February–March 1942, Box 34/Fld 4, Maryknoll Fathers and Brothers Diaries, MMA; Yuki Yamazaki, "St. Francis Xavier School: Acculturation and Enculturation of Japanese Americans in Los Angeles, 1921–1945," *U.S. Catholic Historian* 18 (Winter 2000): 58–60.

22. Takaki, *Strangers*, 218–20.

23. Frank Miyamoto, a former sociology professor at the University of Washington, described the churches filling this "vacuum." Miyamoto, Interview 1, interview by Stephen Fugita, 26 Feb. 1998, DDA.

24. Bulletin IV, Japanese Evacuation Committee of the Church Federation of Los Angeles, 2 Apr. 1942, Box 1/Fld 11, Constantine Panunzio Collection of Material on Japanese American Internment (Collection Number 1636), UCLA; Memorandum on the Work of the Protestant Churches in Japanese Relocation Centers and

Settlements, 20 July 1942, Box 4/Fld 1, Clarence Gillett Papers (Collection 130), UCLA.

25. Brian Hayashi, *For the Sake of Our Japanese Brethren* (Stanford, Calif.: Stanford University Press, 1995).

26. Official tabulations of adherents and church attendance vary widely. A 1943 study states that 22 percent of the first generation and 35 percent of the second generation were currently Christian. For detailed charts of adherence rates (arranged by generation, occupation, and camp) compiled by sociologists working in the camps, consult Dorothy Swaine Thomas, *The Salvage* (Berkeley: University of California Press, 1952), 65–71. "Nisei Assimilation," WRA Community Analysis Report No. 9, 21 June 1943, Box 6/Fld 19, Gillett Papers, UCLA.

27. Over half of the 101 Japanese Protestant congregations in the United States were Methodist or Presbyterian. Memorandum on the Work of the Protestant Churches, 20 July 1942.

28. Fiset, *Camp Harmony*, 13–14.

29. Yosh Nakagawa, interview by Tom Ikeda, 7 Dec. 2004, DDA; Roy Nakagawa, interview by Martha Nakagawa, 20 July 2011, DDA.

30. Virginia Green, "Japanese Americans in Salem," Salem Online History, accessed May 22, 2015, http://www.salemhistory.net/people/japanese_americans .html.

31. Sidney L. Gulick, *Should Congress Enact Special Laws Affecting Japanese? A Critical Examination of the Hearings before the Committee on Immigration and Naturalization Held in California, July 1920* (New York: National Committee on American Japanese Relations, 1922).

32. Gulick, *The Evolution of the Japanese: A Study of Their Characteristics in Relation to the Principles of Social and Psychic Development* (New York: Fleming H. Revell, 1903); Sandra C. Taylor, *Advocate of Understanding: Sidney Gulick and the Search for Peace with Japan* (Kent, Ohio: Kent State University Press, 1984).

33. Tibesar, Autobiographical Writings, undated, Box 3/Vol. 1/Section 2 and Box 4/Vol. 8/Fld 4, QU.

34. For the greater complexity of this issue, see Paddison, *American Heathens*, and Jennifer Snow, *Protestant Missionaries, Asian Immigrants, and Ideologies of Race in America, 1850–1924* (New York: Routledge, 2007).

35. Flowers, "Do Americans Know?," undated, Box 36/Fld 4, RG 18, PHS.

36. FCC, "Message to Christians of All Lands," 1929, Box 36/Fld 20, RG 18, PHS; Minutes, Special Committee on Plans, 9 Feb. 1921, and National Committee on American Japanese Relations, "American Japanese Relations as Affected by the Washington Conference," undated, Box 36/Fld 1, RG 18, PHS.

37. Richard H. Immerman, *John Foster Dulles: Piety, Pragmatism, and Power in U.S. Foreign Policy* (Wilmington, Del.: Scholarly Resources, 1999), 21; Mark G. Toulouse, *The Transformation of John Foster Dulles: From Prophet of Realism to Priest of Nationalism* (Macon, Ga.: Mercer University Press, 1985), 69, 73.

38. Bill Hata, quoted in Sumio Koga, *A Decade of Faith: The Journey of Japanese Christians in the USA (1936–1946)* (New York: Vantage Press, 2002), 24; Toulouse, *Transformation*, 66–67, 121–22; Schultz, *Tri-Faith America*, 63; Andrew Preston, *Sword of the Spirit, Shield of Faith: Religion in American War and Diplomacy* (New York: Alfred A. Knopf, 2012), 319.

39. Quoted in Curtis Evans, "Demonstrating the Sufficiency of Christianity to Solve the Race Problem: The Federal Council of Churches and Race Relations, 1920–1950" (paper presented at American Religious History Workshop, University of Chicago, 1 Dec. 2011).

40. "The Record of a Year: Official Report to the Constituent Bodies of the Federal Council," *Federal Council Bulletin* 5, no. 3 (1922): 28.

41. Newsletters, Box 59/Flds 8 and 9, RG 18, PHS; Clarence Pickett, *For More than Bread: An Autobiographical Account of Twenty-Two Years' Work with the American Friends Service Committee* (Boston: Little, Brown, 1953), 373.

42. "A Grange Member Speaks for Japanese Americans," 26 Aug. 1944, Jerome County Historical Society, Jerome, Idaho.

43. These notions can be seen in *Christian Century* and *Christianity and Crisis*, which in 1942 published the series "How Shall the Christian Church Prepare for the New World Order?" and Paul Tillich's article "Spiritual Problems of Post-War Reconstruction" respectively. Toulouse, *Transformation*, 62.

44. Tibesar to John Walsh, 5 May 1944, Box 6/Fld 7, Topical Misc., MMA.

45. William R. Hutchison, ed., *Between the Times: The Travail of the Protestant Establishment in America, 1900–1960* (New York: Cambridge University Press, 1989), 19.

46. Greg Robinson, *A Tragedy of Democracy*, 53; "LA Evangelist Protests Release," *Granada Pioneer*, 16 June 1943, 3.

47. Minutes of the Monthly Meeting of the AFSC Pacific Coast Branch, 11 July and 1 Aug. 1942, Box 32/Fld 2, Esther Rhoads Collection, HC; "Looking for a Better World," undated, Box 32/Fld 4, Rhoads Collection, HC.

48. Leonard J. Arrington, "Utah's Ambiguous Reception: The Relocated Japanese Americans," in *Japanese Americans: From Relocation to Redress*, ed. Roger Daniels, Sandra C. Taylor, and Harry H. L. Kitano (Salt Lake City: University of Utah Press, 1986), 92–98; Masaoka with Bill Hosokawa, *They Call Me Moses Masaoka* (New York: William Morrow, 1987), 98.

49. Cheryl Greenberg, "Black and Jewish Responses to Japanese Internment," *Journal of American Ethnic History* 14 (Winter 1995): 3–37.

50. See Norman H. Osumi, *Today's Thought: Rev. Paul Osumi—the Man and His Message* (Honolulu: Watermark, 2013).

51. For this perspective, consult Israel A. S. Yost, *Combat Chaplain: The Personal Story of the World War II Chaplain of the Japanese American 100th Battalion* (Honolulu: University of Hawaii Press, 2006).

## Chapter One

1. Monica Sone, *Nisei Daughter* (Boston: Little, Brown, 1953), 146.

2. Floyd Schmoe, "Seattle Peace Churches and Relocation," in *Japanese Americans: From Relocation to Redress*, rev. ed., ed. Roger Daniels, Sandra C. Taylor, and Harry H. L. Kitano (Seattle: University of Washington Press, 1989), 117; Tibesar, Autobiographical Writings, undated, Box 3/Vol. 1/Section 2, QU.

3. Louis Fiset, *Camp Harmony: Seattle's Japanese Americans and the Puyallup Assembly Center* (Urbana: University of Illinois Press, 2009), 28; Tibesar, Seattle Diary, 7–10 Dec. 1942, Box 44/Fld 9, MFBD.

4. Daniels, Taylor, and Kitano, *Japanese Americans*, xvi.

5. Fiset, *Camp Harmony*, 80.

6. Bodine, Japanese Evacuation Report No. 7, 26 Mar. 1942, Branch Office: Seattle—Reports, SIS-JAR 1942.

7. Tamie Tsuchiyama, "Preliminary Report: Santa Anita," 31 July 1942, Reel 016, JAER; Herbert and Margaret Wilke Nicholson, *Comfort All Who Mourn: The Life Story of Herbert and Madeline Nicholson* (Fresno, Calif.: Bookmates International, 1982), 83; Yuki Yamazaki, "St. Francis Xavier School: Acculturation and Enculturation of Japanese Americans in Los Angeles, 1921–1945," *U.S. Catholic Historian* 18 (Winter 2000): 64.

8. Gary Okihiro, "Religion and Resistance in America's Concentration Camps," *Phylon* 45 (Third Quarter 1981): 223.

9. Clarence Gillett, "The Press and the American Japanese," Box 8/Fld 1, Clarence Gillett Papers (Collection 130), UCLA.

10. Frank J. Taylor, "The People Nobody Wants," *Saturday Evening Post*, 9 May 1942, 66.

11. "Waiting for the Signal from Home," *PM*, 13 Feb. 1942.

12. John L. DeWitt, "Final Report: Japanese Evacuation from the West Coast, 1942" (Washington, D.C.: Western Defense Command, 1943), 145.

13. Brian Komei Dempster, ed., *Making Home from War: Stories of Japanese American Exile and Resettlement* (Berkeley, Calif.: Heyday Books, 2011), 199.

14. "Friends and the Japanese Americans," May 1941, Box 1/Fld 42, Floyd Wilfred Schmoe Papers (496-8), UW.

15. Schmoe to James Sakamoto, 8 Apr. 1941, Box 2/Fld 35, James Y. Sakamoto Papers, UW.

16. "A Message to the Society of Friends and Our Fellow Christians," June 1942, Publicity—General, SIS-JAR 1942.

17. "Friends and the Japanese Americans"; "A Message to the Society of Friends and Our Fellow Christians"; Thomas Bodine to Student Relocation Council Executive Committee, 4 Oct. 1944, Box 1/Fld 1, RG 37, PHS.

18. "A Message to the Society of Friends and Our Fellow Christians"; "Opening for Service by the AFSC in Connection with the Japanese Evacuation," 6 Apr.

1942, General, SIS-JAR 1942; Letter to Americans of Japanese ancestry, Box 1/Fld 42, Schmoe Papers (496-8), UW.

19. Letter to Americans of Japanese ancestry; "American Friends Service Committee Sends Greetings," *Minidoka Irrigator*, 25 Dec. 1942, 3.

20. Quoted by Jack Sutters, "American Refugees: The Japanese-American Relocation," AFSC (Feb. 2002); Elmore Jackson to Beatrice Shipley, 16 Dec. 1941, Correspondence, PNW Office, JAA 1941.

21. Kit Oldham, "Schmoe, Floyd W." HistoryLink (revised 25 Feb. 2010), http://www.historylink.org/index.cfm?DisplayPage=output.cfm&File_Id=3876; Schmoe to Booth, 31 Dec. 1941, Wendell Woodward to Raymond Booth, 18 Sept. 1941, and Elmore Jackson to Beatrice Shipley, 16 Dec. 1941, Correspondence, PNW Office, JAA 1941; Joel B. Cox, Report of Sub-Committee for Relief of Destitute Aliens, AFSC—Hawaii Branch, 31 Dec. 1941, Box 10B/Fld 2, Gilbert and Minnie Pickett Bowles Family Papers, HC; Grace Booth, Information Bulletin, AFSC—Pacific Coast Branch, Feb. 1942, Box 1/Fld 13, Constantine Panunzio Collection, UCLA; Regular Meeting of Japanese-American Relations Committee of the AFSC—Pacific Coast Branch, 22 Jan. 1942, Administration—Reports, SIS-JAR 1942.

22. Schmoe to Booth, 31 Dec. 1941; Schmoe to Booth and Clarence Pickett, 16 Jan. 1942, Correspondence, PNW Office, JAR 1942; Pickett to Eleanor Clarke, 8 Jan. 1942, and Reed Cary to Frank Aydelotte, 8 Apr. 1942, Hirabayashi, SIS-JAR 1942; Working or Staff Committee Meeting, 21–22 Jan. 1942, Administration—Reports, SIS-JAR 1942.

23. Bodine to Eleanor Clarke, Raymond Booth, and Mary Kimber, 18 Feb. 1942, Branch Office: Seattle—Reports, SIS-JAR 1942; Booth to Schmoe, Shipley, and Bodine, 9 Mar. 1942, and Booth to Schmoe, 19 Mar. 1942, Correspondence, PNW Office, JAR 1942.

24. Testimony of Schmoe and Waring, AFSC, Tolan Committee, 2 Mar. 1942, 11526–35.

25. Schmoe to Clarence Pickett, 31 Apr. 1942, PNW Office, JAR 1942; Minutes of the Monthly Meeting of the AFSC Pacific Coast Branch, 11 July 1942, Box 32/Fld 2, Esther B. Rhoads Papers, HC.

26. Gordon Hirabayashi, Interview 2, interview by Becky Fukuda and Tom Ikeda, 26 Apr. 1999, DDA; Mark Mullins, *Christianity Made in Japan: A Study of Indigenous Movements* (Honolulu: University of Hawaii Press, 1998), 14–15; John F. Howes, *Japan's Modern Prophet: Uchimura Kanzō, 1861–1930* (Vancouver: University of British Columbia Press, 2005), 222, 200; Carlo Caldarola, "Pacifism among Japanese Non-Church Christians," *Journal of the American Academy of Religion* 41 (Dec. 1973): 506–19; James Hirabayashi, "Four Hirabayashi Cousins: A Question of Identity," in *Nikkei in the Pacific Northwest: Japanese Americans and Japanese Canadians in the Twentieth Century,* ed. Louis Fiset and Gail Nomura (Seattle: University of Washington Press, 2005), 149–50.

27. Hirabayashi Interview 2.

28. Hirabayashi to Eleanor Ring, 18 Feb. 1944, Box 1/Fld 7, Ring Family Papers (4241-2), UW.

29. Hirabayashi, "Why I Refused to Register for Evacuation," 13 May 1942, Box 1/Fld 6, Ring Papers (4241-2), UW.

30. Gordon Hirabayashi with James A. Hirabayashi and Lane Ryo Hirabayashi, *A Principled Stand: The Story of* Hirabayashi v. United States (Seattle: University of Washington Press, 2013), 18.

31. Tom Bodine to Hirabayashi, 24 May 1942, and Woodbury, Character Reference for Hirabayashi, 10 Dec. 1942, Hirabayashi, SIS-JAR 1942.

32. The Northern California branch of the ACLU refused to withdraw its support of Fred Korematsu. Clifford Forster to Harold Evans, 21 Jan. 1943, Hirabayashi—General, SIS-JAR 1943.

33. Alfred G. Scattergood to Friends, 6 May 1943, Hirabayashi—General, SIS-JAR 1943; Marshall Trust representative [name illegible] to Homer Morris, Hirabayashi—Robert Marshall Trust, SIS-JAR 1943.

34. Pickett to Reed Cary, 14 July 1942, Hirabayashi, SIS-JAR 1942.

35. Schmoe, "I Know Gordon Hirabayashi," undated, Box 1/Fld 42, Schmoe Papers (496-8), UW.

36. For more on this trial (*Hirabayashi v. United States*, 320 US 81 [1943]), see Eric L. Muller, "Hirabayashi: The Biggest Lie of the Greatest Generation," UNC Legal Studies Research Paper No. 1233682 (18 Aug. 2008).

37. Hirabayashi, *Principled Stand*, 54.

38. O'Brien wrote a book about the effort after the war. *The College Nisei* (New York: Arno Press, [1949] 1978).

39. Schmoe, interview by Kitty Barragato, 25 Feb. 1989, AFSC Oral History Collection.

40. Schmoe, "Seattle Peace Churches," 117.

41. Yukako Otori, "Faith-Based Relief and Postwar U.S. Foreign Policy: Quäkerspeisung as a Case Study," *Journal of Pacific and American Studies* 12 (Mar. 2012): 97–113; Bodine, Japanese Evacuation Report No. 7.

42. Theodore Wilbur, "American Friends Service Committee Efforts to Aid Japanese American Citizens during World War II" (MA thesis, Boise State University, 2009), 64; O'Brien, interview by Howard Droker, 24 Apr. 1975, Robert W. O'Brien Papers (2420-3), UW; Townsend, "Service with the War Relocation Authority, 1942–46," 1983, Manuscripts 975, HC.

43. Shizue Seigel, *In Good Conscience: Supporting Japanese Americans During the Internment* (San Mateo, Calif.: AACP, 2006), 99.

44. Hirabayashi to Ring, 18 Feb. 1944, Box 1/Fld 7, Ring Papers (4241-2), UW.

45. Seattle Council of Churches Race Relations Department, "Message to the Japanese in the Pacific Northwest," 3 Nov. 1941, Box 15/Fld 11, CCGS; Minutes of the Meeting of the Inter-Council Committee on Japanese Christian Work in the United States, 10 Apr. 1941, Box 8/Fld 17, RG 26, PHS.

46. "Church Leaders Urge Christian Attitude toward Japanese in U.S.," 9 Dec. 1941, and Victor L. Nutley and Gertrude L. Apel, Seattle Council of Churches and Christian Education, Statement for release Monday, December 8, 1941, Box 15/ Fld 11, CCGS.

47. Testimony of Harold V. Jensen, Representing Seattle Council of Churches, Tolan Committee Hearing, 2 Mar. 1942, 11564–73.

48. Exhibit 19—Statement by Mrs. Claude H. Eckart, YWCA President, Tolan Committee Hearing, 27 Feb. 1942, 11613; George Gleason, Tolan Committee Hearing, 6 Mar. 1942, 11623–29; Exhibit 11—Statement by E. W. Thompson, Pastor Japanese Methodist Church, Tolan Committee Hearing, undated, 11607–9; Exhibit 2—Statement by Rev. U. G. Murphy, Tolan Committee Hearing, undated, 11597–98; Biographical Note, Emery E. Andrews Papers, UW.

49. Exhibit 4—Statement by the Portland Council of Churches, Tolan Committee Hearing, 12 Mar. 1942, 11390; Committee Panel, Tolan Committee Hearing, 23 Feb. 1942, 11212–14; Testimony of Dr. W. P. Reagor, Pastor, First Christian Church of Oakland, and President, California Council of Churches," Tolan Committee Hearing, 23 Feb. 1942, 11195–97.

50. Exhibit 18—Resolution Passed by the Japanese Church Federation, Tolan Committee Hearing, 21 Jan. 1942, 11872–73.

51. "Ministers Express Good Will to Japanese Evacuees," *Christian Century*, 8 Apr. 1942, 453; Congregational Christian Churches of the United States, June 1942, and Letter to the President of the United States, 29 Apr. 1942, quoted in *The Concern of the Church for the Christian and Democratic Treatment of Japanese Americans* (New York: Committee on Resettlement of Japanese Americans, 1944), 6–8; John Bennett to Dwight Bradley, 29 Apr. 1942, Box 1/Fld 5, Gillett Papers, UCLA.

52. Santa Maria Ministers on Enemy Alien Control, 4 Feb. 1942, Box 3/Fld 24, Gillett Papers, UCLA; Northern Baptist Convention Resolutions, 30 May 1942, quoted in *The Concern of the Church*, 7; Northwest Oriental Evangelization Society Resolution, 28 May 1942, and Fremont Baptist Church, "Resolution to Be Presented to the Resolutions Committee of the Northern Baptist Convention," 26–31 May 1942, Box 15/Fld 8, CCGS.

53. Report of the Meeting of the Social Welfare and Service Committee, 26 Mar. 1942, Box 15/Fld 5, CCGS.

54. George W. Chessman, "Letter from a Friend in Trouble," *Christian Century*, 22 Apr. 1942, 533; Robert S. Osgood, "Eyewitness Report," *Christian Century*, 15 Apr. 1942, 500; Kenji Okuda to Norio Higano, 4 Apr. 1942, Box 1/Fld 9, Higano Family Papers (2870-1), UW; Elesha Coffman, "The Measure of a Magazine: Assessing the Influence of the *Christian Century*," *Religion and American Culture* 22 (Winter 2012).

55. "Hitlerism Threatens the California Japanese," *Christian Century*, 11 Mar. 1942, 309; "Japanese Ordered from Coastal Areas," *Christian Century*, 18 Mar. 1942, 340.

56. Galen Fisher, "Our Japanese Refugees," *Christian Century*, 1 Apr. 1942, 424–26; Report of the Social Welfare and Service Committee, 26 Mar. 1942.

57. Congregational Committee on Christian Democracy, "You Can Do Something About It," 1945, Box 3/Fld 14, Gillett Papers, UCLA.

58. Mark Hulsether, *Building a Protestant Left:* Christianity and Crisis *Magazine, 1941–1993* (Knoxville: University of Tennessee Press, 1999), 28, 30–31; Henry Smith Leiper, "A Blot on Our Record," *Christianity and Crisis*, 20 Apr. 1942, 1–2; Niebuhr, "The Evacuation of Japanese Citizens," *Christianity and Crisis*, 18 May 1942, 2–5; Bennett to Bradley, 29 Apr. 1942, and Bennett to Truman Douglass, 18 May 1942, Box 1/Fld 5, Gillett Papers, UCLA.

59. Smith to pastors and religious leaders, 26 Mar. 1942, Box 15/Fld 27, CCGS.

60. Salem Japanese Community Church Bulletins and Young People's Bulletins, Dec. 1941–24 May 1942, Box 75/Fld 6, Hoshimiya Family Papers, JARP.

61. Andrew Kuroda, Young People's Bulletin, 22 Mar. 1942, Box 76/Fld 2, Hoshimiya Family Papers, JARP; Royden Susu-Mago, "Reweaving Our Lives," and Kenzon Tajima, "New Pilgrims," in *The Sunday Before*, ed. Allan Hunter and Gurney Binford (Los Angeles: n.p., May 1945), 23–26, 39–42.

62. Sohei Kowta, "Abraham, the Migration Leader," undated; Hideo Hashimoto, "The Babylonian Exile and the Love of God," 10 May 1942; and John M. Yamazaki, "We Shall Have Our Easter or Easter before Evacuation," 5 Apr. 1942, in Hunter and Binford, *Sunday Before*, 28, 33–38, 43–48.

63. Suzuki, "Facing Evacuation," in Hunter and Binford, *Sunday Before*, 16.

64. Suzuki, "The Methodist Voice," 25 Mar. 1942, Box 1/Fld 5, Panunzio Collection, UCLA.

65. The New Revised Standard Version of the New Testament translates the King James Bible's "froward" as "harsh."

66. Suzuki, "Facing Evacuation," 16–17.

67. Hashimoto, "The Babylonian Exile," 27–32; Tajima, "New Pilgrims," 39–42.

68. Kuroda to Friends, 6 May 1942, Box 155/Fld 3, Kuroda Papers, JARP; Quoted by A. Hunter in "Japanese Taken to Owens Valley," *Christian Century*, 15 Apr. 1942, 510.

69. Kuroda to Friends, 6 May 1942; Letter to the *Oregon Statesman*, 1 June 1942, and Letter to Those on the Outside, Summer 1942, Box 155/Fld 3, Kuroda Papers, JARP.

70. Bennett to Bradley, 29 Apr. 1942.

71. Congregational leaders also unsuccessfully sought homes for Nikkei in the country's interior before their incarceration. Robert Inglis to Douglass Horton, 20 Mar. 1942, Box 1/Fld 5, Gillett Papers, UCLA.

72. Tibesar, "Of All Persons," July 1940, Box 6/Fld 3, Series 423, Deceased Society Members Media Files, MMA; James Y. Sakamoto, "Report on Seattle's Maryknoll," in *Chibes a-shi no kotodomo: About Father Tibesar*, ed. Takeo Koiwa (Tokyo: Gengokai, 1968), 24–25.

73. Shaughnessy, "Official Pastoral Letter," NWCP, 12 Dec. 1941; Tibesar, Seattle Diary, Dec. 1941, Box 44/Fld 9, MFBD; National Catholic Welfare Conference News Service, "Editor Expresses U.S. Loyalty of American-Born Japanese," 22 Dec. 1942, Box 3/Vol. 1/Fld 9, QU; "Vincentians Meet Acclaims Loyalty of U.S. Japanese," NWCP, 19 Dec. 1941, 5; "Catholic Group Seeks Employment of Loyal Japanese, NWCP, 16 Jan. 1942, 3; "Maryknoll Pupils Say 'Goodbye' to Their School Here," NWCP, 24 Apr. 1942, 1.

74. Tibesar to Walsh, 7 Mar. 1942, Box 5/Fld 10, Topical Misc., MMA; Gill to Tolan, 16 Mar. 1942, Tolan Committee Hearings; Tibesar, Seattle Diary, January–March 1942, Box 45/Fld 1, MFBD; Tibesar, Seattle Diary, Dec. 1941.

75. Lavery to Walsh, 27 Jan. 1942; Drought to Lavery, 30 Jan. 1942; and Walsh to James Drought, 31 Jan. 1942, Box 4/Fld 10, Topical Misc., MMA.

76. Lavery to Walsh, 27 Jan. 1942.

77. Lavery to Drought, 1 Mar. 1942, and Walsh to Lavery, telegram, 3 Mar. 1942, Box 5/Fld 10, Topical Misc., MMA.

78. Caffrey to Drought, 29 June 1942, Box 5/Fld 12, Topical Misc., MMA.

79. Walsh to Tibesar, 12 Mar. 1943, Box 6/Fld 6, Topical Misc., MMA.

80. Agenda on Japanese Evacuation, May 1942, Box 5/Fld 11, Topical Misc., MMA.

81. Drought to Tibesar, 3 Mar. 1942, Box 5/Fld 10, Topical Misc., MMA.

82. Drought to Lavery, 3 July 1942, Box 5/Fld 12, Topical Misc., MMA.

83. Thomas Kiernan, Report to the Maryknoll Council: Survey of the Japanese Evacuation and Resettlement, 27 May 1942, Box 5/Fld 11, Topical Misc., MMA.

84. Tibesar, 1942–45, Box 6/Fld 4, Series 423, Deceased Society Members Media Files, MMA.

85. Dorothy Day, "Grave Injustice Done Japanese on West Coast," *Catholic Worker*, June 1942, 3.

86. Fiset, *Camp Harmony*, 54; John Martin to Tibesar, telegram, 16 Feb. 1942, Box 4/Fld 10, Topical Misc., MMA; Yamazaki, "St. Francis Xavier School," 64; Barbara Johns, *Signs of Home: The Paintings and Wartime Diary of Kamekichi Tokita* (Seattle: University of Washington Press, 2011), 209–10; Drought to Lavery, 3 Mar. 1942, and "Work Sheet," Mar. 1942, Box 5/Fld 10, Topical Misc., MMA; Lavery to Drought, 1 Mar. 1942; Catholic Foreign Mission Society of America, Exhibit 19—Tabulation for Evacuation on Community Group Basis, Tolan Committee Hearing, undated, 11873–77.

87. Walsh to Tibesar and Lavery, telegrams, 5 Mar. 1942, Box 5/Fld 10, Topical Misc., MMA; E. R. Fryer, WRA Regional Director, to Tibesar, 18 Apr. 1942, Box 3/Vol. 1/Fld 9, QU.

88. Walsh to Francis Caffrey, 13 Mar. 1942; Caffrey to Walsh and Walsh to Tibesar, 9 Mar. 1942, Box 5/Fld 10, Topical Misc., MMA.

89. Walsh, proposal, 31 Mar. 1942; DeWitt to Walsh, 11 Apr. 1942; Milton Eisenhower to Walsh, 8 Apr. 1942; Hoover to Tibesar, 27 Mar. 1942; Walter Wilson to Caffrey, 28 Mar. 1942; Brother Philip to Father, 16 Apr. 1942; and Drought, "Japanese Work on the West Coast," 18 Apr. 1942, Box 5/Fld 10, Topical Misc., MMA.

90. "Rector Denounces All Missions to Japan," *Christian Century*, 21 Jan. 1942, 93.

91. Eleanor Breed, diary entry, 26 Apr. 1942, quoted in *Only What We Could Carry: The Japanese American Internment Experience*, ed. Lawson Fusao Inada (Berkeley, Calif.: Heyday Books, 2000), 42.

92. Clarence Pickett, *For More than Bread: An Autobiographical Account of Twenty-Two Years' Work with the American Friends Service Committee* (Boston: Little, Brown, 1953), 373–74.

93. "The Record of a Year: Official Report to the Constituent Bodies of the Federal Council," *Federal Council Bulletin* 5, no. 3 (1922): 28; Coordinating Committee for Wartime Service, "Wartime Services of the Churches: A Handbook," Feb. 1943, Box 19/Fld 16, RG 26, PHS; Bennett, *Social Salvation: A Religious Approach to the Problems of Social Change* (New York: Charles Scribner's Sons, 1935).

94. Bennett, "To Our Japanese Friends," late spring 1942, Box 155/Fld 3, Kuroda Papers, JARP.

95. Laurie Maffly-Kipp, "Engaging Habits and Besotted Identity: Viewing Chinese Religions in the American West," *Material Religion* 1 (Mar. 2005): 92.

96. Bennett worked on the Congregational Council for Social Action, which proposed various plans to help people avoid the camps in early 1942. Bennett to Gillett, 2 Apr. 1942, Box 1/Fld 5, Gillett Papers, UCLA.

97. Ibid.

98. Seattle Council of Churches Race Relations Department, "Message to the Japanese in the Pacific Northwest."

99. Nutley and Apel, Statement for release Monday, December 8, 1941.

100. James M. Gillis, "Treating the Colored Man Right," NWCP, 27 Mar. 1942; Lavery to Walsh and Walsh to Lavery, 20 Sept. 1945, Box 6/Fld 8, Topical Misc., MMA; Walsh, "Anonymous Column," 25 June 1942, Box 14/Fld 1, Bishop James E. Walsh Papers, MMA.

101. Tibesar, "America and Its Minorities," Summer 1945, Box 7, QU; Tibesar, untitled, Nov. 1944, Box 6/Fld 7, Topical Misc., MMA; Tibesar, Autobiographical Writings, undated, Box 4/Fld 5 and Box 3/Vol. 1/Section 2, QU.

102. Schmoe, Tolan Committee Hearing, 11527; Exhibit 11, 11608.

103. Greg Robinson, *By Order of the President: FDR and the Internment of Japanese Americans* (Cambridge, Mass.: Harvard University Press, 2001), 38, 7; Report of the Congressional Select Committee Investigating National Defense Migration, May 1942, quoted in *The Concern of the Church*, 3.

104. Biographical Summary, 10 May 1946, Box 2/Fld 4, Andrews Papers (1908-3), UW; Biographical Note, Andrews Papers (1908-1), UW; "History," Japanese Baptist Church (updated May 2014), http:// www.jbcseattle.org/en/2014-04-29 -02-06-0/history.

105. "Instructions to All Japanese Living on Bainbridge Island," 24 Mar. 1942, "Bainbridge Island," Camp Harmony Exhibit, University of Washington Libraries (revised 20 Dec. 1999), https://www.lib.washington.edu/exhibits/harmony /Exhibit/bainbridge.html; Bodine, Seattle Japanese Evacuation Report No. 7;

"Evacuees Sing on Trip," *Bainbridge Review*, 2 Apr. 1942, 1; Paul Ohtaki, "Find Friends at Minidoka," *Bainbridge Review*, 11 Mar. 1943.

106. Seigel, *In Good Conscience*, 27.

107. Storage Receipts, Spring 1942, Box 4/Flds 32–35, Andrews Papers (1908-1), UW; Breed, diary entry, 25 Apr. 1942, in *Only What We Could Carry*, 41.

108. Ralph Smeltzer, "These Are American Refugees: Part Two—Facing Opposition," Reel 082, JAER.

109. Sone, *Nisei Daughter*, 171; Tibesar, Autobiographical Writings, undated, Box 3/Vol. 1/Section 2, QU.

110. Sone, *Nisei Daughter*, 173, 180.

111. "Policy—Religion within WCCA Reception and Assembly Centers," 20 May 1942, Box 15/Fld 21, CCGS; "Japanese Assembly Center at Puyallup," 8 Sept. 1942, Box 15/Fld 4, CCGS.

112. "Japanese Assembly Center at Puyallup"; Sone, *Nisei Daughter*, 188; Doris Hayashi, "JERS Religion Report," Tanforan Assembly Center, Summer 1942, Reel 016, JAER.

113. "Protestants in City and State Unite to Serve Japanese, Call Rev. Everett W. Thompson," 26 Apr. 1942, Box 15/Fld 22, CCGS; Edward Laird Mills, "A Pioneer Woman in a Pioneer Position," 1953, Box 1/Fld 1, Gertrude L. Apel Papers (4350-1), UW; John R. Bootford, "She Wins Cooperation," undated, Box 2/Fld 3, Apel Papers, UW.

114. "Council of Churches Visitor's Agreement before Issuance of Passes to the Japanese Camps," May 1942, Box 15/Fld 21, CCGS.

115. "Japanese Assembly Center at Puyallup."

116. Everett Thompson to Theresa McCoy, 13 and 20 May 1942, and Thompson to Frank Herron Smith, 24 June 1942, Box 15/Fld 1, CCGS; Fiset, *Camp Harmony*, 112; "Japanese Assembly Center at Puyallup"; Thompson to Smith, 24 June 1942; Tibesar, Autobiographical Writings, undated, Box 3/Vol. 1/Section 2, QU; "Chaplain Asks Rules Observance," *Camp Harmony Newsletter*, 23 May 1942, 2.

117. Tom Fukuyama, *My Spiritual Pilgrimage: Autobiographies of Asian American Baptist Ministers*, compiled by the Asian American Baptist Caucus, 1976, Box 10/Fld 8, PACTS Collection, GTU 2001-9-01, GTU.

118. "Japanese Assembly Center at Puyallup"; Thompson to McCoy, 13 and 20 May 1942.

119. Fiset, *Camp Harmony*, 103; Tibesar, Seattle Diary, May–July 1942, Box 45/Fld 1, MFBD; Seattle Diary, June 1942, Box 73/Fld 1, Maryknoll Sisters Diaries, MMA.

120. "Protestants in City and State Unite to Serve Japanese"; Thompson to McCoy, 13 and 20 May 1942; "Japanese Assembly Center at Puyallup."

121. Thompson to Smith, 24 June 1942; "Japanese Assembly Center at Puyallup."

122. "Japanese Assembly Center at Puyallup."

123. Sone, *Nisei Daughter*, 185–86.

124. Ibid., 186.

125. "Harmony Residents Slated for Tulelake," *Camp Harmony Newsletter*, 12 June 1942, 1; Thompson to Smith, 24 June 1942.

126. Sone, *Nisei Daughter*, 189.

127. Report of the Social Welfare and Service Committee, 26 Mar. 1942.

## Chapter Two

1. Coordinating Committee for Wartime Service, "Wartime Services of the Churches: A Handbook," Feb. 1943, Box 19/Fld 16, RG 26, PHS.

2. Gerald L. Sittser, *A Cautious Patriotism: The American Churches and the Second World War* (Chapel Hill: University of North Carolina Press, 1997), 2–6; Andrew Preston, *Sword of the Spirit, Shield of Faith: Religion in American War and Diplomacy* (New York: Alfred A. Knopf, 2012), part 6.

3. Minutes of Inter-Council Committee on Japanese Christian Work, 10 Apr. and 18 Dec. 1941, Box 8/Fld 17, RG 26, PHS.

4. Emergency Meeting of Board Secretaries Concerned with the Situation among the Japanese in New York City, 8 Dec. 1941, Box 8/Fld 17, RG 26, PHS.

5. Kevin Schultz notes strained exceptions to this independence in *Tri-Faith America: How Catholics and Jews Held Postwar America to Its Protestant Promise* (Oxford: Oxford University Press, 2011).

6. After a year, Congregational leaders renamed this group the Citizens' Committee for Resettlement; in 1945, it became the Congregational Committee for Christian Democracy to reflect its broadening scope. For clarity, this book refers to it as the Congregational Committee throughout. Gillett, "Congregational Committee for Christian Democracy: Background and History," 1945, and "Changes in Organization," 24 Aug. 1945, Box 1/Fld 2, Clarence Gillett Papers (Collection 130), UCLA.

7. Leaders adopted this name after deciding the original title, the Western Area Protestant Church Commission for Wartime Japanese Service, was "too long for most people to remember." Protestant Church Commission Meeting Minutes, 26 June 1942, Box 15/Fld 31, CCGS; Foreign Mission Conference, Notice signed by Roswell Barnes, 2 May 1942, quoted in "Documents Bearing on the Function of the Protestant Commission for Japanese Service," Dec. 1943, Box 4/Fld 2, Gordon K. Chapman: Protestant Church Commission for Japanese Service, GTU 2002-9-01, GTU.

8. Minutes of the Conference of Leaders of Japanese Christian Work, 15–17 Dec. 1943, Box 2/Fld 5, RG 37, PHS.

9. E. J. Kawamorita to Whom It May Concern, 1 May 1942, and Kawamorita to the FCC, telegram, 2 Sept. 1942, Box 1/Fld 48, Chapman Papers, GTU.

10. Chapman to Gillett, 11 Aug. 1942, Box 1/Fld 9, Chapman Papers, GTU; Chapman to Virginia Mackenzie, 17 Nov. 1942, Box 1/Fld 38, Chapman Papers, GTU; Paul Fujihana to Chapman, 27 July 1942, Box 1/Fld 23, Chapman Papers, GTU.

11. Lars Hemingstam, "Drottningholm and Gripsholm: The Exchange and Repatriation Voyages during WWII," accessed May 22, 2015, http://www.salship.se

/mercy.php; Betty Evans to Chapman, 17 Sept. 1942, Box 1/Fld 5, Chapman Papers, GTU; Gladys Kaiser to Chapman, 17 Nov. 1942, Box 1/Fld 39, Chapman Papers, GTU; Yuki Yamazaki, "St. Francis Xavier School: Acculturation and Enculturation of Japanese Americans in Los Angeles, 1921–1945," *U.S. Catholic Historian* 18 (Winter 2000): 64; Laura Bodenhamer to Chapman, 6 Aug. 1942, Box 1/Fld 29, Chapman Papers, GTU; Chapman to Marcia Kerr, 8 July 1942, Box 1/Fld 38, Chapman Papers, GTU.

12. Still to Chapman, 3 June and 27 July 1942, Box 1/Fld 24, Chapman Papers, GTU; [illegible] to Chapman, 9 Apr. 1943, Box 1/Fld 32, Chapman Papers, GTU; Memorandum on the Work of the Protestant Churches, 20 July 1942, Box 4/Fld 1, Gillett Papers, UCLA.

13. Gordon Chapman to Ernest Chapman, 8 Mar. 1945; Douglas W. Noble, Reports to the Board of National Missions, Presbyterian Church, U.S.A., on Wayside Chapel Tour to War Relocation Centers, 15 Mar. to 6 May 1945; and Noble to Chapman, 26 Mar. 1945, Box 1/Fld 13, Chapman Papers, GTU.

14. Chapman to Noble, 4 May 1945, and L. H. Bennett to Chapman, 10 Apr. 1945, Box 1/Fld 13, Chapman Papers, GTU.

15. Paul Osumi to Chapman, 30 Nov. 1943, and Chapman to Smith, 6 Dec. 1943, Box 1/Fld 17, Chapman Papers, GTU; Dawber to Chapman, 16 Oct. 1942, Box 12/Fld 4, RG 301.7, PHS; Chapman, Memorandum on the Scope, Function, and Policies of the PCC, 9 Dec. 1942, Box 36/Fld 5, RG 18, PHS.

16. Thomas to Andrews, 26 July 1943, Box 1/Fld 3, Emery E. Andrews Papers (1908-1), UW.

17. Thomas Alfred Tripp to Harley Gill, 9 Feb. 1943, Box 1/Fld 7, Gillett Papers, UCLA; PCC Meeting Minutes, 13–15 July 1943, Box 15/Fld 3, CCGS.

18. Chapman to Gillett, 4 Feb. 1944, Box 1/Fld 12, Gillett Papers, UCLA; French to Chapman, 22 Sept. and 20 June 1944, and Chapman to French, 6 May 1943, Box 1/Fld 8, Chapman Papers, GTU; Minutes of the Executive Committee of the Congregational Committee, 15 Sept. 1942, Box 1/Fld 1, Gillett Papers, UCLA; Unsigned to A. C. Knudten, 12 Dec. 1942, Box 1/Fld 13, Gillett Papers, UCLA; Bovenkerk to Chapman, 5 Oct. 1944, Box 1/Fld 1, Chapman Papers, GTU.

19. Memorandum on the Work of the Protestant Churches, 20 July 1942; Tibesar, Seattle Diary, Dec. 1941, Box 44/Fld 9, MFBD; Rhoads to E. R. Fryer, 28 Apr. 1942, Box 44/Fld 570, RG 210, NARA.

20. The executive secretary of the Disciples of Christ's Committee on War Services also "found it difficult to cooperate" with the commission and felt the organization overstepped its authority. Willard Wickizer to Chapman, 14 Feb. 1945, Box 1/Fld 18, Chapman Papers, GTU; Hannaford to Chapman, 9 Nov. 1943, Box 1/Fld 11, Chapman Papers, GTU.

21. Memorandum of the PCC, 21 Sept. 1944, Box 4/Fld 1, Gillett Papers, UCLA; Chapman to Gillett, 12 June 1943, Box 4/Fld 3, Gillett Papers, UCLA; PCC Meeting Minutes, 13–15 July 1943.

22. Meeting of Commission on Aliens and Prisoners of War, 24 Sept. 1942, Box 59/Fld 11, RG 18, PHS; "Points Agreed on . . . ," 12 Nov. 1942, quoted in

"Documents Bearing on the Function of the PCC," Dec. 1943, Box 4/Fld 2, Gillett Papers, UCLA.

23. Dawber, Meeting on Christian Work among the Japanese in the USA, 6 Dec. 1942; Dawber to Chapman, 16 Jan. 1943, and Minutes of the Committee on Administration of Japanese Work, 24 Mar. and 12 May 1943, Box 12/Fld 4, RG 301.7, PHS; PCC Meeting Minutes, 18 Jan. and 27 Apr. 1943, and Smith to Dawber, 20 Jan. 1943, Box 12/Fld 11, RG 301.7, PHS; Minutes of the Committee on Administration of Japanese Work, 18 Jan., 1 Mar., and 16 Apr. 1945, Box 8/Fld 18, RG 26, PHS.

24. PCC Meeting Minutes, 11–12 Jan. 1945, Box 15/Fld 30, CCGS.

25. The Granada Christian Church expressed similar sentiments. Y. Tsuda to the FCC and Chapman, 11 Jan. 1943, Box 1/Fld 48, Chapman Papers, GTU; "In Appreciation of the PCC," *Granada Christian Church News*, 21 Feb. 1943, Reel 303, JAER.

26. PCC Meeting Minutes, 11–12 Jan. 1945.

27. Dawber to Clarence Pickett, 22 May 1942, Home Missions Council, SIS-JAR 1942; Morris to Reed Cary, 8 Aug. 1942, and Cary to Morris, 18 Aug. 1942, Morris Correspondence, SIS-JAR 1942; Margaret Jones to Morris, 12 Oct. 1943, Morris— Correspondence, SIS-JAR 1943; Floyd Schmoe, Denver Conference Report, 16–17 Dec. 1943, Branch Office: Seattle, SIS-JAR 1943; Memorandum, 29 Sept. 1942, WRA, SIS-JAR 1942; Jones to Dawber, 5 Aug. 1942, Stanley Jones, SIS-JAR 1942.

28. Chapman, "Meeting the Unexpected," 1942 Annual Report of the Special Representative for Japanese Work, 3 Mar. 1943, Box 17/Fld 8, RG 93, PHS; Minutes of Inter-Council Committee on Japanese Christian Work, 22 Oct. 1941, Box 8/Fld 17, RG 26, PHS.

29. They selected delegates in proportion to the size of each denomination in the camps. For example, since Methodists had the greatest number of ordained Nikkei working in the camps, the commission suggested they send nine Nikkei delegates, while Episcopalians sent two. Chapman to Members of the Japanese Church Committee, 3 June 1943, Box 4/Fld 3, Gillett Papers, UCLA.

30. PCC Meeting Minutes, 13–15 July 1943; Minutes of the Conference of Leaders of Japanese Christian Work, 15–17 Dec. 1943.

31. Nikkei made similar complaints about the WRA. They claimed that if the government had consulted them, a more effective plan may have been possible, resulting in positive gains for both white administrators and Nikkei. Clarence Gillett, Notes Taken at the Conference of Japanese Christian Leaders, 16 Dec. 1943, Box 4/Fld 1, Gillett Papers, UCLA.

32. Matsumoto and Marion Olive Lerrigo, *A Brother Is a Stranger* (New York: John Day, 1946).

33. Chapman to Fisher, 12 July 1944, Box 1/Fld 6, Chapman Papers, GTU.

34. Proposed letter to Dillon Myer, 4 July 1942, Box 5/Fld 12, Topical Misc., MMA; J. Kimmett to Bishop P. A. McGovern, 7 Sept. 1942, Box 6/Fld 3, Topical Misc., MMA; Lavery to Drought, 19 Jan. 1943, Box 6/Fld 4, Topical Misc., MMA;

James T. O'Dowd, Report to National Catholic Welfare Conference, Spring 1944, Box 6/Fld 7, Topical Misc., MMA.

35. Seattle's and Portland's Buddhist and Protestant churches and schools loaned Minidokans eighteen pianos, four organs, over two thousand folding chairs, and many benches and tables. Report for quarter ending 31 Dec. 1942 and 29 Jan. 1943, Reel 330, JAER; "Over 2,000 Chairs Coming—Townsend," *Minidoka Irrigator*, 28 Oct. 1942, 3; Minutes of the Monthly Meeting, AFSC Pacific Coast Branch, 1 Aug. 1942, Box 1/Fld 13, Constantine Panunzio Collection (Collection Number 1636), UCLA; Drought to Maurice Ahern, Maryknoll College, 4 May 1942, Box 5/Fld 11, Topical Misc., MMA.

36. Robert W. O'Brien, *The College Nisei* (New York: Reprinted by Arno Press, [1949] 1978), 135–36.

37. Remsen Bird to Guy Snavely, Association of American Colleges, 18 May 1942, and Bird to Clarence Pickett, 27 May 1942, Box 1/Fld 1, JAR; Eisenhower to Clarence Pickett, 5 May 1942, Box 2/Fld 5, RG 37, PHS; Pickett to Eisenhower, 10 May 1942, WRA, SIS-JAR 1942; "A Message to the Society of Friends and Our Fellow Christians," June 1942, Publicity—General, SIS-JAR 1942; Information Bulletins, AFSC Pacific Coast Branch, 3 June 1942, Box 1/Fld 13, Panunzio Collection, UCLA; Caffrey to Drought, 29 June 1942, Box 5/Fld 12, Topical Misc., MMA.

38. Allan Austin, *From Concentration Camp to Campus: Japanese American Students and World War II* (Champaign: University of Illinois Press, 2004), 28–29.

39. Ibid., 63–66.

40. The Catholic, Congregational, Episcopal, Reformed, and Methodist churches donated between $41,000 and $16,000 each. The AFSC, Disciples of Christ, Free Methodists, and Lutherans gave $1,000 to $2,000 each, and the United Brethren gave $325. Report of the National Student Relocation Council, Box 4/Fld 1, Gillett Papers, UCLA.

41. Report on Scholarship Allocations, July 1942 to June 30, 1946, Box 1/Fld 1, RG 37, PHS; O'Brien, *The College Nisei*, 135–48.

42. Pickett, *For More than Bread* (Boston: Little, Brown, 1953), 159.

43. Austin, *From Concentration Camp to Campus*, 44, 165; Bryant Drake to Gillett, 7 Aug. 1943, Box 2/Fld 2, Gillett Papers, UCLA; "Do the Buddhist Students Feel Left Out?" undated, Box 4/Fld 6, Gillett Papers, UCLA; Herbert and Margaret Nicholson, *Comfort All Who Mourn: The Life Story of Herbert and Madeline Nicholson* (Fresno, Calif.: Bookmates International, 1982), 83; "Distribution by Denomination of Students Who Have Applied to NJASRC," undated, Box 4/Fld 5, Gillett Papers, UCLA.

44. Leopold Tibesar to Seraphin Tibesar, 7 Jan. 1945, Box 3/Vol. 1/Fld 12, QU; L. Tibesar to S. Tibesar, 26 Oct. 1943; Myer to John Koebele, President of Quincy College, 20 July 1943; and Joanne Oyabe to S. Tibesar, 27 July 1943, Box 3/Vol. 1/Fld 11, QU; Perry Hall to S. Tibesar, 28 May 1943, Box 3/Vol. 1/Fld 10, QU.

45. Drought to Lavery, 7 Aug. 1942, and Drought to O'Dowd, 13 Aug. 1942, Box 6/Fld 3, Topical Misc., MMA; Lavery to Walsh, 25 June 1943, Box 6/Fld 4, Topical Misc., MMA.

46. Drought to Lavery, 7 Aug. 1942; Lavery to Walsh, 25 June 1943; Tibesar to Considine, 22 June 1943, Box 6/Fld 4, Topical Misc., MMA; O'Dowd, Report to National Catholic Welfare Conference.

47. Toru Matsumoto, *Beyond Prejudice: A Story of the Church and Japanese Americans* (New York: Friendship Press, 1946), 40–42; WRA Semi-Annual Report, January–June 1943, Box 7/Fld 11, Gillett Papers, UCLA; Yoosun Park, "The Role of the YWCA in the World War II Internment of Japanese Americans: A Cautionary Tale for Social Work," *Social Service Review* 87 (Sept. 2013): 477–524.

48. American Bible Society, undated, Box 4/Fld 2, Gillett Papers, UCLA; PCC Meeting Minutes, 26 June 1942; Chapman to Eric North, 25 Apr. 1944, Box 1/Fld 47, Chapman Papers, GTU; PCC Meeting Minutes, 21 Aug. 1942, Box 15/Fld 31, CCGS; Chapman to E. Marshal Taylor, 12 Dec. 1943, Box 1/Fld 55, Chapman Papers, GTU.

49. John Bennett suggested that the Pacific School of Religion Library coordinate the effort. Congregational Committee Meeting Minutes, 15 Sept. 1942; PCC Meeting Minutes, 2 Dec. 1942, Box 1/Fld 1, J. Stillson Judah: Japanese Camp Books collection, GTU 2001-3-01, GTU; Correspondence between librarians and Judah, Fall 1942, Box 1/Fld 2, Judah Papers, GTU.

50. Yoshikazu Horikoshi to Judah, 26 Jan. 1943, Box 1/Fld 11, Judah Papers, GTU; Junichi Fujimori to Judah, 18 Feb. 1943, Box 1/Fld 13, Judah Papers, GTU.

51. Judah to Martin Rist, 15 Nov. 1942 and 17 Mar. 1943, Box 1/Fld 2, Judah Papers, GTU; Bovenkerk to Judah, 24 Jan. 1944, Box 1/Fld 24, Judah Papers, GTU; Judah to Aki, 17 Mar. 1943, Box 1/Fld 12, Judah Papers, GTU.

52. Aki worked with Judah at the Berkeley library before the war, so they had an established relationship. Judah to Aki, 15 and 17 Mar. and 14 Apr. 1943, Box 1/Fld 12, Judah Papers, GTU.

53. Home Missions Council, "America's Biggest Christmas Party," Box 2/Fld 3, Kaoru Ichihara Papers (1839-1), UW; Gordon Chapman, "Meeting the Unexpected," 1942 Annual Report of the Special Representative for Japanese Work, 3 Mar. 1943, Box 17/Fld 8, RG 93, PHS; "7,000 Gifts Received through Two Churches," *Minidoka Irrigator*, 19 Dec. 1942, 8; "17,000 Gifts Donated Hunt," *Minidoka Irrigator*, 30 Dec. 1942, 2; Schmoe to Homer Morris, 4 Jan. 1943, Branch Office: Seattle, SIS-JAR 1943.

54. Interview with Kalvin K. Hara, Apr. 1982, Series 3/Box 5/Fld 16, Rosalie H. Wax Papers, BANC MSS 83/115 c, UCB.

55. Information Bulletin, AFSC Southern California Branch, 10 Oct. 1944, Reel 082, JAER.

56. Sandra C. Taylor, *Jewel of the Desert: Japanese American Internment at Topaz* (Berkeley: University of California Press, 1993), 157.

57. "Variety of Events Marks Second Christmas in Hunt," *Minidoka Irrigator*, 25 Dec. 1943, 1.

58. Shizue Seigel, *In Good Conscience: Supporting Japanese Americans During the Internment* (San Mateo, Calif.: AACP, 2006), 264.

59. Nicholson, *Comfort All Who Mourn*, 95.

60. Fisher to Chapman, 31 Aug. 1942, Box 1/Fld 51, Chapman Papers, GTU; "Colorado Church Council Visits the Granada Center," *Granada Christian Church News*, 1 Nov. 1942 [misdated 1 Nov. 1941], Reel 303, JAER; Religious Services, undated, Reel 330, JAER; Reifsnider to Chapman, Nov. 1942, Box 1/Fld 14, Chapman Papers, GTU; Tibesar, Minidoka Diary, Nov. 1942 and Mar. 1944, Box 35/Fld 6, MFBD; Fukuyama to Adkins, 19 Sept. 1944, Box 1/Incoming Letters, Betty Fukuyama Papers (4411-1), UW; Andrews to Thomas, 11 Aug. 1943 and 14 Aug. 1944, Box 2/Fld 4, Andrews Papers (1908-3), UW.

61. T. L. Harris, "Thinking of Rohwer and Jerome," *Arkansas Baptist*, 17 Mar. 1943, 3; Mitchell, "Our Japanese Visitors," *Arkansas Churchman*, Nov. 1942, 3; Chapman to Jacob Long, 31 Dec. 1942, Box 11/Fld 42, RG 301.7, PHS.

62. Community Activities Section, History/Final Report, Box 1/Series 2/Fld 2, Nathaniel R. Griswold Papers, UA; William Cary Anderson, "Early Reaction in Arkansas to the Relocation of Japanese in the State," *Arkansas Historical Quarterly* 23 (Autumn 1964): 207; R. Bland Mitchell to Reifsnider, 5 Aug. 1942, Box 1/Fld 26, Chapman Papers, GTU.

63. John Howard, *Concentration Camps on the Home Front: Japanese Americans in the House of Jim Crow* (Chicago: University of Chicago Press, 2008), 168.

64. "Gas Rationing Hits Amache," *Granada Christian Church News*, 13 Dec. 1942, Reel 303, JAER.

65. Howard, *Concentration Camps*, 127.

66. Highlights of Community Activities from 20 Sept. to 31 Dec. 1942, Box 1/Series 2/Fld 18, Griswold Papers, UA.

67. Ward, "'No Jap Crow': Japanese Americans Encounter the World War II South," *Journal of Southern History* 73 (February 2007); Howard, *Concentration Camps*, 149; "Minstrel Show Is Held," *Denson Tribune*, 5 May 1944, 1.

68. Bulletin of the Young People's Missionary Society of the Free Methodist Church, 4 June 1943, Box 4/Fld 5, Japanese-American Internment Camp Church Bulletins and Newsletters Collection, GTU 94-9-02, GTU; "Clearwater Clarion Call: Clearwater Baptist Church News," 25 Aug. 1943, Box 4/Fld 7, Bulletins and Newsletters Collection, GTU.

69. Kazuo Ikebasu, History of Rohwer Community Activities Section, 20 May 1943, Box 5/Fld 3, Gillett Papers, UCLA.

70. Minutes of the Executive Committee of the Committee for Work with the Japanese Evacuees, 21 July 1942, Box 1/Fld 1, Gillett Papers, UCLA; Booth to Janet McKelvie, 7 July 1942, Denver Council of Churches, SIS-JAR 1942; Memorandum on the Work of the Protestant Churches, 20 July 1942; Galen Fisher, *Round Table on Japanese Evacuation* (New York: American Council Institute of Pacific Relations, October 1942), 9; Meeting of Special Group Called to Consider Plans for Japanese Resettlement, 24 Sept. 1942, Box 59/Fld 11, RG 18, PHS; Meeting of

the Committee on Resettlement of Japanese Americans, 6 Apr. 1944, Committee on Resettlement of Japanese Americans—Printed Items, SIS-JAR 1944.

71. Harper Sakaue, "Clearwater Clarion Call: Clearwater Baptist Church News," Sept./Oct. 1944, Box 4/Fld 7, Bulletins and Newsletters Collection, GTU.

72. "The Japanese in Our Midst," 1942, updated in 1943, Box 53/Fld 2, William C. Carr Papers, JARP.

73. Toru Matsumoto to Jacob Long, 8 Apr. 1943, Box 12/Fld 5, RG 301.7, PHS.

74. Clarence Gillett, ed., "A Touchstone of Democracy: The Japanese in America" (New York: Council for Social Action of the Congregational Christian Churches, June 1942 [updated in June 1943]), 3; Nagata, "O California, Dear California," undated, Box 8/Fld 2, Gillett Papers, UCLA; Seigel, *In Good Conscience*, 48.

75. American Baptist Home Mission Society, "Democracy Demands," 1944, JAR; Adams, *Born Free and Equal: The Story of Loyal Japanese Americans, Manzanar Relocation Center, Inyo County, California* (Bishop, Calif.: Spotted Dog Press, 2001); Galen Fisher, "The Drama of Japanese Evacuation," in "A Touchstone of Democracy," 30.

76. Tibesar, untitled, Nov. 1944, Box 6/Fld 7, Topical Misc., MMA.

77. Benedict and Weltfish, "The Races of Mankind," Public Affairs Pamphlet No. 85 (New York: Public Affairs Committee, 1943). Weltfish also published "Racism: Japan's Secret Weapon," *Far Eastern Survey* 14 (29 Aug. 1945): 233–37.

78. Schultz, *Tri-Faith America*, 56.

79. American Board of National Missions of the Presbyterian Church in the USA, "What Does Race Matter? To a Chinese American, to a Japanese American," 2nd ed., 1947, Box 8/Fld 8, Gillett Papers, UCLA; Hedstrom, *The Rise of Liberal Religion: Book Culture and American Spirituality in the Twentieth Century* (New York: Oxford University Press, 2012), 156–57.

80. Charles McCarthy, "No New Acadia," *Field Afar*, June 1942, 12–13, 32; Tibesar, "Minidoka Sanctuary," *Field Afar*, April 1944, 28–29; Lavery, "Ten-Thousand-Mile Parish," *Field Afar*, Jan.–Feb. 1945, 6–8; "Says American Born Japanese Are Loyal to the U.S.," *Our Sunday Visitor*, 28 Dec. 1941, 5; Mary Just to Considine, 10 Aug. 1943; Considine to Tibesar, 12 Aug. 1943; and Tibesar to Considine, 28 Dec. 1943, Box 6/Fld 5, Topical Misc., MMA; Considine to Tibesar, 20 Nov. 1944, Box 6/Fld 7, Topical Misc., MMA; Tibesar to Considine, 8 Jan. 1945, Box 6/Fld 8, Topical Misc., MMA.

81. Requests for Publicity Materials, Box 1/Fld 49, Chapman Papers, GTU; Congregational Committee for Christian Democracy Meeting Minutes, 10 Sept. 1946, Box 1/Fld 1, Gillett Papers, UCLA.

82. Congregational Committee on Christian Democracy, "You Can Do Something about It," 1945, Box 3/Fld 14, Gillett Papers, UCLA; Resolutions from Deering on the Pilgrim Fellowship and Aid to the Japanese Americans and the National Pilgrim Fellowship's Program of Assistance to the Japanese Americans, undated, Box 1/Fld 5, Gillett Papers, UCLA; "That Fellowship May Not Be Broken," Apr. 1943, Box 1/Fld 52, Chapman Papers, GTU.

83. Tibesar, Minidoka Diary, Oct. 1942, Box 35/Fld 6, MFBD; Tibesar to Considine, 8 Jan. 1945; Tibesar, "Which Way Democracy," summer 1945, Box 6, QU; Tibesar, untitled essay, undated, Box 6/Fld 2, Series 423, Deceased Society Members Media Files, MMA.

84. Citizens' Committee for Resettlement: Minutes of the Executive Committee Meeting, 21 Jan. 1944, Box 1/Fld 1, Gillett Papers, UCLA; Letter from the Publicity Chairman of the Citizens' Committee for Resettlement, Box 1/Fld 5, Gillett Papers, UCLA; PCC Meeting Minutes, 13–15 July 1943; *The Minidoka Churchman*, 24 June 1944, Bulletins and Newsletters Collection, GTU.

85. Klancy Clark de Nevers, *The Colonel and the Pacifist: Karl Bendetsen, Perry Saito, and the Incarceration of Japanese Americans during World War II* (Salt Lake City: University of Utah Press, 2004), 12, 226–30, 235–36.

86. "Hostile Japs Hoodwink Churches: Spread Propaganda for Jobs in War Centers," *International Teamster*, Feb. 1944, 17–18.

87. Quoted in FOR Northern California Office, "Church Measures the Evacuation," 26 Oct. 1942, Box 53/Fld 2, JARP; Resolutions Favoring Immediate Return of Evacuees as Passed by the Presbyterian Synod of California, 25–27 July 1944, Box 78/Fld 325, RG 210, NARA; National Inter-Collegiate Christian Council, Sept. 1942, and Board of Missions and Church Extension of the Methodist Church, 5 Dec. 1942, quoted in *The Concern of the Church for the Christian and Democratic Treatment of Japanese Americans* (New York: Committee on Resettlement of Japanese Americans, April 1944), 11, 15.

88. Alfred Tonness, 2 Sept. 1943, Box 53/Fld 4, Carr Papers, JARP; Alphonzo E. Bell and Donald H. Tippett to members of the California legislature, 30 Jan. 1943, Reel 082, JAER; Congregational Committee for Christian Democracy Meeting Minutes, 10 Sept. 1946, Box 1/Fld 1, Gillett Papers, UCLA; PCC Meeting Minutes, 27 Apr. 1943.

89. Seattle AFSC Office, Information and Suggestions Concerning the Return of Our Japanese American Neighbors, 23 May 1944, Branch Office: Seattle—General, SIS-JAR 1944; Resolution Adopted at the Annual Meeting of the Washington State Council of Churches and Christian Education, 11 Jan. 1944, and Apel to Delos Emmons, Commanding General of the Western Defense Command, 21 Feb. and 28 Mar. 1944, Box 15/Fld 2, CCGS; Douglas Dye, "For the Sake of Seattle's Soul: The Seattle Council of Churches, the Nikkei Community, and World War II," *Pacific Northwest Quarterly* 93 (Summer 2002): 133.

90. Resolution of the Catholic Interracial Council of LA on the Subject of American Citizens of Japanese Descent and Alien Japanese, 6 Sept. 1944, Reel 082, JAER; "What of President's Promise?" and "'Return the Evacuees,' Say the Churches," *Church Call*, a newsletter of the First Methodist Church, 22 Sept. 1944, Box 53/Fld 3, Carr Papers, JARP.

91. Tibesar to Considine, 8 Jan. 1945, Box 6/Fld 8, Topical Misc., MMA; Tibesar, Minidoka Diary, May–Sept. 1943, Box 35/Fld 6, MFBD; Tibesar to Considine, 28 Dec. 1943, Box 6/Fld 5, Topical Misc., MMA; Tibesar, Relocation Survey, 9

Aug. 1944, and Tibesar to Considine, 19 Nov. 1944, Box 6/Fld 7, Topical Misc., MMA.

92. Linda Tamura, *Nisei Soldiers Break Their Silence: Coming Home to Hood River* (Seattle: University of Washington Press, 2012), 146–49, 153–54, 176, 191–92.

93. Day, "God's Design for Living or Americanism and Christianity Begin at Home," 7 Nov. 1943, Box 8/Fld 10, Gillett Papers, UCLA.

94. Gillett, Correspondence with Media Representatives, 1943–44, Box 3/Fld 1, Gillett Papers, UCLA; Gillett to William Loeb, 18 Mar. 1943, Burlington, Vt., Box 2/Fld 1, Gillett Papers, UCLA.

95. "Orange County Citizens Protest Return of Japs," *Santa Ana Register*, 1944; Jack Hall, "As It Looks to Jack Hall," *Japanese Exclusion League Journal*, May 1945; Schmoe, untitled, 1944, Box 1/Fld 43, Floyd Wilfred Schmoe Papers (496-8), UW.

96. Tibesar, "Are Japanese Evacuees Getting a Fair Break?," *Seattle Times*, 14 Nov. 1943, magazine section; Denver and Colorado Councils of Churches, "Hate Is Moral Poison: The Church Answers Propaganda against Americans of Japanese Ancestry with These Facts," undated, Box 3/Fld 14, Gillett Papers, UCLA; Minutes of the Conference of Leaders of Japanese Christian Work, 15–17 Dec. 1943.

97. Bernard Waring to Twentieth Century Fox Film Corp., 20 Sept. 1942, Publicity—Correspondence, SIS-JAR 1942; Ruth Gefwort to Morris, 18 June 1943; Morris to McClure Syndicate, 15 July 1943; Jerry Siegel and Joe Shuster, *Superman*, 1943 (undated clipping); and Leman to Morris, 18 July 1943, Publicity—General, SIS-JAR 1943; "Superman May Help Evacuees," *Gila News-Courier*, 31 July 1943, 1–2; Jerry Siegel and Joe Shuster, *Superman*, released 18 Aug. 1943, McClure Newspaper Syndicate.

98. Robert Leffingwell, "Little Joe: Give till It Hurts?," *San Francisco Chronicle*, 26 Dec. 1943.

99. Andrews to Leffingwell, 29 Dec. 1943, Box 1/Fld 4, Andrews Papers (1908-3), UW.

100. Royal J. Montgomery to Thom B. Keehn, 19 Apr. 1943, Box 1/Fld 5, Gillett Papers, UCLA; PCC Meeting Minutes, 13–15 July 1943.

101. "Many Churchmen Anti," *Japanese Exclusion League Journal*, July 1945.

102. Walt Godfrey to Raymond Booth, 28 Jan. 1945, Box 78/Fld 324, RG 210, NARA.

103. Charles Warren to Ross Sanderson, 10 Aug. 1942, and Ross Sanderson to Charles Warren, 17 Aug. 1942, Box 15/Fld 1, CCGS.

104. Montgomery to Keehn, 19 Apr. 1943.

105. Riichi Satow, quoted in Eileen Sunada Sarasohn, ed., *The Issei: Portrait of a Pioneer, an Oral History* (Palo Alto, Calif.: Pacific Books, 1983), 245–46.

106. Coffman, *The Christian Century and the Rise of the Protestant Mainline* (New York: Oxford University Press, 2013), 3.

107. Seigel, *In Good Conscience*, 48.

108. Mrs. Winburn Thomas to Myers, 14 May 1943, Box 415/Fld 68.01, RG 210, NARA.

109. Ray Gibbons to Z. Okayama, 25 May 1944, Box 416/Fld 68.01, RG 210, NARA.

110. Chapman, Annual Report, 1943, Box 18/Fld 8, RG 93, PHS.

111. Chapman to Provinse, 9 Mar. 1944, Box 416/Fld 68.01, RG 210, NARA.

112. Gillett, Notes taken at the Conference of Japanese Christian Leaders.

113. Osteen, ed., *The Question of the Gift: Essays across Disciplines* (London: Routledge, 2002), 18.

114. Mauss, *The Gift: The Form and Reason for Exchange in Archaic Societies* (New York: W. W. Norton, 1990), 5.

115. Minutes of the Monthly Meeting of the AFSC Pacific Coast Branch, 11 July 1942, Box 32/Fld 2, Rhoads Collection, HC; Hollinger, *After Cloven Tongues of Fire: Protestant Liberalism in Modern American History* (Princeton, N.J.: Princeton University Press, 2013); Collier-Thomas, *Jesus, Jobs, and Justice: African American Women and Religion* (New York: Alfred A. Knopf, 2010).

## Chapter Three

1. Monica Sone, *Nisei Daughter* (Boston: Little, Brown, 1953), 192–93.

2. "Looking Back through the Files: September 1942," *Minidoka Irrigator*, 25 Sept. 1943, 4.

3. U.S. Department of the Interior, *Minidoka National Monument: General Management Plan* (Seattle: National Park Service, 2006), 20–27; Jeffery F. Burton, Mary M. Farrell, Florence B. Lord, and Richard W. Lord, *Confinement and Ethnicity: An Overview of World War II Japanese American Relocation Sites* (Seattle: University of Washington Press, 2002), 205.

4. WRA Administrative Instruction No. 32, 24 Aug. 1942, Box 1/Fld 12, Kaoru Ichihara Papers (1839-1), UW.

5. Glick to Provinse, 27 July 1942, and Kneier to Provinse, 24 July 1942, Box 415/Fld 68.01, RG 210, NARA.

6. Dolan Kimball to M. Hidashima, 25 Aug. 1943, Box 415/Fld 68.01, RG 210, NARA.

7. "Religion," July 1942, Box 415/Fld 68.01, RG 210, NARA.

8. Philip Schafer to Stafford, 25 May 1943, Box 2/Fld 1, Harry L. Stafford Papers: Records, 1942–46, CSI.

9. WRA, Office of War Information and Office of Strategic Services, *A Challenge to Democracy*, 1944.

10. Andrew Preston, *Sword of the Spirit, Shield of Faith: Religion in American War and Diplomacy* (New York: Alfred A. Knopf, 2012), 319.

11. Correspondence, Box 44, RG 210, NARA.

12. WRA Committee on Religion, "The Problem of Setting up a Policy for Religious Worship," Files of the Poston Christian Church III, Reel 213, JAER.

13. Gordon Chapman to Charles Reifsnider, 26 Oct. 1942, Box 1/Fld 14, Gordon K. Chapman: Protestant Church Commission for Japanese Service, GTU 2002-9-01, GTU; Kiernan, Report to the Maryknoll Council: Survey of the Japanese Evacuation and Resettlement Problem, 27 May 1942, Box 5/Fld 11, Topical Misc., MMA; Questionnaires and responses, 1943, Box 415/Fld 68.01, RG 210, NARA.

14. J. Kimmett to Bishop P. A. McGovern, 7 Sept. 1942, Box 6/Fld 3, Topical Misc., MMA; James O'Dowd to Francis Caffrey, 29 Apr. 1942, Box 5/Fld 10, Topical Misc., MMA; Letter proposed for WRA, 4 July 1942, Box 5/Fld 12, Topical Misc., MMA; Kiernan, Religious Care of the Japanese under the War Relocation Authority, 14 July 1942, Box 5/Fld 11, Topical Misc., MMA.

15. Eisenhower to Walsh, 8 Apr. 1942, Box 5/Fld 10, Topical Misc., MMA.

16. Kiernan, Religious Care.

17. Toru Matsumoto, *Beyond Prejudice: A Story of the Church and Japanese Americans* (New York: Friendship Press, 1946), 98–99; WRA Committee on Religion, "Problem of Setting up a Policy."

18. S. T. Kimball to Provinse, 22 May 1943, Box 415/Fld 68.01, RG 210, NARA.

19. "Religious Workers Meeting," 12 Jan. 1943, Reel 330, JAER.

20. Robertson to Myer, 20 Mar. 1943, Box 415/Fld 68.01, RG 210, NARA.

21. Powell to Provinse, 2 Jan. 1943; Ralph Merritt to Myer, 19 Mar. 1943; Kowta to Provinse, 3 Nov. 1942; and Provinse to Mark Dawber, 25 Nov. 1942, Box 415/Fld 68.01, RG 210, NARA; Shirrell to Fryer, 30 July 1942, Box 44/Fld 571, RG 210, NARA.

22. Shirrell to Fryer, 30 July 1942; Tibesar, Autobiographical Writings, undated, Box 3/Vol. 1/Section 2, QU; Tibesar, Minidoka Diary, Nov. 1942, Box 35/Fld 6, MFBD.

23. John Howard, *Concentration Camps on the Home Front: Japanese Americans in the House of Jim Crow* (Chicago: University of Chicago Press, 2008), 151, 172.

24. Kiernan, Report to Council on Discussion with Msgr. Ready of NCWC, 1 May 1942, Box 5/Fld 11, Topical Misc., MMA.

25. WRA Administrative Order No. 23, 24 Aug. 1942, Box 1/Fld 12, Ichihara Papers, UW; Drought to O'Dowd, 13 Aug. 1942, Box 6/Fld 3, Topical Misc., MMA.

26. Drought to Lavery, 3 July 1942, Box 5/Fld 12, Topical Misc., MMA.

27. Kiernan, Report to the Maryknoll Council; Secretary General to James O'Dowd, 9 June 1943, and Caffrey to Kiernan, 1 June 1942, Box 5/Fld 12, Topical Misc., MMA; Drought to Lavery, 7 Aug. 1942.

28. James Sakoda, "The Christian Church in Tule Lake," 1 Oct. 1942, Reel 181, JAER.

29. Protestants used words like "union," "ecumenical," "community," and "federated" inconsistently, making it difficult to understand what they were discussing. Seattleites apparently differentiated between "united" and "federated," but Minidoka Federated Church operated identically to Tule Lake Union Church. Minutes of the

Inter-Area Church Council Meeting with the Church School Faculty, 7 Aug. 1942, Box 1/Fld 3, Ichihara Papers, UW; Sakoda, "Christian Church in Tule Lake."

30. Minutes of the Inter-Area Church Council Meeting, 7 Aug. 1942.

31. G. H. Powers to Robert M. Cozzens, 15 June 1942, Box 44/Fld 571, RG 210, NARA.

32. "Center Churches to be Constructed by WRA," *Gila News-Courier,* 12 Sept. 1942, 3; Royden Susu-Mago, "A Letter to the Editor," *Gila News-Courier,* 14 Oct. 1942, 2.

33. Heart Mountain Relocation Center, the only exception, received $10,000 from the Board of National Missions of the Presbyterian Church for an "attractively planned church" in December 1942. E. R. Fryer to Robert Cozzens, 11 June 1942, Box 44/Fld 571, RG 210, NARA; WRA Quarterly Report, Oct.–Dec. 1942, Box 7/Fld 10, Clarence Gillett Papers (Collection 130), UCLA; Memorandum on the Work of the Protestant Churches in Japanese Relocation Centers and Settlements, 20 July 1942, Box 4/Fld 1, Gillett Papers, UCLA.

34. Article from *Missions,* Jan. 1943, 26, Box 1/Fld 1, Betty Fukuyama Papers (4411), UW.

35. WRA Administrative Instruction No. 32.

36. Reply to Questions of Religious Policies, 30 Mar. 1943, and Interfaith Council Meeting, 14 Sept. 1943, Reel 330, JAER.

37. Sohei Kowta to Friend, 25 May 1943, Box 12/Fld 3, RG 301.7, PHS.

38. George Townsend, "Service with the War Relocation Authority, 1942–46," 1983, Manuscripts 975, HC.

39. Chapman to Clarence Gillett, 4 Feb. 1944, Box 1/Fld 12, Gillett Papers, UCLA; Kodaira to Townsend, 1 Sept. 1942, Reel 330, JAER.

40. Phillip Schafer to James Sakamoto, 21 June 1943, Box 10/Fld 27, James Y. Sakamoto Papers, UW.

41. "First Communion Class" (denshopd-i37-00684), 1943, NARA, DDA.

42. Tibesar, Minidoka Diary, June 1943, Nov. and Dec. 1942, Box 35/Fld 6, MFBD; Tibesar, summary of work, Oct. 1943, and Clement Boesflug, Newsletter of Minidoka's Catholic Church, 1 Apr. 1945 and 1 May 1945, Reel 331, JAER; "First Communion Class" (denshopd-i37-00683), 1943, Minidoka Catholic Church, NARA, DDA.

43. Tibesar, Minidoka Diary, Oct. 1942, Box 35/Fld 6, MFBD.

44. Kenneth I. Helphand, *Defiant Gardens: Making Gardens in Wartime* (San Antonio, Tex.: Trinity University, 2006), 12–13; Jane E. Dusselier, *Artifacts of Loss: Crafting Survival in Japanese American Concentration Camps* (New Brunswick, N.J.: Rutgers University Press, 2008), 1–5, 154–61.

45. "The Altar of the Church of the Holy Apostles," *The Minidoka Churchman,* 1 Apr. 1945, Reel 331, JAER.

46. Kuroda, Memorandum, Fall 1942, Box 155/Fld 3, Kuroda Papers, JARP.

47. Smith, Notes on Sermon, 17 Aug. 1942, Box 44/Fld 571, RG 210, NARA; Kuroda, Memorandum, Fall 1942; Kuroda, "Tule Lake Union Christian Church," 12 Nov. 1942, Box 155/Fld 3, Kuroda Papers, JARP.

48. Fukuyama to Adkins, 10 Nov. 1944 and 1 and 10 Oct. 1944, Box 1/Incoming Letters, Fukuyama Papers, UW.

49. PCC Meeting Minutes, 21 Aug. 1942, Box 15/Fld 31, CCGS; Tentative Constitution of . . . Protestant Church, undated, Box 4/Fld 2, Gillett Papers, UCLA; Kojiro Unoura to Chapman, 6 and 13 Feb. 1943, Box 1/Fld 51, Chapman Papers, GTU; Constitution of the Community Christian Church, Jerome Relocation Center, undated, Box 12/Fld 6, RG 301.7, PHS.

50. Kowta to Friend, 25 May 1943.

51. PCC Meeting Minutes, 21 Aug. 1942.

52. Chapman to Jutaro Yokoi, 19 May 1944, Box 1/Fld 9, Chapman Papers, GTU; WRA Semi-Annual Report, January–June 1943, Box 7/Fld 11, Gillett Papers, UCLA.

53. Doris Hayashi, Notes on Tanforan Young People's Council, Summer 1942, Reel 016, JAER.

54. Bovenkerk to Chapman, 6 May 1943, Box 1/Fld 1, Chapman Papers, GTU.

55. Fukuyama to Adkins, 18 Oct. 1944, Box 1/Incoming Letters, Fukuyama Papers, UW.

56. Reply to Questions of Religious Policies.

57. Chapman to Roy P. Adams, 16 May 1944, Box 1/Fld 31, Chapman Papers, GTU.

58. Thompson to Frank Herron Smith, Bishop Baker, the Seattle Council of Churches, and the Methodist Board of Missions, 14 Dec. 1943, Box 15/Fld 5, CCGS.

59. "Sunday Church Services," *Minidoka Irrigator*, 21 Nov. 1942, 2; Memorandum on the Work of the Protestant Churches, 20 July 1942.

60. "Christian Summer Schools Offer Many Courses," *Minidoka Irrigator*, 31 July 1943, 6.

61. Of the 329 students at Huntville Elementary School (one of the Minidoka's two elementary schools), 240 enrolled in the two-week summer school. "Church Vacation Schools to Start," *Minidoka Irrigator*, 27 June 1943, 3; Thompson to Gertrude Apel, 18 June 1943, Box 15/Fld 2, CCGS; Arthur Kleinkopf, *Relocation Center Diary*, 28 June 1943, 218; "Catholic Summer Schools Start," *Minidoka Irrigator*, 14 Aug. 1943, 8; "Federated Church Summer School," 3–13 Aug. 1943, Reel 331, JAER; "Church Vacation Schools Hold Commencement," *Minidoka Irrigator*, 17 July 1943, 5.

62. Fukuyama, "A Report of My Work at Minidoka," Aug. 1942–Aug. 1945, Box 7/Evacuation, Fukuyama Papers, UW.

63. Jane Chase, "My Dear Bishop: A Report from Minidoka, 23 Nov. 1942," *Idaho Yesterdays* 44 (Summer 2000): 6.

64. Chapman to Jesse Bader, 26 Oct. 1943, Box 1/Fld 46, Chapman Papers, GTU; Chase, "My Dear Bishop," 6.

65. A sociologist observed a similar "schism" at an Arizona camp. Church services listed in camp newspapers reveal this pattern in all ten incarceration centers. "Bishops Will Visit Project," *Minidoka Irrigator*, 7 Nov. 1942, 5; "Religious Life in the Gila Community," 2 Nov. 1942, Reel 284, JAER.

66. Chase, "Dear Bishop," 6; Thompson to Smith, 14 Dec. 1943; Thompson to Apel, 18 June 1943; "Special Episcopal Christmas Service," *Minidoka Irrigator*, 18 Dec. 1943, 3; "Church Program," *Minidoka Irrigator*, 18 Dec. 1943, 4; Andrew N. Otani, *A History of Japanese-American Episcopal Churches* (n.p., 1980).

67. Lester Suzuki, *Ministry in the Assembly and Relocation Centers of World War II* (Berkeley, Calif.: Yardbird Press, 1979), 232–33.

68. Unoura to Chapman, 6 Feb. 1943; Bill Knott, "Surviving Injustice" and "Prisoners of Hope," *Adventist Review*, 28 Sept. 2000, 8–17; "Protestant Ministers and Missionaries Now Laboring in WRA Relocation Centers," Mar. 1944, Box 4/Fld 2, Gillett Papers, UCLA; "We Are Seventh Day Adventists," *Granada Christian Church News*, 13 Dec. 1942, and "Seventh Day Adventists News," *Granada Christian Church News*, 1 Nov. 1942 [misdated 1 Nov. 1941], Reel 303, JAER; "Radio Preacher to Speak at Rally," Heart Mountain General Information Bulletin, 15 Oct. 1942, Box 1/Fld 12, Constantine Panunzio Collection (Collection Number 1636), UCLA.

69. Chapman to Reifsnider, 26 Oct. 1942; "Issei–Nisei Christmas Services," *Minidoka Herald*, 19 Dec. 1943, 1.

70. Thompson to Smith, 14 Dec. 1943; Marie Jeurgensen to Chapman, 5 Dec. 1942, and Chapman to Thompson, 16 Dec. 1942, Box 1/Fld 20, Chapman Papers, GTU; "Protestant Ministers and Missionaries Now Laboring."

71. Yosh Nakagawa, interview by Tom Ikeda, 7 Dec. 2004, DDA; Okuda to the Farquharsons, 8 Nov. 1942, Box 1/Fld 1, Mary Farquharson Records (397-5), UW.

72. Memorandum on the Work of the Protestant Churches, 20 July 1942; Kodaira to Townsend, 1 Sept. 1942; Thompson to Smith, 14 Dec. 1943; Andrews to Thomas, 9 Mar. 1943, Box 2/Fld 4, Andrews Papers (1908-3), UW; Tibesar, Minidoka Diary, Dec. 1942, Box 35/Fld 6, MFBD.

73. Chapman to Hannaford, 12 Nov. 1943, Box 1/Fld 11, Chapman Papers, GTU; Thompson to Smith, 14 Dec. 1943.

74. Warren to Harvey Coverley, 31 Mar. 1942, Box 1/Fld 9, Gillett Papers, UCLA; Andrews to Thomas, 13 Apr. 1943, Box 2/Fld 4, Andrews Papers (1908-3), UW; Andrews to Thomas, 9 Mar. 1943.

75. Morikawa, "Jesus Is Lord," 21 June 1977, reprinted in *Jitsuo Morikawa: A Prophet for the Twenty-First Century: A Legacy of Sixty Inspiring Sermons*, ed. Paul Nagano and William L. Malcomson (Richmond, Calif.: Council for Pacific Asians Theology, 2000), 263.

76. Matsumoto, *Beyond Prejudice*, 97–98.

77. Gordon Chapman, Annual Report, 1943, Box 18/Fld 8, RG 93, PHS.

78. A congregational history written a decade after the war remembered the camp's ecumenism in a similarly interested but not fervent manner. *Watsonville Westview Presbyterian Church: The 60th Anniversary, 1895–1958* (Watsonville, Calif.: n.p., 1958).

79. Paul Nagano, interview by Stephen Fugita (primary) and Becky Fukuda, 25 May 1999, DDA; Matsumoto, *Beyond Prejudice*, 98.

80. "Religious Activities in Minidoka," *Minidoka Irrigator*, 25 Sept. 1943, 4.

81. Fukuyama to DeYoung, 14 Dec. 1943, Reel 330, JAER.

82. "Busiest Office in Hunt," *The Federated Church Herald*, 2 Jan. 1944, Box 1/Fld 6, Ichihara Papers, UW.

83. James Sakoda, "The 'Residue': The Unresettled Minidokans, 1943–1945," in *Views from Within: The Japanese American Evacuation and Resettlement Study*, ed. Yuji Ichioka (Los Angeles: University of California, Los Angeles, 1989), 263; Ralph Merritt to Chapman, 18 June 1943, Box 1/Fld 1, Chapman Papers, GTU.

84. Robert W. Coombs, interview by Heny Yui, 3 June 1993, Florin Japanese-American Citizens League Oral History Project.

85. Nagano, interview by Fugita and Fukuda, 25 May 1999.

86. Daisuke Kitagawa, *Issei and Nisei* (New York: Seabury Press, 1967), 71.

87. Poston religion report, 2 Aug. 1942, Reel 259, JAER; Nagano, "United States Concentration Camps," *American Baptist Quarterly* 13 (Mar. 1994): 48.

88. Kitagawa, *Issei and Nisei*, 140–41.

89. Sermon by Frank Herron Smith, Poston Religion Report, 16 Aug. 1942, Reel 259, JAER.

90. Fukuyama, "A Report of My Work"; Fukuyama to Adkins, 3 Dec. 1944, and Fukuyama, Christmas Letter, 16 Dec. 1944, Box 1/Incoming Letters, Fukuyama Papers, UW.

91. PCC to Japanese Ministers in the United States, 9 June 1943, Box 4/Fld 3, Gillett Papers, UCLA.

92. As recorded in Fukuyama to Adkins, 1 Oct. 1944.

93. Fukuyama to the Reverend and Mrs. Andrews, 16 Dec. 1942, Box 1/Fld 44, Andrews Papers (1908-1), UW.

94. Tibesar, sermons, 7, 21, and 31 Mar. 1943, Box 3/Vol. 1, QU.

95. "Re-Dedicatory Meetings Scheduled for This Week," *Minidoka Irrigator*, 29 Mar. 1943, 2; Thompson to Apel, 18 June 1943; Fukuyama, "A Report of My Work"; Andrews to Thomas, 9 Feb. 1944, Box 2/Fld 4, Andrews Papers (1908-3), UW; Mary Hirashige to Andrews, 25 June 1942, Box 1/Fld 45, Andrews Papers (1908-3), UW; Thomas to Andrews, 8 Sept. 1944, Box 1/Fld 4, Andrews Papers (1908-1), UW; James Sakamoto, "Report on Seattle's Maryknoll," Apr. 1944, in *Chibes_a-shi no kotodomo: About Father Tibesar*, ed. Takeo Koiwa (Tokyo: Gengokai, 1968), 59.

96. Tibesar to Walsh, 20 Sept. 1943, Box 6/Fld 5, Topical Misc., MMA; Lavery to Drought, 27 Apr. 1942, Box 5/Fld 10, Topical Misc., MMA.

97. Fukuyama to Adkins, 20 Nov. 1944, Box 1/Incoming Letters, Fukuyama Papers, UW.

98. Nagano, interview by Fugita and Fukuda, 25 May 1999.

99. Tamie Tsuchiyama, "Preliminary Report: Santa Anita," 31 July 1942, Reel 016, JAER; Bob Okazaki to Andrews, 24 Feb. 1943, Box 2/Fld 2, Andrews Papers (1908-1), UW; Gary Okihiro, "Religion and Resistance in America's Concentration Camps" *Phylon* 45 (Third Quarter 1981): 224.

100. Nagano, interview by Fugita and Fukuda, 25 May 1999.

101. Yosh to Andrews, 3 Nov. 1943, Box 2/Fld 1, Andrews Papers (1908-1), UW; Takeo and Leatice Nakano, *Within the Barbed Wire Fence: A Japanese Man's Account of His Internment in Canada* (Seattle: University of Washington Press, 1981), 84; Victor N. Okada, ed., *Triumphs of Faith: Stories of Japanese-American Christians During World War II* (Los Angeles: Japanese-American Internment Project, 1998).

102. Tibesar to Considine, 2 June 1943, Box 6/Fld 4, Topical Misc., MMA.

103. Tibesar, Autobiographical Writings, undated, Box 3/Vol. 1/Section 2, QU; Tibesar, Minidoka Diary, Feb. 1944, Box 35/Fld 6, MFBD.

104. Tibesar, Minidoka Diary, Oct. 1944, Box 35/Fld 6, MFBD.

105. Kiernan, Report to the Maryknoll Council.

106. Jeanne Wakatsuki Houston and James D. Houston. *Farewell to Manzanar* (Boston: Houghton Mifflin, 1973), 36–37; Theophane, L.A. Japanese Mission Diary, March–July 1942, Box 34/Fld 4, MFBD; Sister Paul Miki's "Account of Manzanar, 1940s," in *Keeping Faith: European and Asian Catholic Immigrants*, ed. Jeffrey M. Burns, Ellen Skerrett, and Joseph M. White (Maryknoll, N.Y.: Orbis, 2000), 254.

107. Sakamoto, "Report on Seattle's Maryknoll."

108. Tibesar, Minidoka Diary, Dec. 1942 and Apr. 1943, Box 35/Fld 6, MFBD.

109. Tibesar, Minidoka Diary, Sept. 1944, Box 35/Fld 6, MFBD.

110. Tibesar to Walsh, 20 Sept. 1943, Box 6/Fld 5, Topical Misc., MMA.

111. Howard, *Concentration Camps*, 170.

112. "Lost Opportunities," Poston III Christian Church newsletter, 23 July 1944, and George Takaoka, Sermonette, Poston III Christian Church newsletter, 22 Aug. 1943, Box 5/Fld 2, Japanese-American Internment Camp Church Bulletins and Newsletters collection, GTU 94-9-02, GTU; Andrews to Thomas, 11 June 1943, Box 2/Fld 4, Andrews Papers (1908-3), UW.

113. Machida to Gertrude Apel, 8 Dec. 1943, Box 15/Fld 25, CCGS.

114. Aki to Stillson Judah, Spring 1943, Box 1/Fld 12, J. Stillson Judah: Japanese Camp Books Collection, GTU 2001-3-01, GTU.

115. Ernie T. Yamamoto to Andrews, 31 Jan. 1943 [mistakenly dated 1942], Box 1/Fld 52, Andrews Papers (1908-1), UW; Beth Hessel, "The Challenge of Justice and Comity: The Work of the Protestant Church Commissions for Japanese Service during World War II" (paper presented at the World War II and Religion Conference, Tallahassee, Fla., 1 Dec. 2012).

116. Merritt to Chapman, 18 June 1943, Box 1/Fld 1, Chapman Papers, GTU.

117. Townsend to Chapman, 27 June 1945, Box 4/Fld 3, Gillett Papers, UCLA.

118. Regina to Penny Lernoux, 20 Sept. 1988, Box 3/Fld 12, Maryknoll Sisters History Western USA, MMA; Mary Suzuki Ichino, Interview 2, interview by Richard Potashin, 3 Dec. 2008, Manzanar National Historic Site Collection, DDA.

119. Chapman to Unoura, 20 Oct. 1942, Box 1/Fld 51, Chapman Papers, GTU; Fukiko Seki to Andrews, 3 Feb. 1943, Box 2/Fld 3, Andrews Papers (1908-1), UW.

120. Thompson to Apel, 18 June 1943; Andrews, Summary of Tasks, undated, and Andrews to Thomas, 6 Jan. 1943 and July 1944, Box 2/Fld 4, Andrews Papers (1908-3), UW.

121. Biographical Summary, 10 May 1946, Box 2/Fld 4, Andrews Papers (1908-3), UW; Gordon Lahrson to Andrews, 17 Jan. 1945, Box 1/Fld 7, Andrews Papers (1908-3), UW; Thomas to Andrews, 26 July 1943 and 27 Oct. 1943, Box 1/Fld 3, Andrews Papers (1908-1), UW; Bovenkerk to Chapman, 12 June 1943, Box 1/Fld 1, Chapman Papers, GTU.

122. Tibesar, Minidoka Diary, May–Sept. 1943; Tibesar to Considine, 2 June 1943, and Tibesar to John Walsh, 12 June 1943, Box 6/Fld 4, Topical Misc., MMA; Tibesar to Walsh, 20 Sept. 1943, Box 6/Fld 5, Topical Misc., MMA.

123. Tibesar to Walsh, 12 June 1943; Tibesar to Walsh, 31 Oct. 1943, Box 6/Fld 5, Topical Misc., MMA; Tibesar, Minidoka Diary, Oct. 1943, Box 35/Fld 6, MFBD; L. Tibesar to Seraphin Tibesar, 26 Oct. 1943, Box 3/Vol. 1/Fld 11, QU; L. Tibesar to S. Tibesar, 11 Apr. 1944 and 7 Jan. 1945, Box 3/Vol. 1/Fld 12, QU.

124. Seattle Diaries, 8 and 9 Feb. 1945, Box 73/Fld 1, Maryknoll Sisters Diaries, MMA.

125. Okazaki to Andrews, 24 Feb. 1943; Fukiko Seki to Andrews, 1 Mar. 1943, Box 2/Fld 3, Andrews Papers (1908-1), UW.

126. Yukie Yumibe to Andrews, 22 Jan. 1944, Box 2/Fld 21, Andrews Papers (1908-1), UW.

127. Andrews, Summary of Tasks.

128. Thank you letters from families, Box 1/Fld 43 to Box 3/Fld 42, Andrews Papers (1908-1), UW; Theophane, L.A. Japanese Mission Diary, March–July 1942; Tibesar, Minidoka Diary, May–Sept. 1943.

129. Ingress/Egress permits for the week beginning May 10, 1943, Box 2/Fld 10, Stafford Papers, CSI.

130. "Haven of Rest: Welcome Sign up for Visitors," *Minidoka Irrigator*, 10 Apr. 1943, 3.

131. Andrews to Thomas, 3 Mar. 1944, Box 2/Fld 4, Andrews Papers (1908-3), UW.

132. Fukuyama to Adkins, 19 Dec. 1944, Box 1/Incoming Letters, Fukuyama Papers, UW.

133. Sone, *Nisei Daughter*, 201–15; "Weddings: Yokoyama—Itoi," *Minidoka Irrigator*, 6 Mar. 1943, 5.

134. Monthly Activity Reports, Box 2/Fld 4, Andrews Papers (1908-3), UW; Biographical Summary, 10 May 1946; Emery Brooks Andrews, interview by Tom Ikeda, 24 Mar. 2004, DDA; Biographical note, Andrews Papers, UW; Kazuko Hoshide to Mary Andrews, 19 Sept. 1942, Box 1/Fld 45, Andrews Papers (1908-1), UW; Marian Ohno to Emery Andrews, 2 Dec. 1943, and Ohno to Mary Andrews, 8 Dec. 1943, Box 2/Fld 2, Andrews Papers (1908-1), UW.

135. "Federated Christian Church: Organizations and its Officers," undated, Reel 330, JAER.

136. Thompson to Frank Herron Smith, 24 June 1942, Box 15/Fld 1, CCGS.

137. Linda Popp Di Biase, "Neither Harmony nor Eden: Margaret Peppers and the Exile of the Japanese Americans," *Anglican and Episcopal History* 70 (Mar. 2001): 116.

138. S. Arthur Huston, Bishop of Olympia, to Reifsnider, 11 July 1942, Box 1/Fld 26, Chapman Papers, GTU.

139. Esther Mary McCullough Papers (2236-1), UW.

140. Tibesar, Autobiographical Writings, undated, Box 3/Vol. 1/Section 2, QU.

141. Tibesar to Considine, 22 Sept. 1943, Box 6/Fld 5, Topical Misc., MMA; Tibesar, Minidoka Diary, May–Sept. 1943, Box 35/Fld 6, MFBD.

142. See Guy and Marguerite Cook Nisei Collection (Mss33); Elizabeth Carden Japanese Relocation Papers (C266), Small California Collections (Mss3); and Marie Mitsuda Papers (Mss314), Holt-Atherton Department of Special Collections, University of the Pacific; Virginia Tidball Papers, UA. Memoirs of incarcerated women and girls include May Matsuda Gruenewald, *Looking Like the Enemy: My Story of Imprisonment in Japanese-American Internment Camps* (Troutdale, Ore.: New Sage, 2005); and Yoshiko Uchida, *Desert Exile: The Uprooting of a Japanese-American Family* (Seattle: University of Washington Press, 1982).

143. Eric Muller, "Americanism behind Barbed Wire," *Nanzan Review of American Studies* 31 (2009): 13–31.


## Chapter Four

1. De Certeau, *The Practice of Everyday Life* (Berkeley: University of California Press, 1984), ix.

2. Doris Hayashi, Notes on Young People's Council, Summer 1942, Tanforan Assembly Center, Reel 016, JAER.

3. Journal clipping, Jan. 1943, Box 7, Betty Fukuyama Papers (4411-1), UW.

4. Hayashi, Notes on Young People's Council.

5. Thompson to Frank Herron Smith, Bishop Baker, the Seattle Council of Churches, and the Methodist Board of Missions, 14 Dec. 1943, Box 15/Fld 5, CCGS.

6. Fukuyama to Adkins, 5 Nov. 1944, Box 1/Incoming Letters, Fukuyama Papers, UW.

7. Daisuke Kitagawa to Gordon Chapman, 2 Nov. 1942, Box 1/Fld 44, Gordon K. Chapman: Protestant Church Commission for Japanese Service Records, GTU 2002-9-01, GTU.

8. Religious Activity in Tule Lake: Preliminary Report, Nov. 1942, Reel 181, JAER.

9. Frank Miyamoto, Interview III, interview by Stephen Fugita, 29 Apr. 1998, DDA.

10. Eric L. Muller, *American Inquisition: The Hunt for Japanese American Disloyalty in World War II* (Chapel Hill: University of North Carolina, 2007), 46–48.

11. Paul Nagano, interview by Stephen Fugita (primary) and Becky Fukuda, 25 May 1999, DDA; Shigeo Shimada, *A Stone Cried Out* (Valley Forge, Penn.: Judson Press, 1986), 128.

12. Kristine Kim, *Henry Sugimoto: Painting an American Experience* (Berkeley, Calif.: Heyday Books, 2000), 87.

13. The camp newspaper reported that Yamazaki recovered from "slight injuries" in a few days. Andrew N. Otani, *A History of Japanese-American Episcopal Churches* (n.p., 1980), 66; "Assaulters Injure Two Residents," *Densen Tribune*, 9 Mar. 1943, 1; "Attackers Still Sought," *Densen Tribune*, 12 Mar. 1943, 1.

14. Historical Note, "Reverend Yamazaki Was Beaten in Camp Jerome," Henry Sugimoto Collection: A Life Transformed 1941–1945, Hirasaki National Resource Center, JANM.

15. John Howard, *Concentration Camps on the Home Front: Japanese Americans in the House of Jim Crow* (Chicago: University of Chicago Press, 2008), 208.

16. Kim, *Henry Sugimoto*, 87.

17. Muller, *American Inquisition*, 3–4.

18. Andrews to Thomas, 17 Sept. 1943, Box 2/Fld 4, Emery E. Andrews Papers (1908-3), UW.

19. Interfaith Council Meeting, 14 Sept. 1943, Reel 330, JAER.

20. Suzuki to Friends, 17 Aug. 1943, Box 5/Fld 6, Clarence Gillett Papers (Collection 130), UCLA.

21. Tamiko Sano to Mrs. Kozelka, 13 Sept. 1945, Box 1/Fld 15, Gillett Papers, UCLA.

22. Choichi Nitta, quoted in Eileen Sunada Sarasohn, ed., *The Issei: Portrait of a Pioneer, an Oral History* (Palo Alto, Calif.: Pacific Books, 1983), 191; Klancy Clark de Nevers, *The Colonel and the Pacifist: Karl Bendetsen, Perry Saito, and the Incarceration of Japanese Americans during World War II* (Salt Lake City: University of Utah Press, 2004), 203.

23. Ai Miyasaki, quoted in Sarasohn, *Issei*, 209.

24. Daisuke Kitagawa, *Issei and Nisei* (New York: Seabury Press, 1967), 121.

25. De Nevers, *Colonel and the Pacifist*, 203.

26. Kitagawa to Gillett, 9 Sept. 1943, Box 1/Fld 10, Gillett Papers, UCLA; Hannaford to Chapman, 3 Nov. 1943, Box 1/Fld 11, Chapman Papers, GTU.

27. Hannaford to Gillett, 24 Sept. 1943, Box 1/Fld 7, Gillett Papers, UCLA.

28. Hannaford to Chapman, 17 Nov. 1943, Box 1/Fld 11, Chapman Papers, GTU; Hannaford to Chapman, 3 Nov. 1943.

29. A. J. to Marcia Kerr, 24 Aug. 1943, Box 1/Fld 11, Chapman Papers, GTU; Hannaford to Gillett, 5 Nov. 1943, Box 1/Fld 7, Gillett Papers, UCLA; Jacob Long to Hannaford, 23 Nov. 1943, Box 18/Fld 8, RG 93, PHS.

30. Hannaford to Chapman, 26 July 1943, Box 1/Fld 11, Chapman Papers, GTU.

31. Hannaford to Chapman, 29 Sept. 1943, Box 4/Fld 3, Gillett Papers, UCLA; Gary Okihiro, "Religion and Resistance in America's Concentration Camps," *Phylon* 45 (Third Quarter 1984): 223; Thomas W. Grubbs, Report on Tule Lake

Segregation Center, June–Oct. 1944, Box 12/Fld 8, RG 301.7, PHS; Ai Miyasaki, quoted in Sarasohn, *Issei*, 210.

32. Shigeko Fukuye, interview by Rosalie Wax, Dec. 1981, Box 5/Fld 13, Rosalie H. Wax Papers, BANC MSS 83/115 c, UCB.

33. Chapman to Members of the PCC, 12 Apr. 1944, Box 4/Fld 3, Gillett Papers, UCLA; Douglas W. Noble, Report to the Board of National Missions, PCUSA on Wayside Chapel Tour to War Relocation Centers, 15 Mar. to 6 May 1945, Box 1/Fld 13, Chapman Papers, GTU; Sandra C. Taylor, *Jewel of the Desert: Japanese American Internment at Topaz* (Berkeley: University of California Press, 1993), 157.

34. James M. Sakoda, interview by Arthur A. Hansen, 9 Aug. 1988, in Hansen, ed., *Japanese American World War II Evacuation Oral History Project, Part III* (Westport, Conn.: Meckler Publishing, 1991), 394.

35. Hirabayashi to Eleanor Ring, 15 Apr. 1943, Box 1/Fld 6, Ring Family Papers (4241-2), UW.

36. This difference was not only due to Minidoka's greater number of Christians, most of whom answered in the affirmative nationwide. The government segregated only 56 percent of the male Buddhists educated in Japan with a background in agriculture (the group least likely to agree to military service) from Minidoka, while sending 79 percent of those from California to Tule Lake. Northwesterners at other camps responded similarly. Dorothy Swaine Thomas, *The Salvage* (Berkeley: University of California Press, 1952), 100.

37. Eric Muller, *Free to Die for Their Country: The Story of the Japanese American Draft Resisters in World War II* (Chicago: University of Chicago Press, 2001), 54.

38. Hirabayashi to Ring, 15 Apr. 1943; Schmoe, Report to Homer Morris, 3 May 1944, Branch Office: Seattle—General, SIS-JAR 1944.

39. Tats Kojima, interview by Debra Grindeland, 22 Oct. 2006, Bainbridge Island Japanese American Community Collection, DDA.

40. Andrews to E. R. Fryer, 20 Jan. 1943, Box 4/Fld 28, Andrews Papers (1908-1), UW.

41. Ibid.

42. Kojima, interview by Debra Grindeland.

43. Andrews to Fryer, 20 Jan. 1943.

44. Arthur Kleinkopf, *Relocation Center Diary* (Hunt, Idaho: privately printed, 1945), 9 Dec. 1943, 308.

45. Perry Saito to Norio Higano, 14 Apr. 1942, Box 1/Fld 13, Higano Family Papers (2870-1), UW.

46. De Nevers, *Colonel and the Pacifist*, 202.

47. Saito to Higano, 14 Apr. 1942.

48. Saito to Higano, 23 Apr. 1942, Box 1/Fld 13, Higano Papers, UW.

49. Hirabayashi to Eleanor Ring, 6 June 1944, Box 1/Fld 7, Ring Papers (4241-2), UW.

50. Hirabayashi to Ring, 18 Feb. 1944, Box 1/Fld 7, Ring Papers, (4241-2), UW.

51. Hirabayashi to Morris, 23 May 1944, Hirabayashi, SIS-JAR 1944.

52. "Deny Acquittal of Hirabayashi," *Spokane Chronicle*, 1 Dec. 1944.

53. Schmoe to Roy Kurta, 22 Nov. 1944, and Morris to Kurta, 27 Nov. 1944, Hirabayashi, SIS-JAR 1944.

54. Saito to Higano, 14 Apr. 1942.

55. Kinya Okajima, "Volunteers' Banquet," 19 Mar. 1943, Reel 330, JAER; "Testimonial Banquets Held: 1200 Toast Volunteers," *Minidoka Irrigator*, 20 Mar. 1943, 5; Muller, *Free to Die*, 1.

56. Kleinkopf, *Relocation Center Diary*, 29 July 1944, 414.

57. "Memorial Service Honoring Fallen Nisei Soldiers" (denshopd-p2-00035), 11 Aug. 1944, Bain Family Collection, DDA.

58. "Memorial Service for a Nisei Soldier," 1944, Hatate Collection, Wing Luke Museum.

59. "The Niseis' Stars and Stripes," printed in the Memorial Service Program, 11 Aug. 1944, Reel 330, JAER.

60. Memorial Service Program, 11 Aug. 1944.

61. "Memorial Services Honor Twelve Hunt Servicemen," *Minidoka Irrigator*, 26 May 1945, 1, 4.

62. "Second Memorial Service: 16 Servicemen to Be Honored by Centerites," *Rohwer Outpost*, 16 Dec. 1944, 1.

63. "Funeral for Nisei Soldier" (denshopd-i37-00733), NARA, DDA.

64. Thompson to Smith, 14 Dec. 1943.

65. Anne M. Blankenship, "Civil Religious Dissent: Patriotism and Resistance in a Japanese American Incarceration Camp," *Material Religion* 10 (Sept. 2014): 264–93.

66. "Gala Bon Odori Slated for Obon," *Minidoka Irrigator*, 14 Aug. 1943, 5.

67. Peggy S. Furukawa, interview by Tom Ikeda, 20 Mar. 2012, DDA; Betty Fujimoto, interview by Jill Shiraki and Tom Ikeda, Preserving California's Japantowns Collection, DDA.

68. Kleinkopf, *Relocation Center Diary*, 3 May 1945, 515.

69. Kleinkopf, *Relocation Center Diary*, 28 June 1943, 218.

70. Tibesar, Minidoka Diary, Sept. 1944, Box 35/Fld 6, MFBD.

71. Kevin M. Schultz, *Tri-Faith America: How Catholics and Jews Held Postwar America to Its Protestant Promise* (Oxford: Oxford University Press, 2011), 34.

72. Schmoe to Tibesar, 22 Oct. 1944, and Tibesar to Considine, 26 Oct. 1944, Box 6/Fld 7, Topical Misc., MMA.

73. Program, Conference on Problems of Minorities, 15–17 Nov. 1944, Box 6/Fld 7, Topical Misc., MMA.

74. Seattle Diaries, 26 Oct. 1944, Box 73/Fld 1, Maryknoll Sisters Diaries, MMA.

75. Drought to Lavery, 7 Aug. 1942, Box 6/Fld 3, Topical Misc., MMA.

76. Tibesar, Seattle Diary, 10 June 1942, Box 45/Fld 1, MFBD; Tibesar, Minidoka Diary, Oct. 1943, Box 35/Fld 6, MFBD.

77. Fukuyama to the Rev. and Mrs. Andrews, 16 Dec. 1942, Box 1/Fld 44, Andrews Papers, (1908-1), UW.

78. Doris Hayashi, JERS Religion Report, Tanforan Assembly Center, Summer 1942, Reel 016, JAER.

79. Hayashi, Notes on Young People's Council.

80. Manzanar Baccalaureate Program, 27 May 1945, Manzanar National Historic Site Virtual Museum Exhibit, accessed June 13, 2015, http://www.nps.gov /museum/exhibits/manz/exb/Camp/school/MANZ_0170_015_ProgramOutside .html.

81. Russell Cartwright Stroup, *Letters from the Pacific: A Combat Chaplain in World War II* (Columbia: University of Missouri, 2000), 78–79.

82. Philip Gleason, "Americans All: World War II and the Shaping of American Identity," *Review of Politics* 43 (Oct. 1981): 499–502.

83. Schultz, *Tri-Faith America*, 35–41.

84. Mark Silk, "Notes on the Judeo-Christian Tradition in America," *American Quarterly* 36 (Spring 1984): 65, 69; Schultz, *Tri-Faith America*, 35, 54–57; Roxworthy, *The Spectacle of Japanese American Trauma: Racial Performativity and World War II* (Honolulu: University of Hawaii Press, 2008), 102.

85. George Aki, "Memoir: My Thirty Months (1944–1946)," undated, George Aki Collection (AFC/2001/001/11135), Veterans History Project, American Folklife Center, Library of Congress.

86. Nagano, "United States Concentration Camps," 73–74.

87. Ernie T. Yamamoto to Andrews, 31 Jan. 1943 [misdated 1942], Box 1/Fld 52, Andrews Papers (1908-1), UW.

88. Joseph D. Hughes to Andrews, 4 Mar. 1943, Box 1/Fld 3, Andrews Papers (1908-3), UW; E-mail from Brooks Andrews to the author, 1 Sept. 2011.

89. Andrews to Thomas, 9 Mar. 1943, Box 3/Fld 4, Andrews Papers (1908-3), UW.

90. Tibesar to Walsh and Walsh to Tibesar, 6 Mar. 1943, Box 6/Fld 4, Topical Misc., MMA.

91. Fukuyama to Adkins, 11 Nov. 1944, Box 1/Incoming Letters, Fukuyama Papers, UW; Andrews to Thomas, 8 May and 9 Feb. 1944, Box 2/Fld 4, Andrews Papers (1908-3), UW.

92. Thompson to Gertrude Apel, 18 June 1943, Box 15/Fld 2, CCGS.

93. Thompson to Smith, 14 Dec. 1943.

94. Thompson to Apel, 18 June 1943.

95. James Sakoda, "The 'Residue': The Unresettled Minidokans, 1943–1945," in *Views from Within: The Japanese American Evacuation and Resettlement Study*, ed. Yuji Ichioka (Los Angeles: University of California at Los Angeles, 1989), 260, 269.

96. Suzuki to Friends, 27 Apr. 1944, Box 5/Fld 6, Gillett Papers, UCLA.

97. Thompson to Scattered Members, 24 Aug. 1943, Box 1/Fld 6, Kaoru Ichihara Papers (1839-1), UW.

98. Chapman to Bovenkerk, 16 Dec. 1944, Box 1/Fld 1, Chapman Papers, GTU; Rowena Kubo to Mark Dawber, 16 May 1945, Box 4/Fld 3, Gillett Papers, UCLA.

99. Manzanar church bulletins, Box 59/Fld 8, Manzanar War Relocation Center Records (Collection 122), UCLA.

100. Asako Tokuno, ed., *Issei Christians: Selected Interviews from the Issei Oral History Project* (Sacramento, Calif.: Issei Oral History Project, 1977); Victor N. Okada, ed., *Triumphs of Faith: Stories of Japanese-American Christians During World War II* (Los Angeles: Japanese-American Internment Project, 1998).

101. Tibesar, Minidoka Diary, Nov. 1942, Box 35/Fld 6, MFBD.

102. Ibid.

103. Hayashi, Notes on Young People's Council.

104. James Sera, "Religion in Poston," 6 Mar. 1944, Reel 213, JAER.

105. Kowta to Friend, 25 May 1943, Box 12/Fld 3, RG 301.7, PHS.

106. Joshua Shimomura, ed., *Desert Echoes*, Poston Junior Church, Reel 215, JAER.

107. Nagano, "United States Concentration Camps," *American Baptist Quarterly* 13 (Mar. 1994): 71.

108. Hayashi, JERS Religion Report.

109. Asako Takusagawa and Carl Yoshimine, eds., *Streams in the Desert*, Poston III Christian Endeavor Society, Aug. 1943, Box 1/Fld 4, Japanese-American Internment Camp Church Bulletins and Newsletters collection, GTU 94-9-02, GTU.

110. Champions of the organization viewed Endeavor's "adaptation to all races, . . . churches and ages" as "proof . . . of [the organization's] divine origin." "Religion: Christian Endeavor," *Time*, 11 July 1927; Henry B. F. MacFarland, "The Christian Endeavor Movement," *North American Review* 182 (Feb. 1906): 196–98.

111. Takusagawa and Yoshimine, *Streams in the Desert*.

112. Francis E. Clark, *The Christian Endeavor Manual: A Text-Book on the History, Theory, Principles and Practice of the Society* (Boston: United Society of Christian Endeavor, 1903), 11–13, 124–25.

113. Shimomura, *Desert Echoes*.

114. Takusagawa and Yoshimine, *Streams in the Desert*.

115. "Testimony," "Poston Christian Church Bulletin," 14 Mar. 1943, Reel 260, JAER.

116. "Testimony," "Poston Christian Church Bulletin," 7 Mar. 1943, Reel 260, JAER.

117. Takusagawa and Yoshimine, *Streams in the Desert*.

118. Paul S. Osumi, Foreword, *Rich Life in a Barren Desert*, July 1945, Box 5/Fld 8, Gillett Papers, UCLA.

119. Shimomura, *Desert Echoes*.

120. Yosh to Andrews, 3 Nov. 1943, Box 2/Fld 1, Andrews Papers (1908-1), UW.

121. Yoshisada Kayai, quoted in Tokuno, *Issei Christians*, 15–19.

122. Okazaki to Andrews, 24 Feb. 1943, Box 2/Fld 2, Andrews Papers (1908-1), UW.

123. Kowta to Friend, 25 May 1943.

124. Gordon Chapman, Annual Report, 1943, Box 18/Fld 8, RG 93, PHS.

125. See Judith Perkins, *The Suffering Self: Pain and Narrative Representations in the Early Christian Era* (London: Routledge, 1995); Elizabeth Anne Castelli, *Martyrdom and Memory: Early Christian Culture Making* (New York: Columbia University Press, 2004).

126. Masakazu Konatsu, Testimony, Poston III Christian Church newsletter, 12 Sept. 1943, Box 5/Fld 2, Bulletins and Newsletters collection, GTU.

127. Takusagawa and Yoshimine, *Streams in the Desert*.

128. Mary Nakahara, "The Exit We Search," 18 July 1945, Jerome Christian High School Fellowship, JANM.

129. Diane C. Fujino, *Heartbeat of Struggle: The Revolutionary Life of Yuri Kochiyama* (Minneapolis: University of Minnesota Press, 2005).

130. Quoted in Roger Daniels, *Concentration Camp USA: Japanese Americans and World War II* (New York: Holt, Rinehart and Winston, 1972), 119.

131. Sumio Koga, *A Decade of Faith: The Journey of Japanese Christians in the USA (1936-1946)* (New York: Vantage Press, 2002), 54.

132. Alice Kono, "The Wilderness Experience," *Young People's Fellowship News*, Ogden Christian Union Church, July 1944, Box 5/Fld 15, Gillett Papers, UCLA.

133. Jackson, *The Politics of Storytelling: Violence, Transgression and Intersubjectivity* (Copenhagen: Museum Tusculanum Press-University of Copenhagen, 2002), 59.

134. Psychologists disagree whether writing about trauma later in life helps victims reconcile events or increases suffering as they are relived. Writing during trauma has not been adequately studied, particularly in terms of its relationship to religion. Dominick LaCapra, *Writing History, Writing Trauma* (Baltimore: Johns Hopkins University Press, 2001); Peter N. and Maureen Daly Goggin, "Presence in Absence: Discourses and Teaching (In, On, About) Trauma," in *Trauma and the Teaching of Writing*, ed. Shane Borrowman (Albany: State University of New York Press, 2005), 29-51.

135. Hannah Arendt, *The Human Condition*, 2nd ed. (Chicago: University of Chicago Press, [1958] 1998), 184-86.

136. Daphne Desser, "Teaching Writing in Hawaii after Pearl Harbor and 9/11: How to 'Make Meaning' and 'Heal' Despite National Propaganda," in Borrowman, *Trauma and the Teaching of Writing*, 85-97.

137. Yoo described how religious groups "acted as racial-ethnic centers of protest." Okihiro, "Religion and Resistance in America's Concentration Camps," *Phylon* 45 (Third Quarter 1984): 220-33; Yoo, *Growing Up Nisei: Race, Generation, and Culture among Japanese Americans of California: 1924-1949* (Urbana: University of Illinois Press, 2000), 114-23.

138. Sermonette, Poston III Christian Church newsletter, 25 Apr. 1943, Box 5/Fld 2, Bulletins and Newsletters collection, GTU.

139. Howard, *Concentration Camps*, 150.

140. Brian Masaru Hayashi, *Democratizing the Enemy: The Japanese American Internment* (Princeton, N.J.: Princeton University Press, 2004), 169.

141. Frank Herron Smith, Notes on Sermon, 17 Aug. 1942, Box 44/Fld 571 Churches, RG 210, NARA; Andrew Kuroda, Memorandum, Fall 1942, Box 155/Fld 3, Kuroda Papers, JAER.

142. James C. Scott, *Domination and the Arts of Resistance* (New Haven, Conn.: Yale University, 1990).

143. De Certeau, *Practice of Everyday Life*, xiv–xv.


## Chapter Five

1. "The Resettlement of American-Born Japanese," Box 59/Fld 11, RG 18, PHS.

2. Minutes of the Conference of Leaders of Japanese Christian Work, 15–17 Dec. 1943, Box 2/Fld 5, RG 37, PHS.

3. WRA director Dillon Myer outlined plans for resettlement on 31 July 1942. Office of War Information News Release, 31 July 1942, Box 2/Fld 5, RG 37, PHS.

4. Andrews to Thomas, 19 July 1943, Box 2/Fld 4, Emery E. Andrews Papers (1908-3), UW.

5. Alison Greene, "The End of 'The Protestant Era'?," *Church History* 80 (Sept. 2011): 600–10.

6. Galen Fisher, *Round Table on Japanese Evacuation* (New York: American Council Institute of Pacific Relations, October 1942), 10.

7. Minutes of the Conference of Leaders of Japanese Christian Work, 15–17 Dec. 1943.

8. Ibid.; Jensen to Fukuyama, 4 May 1945, Box 15/Fld 24, CCGS.

9. Minutes of the Conference of Leaders of Japanese Christian Work, 15–17 Dec. 1943.

10. Minutes of Section Meeting No. 1: The Future of Japanese in American Churches, 16 Dec. 1943, Reel 082, JAER; Paul Nagano, interview by Stephen Fugita and Becky Fukuda, 25 May 1999, DDA.

11. Minutes of the Conference of Leaders of Japanese Christian Work, 15–17 Dec. 1943.

12. Philip Gleason, "Americans All: World War II and the Shaping of American Identity," *Review of Politics* 43 (Oct. 1981): 483–518; Minutes of Section Meeting No. 1, 16 Dec. 1943; Harold Jensen to Lincoln Wadsworth, 10 Nov. 1945, Box 15/Fld 2, CCGS.

13. Minutes of the Conference of Leaders of Japanese Christian Work, 15–17 Dec. 1943.

14. Gillett, Notes Taken at the Conference of Leaders of Japanese Christian Work, 16 Dec. 1943, Box 4/Fld 1, Clarence Gillett Papers (Collection 130), UCLA; Chapman to Gillett, 23 Jan. 1945, Box 1/Fld 9, Gordon K. Chapman: Protestant Church Commission for Japanese Service, GTU 2002-9-01, GTU; Memorandum of the PCC, 21 Sept. 1944, Box 4/Fld 1, Gillett Papers, UCLA; Toru Matsumoto, AB-HMS Report, 25 Mar. 1945, Reel 082, JAER.

15. Minutes of the United Church Ministry to Returning Japanese (UCM), 19 July 1945, Box 15/Fld 2, CCGS; "Congregational Christians Aid American-Japanese Evacuees," undated, Box 1/Fld 2, Gillett Papers, UCLA; Joseph Fukushima to Clarence Gillett, 13 Nov. 1943, Box 1/Fld 10, Gillett Papers, UCLA; Matsumoto, ABHMS Report, 25 Mar. 1945; Osame Doi, interview, 17 Sept. 1986, in *Nisei Christian Journey: Its Promise and Fulfillment* (n.p.: Nisei Christian Oral History Project, 1988), 12.

16. Memorandum of the PCC, 21 Sept. 1944; Minutes of the Conference of Leaders of Japanese Christian Work, 15–17 Dec. 1943.

17. Minutes of the Conference of Leaders of Japanese Christian Work, 15–17 Dec. 1943; Statement of Policies, 18 Jan. 1945, Box 2/Fld 10, Andrews Papers (1908-3), UW.

18. Chapman to Long, 9 Apr. 1945, Box 12/Fld 9, RG 301.7, PHS; Gordon Chapman, Annual Report, 1943, Box 18/Fld 8, RG 93, PHS.

19. Walsh to Lavery, 5 and 20 Sept. 1945, and Sister Mary Susanna to Sister Columba, 10 Sept. 1945, Box 6/Fld 8, Topical Misc., MMA.

20. Greg Robinson, *By Order of the President: FDR and the Internment of Japanese Americans* (Cambridge, Mass.: Harvard University Press, 2001), 118, 221.

21. Fisher, *Round Table*, 7.

22. Memorandum on the Work of the Protestant Churches in Japanese Relocation Centers and Settlements, 20 July 1942, Box 4/Fld 1, Gillett Papers, UCLA.

23. Clarence Gillett to Robert Inglis, 4 Apr. 1942, Box 1/Fld 6, Gillett Papers, UCLA; "Congregational Christians Aid American-Japanese Evacuees," undated.

24. Jones to Pickett, 6 July and 7 Aug. 1942, and Pickett to Jones, 14 July 1942, Stanley Jones, SIS-JAR 1942.

25. Jones to Sam Cavert and Roswell Barnes, 16 July 1942, Stanley Jones, SIS-JAR 1942.

26. Minutes of the FCC Executive Committee, 16 Mar. 1943, in "The Concern of the Church for the Christian and Democratic Treatment of Japanese Americans" (New York: Committee on Resettlement of Japanese Americans, April 1944), 6; Committee on Resettlement, "Planning Resettlement of Japanese Americans, July 1943, Box 8/Fld 17, RG 26, PHS; Jacob Long, untitled, undated, Box 12/Fld 5, RG 301.6, PHS.

27. Report of the Rev. Daisuke Kitagawa, undated, Box 5/Fld 4, Gillett Papers, UCLA.

28. Unsigned to Steve, 21 June 1943, Box 1/Fld 6, Gillett Papers, UCLA.

29. Examples include: Clement Boesflug, letters from Minidoka, 1945, Reel 331, JAER; Carl Nugent's *Your Visiting Pastor*, Box 5/Fld 10, Gillett Papers, UCLA; and the literary editions of the *Rohwer Transmitter*, Japanese-American Internment Camp Church Bulletins and Newsletters collection, GTU 94-9-02, GTU.

30. Schmoe, notes for speech, "The Role of Local Churches and Religious Leaders in the Evacuation, Internment, and Final Settlement of Americans of Japanese Ancestry," Anniversary Conference: Topaz, Mar. 1983, Box 1/Fld 48, Floyd Wilfred Schmoe Papers (496-8), UW.

31. Community Christian Church Bulletin, Jerome Relocation Center, 11 July 1943, Box 5/Fld 7, Gillett Papers, UCLA.

32. Tibesar, Relocation Survey, 9 Aug. 1944, Box 6/Fld 7, Topical Misc., MMA.

33. Everett Thompson to Scattered Members, 24 Aug. 1943, Box 1/Fld 6, Kaoru Ichihara Papers (1839-1), UW.

34. Marion Kline to Hashimoto, 25 May 1943, Box 1/Fld 53, Andrews Papers (1908-1), UW.

35. Notice to Assistant Project Directors, 2 Oct. 1943, Box 6/Fld 18, Gillett Papers, UCLA.

36. Jean Endo to Andrews, Fall 1942, Box 1/Fld 44, Andrews Papers (1908-1), UW; Yoshie Oshite to Gillett, 7 Aug. 1943, Box 1/Fld 17, Gillett Papers, UCLA; Gillett to Edward G. Marks, 24 Aug. 1944, Box 1/Fld 21, Gillett Papers, UCLA; Citizens Committee for Resettlement: Meeting of the Executive Committee, 20 Mar. 1944, Box 1/Fld 1, Gillett Papers, UCLA; Tibesar to Father John, 5 May 1944, Box 6/Fld 7, Topical Misc., MMA.

37. Drought to Tibesar, 4 Sept. 1942, and Buck to James G. Keller, 11 Aug. 1942, Box 6/Fld 3, Topical Misc., MMA.

38. Tibesar to Walsh, 19 Oct. 1942, and Walsh to Tibesar, 27 Oct. 1942, Box 6/Fld 3, Topical Misc., MMA; Leopold Tibesar to Seraphin Tibesar, 26 Apr. 1943, Box 3/Vol. 1/Fld 10, QU; S. Tibesar to Perry Hall, 26 Apr. 1943, Box 3/Vol. 1/Fld 10, QU.

39. L. Tibesar to S. Tibesar, 19 Oct. 1942, Box 3/Vol. 1/Fld 9, QU.

40. Tibesar, Relocation Survey, 9 Aug. 1944, Box 6/Fld 7, Topical Misc., MMA; L. Tibesar to S. Tibesar, 2 Aug. 1944, Box 3/Vol. 1/Fld 12, QU; L. Tibesar to Malone, 11 Oct. 1944, Lavery to Considine, 22 Nov. 1944, and "Plan of Work for Father Tibesar," 13 Dec. 1944, Box 6/Fld 7, Topical Misc., MMA; L. Tibesar to S. Tibesar, 11 Apr. 1945, Box 3/Vol. 1/Fld 12, QU; Theophane to Considine, 14 Feb. 1945 and 13 Apr. 1945, Box 6/Fld 8, Topical Misc., MMA; Tibesar to Considine, 21 May 1945, Box 6/Fld 8, Topical Misc., MMA.

41. AFSC Midwest Branch Office, Report on Chicago Resettlement, Nov. 1944, Reel 082, JAER.

42. Myer to Homer Morris, 11 Jan. 1943, WRA, SIS-JAR 1942.

43. Ralph E. Smeltzer, speech to center residents, 16 Nov. 1943; Helpful Information about the Hostel, undated; Instructions and Procedure Regarding the

Brethren Relocation Hostel, 15 July 1943; and "Travel Hints to Brethren Hostelers," 23 July 1943, Reel 082, JAER; Relocation through the Brethren Hostel, Fall 1943, 53/Fld 4, William C. Carr Papers, JARP.

44. WRA, "When You Leave the Relocation Center," undated, Box 1/Instruction and Policy Manuals, Toshiyuki Fukushima Correspondence and Papers (5554-1), UW; Resettler Group Discussion No. 1: "How Can I Adjust My Personal Life to This New Community?," 9 May 1943, Reel 082, JAER.

45. Monica Sone, *Nisei Daughter* (Boston: Little, Brown, 1953), 223; Mrs. Perry to Gillett, 14 Apr. 1943, Box 1/Fld 45, Gillett Papers, UCLA; Charles E. Mace, photographer, WRA no. H-180, 25 Aug. 1943, Series 12, WRA Photographs of Japanese-American Evacuation and Resettlement, UCB.

46. Sone, *Nisei Daughter*, 216–17; Perry to Gillett, 14 Apr. 1943; Mrs. Howard Wright to Mr. and Mrs. Higano, 24 May 1943, Box 3/Fld 4, Higano Family Papers (2870-1), UW; Thomas Sasaki to Tibesar, 28 May 1944, Box 6/Fld 8, Topical Misc., MMA.

47. Sone, *Nisei Daughter*, 225–27; Robert W. O'Brien, *The College Nisei* (New York: Reprinted by Arno Press, [1949] 1978), 91, 116; Allan Austin, *From Concentration Camp to Campus: Japanese American Students and World War II* (Champaign: University of Illinois Press, 2004), 15.

48. U.S. Department of the Interior and War Agency Liquidation Unit (formerly WRA), *People in Motion: The Postwar Adjustment of the Evacuated Japanese Americans* (Washington, D.C.: Dept. of the Interior, 1947), 145–46, 71–72, 76.

49. Aromura estimated that 380 Nisei lived in Ann Arbor by early 1944. Aromura to Andrews, 11 Jan. 1944, Box 2/Fld 7, Andrews Papers (1908-1), UW.

50. Andrews to Thomas, 13 Apr. and 12 May 1943, Box 2/Fld 4, Andrews Papers (1908-3), UW.

51. Bob Kiino to Virginia Tidball, 3 Oct. and 7 Nov. 1943, Box 1/Fld 1, Virginia Tidball Papers, MS T348274, UA.

52. Tibesar, Relocation Survey, 9 Aug. 1944, Box 6/Fld 7, Topical Misc., MMA.

53. Tibesar, Minidoka Diary, Feb. 1944, Box 35/Fld 6, MFBD.

54. Greg Robinson, *After Camp: Portraits in Midcentury Japanese American Life and Politics* (Berkeley: University of California Press, 2012).

55. PCC Meeting Minutes, 13–15 July 1943, Box 15/Fld 3, CCGS.

56. Rundquist to Homer Morris, 20 Mar. 1944, Committee on the Resettlement of Japanese Americans—General, SIS-JAR 1944.

57. Report, Open Meeting of Seattle Office, 6 Aug. 1943, Branch Office: Seattle, SIS-JAR 1943.

58. Akira Kikuchi to unnamed, prior to 26 Nov. 1943, Box 1/Fld 7, Gillett Papers, UCLA.

59. Tom Fukuyama to Betty Adkins, 22 Sept. 1944, Box 1/Incoming Letters, Betty Fukuyama Papers (4411-1), UW.

60. Fukuyama, "The Dispersion of the Nisei," *Federated Church Herald*, 12 Dec. 1943, Box 1/Fld 6, Ichihara Papers, UW.

61. Clarence Gillett to Robert Inglis, 4 Apr. 1942, Box 1/Fld 6, Gillett Papers, UCLA; "Congregational Christians Aid American-Japanese Evacuees," undated; Resettler Group Discussion No. 1; Fukuyama to Adkins, 22 Sept. 1944.

62. Schmoe, "Dispersal No Solution," 29 Nov. 1944, Branch Office Seattle— General, SIS-JAR 1944; Schmoe, Memo to Members of the Japanese Relocation Committee, 3 Feb. 1943, Branch Office: Seattle, SIS-JAR 1943; Schmoe to Homer Morris, 17 Apr. 1944, Branch Office: Seattle—Correspondence, SIS-JAR 1944; AFSC Midwest Branch Office, Report on Chicago Resettlement, Nov. 1944.

63. Tibesar to Walsh, 19 Oct. 1942, Box 6/Fld 3, Topical Misc., MMA.

64. Walsh to Tibesar, 12 Mar. 1943, Box 6/Fld 6, Topical Misc., MMA.

65. Toru Matsumoto, *Beyond Prejudice: A Story of the Church and Japanese Americans* (New York: Friendship Press, 1946), 131–33.

66. Tibesar to Considine, 19 July 1943, Box 6/Fld 5, Topical Misc., MMA.

67. Tibesar, Minidoka Diary, Feb. 1944, Box 35/Fld 6, MFBD, MMA.

68. Minutes of the Committee of the United Ministry to Evacuees, 15 and 28 June 1943, and Ralph E. Smeltzer and John M. Yamazaki to Friends, undated, Reel 082, JAER; Joint Conference on Future of Japanese Church Work, Resettlement and Return, 24–25 Apr. 1945, Box 4/Fld 1, Gillett Papers, UCLA; Donald Toriumi to Chapman, 17 Feb. 1945, Box 12/Fld 10, RG 301.7, PHS; Morikawa, "My Spiritual Pilgrimage," 23 May 1973, reprinted in *Jitsuo Morikawa: A Prophet for the Twenty-First Century: A Legacy of Sixty Inspiring Sermons*, ed. Paul Nagano and William L. Malcomson (Richmond, Calif.: Council for Pacific Asians Theology, 2000), 107–9.

69. Joint Conference on Future of Japanese Church Work, 24–26 Apr. 1945.

70. Chapman to Royal Fisher, 3 Feb. 1944, Box 1/Fld 7, Chapman Papers, GTU.

71. Chapman to Gillett, 12 June 1943, Box 4/Fld 3, Gillett Papers, UCLA.

72. Chapman to Herrick Young, 20 June 1944, Box 1/Fld 39, Chapman Papers, GTU.

73. Riichi Satow, quoted in Eileen Sunada Sarasohn, ed., *The Issei: Portrait of a Pioneer, an Oral History* (Palo Alto, Calif.: Pacific Books, 1983), 245–46; Colorado Council of Churches, "The Japanese in Our Midst," 1942, Box 53/Fld 2, Carr Papers, JARP.

74. Fukuyama, "Dispersion of the Nisei."

75. Andrews to John Thomas, 8 Dec. 1944, and Andrews to Jobu Yasumura, 28 Dec. 1944, Box 2/Fld 4, Andrews Papers (1908-3), UW.

76. Fisher to Gillett, 18 Dec. 1944, Box 3/Fld 7, Gillett Papers, UCLA; M. Okimura to Gillett, 15 Feb. 1945, Box 1/Fld 10, Gillett Papers, UCLA.

77. Joint Conference on Future of Japanese Church Work, 24–26 Apr. 1945; Kitagawa, "One Day's Observation of White River Valley Situation," 20 Apr. 1945, Reel 064, JAER.

78. Floyd Schmoe, Statement Regarding Return of Evacuees to Seattle Area during One Month, 14 Feb. 1945, Box 2/Fld 4, Andrews Papers (1908-3), UW; Min-

utes of the UCM, 19 July 1945; "Japanese Baptist Church Journal," Sept. 1945, Box 15/Fld 10, CCGS.

79. Robinson, *After Camp*, 4.

80. Schmoe, Statement Regarding Return.

81. Remember Pearl Harbor League, Inc., open letter to all ministerial associations, 11 May 1945, Box 1/Fld 22, Ring Family Papers (4241-2), UW.

82. U. G. Murphy to Remember Pearl Harbor League, undated, Box 1/Fld 22, Ring Papers (4241-2), UW.

83. Church Federation of Los Angeles, "Fair Treatment for Persons of Japanese Ancestry," 18 Jan. 1945, Box 3/Fld 24, Gillett Papers, UCLA.

84. Joint Conference on Future of Japanese Church Work, 24–25 Apr. 1945.

85. Hostel Directory: Los Angeles Area, 27 Sept. 1945, Box 6/Fld 17, Gillett Papers, UCLA.

86. Clarence Gillett, Recent Developments in the Metropolitan Los Angeles Area, 15 May 1946, Box 1/Fld 1, Gillett Papers, UCLA.

87. Ibid.

88. The Resettlement Staff Workers Conference, 5 Sept. 1945, Box 8/Fld 18, RG 26, PHS; George Wieland, Mark Dawber, and Toru Matsumoto to Truman, 27 Nov. 1945, and WRA Comments on Recommendations of the All Center Conference, 1 Aug. 1945, Committee on Resettlement of Japanese Americans, SIS-JAR 1945.

89. Andrews to Yasumura, 28 Dec. 1944.

90. PCC Meeting Minutes, 11–12 Jan. 1945, Box 15/Fld 30, CCGS.

91. Douglas M. Dye, "For the Sake of Seattle's Soul: The Seattle Council of Churches, the Nikkei Community, and World War II," *Pacific Northwest Quarterly* 93 (Summer 2002): 134; Schmoe, Statement Regarding Return.

92. Helen Amerman and Elmer R. Smith, Survey of Nisei in Seattle, 31 Dec. 1945, Box 15/Fld 23, CCGS.

93. Schmoe, A New Work Camp Opportunity, May 1945, Branch Office: Seattle—General, SIS-JAR 1945.

94. Resettlement Council Newsletter, 5 July 1945, Box 15/Fld 24, CCGS.

95. Emery Brooks Andrews, interview by Joyce Nishimura, 7 Oct. 2006, Bainbridge Island Japanese American Community Collection, DDA.

96. Emery Brooks Andrews, interview by Tom Ikeda, 24 Mar. 2004, DDA; Andrews to Wadsworth, 29 Oct. 1945, Box 4/Fld 30, Andrews Papers (1908-1), UW.

97. Walsh claimed to place only one returnee during these early months, but oral histories record more successes. Thomas T. Kobayashi, interview by Tom Ikeda, 30 Apr. 2009, DDA; Kajiko Hashisaki, interview by Brian Hashisaki and Tom Ikeda, 26 Mar. 2007, DDA; Walsh, Seattle Diary, June–July 1945, Box 45/Fld 1, MFBD; Seattle Diaries, 8 Feb. 1945, Box 73/Fld 1, Maryknoll Sisters Diaries, MMA.

98. Report on Activities of the UCM to Returning Japanese, 22 Oct. 1945, Box 12/Fld 8, Washington Association of Churches Records (1567-1), UW.

99. Schmoe to Robertson Fort, 2 Jan. 1945, Branch Office: Seattle—General, SIS-JAR 1945.

100. Action Taken at the Regular Executive Meeting of the Seattle Council of Churches and Christian Education, 19 Feb. 1945, Box 15/Fld 3, CCGS.

101. John Eubank, Report on the Annual Meeting of the Washington State Council of Churches and Christian Education, 4–8 Jan. 1946, Box 24/Fld 203.3, RG 210, NARA.

102. Action Taken, 19 Feb. 1945.

103. Gorman Y. Doubleday to Fellow Ministers of the Northern California Council of Churches, 15 Mar. 1945, Box 3/Fld 20, Gillett Papers, UCLA.

104. Jensen to Wadsworth, 10 Nov. 1945.

105. Meeting of Denominational Executives, 15 Apr. 1946, 22 Oct. 1945, Box 15/Fld 29, CCGS.

106. Minutes of the UCM, 19 and 26 July 1945, Box 15/Fld 2, CCGS; Minutes of the Conference of Leaders of Japanese Christian Work, 15–17 Dec. 1943; Jensen to G. K. Watanabe, 27 July 1945, Box 15/Fld 2, CCGS.

107. Paul Osumi to Gillett, 1 Apr. 1942, Box 1/Fld 14, Gillett Papers, UCLA.

108. Jensen to Alice Brimson, 17 May 1945, Box 15/Fld 24, CCGS.

109. Washington Baptist Convention to G. K. Watanabe, 29 June 1945, Box 1/Fld 7, Andrews Papers (1908-1), UW.

110. Jensen to Wada, 14 Aug. 1946, Box 15/Fld 2, CCGS.

111. Most but not every Japanese congregation on the Pacific Coast encountered this problem. The Japanese leaders of a Presbyterian church south of San Jose explained that they were not interested in integration, asked the city to return their building, and reopened in January 1945. The Quaker missionary Herbert Nicholson maintained a Japanese Methodist church in Los Angeles during the incarceration and helped the congregation reopen its buildings on 28 Aug. 1945. *Watsonville Westview Presbyterian Church: The 60th Anniversary, 1895–1958* (Watsonville, Calif.: n.p., 1958); *West Los Angeles Community Methodist Church, 30th Anniversary Dedication, 1930–1960*, Box 381, JARP.

112. Amerman and Smith, Survey of Nisei, 46.

113. "JBC Journal," Dec. 1945, Box 15/Fld 10, CCGS.

114. Ruth Mayasaka to Joseph Kitagawa, reprinted in *The Minidoka Churchman*, 19 Aug. 1944, Bulletins and Newsletters Collection, GTU.

115. Toriumi to Chapman, 17 Feb. 1945.

116. Hirabayashi to Eleanor Ring, 6 June 1944, Box 1/Fld 7, Ring Papers (4241-2), UW.

117. Andrews to Wadsworth, 29 Oct. 1945, and Andrews to Caldwell, 25 Mar. 1946, Box 4/Fld 30, Andrews Papers (1908-1), UW; Jensen to Brimson, 17 May 1945.

118. Andrews to Thomas, 3 Mar. 1945, Box 2/Fld 4, Andrews Papers (1908-3), UW; Jensen to Watanabe, 27 July 1945.

119. "JBC Journal," July 1945, and Joseph K. Watanabe, Seattle Baptist Church Board of Deacons Meeting, Hunt, Idaho, 26 May 1945, Box 15/Fld 24, CCGS; Jen-

sen to Brimson, 17 May 1945; Shigeko Sese Uno, interview by Beth Kawahara and Alice Ito, 18 Sept. 1998, DDA.

120. Jensen to Wadsworth, 10 Nov 1945.

121. Jensen to Brimson, 17 May 1945.

122. Presented by Alice W. S. Brimson to the UCM, 12 June 1945, Box 15/Fld 24, CCGS.

123. Pricilla Fornia et al. to Jensen, and Mrs. F. R. Leach to Jensen, 4 June 1945, Box 15/Fld 2, CCGS.

124. Emery Brooks Andrews, interview by Ikeda; Andrews to Wadsworth, 29 Oct. 1945; Andrews, Report to the ABHMS, 2 Apr. 1945, Box 2/Fld 4, Andrews Papers (1908-3), UW.

125. Andrews to Caldwell, 25 Mar. 1946; Andrews to Wadsworth, 29 Oct. 1945.

126. Apel to Jensen, 21 July 1945, Box 15/Fld 2, CCGS; "Difficulties Involved in Carrying on the United Church Ministry to the Returning Japanese," 21 Sept. 1945, Box 15/Fld 29, CCGS; Apel to Jensen, telegram, 17 July 1945, Box 15/Fld 24, CCGS.

127. Andrews to Wadsworth, 29 Oct. 1945; Wadsworth to Andrews, 1 Oct. 1945, Box 1/Fld 5, Andrews Papers (1908-1), UW.

128. Amerman and Smith, Survey of Nisei, 44, Survey Outline; Christian Work: Japanese and Japanese-Americans in Seattle Area, 6 Feb. 1946, Box 15/Fld 23, CCGS.

129. Untitled biographical summary, 10 May 1946, Box 2/Fld 4, Andrews Papers (1908-3), UW; Andrews to Caldwell, 25 Mar. 1946.

130. Andrews to Caldwell, 25 Mar. 1946; "JBC Journal," Apr. 1946, Box 15/Fld 10, CCGS.

131. Meeting of Denominational Executives, 15 Apr. 1946; "Seattle Baptist Church" (denshopd-i35-00203), DDA.

132. Minutes of the Congregational Committee, 10 Sept. and 4 June 1946, Box 1/Fld 1, Gillett Papers, UCLA.

133. Shigeo Shimada, *A Stone Cried Out* (Valley Forge, Penn.: Judson Press, 1986), 146; Chapman to Fisher and Kojiro Unoura, 6 Apr. 1945, Box 1/Fld 7, Chapman Papers, GTU.

134. Frank Herron Smith, "Integration," 25 July 1956, Box 136/Fld 3, Shima Papers, JARP.

135. Paul Nagano and Joan Thatcher, *The Asian American Experience* (Valley Forge, Penn.: Fund for Renewal, 1973), 20.

136. Untitled records, 1950, 27 Feb. and 1 Sept. 1951, Box 3/Fld 12, Maryknoll Sisters History, Western USA, MMA; Mary Suzuki Ichino, Interview 2, interview by Richard Potashin, 3 Dec. 2008, Manzanar National Historic Site Collection, DDA; John Hayatsu, "The Role of the Japanese American in the Church," 1992, in *Keeping Faith: European and Asian Catholic Immigrants*, ed. Jeffrey M. Burns, Ellen Skerrett, and Joseph M. White (Maryknoll, N.Y.: Orbis, 2000), 262–63.

137. Walsh to Lavery and Lavery to Walsh, 20 Sept. 1945, Box 6/Fld 8, Topical Misc., MMA.

138. Lavery to Walsh, 23 Aug. 1945; Minnie Ono to Walsh, 24 Sept. 1945; and Steinbach to Walsh, 19 Sept. 1945, Box 6/Fld 8, Topical Misc., MMA.

139. Lavery to Walsh, 20 Sept. and 25 Aug. 1945, and Walsh to Lavery, 5 Sept. 1945, Box 6/Fld 8, Topical Misc., MMA.

140. Nagano, interview by Fugita and Fukuda.

141. Lester Suzuki, "Persecution Alienation, and Resurrection: History of Japanese Methodist Churches," in *Asian American Christianity Reader*, ed. Viji Nakka-Cammauf and Timothy Tseng (Castro Valley, Calif.: Institute for the Study of Asian American Christianity, 2009), 69.

142. St. Peter's Episcopalian parish is no longer a Japanese mission church, but people of Asian descent comprise 70 percent of the congregation. "St. Peter's Episcopal Parish: About Us" (2007).

143. "The Japanese Presbyterian Church," undated, Box 12/Fld 11, RG 301.7, PHS.

144. Chapman to Fisher, 13 Dec. 1945, Box 1/Fld 6, Chapman Papers, GTU; Lester Suzuki, *Ministry in the Assembly and Relocation Centers of World War II* (Berkley, Calif.: Yardbird, 1979), 18.

145. Through an ironic twist of fate, Thurman's church, the Church for the Fellowship of All Peoples, met in a former Japanese Presbyterian church building. Thurman, *With Head and Heart: The Autobiography of Howard Thurman* (Boston: Harcourt Brace Jovanovich, 1979), 139; Thurman, *Jesus and the Disinherited* (Boston: Beacon Press, [1949] 1976), 98.

146. Hirabayashi to Ring, 6 June 1944; Thurman, *Jesus and the Disinherited*, 101.

147. Toriumi to Chapman, 17 Feb. 1945.

148. Nagano, interview by Fugita and Fukuda.

149. Tibesar, autobiographical writings, undated, Box 3/Vol. 1/Section 2, QU.

## Epilogue

1. Clarence Gillett, Notes Taken at the Conference of Japanese Christian Leaders, 16 Dec. 1943, Box 4/Fld 1, Clarence Gillett Papers (Collection 130), UCLA; Tibesar, autobiographical writings, undated, Box 3/Vol. 1/Section 2, QU.

2. Minutes of Inter-Council Committee on Japanese Christian Work, 22 Oct. 1941, Box 8/Fld 17, RG 26, PHS.

3. Okuda to Farquharsons, 8 Nov. 1942 and 1 Jan. 1943, Box 1/Fld 1, Mary Farquharson Papers (397-5), UW.

4. Seido Ogawa, Report of the Congregational Committee for Christian Democracy, June 1948, Box 1/Fld 2, Gillett Papers, UCLA; Committee for Christian Democracy, "A Primer on Prejudice by Law," 4 Mar. 1946, Box 3/Fld 14, Gillett Papers, UCLA.

5. Toru Matsumoto to Harold Choate, 25 Apr. 1945, Box 470/Fld 71.501, RG 210, NARA.

6. Program, Conference on Problems of Minorities, 15–17 Nov. 1944, Box 6/Fld 7, Topical Misc., MMA.

7. Rhoads to Elizabeth Page, 8 Mar. 1944, Box 20/Letters from Rhoads July–Dec. 1944, Esther B. Rhoads Collection, HC.

8. Meeting Minutes of the Advisory Committee of the Congregational Committee on Christian Democracy, 4 Sept. and 9 Oct. 1945, Box 1/Fld 1, Gillett Papers, UCLA.

9. LeGrand Dunkley to Bethel Baptist Church, 7 Feb. 1945, Box 24/Fld 203.3, RG 210, NARA.

10. Ralph Rose, *American Friends and Race Relations* (London: Hereford Times, 1954), 5; AFSC, "Some Quaker Approaches to the Race Problem" (Philadelphia: AFSC, 1946).

11. Barnes to G. Murray Bernhardt, 23 May 1947, and Melvin Harter to Barnes, 6 May 1946, Box 12/Fld 3, RG 18, PHS; Douglas Horton, James C. Baker, Luman Shafer, and Walter Van Kirk, "The War Time Activities of the Churches of the United States Bearing upon Matters of Concern to the Christian Community in Japan," undated, Box 36/Fld 9, RG 18, PHS.

12. Historian William Wei states that the incarceration fueled the civil rights activism of many Japanese Americans. Wei, *The Asian American Movement* (Philadelphia: Temple University Press, 1993), 21; Greg Robinson, *After Camp: Portraits in Midcentury Japanese American Life and Politics* (Berkeley: University of California Press, 2012), 226; Mark D. Jordan, *Blessing Same-Sex Unions: The Perils of Queer Romance and the Confusions of Christian Marriage* (Chicago: University of Chicago Press, 2013), 132; Diane C. Fujino, *Heartbeat of Struggle: The Revolutionary Life of Yuri Kochiyama* (Minneapolis: University of Minnesota Press, 2005); Tom Fukuyama, in *My Spiritual Pilgrimage: Autobiographies of Asian American Baptist Ministers*, compiled by the Asian American Baptist Caucus, 1976, Box 10/Fld 8, PACTS, GTU 2001-9-01, GTU.

13. Klancy Clark de Nevers, *The Colonel and the Pacifist: Karl Bendetsen, Perry Saito, and the Incarceration of Japanese Americans during World War II* (Salt Lake City: University of Utah Press, 2004), 11, 235–37, 265.

14. James F. Findlay, *Church People in the Struggle: The National Council of Churches and the Black Freedom Movement, 1950–1970* (New York: Oxford University Press, 1993); Stephen L. Longnecker, *Selma's Peacemaker: Ralph Smeltzer and Civil Rights Mediation* (Philadelphia: Temple University Press, 1987); Biographical Note, Rhoads Papers, HC.

15. Herbert Nicholson, *Treasure in Earthen Vessels* (Upland, Calif.: n.p., 1972), 66, 70.

16. South Pasadena Council for Civic Unity, undated, Box 78/Fld 321, RG 210, NARA; Council meeting minutes and membership lists, Box 24/Fld 200.2, RG 210, NARA; Kit Oldham, "Floyd W. Schmoe," HistoryLink (revised 25 Feb. 2010), http://www.historylink.org/index.cfm?DisplayPage=output.cfm&File_Id =3876.

17. Haruyama, "Tsukemono Theology," quoted in Andrew N. Otani, *A History of Japanese-American Episcopal Churches* (n.p., 1980), 98; "Justin Haruyama Scholarship Fund," Japanese American United Church, accessed 20 May 2015, http://www.jauc.org/haruyama.

18. Otani, *History of Japanese-American Episcopal Churches*, 98, 104.

19. Nagano, interview by Stephen Fugita and Becky Fukuda, 25 May 1999, DDA.

20. Nagano, "Identity, Identification and Initiative," in *The Theologies of Asian Americans and Pacific Peoples: A Reader,* ed. Roy I. Sano (Berkeley, Calif.: Asian Center for Theology and Strategies, 1976), 221.

21. Kevin Omi, "Final Paper: Rev. Paul Nagano" (term paper for Theologies of Asian American Faith Communities, Graduate Theological Union, 2009), 14–15.

22. Nagano, interview by Fugita and Fukuda, 25 May 1999.

23. Paul Nagano, in *My Spiritual Pilgrimage.*

24. Shizue Seigel, *In Good Conscience: Supporting Japanese Americans During the Internment* (San Mateo, Calif.: AACP, 2006), 166; de Nevers, *Colonel and the Pacifist,* 266; Frank Ichishita, "I Know Who I Am," *Trends,* Mar./Apr. 1973, 10.

25. Marshall Sumida and Paul Nagano, "Review, Resolve and Redress of the Internment of Japanese Americans During World War II," *American Baptist Quarterly* 13 (Mar. 1994): 84; Roy I. Sano, "Yes, We'll Have No More Bananas in Church!" Aug. 1969, in Sano, *Theologies of Asian Americans and Pacific Peoples,* 54.

26. Russell Jeung, *Faithful Generations: Race and New Asian American Churches* (New Brunswick, N.J.: Rutgers University Press, 2005); Paul Nagano, "A Japanese-American Pilgrimage: Theological Reflections," in *Journeys at the Margin: Toward an Autobiographical Theology in American-Asian Perspective,* ed. Peter C. Phan and Jung Young Lee (Collegeville, Minn.: Liturgical Press, 1999), 78–79.

27. Biography/Administrative History, PACTS, GTU.

28. Kawata, "Address Delivered at the Council of Japanese American Churches Annual Meeting," 5 May 1975, in Sano, *Theologies of Asian Americans and Pacific Peoples,* 462.

29. Matsuoka, "Creating Community amidst the Memories of Historic Injuries," in *Realizing the America of Our Hearts: Theological Voices of Asian Americans,* ed. Fumitaka Matsuoka and Eleazar S. Fernandez (St. Louis: Chalice Press, 2003), 39.

30. Andrew Sung Park, "Asian American Theology," in *Liberation Theologies in the United States: An Introduction,* ed. Stacey M. Floyd-Thomas and Anthony B. Pinn (New York: New York University Press, 2010), 116.

31. Morikawa, "Toward an Asian-American Theology," 3 Jan. 1986, reprinted in *Jitsuo Morikawa: A Prophet for the 21$^{st}$ Century: A Legacy of Sixty Inspiring Sermons,* ed. Paul Nagano and William L. Malcomson (Richmond, Calif.: Council for Pacific Asians Theology, 2000), 200–201.

32. Nagano, "Japanese-American Pilgrimage," 78.

33. Jonathan Y. Tan, *Introducing Asian American Theologies* (Maryknoll, N.Y.: Orbis Books, 2008), 134–38.

34. Paul Nagano and Joan Thatcher, *The Asian American Experience* (Valley Forge, Penn.: Fund for Renewal, 1973), 20–21, 25.

35. Sumida and Nagano, "Review, Resolve and Redress," 96.

36. Horton, Baker, Shafer, and Van Kirk, "The War Time Activities."

37. Floyd Schmoe, "Seattle Peace Churches and Relocation," in *Japanese Americans: From Relocation to Redress*, rev. ed., ed. Roger Daniels, Sandra C. Taylor, and Harry H. L. Kitano (Seattle: University of Washington Press, 1989), 117.

38. June Toshiyuki, interview, 10 Oct. 1983, and Nobuko Lillian Omi, interview, 27 Nov. 1983, in *Nisei Christian Journey: Its Promise & Fulfillment* (n.p.: Nisei Christian Oral History Project, 1988), 63, 100.

39. Sumida and Nagano, "Review, Resolve and Redress," 96.

40. Ibid., 95, 103.

41. Stephanie Bangarth, *Voices Raised in Protest: Defending North American Citizens of Japanese Ancestry, 1942–49* (Vancouver: University of British Columbia Press, 2008); Roland Kawano, ed., *Ministry to the Hopelessly Hopeless: Japanese Canadian Evacuees and Churches in WWII* (Scarborough, Ontario: Japanese Canadian Christian Churches Historical Project, 1997); Muriel Kitagawa and Roy Miki, eds., *This Is My Own: Letters to Wes & Other Writings on Japanese Canadians, 1941–1948* (Vancouver: Talonbooks, 1985); Frank Moritsugu and the Ghost-Town Teachers Historical Society, *Teaching in Canadian Exile: A History of the Schools for Japanese-Canadian Children in British Columbia Detention Camps during the Second World War* (Toronto: Ghost-Town Teachers Historical Society, 2001); Patricia E. Roy, "Lessons in Citizenship, 1945–1949: The Delayed Return of the Japanese to Canada's Pacific Coast," *Pacific Northwest Quarterly* 93 (Spring 2002): 69–80; Shichan Takashima, *A Child in Prison Camp* (New York: Tundra Books, 1971).

42. Biographical Note, Rhoads Papers, HC; Paul J. Clark, "Japan Honors Priest," 19 Jan. 1968, unlabeled newspaper clipping, Box 4/Vol. 9/Fld 7, QU; "Father Lavery to Accept Tokyo Award at Home, 25 Apr. 1966, *Bridgeport Telegram*, clipping in Box 41/Fld 1, Series 237, Deceased Society Members Media Files, MMA; Emery Brooks Andrews, interview by Tom Ikeda, 24 Mar. 2004, DDA.

43. "History," Japanese Baptist Church (updated May 2014), http://www.jbcseattle.org/en/2014-04-29-02-06-07/history.

44. Emery Brooks Andrews, interview by Ikeda and interview by Joyce Nishimura, 7 Oct. 2006, Bainbridge Island Japanese American Community Collection, DDA; Seigel, *In Good Conscience*, 162–63.

# Index

Baptists (cont.)

congregations, 31, 45, 172, 188, 202; Northern Baptist Convention, 30, 89, 201; in Seattle, 194, 196–99, 201; Southern, 77–78, 94; Washington Baptist Convention, 49, 194–95. *See also* American Baptist Home Mission Society; Churches, Japanese ethnic; *names of individuals*

Barnes, Roswell, 209

Barnett, Arthur, 89

Beale, Howard K., 177

Bennett, John C., 33, 37, 43–46, 59, 81, 234n96, 240n49

Berkeley, California, 42, 49, 53

Bible, 35, 55, 112, 145, 148; colleges, 25, 48; as a physical object, 51, 54, 63, 74, 116, 140, 149, 160; study groups, 52, 117–19, 123, 139, 145. *See also* American Bible Society; Sermons

Biddle, Francis, 2

Binford, Gurney and Elisabeth, 81

Black Power, 209

Bodine, Thomas, 20

Boesflug, Clement, 181

Bon Odori, 153

Booth, Raymond, 79, 96, 210–11

Bovenkerk, Henry, 114

Bowles, Gilbert and Minnie, 95

Bowman, Nora, 128, 131, 134

Boy Scouts of America, 73, 79

Brethren, Church of the, 11, 181–82, 210, 239n40

Buck, Pearl S., 180

Buddhism, 4, 95; prior to incarceration, 6–7, 16–17, 49; during incarceration, 51, 62–63, 72, 95, 100–104, 107–9, 115–16, 144–45, 168–69, 239n35, 255n36; postwar, 195, 199, 202. *See also* Evangelism; Interfaith cooperation

Burgoyne, W. Sherman, 90

Caffrey, Francis, 39, 41–42

Camp Harmony. *See* Puyallup WCCA center

Camp Shelby, 156

Canada, 20, 216–17

Catholic Foreign Mission Society of America. *See* Maryknoll Mission

Catholic Youth Organization (Chicago), 86, 181

Chaplains, 53, 102, 147, 156–58

Chapman, Gordon, 61–68, 95, 100, 111, 115, 119–20, 144–45, 178, 188, 208

Charity, 19, 84, 130, 180

Chicago, Illinois, 51, 65, 86, 140, 179, 181–83, 185, 188, 204

*Christian Century*, 31–33, 227n43

Christian Endeavor Society, 59, 159–67, 258n110

*Christianity and Crisis*, 33, 227n43

Christmas: prior to incarceration, 15; during incarceration, 75–76, 93, 108, 117, 127, 138, 152–53, 160; postwar, 195

Churches, Japanese ethnic: prior to incarceration, 6–7, 34, 48, 94, 226n27; resettlement and return to the West Coast, 188, 195–96, 266n111; postwar, 204–6, 211, 213–14; Salem Japanese Community Church, 36, 105; Seattle Japanese Baptist, 7, 16, 48–49, 53, 191, 194–202, 204, 217–18; Seattle Japanese Methodist, 1, 7, 15, 29, 196. *See also* Integration; Segregation

Church of Jesus Christ of Latter-day Saints, 12, 83

Church for the Fellowship of All Peoples, 204–5, 268n145

Citizenship, 6, 27, 30, 45–47, 81, 88, 92, 142–43, 148–49, 209

Civil rights activism, 2–4, 7; fighting for Nikkei rights, 7–8, 12, 18–19, 22–25, 88–91; postwar activism,

Methodists (cont.)
239n40; resettlement and return to the West Coast, 176, 191, 193, 202, 266n111; postwar, 204, 210, 214; Free, 77, 112, 239n40. *See also* Churches, Japanese ethnic; *and names of individuals*

Michigan, 185, 263n49

Minidoka incarceration center, 56, 75–77, 85–86, 91, 97–98; Federated Church, 106, 109, 115–17, 122–23, 125–26; interfaith programs, 149–55; lay Nikkei Protestants, 63, 106, 108–9, 139, 158; Nikkei pastors, 101, 105–7, 114, 118, 125–26, 158, 186, 209; Roman Catholics, 69, 72, 77, 102, 107–9, 115–16, 126, 159; segregation, 142–43, 146, 255n36; unique atmosphere of, 145–47; white religious workers at, 62, 102, 106, 115, 119, 128–34

*Minidoka Irrigator*, 97, 131–32, 149

Missionaries, Protestant: prior to incarceration, 7–10, 16, 23, 43; during incarceration, 61–65, 67, 77–78, 103, 105–6, 122, 128, 133–34, 143, 158, 175; resettlement and return to the West Coast, 179, 197; postwar, 208, 213. *See also names of individuals*

Missions: home, 7, 48, 77; foreign, 2, 11–12, 42, 103, 162, 180, 213; societies, 11, 43, 64, 88, 174, 202, 209. *See also specific missionary societies and boards*

Morale, 14, 75, 99, 102, 122, 136, 152, 159, 171, 177, 185

Morikawa, Jitsuo, 121, 123–24, 188, 215

Mormons, 12, 83

Morris, Homer, 68, 92, 149

Mukyōkai, 22–24, 113, 135

Murphy, U. G., 29, 190

Myer, Dillon S., 99–101, 131, 151

Nagano, Paul: during incarceration, 121, 123–24, 126, 140, 161; leaving Poston, 156–57; postwar, 161, 206, 213, 215–16, 218

Nakahara, Mary, 164–65, 209

National Conference of Christians and Jews (NCCJ), 83–84, 155–56

Native Sons and Daughters of the Golden West, 8, 17, 39

Naturalization, 6, 8, 19, 209

New Deal, 171

New York, 38, 67–68, 94, 129, 204, 210

Nicholson, Herbert, 49, 72, 210, 266n111

Niebuhr, H. Richard, 59

Niebuhr, Reinhold, 33, 59

Noble, Douglas, 63, 145

*Northwest Catholic Progress*, 38

Northwest Oriental Evangelization Society, 29, 45

Oberlin College, 183

O'Brien, Robert, 25–26, 230n38

Okajima, Kinya, 149

Okuda, Kenji, 120, 183, 208

Pacific School of Religion, 43, 74, 240n49

Pacifism, 22–23, 32, 87, 147–49, 157, 168. *See also* Fellowship of Reconciliation; Quakers

Patriotism: Nikkei expressions of, 37, 87, 148–55, 164; Christianity and, 2, 27–31, 34, 39, 148, 178; white supremacy and, 31, 57, 85, 190. *See also* Public relations

Pentecostalism, 110, 114, 119. *See also* Holiness

Peppers, Margaret, 115, 117, 128, 133

Pickett, Clarence, 19, 24, 43, 70–72, 178

Portland, Oregon, 204, 225n20, 239n35; Council of Churches, 29, 90